Bickford

THE ADIRONDACK GUIDE

THE ADIRONDACK GUIDE

AN ALMANAC
OF
ESSENTIAL INFORMATION
AND
ASSORTED TRIVIA

Howard Kirschenbaum
Susan Schafstall
Janine Stuchin
Editors

SAGAMORE INSTITUTE
Raquette Lake, New York

To
Edward E. Wright
(1888-1978)
Adirondack friend and neighbor
who lived 90 years
on the same site
near Au Sable Forks, New York

ISBN 0-913393-00-2

Printed in the
Adirondack Park by
Adirondack Press, Inc.
Lake George, New York

CONTENTS

EDUCATION

ORGANIZATIONS AND AGENCIES

ENVIRONMENT

ARTS AND CRAFTS

ENTERTAINMENT

RECREATION

TRANSPORTATION

ASSISTANCE

MISCELLANEOUS

FOREWORD

One person's essential information is another person's trivia.

In the Adirondacks these categories are often hard to distinguish. When an Adirondacker comments upon the weather (Section 55), it is not small talk; he or she really cares. When a hiker is lost (Section 113), it is not just another statistic, but a reminder of the clear and present danger each of us encounters as we venture into the Adirondack wilderness. When an Adirondack-lover reads a list of waterfalls and their elevations (Section 53), it is a reminder of past adventures at some of these very falls and a beckoning call to see the others, to experience every treat the vast and wild Adirondacks have to offer.

In short, for lovers of the Adirondacks—and there are many—no fact is trivial, no local subject irrelevant. Living in these mountains—for days or for years—is a total experience and all the pieces are connected.

The Adirondack Guide is designed to help enrich that total experience of living and being in the Adirondacks. The book is meant equally for the 125,000 residents of the Park and the millions of visitors who cross the "Blue Line" each year.

It will not be accidental if this book's title brings to mind images of the Adirondack guides of old—who guided visitors in where to go and what to do there; who helped them notice things along the way; who provided essential information for surviving and thriving in the wilderness; who told stories around the campfire or on the lake and related interesting facts about the region—in some cases neither essential nor accurate, a tradition we shall try not to emulate; and who provided, here and there, a touch of humor and a new perspective.

If *The Adirondack Guide* continues at least a part of this rich tradition, the work will have been amply rewarded.

Howard Kirschenbaum
Susan Schafstall
Janine Stuchin

Raquette Lake, New York

SOURCES AND ACKNOWLEDGEMENTS

A book like this would not be possible without the help of literally hundreds of people providing and verifying the thousands of pieces of information contained in it. Mentioning all by name would require pages. A few individuals and organizations, however, deserve special appreciation.

The Adirondack Museum is considered by many to be one of the finest regional museums in the United States. It is a well-designed and attractive treasure house of information on the history of the Adirondacks. We have drawn heavily on the Museum's resources for about ten sections of *The Guide.*

Two state agencies—The Department of Environmental Conservation and the Adirondack Park Agency—were particularly helpful in providing copious information on numerous aspects of the Adirondacks. Many sections of *The Guide* are drawn directly from the published information these agencies provide. Special thanks are due to Mike Storey, Park Agency Naturalist, and Bob Inslerman, Supervising Wildlife Biologist in DEC's Division of Fish and Wildlife, for the time they took personally to gather information and for mobilizing the resources of their respective agencies. Thanks also to APA's Robert Glennon and to DEC staff members Mark Brown, Lawrence J. Nashett, Ernie Lantiegne, Robert E. Wilson and Patricia Riexinger.

Two authorities on the Adirondacks graciously agreed to review the manuscript of *The Guide* and to make corrections, additions or suggestions they thought warranted. To Bernard Carmen, former editor of *Adirondack Life,* and to Craig Gilborn, Director of the Adirondack Museum, our great appreciation for the hours they spent carefully reviewing the text. Any remaining errors or omissions, however, are the full responsibility of the editors.

Each of the following individuals deserves special thanks for generously consenting to write a section for *The Guide* in his or her area of expertise: Robert Venables, Norman Hess, Warder Cadbury, Barbara McMartin, Grace Leach Hudowalski and Paul Jamieson. Also special thanks to Maitland deSormo for his gracious assistance on several sections.

We would also like to thank the following individuals for their help in providing considerable information for one or more sections of *The Guide* or for other assistance rendered: Tim Barnett of the Adirondack Conservancy, Gary Randorf of the Adirondack Council, Doris M. Herwig of the Warren County Department of Tourism, Betsy Boyd of the "I Love New York" Tourism Office of New York State Department of Commerce, Dr. E. W. Cupp of of Cornell University, Raymond G. Paolino of the Bureau of Business Research at the Department of Commerce, Charlotte McCormick of the Essex County Historical Society, Senator Hugh T. Farley, Edward Winslow of the NYS Education Department, Geoff Knapp of the Olympic Regional Development Authority, and to Murray Heller, Ronnie Renoni, John M.C. Peterson, Heidi Miller, Sally Packard and Bill Pearson.

Thanks also to Joanna Darling and Susan Keeler for their many hours of typing the manuscript and dealing with the inevitable frustrations of a new word processor, to Jean Marie Byrne for her help in the verification process, to Elliott Masie and Gregg Laird for their technical assistance in word processing, and to Bob and Linda Miner for their care in proofreading.

Finally, we extend thanks to the hundreds of individuals who returned our request for verification of the entry on their particular organization, event, facility or resource. Over one thousand such information requests were sent out to verify any entry about which we had the slightest doubt as to its accuracy. Most of these verifications were returned in a timely manner. After a period of waiting, a second request was sent to those who had not been heard from, and many telephone calls were made.

As press time approached and 40 or so entries remained un-verified, we had a dilemma. In some cases, when we were somewhat skeptical about the entry to begin with, it was dropped. In other cases, when we were fairly certain of the entry's accuracy, we took the risk of including it as originally written. Almost every entry throughout *The Adirondack Guide,* however, has been verified and, aside from changes that occurred after going to press, we believe the information on these pages is as accurate as it could possibly be.

Thinking ahead to future editions of *The Adirondack Guide,* any additions or corrections from readers would be most welcome. When submitting additions, please keep in mind that we have attempted to limit the scope of *The Guide,* with rare exceptions, to organizations, events, people and places within the Adirondack Park boundary ("the Blue Line"). Correspondence may be addressed to the editors at Sagamore Lodge and Conference Center, Sagamore Road, Raquette Lake, NY 13436.

GEOGRAPHY AND GOVERNMENT

(1)
POPULATION STATISTICS

Except for Essex and Hamilton Counties, which lie entirely within the Adirondack Park, the county population and land area statistics include areas which lie outside the Park. Town and village statistics are given only for those towns and villages which lie within the Park. All population figures are based on the 1980 census.

CLINTON COUNTY

County Seat	Plattsburgh
Land Area (sq. miles)	1,059
Population	80,750
Percent of State Population	.46 %

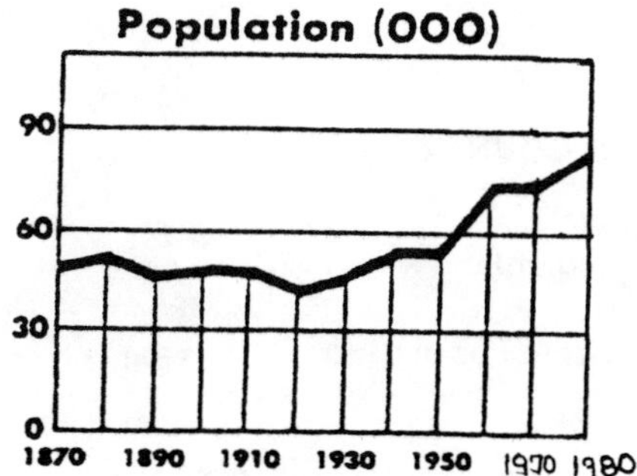

Town of AuSable	2,792
Town of Black Brook	1,505
Town of Dannemora	4,717
Town of Ellenburg	1,751
Town of Saranac	3,389
Village of Dannemora	3,770
Village of Keeseville	1,055

ESSEX COUNTY

County Seat	Elizabethtown
Land Area (sq. miles)	1,823
Population	36,176
Percent of State Population	.21%

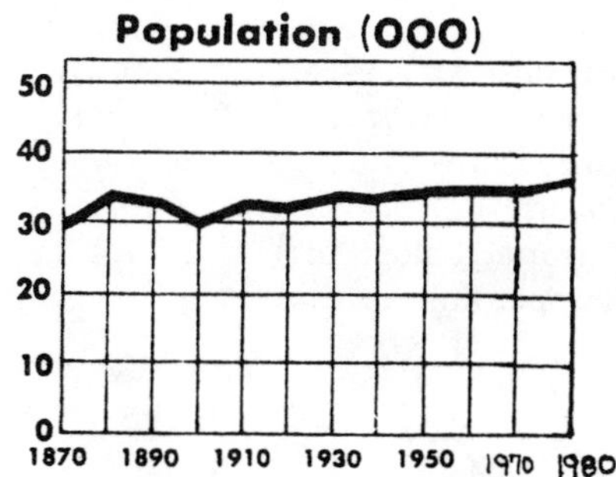

In 1915 part of Essex was annexed to Hamilton and part of Hamilton to Essex.

Town of Chesterfield	2,398
Town of Crown Point	1,837
Town of Elizabethtown	1,267
Town of Essex	880
Town of Jay	2,221
Town of Keene	919
Town of Lewis	922
Town of Minerva	781
Town of Moriah	5,139
Town of Newcomb	681
Town of No. Elba	6,597
Town of No. Hudson	179
Town of St. Armand	1,064
Town of Schroon	1,606
Town of Ticonderoga	5,436
Town of Westport	1,439
Town of Willsboro	1,759
Town of Wilmington	1,051
Village of Bloomingdale	608
Village of Elizabethtown	659
Village of Keeseville (Part)	970
Village of Lake Placid	2,490
Village of Port Henry	1,450
Village of Saranac Lake (Part)	1,462
Village of Ticonderoga	2,938
Village of Westport	613

FRANKLIN COUNTY

County Seat .... Malone
Land Area (sq. miles) 1,674
Population 44,929
Percent of State Population .... .26%

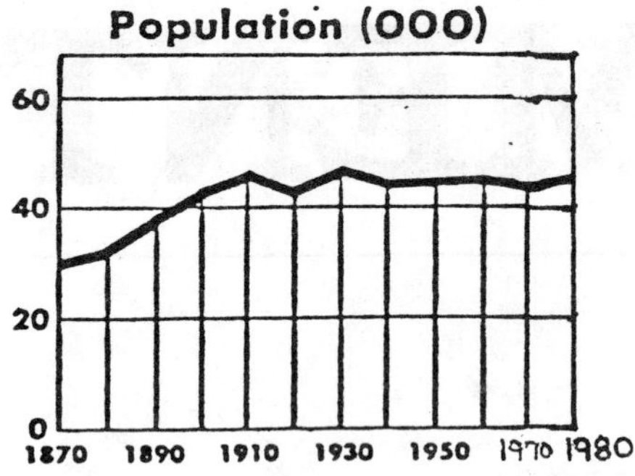

Town of Altamont 6,318
Town of Bellmont 1,045
Town of Brighton 1,625
Town of Duane 184
Town of Franklin 926
Town of Harrietstown 5,604
Town of Santa Clara 310
Town of Waverly 1,110
Village of Saranac Lake (Part) 4,116
Village of Tupper Lake 4,478

FULTON COUNTY

County Seat .... Johnstown
Land Area (sq. miles) 498
Population 55,153
Percent of State Population .... .32%

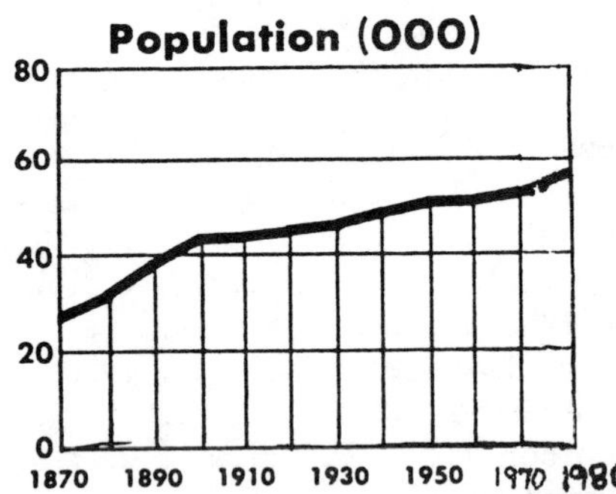

Town of Bleeker 463
Town of Caroga 1,177
Town of Mayfield 5,439
Town of Northampton 2,829
Town of Stratford 625
Village of Mayfield
(within Town of Mayfield) 944
Village of Northville
(within Town of Northampton) 1,304

HAMILTON COUNTY

County Seat .... Lake Pleasant
Land Area (sq. miles) 1,735
Population. 5,034
Percent of State Population .... .03%

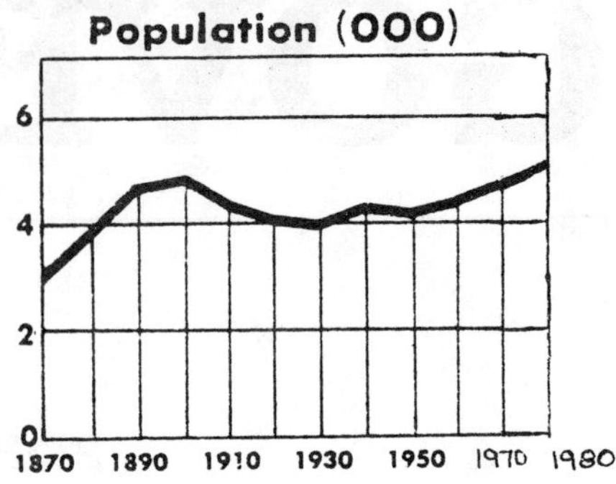

In 1915 part of Essex was annexed to Hamilton and part of Hamilton to Essex

Town of Arietta 314
Town of Benson 156
Town of Hope 311
Town of Indian Lake 1,410
Town of Inlet 320
Town of Lake Pleasant 859
Town of Long Lake 935
Town of Morehouse 102
Town of Wells 627
Village of Speculator 408

HERKIMER COUNTY

County Seat .... Herkimer
Land Area (sq. miles) 1,435
Population 66,714
Percent of State Population .... .38%

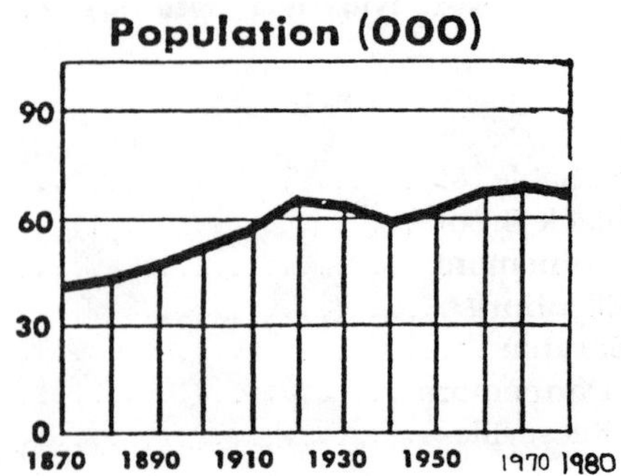

Town of Ohio 468
Town of Salisbury 1,741
Town of Webb 1,616

LEWIS COUNTY

County Seat .... Lowville
Land Area (sq.miles) 1,291
Population 25,035
Percent of State Population .... .14%

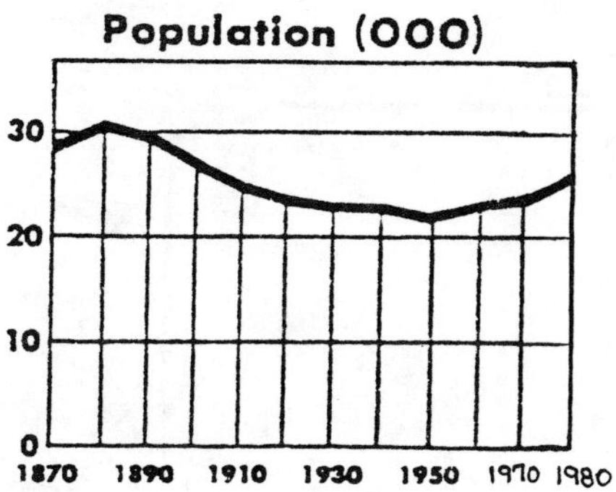

Town of Greig 1,115
Town of Lyonsdale 1,135
Town of Watson 1,272

ONEIDA COUNTY

County Seat .... Utica
Land Area (sq. miles) 1,223
Population 253,466
Percent of State Population 1.45%

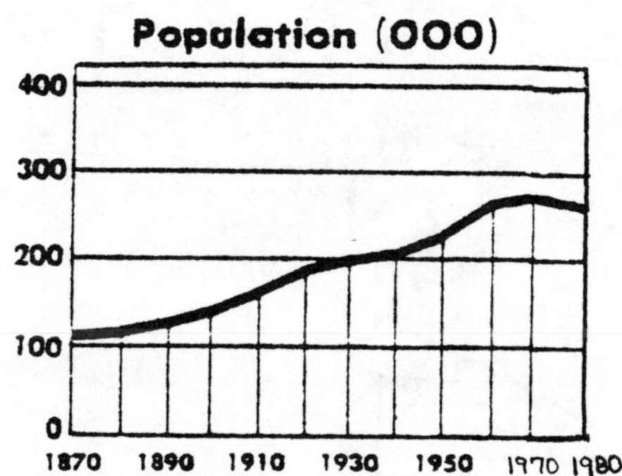

No towns or villages totally in the Adirondack Park.

ST. LAWRENCE COUNTY

County Seat .... Canton
Land Area (sq.miles) 2,768
Population 114,254
Percent of State Population .... .65%

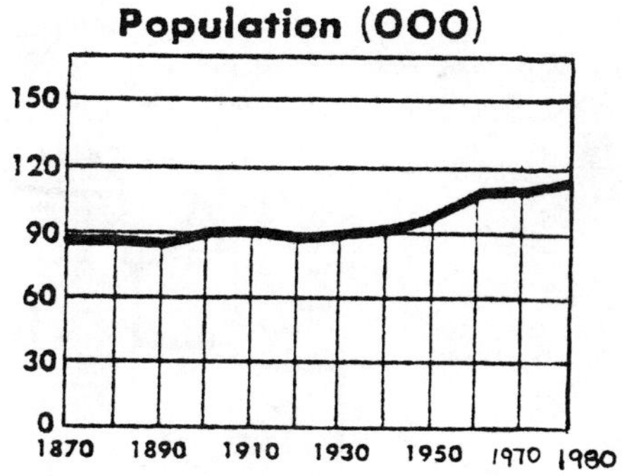

Town of Clare 121
Town of Clifton 1,009
Town of Colton 1,293
Town of Fine 2,243
Town of Hopkinton 1,057
Town of Piercefield 365

SARATOGA COUNTY

County Seat .... Ballston Spa
Land Area (sq. miles) 818
Population 153,759
Percent of State Population .... .88%

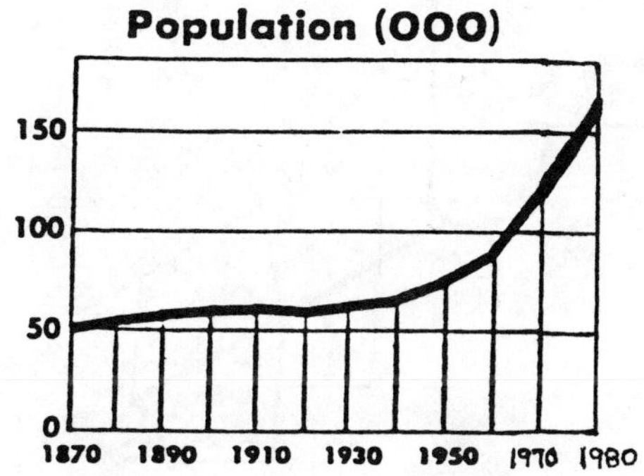

Town of Corinth 2,370
Town of Day 609
Town of Edinburg 1,104
Town of Hadley 1,385
Village of Corinth 2,626

ADIRONDACK REGION POPULATION GAINS AND LOSSES 1970-1980

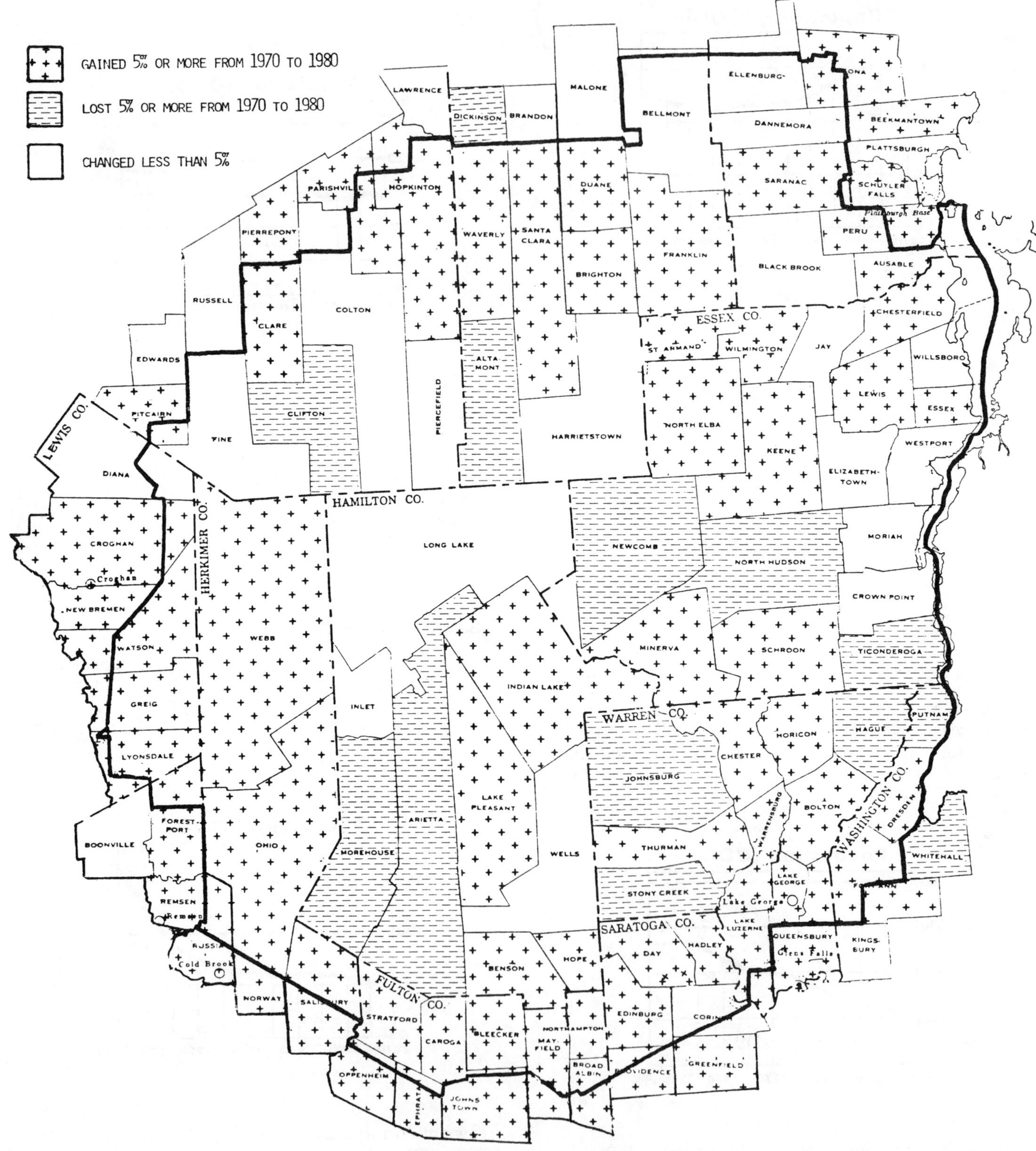

This map contains towns that are inside as well as outside the Blueline. Population gains and losses shown come from United States Census figures. Source: Dept. of Rural Sociology, Cornell University.

WARREN COUNTY

County Seat .... Lake George
Land Area (sq. miles) 887
Population 54,854
Percent Of State Population .... .31%

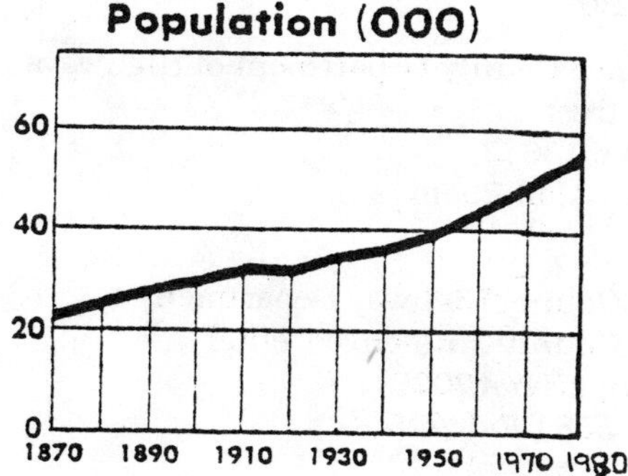

Town of Bolton 1,793
Town of Chester 2,909
Town of Hague 766
Town of Horicon 1,082
Town of Johnsburg 2,173
Town of Lake George 3,394
Town of Lake Luzerne 2,672
Town of Stony Creek 528
Town of Thurman 852
Town of Warrensburg 3,810

WASHINGTON COUNTY

County Seat .... Hudson Falls
Land Area (sq. miles) 836
Population 54,795
Percent of State Population .... .31%

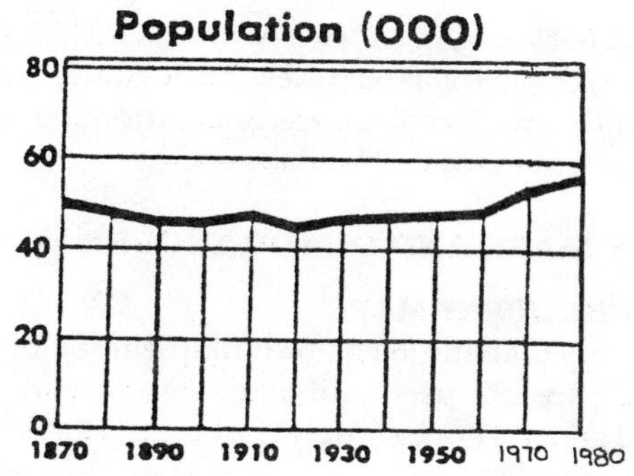

Town of Dresden 557
Town of Fort Ann 4,422
Town of Putnam 496
Village of Fort Ann 510

(2)
MAPS

NEW YORK STATE MAPS

I LOVE NEW YORK TOURISM MAP. A 26x36 multi-color map giving tourist information for Adirondacks and other regions, insets for major cities. Available from NYS Dept of Commerce, Division of Tourism, 99 Washington Ave., Albany, NY 12245 and the Chamber of Commerce, Lake Placid, NY 12943. No charge. (518)474-4116.

NEW YORK STATE WALL MAP. A 40x52 multi-color map that is highly detailed, yet easy to read. Towns indexed with population figures. Major roads, waters, boundaries, landmarks, parks, airports and other sites shown. Available from the publisher: The National Survey, Chester, VT 05143. $12.00.

ADIRONDACK REGIONAL MAPS

ADIRONDACK ATLAS. A 42x48 4-color map of the Adirondack region, fully indexed with separate indices for major roads, bodies of water, parks, airports, hiking trails, other attractions and facilities. Available at most Adirondack bookstores for $3.95, or directly from publisher for $6.00, price includes tax and postage. Marshall-Penn Co., Inc., 585 Eric Blvd. West, Syracuse, NY 13204. (315)422-2162.

ADIRONDACK MAP. Prepared by Preserve, Protection and Management Division, Department of Environmental Conservation. In four sections, each 55x19 inches. Map shows original surveys—townships, patents, grants, Totten and Crossfield's Purchase, great lots, etc.—with current state-owned lands also shown. Most recent edition is dated 1976, but new, updated map should be published soon. No price for new edition has been set as yet. Map available from Department of Environmental Conservation, 50 Wolf Rd., Albany, NY 12233. (518)457-7433.

ADIRONDACK PARK LAND USE AND DEVELOPMENT PLAN MAP. A 36x48 multi-color wall map updated from time to time which shows state lands according to classification as wilderness, wild forest, etc. and private lands according to their zoning as hamlet, moderate intensity, rural use, etc. Available from Adirondack Park Agency, Box 99, Ray Brook NY 12977. No charge. (518)891-4050.

RECREATIONAL MAP OF THE ADIRONDACKS. A 34 x 43 color map of northeastern New York State. Watershed regions indicated by color code. Recreational trails listed. Available from many Adirondack stores.

COUNTY MAPS AND QUADRANGLES

COUNTY HIGHWAY MAPS

Each county distributes its own map; therefore uniform standards are not used and maps will vary in fee, date, scale and general appearance. They are available from the following sources:

Clinton County Highway Department
RD #1, Box 366
Plattsburgh, NY 12901
(518)561-8800 Ext. 300

Essex County Highway Department
Government Center
Elizabethtown, NY 12932
(518)873-6301 Ext. 318

Franklin County Highway Department
RD #2, Constable Rd.
Malone, NY 12953
(518)483-1140

Fulton County Highway Department
PO Box 127
Johnstown, NY 12095
(518)762-7120

Hamilton County Highway Department
Route 8
Lake Pleasant, NY 12108
(518)548-7141

Herkimer County Highway Department
Third Ave., PO Box 167
Herkimer, NY 13350
(315)867-1191

Lewis County Highway Department
Court House
State Street
Lowville, NY 13367
(315)376-3563

Oneida County Department of Public Works
Box 400
Airport Road
Oriskany, NY 13424
(315)736-3071

St. Lawrence County Department of Highways
44 Park Street
Canton, NY 13617
c/o County Mail Room
(315)379-2315

Saratoga County Highway Department
Saratoga County Municipal Center
Ballston Spa, NY 12020
(518)885-5381 Ext. 235

Warren County Municipal Center
Central Stockman
Lake George, NY 12845
(518)761-6499

Washington County Planning Department
County Office Building
Fort Edward, NY 12828
(518)747-4687

DEPARTMENT OF ENVIRONMENTAL CONSERVATION COUNTY MAPS.

Approximately 19x24, these maps show locations of all state lands, stream easements, boat launch sites, and special use areas. County maps for Clinton, Franklin, Essex, Hamilton, Warren, Washington, Saratoga, and Fulton can be obtained from the Department of Environmental Conservation, Ray Brook, NY 12977. Herkimer, Lewis, Oneida, and St. Lawrence County maps can be obtained from the Department of Environmental Conservation, 317 Washington St., Watertown, NY 13601. They are available at no charge while supply lasts.

U.S. TOPOGRAPHICAL SURVEY MAPS.

Adirondack Region is charted in a series of quadrangle maps; shape and elevation of the terrain are marked; location and shape of mountains, valleys, woods, roads, streams and rivers are shown. Essential for hiking, exploring. Available at many Adirondack stores and from Branch of Distribution, U.S. Geological Survey, 1200 S. Eads St., Arlington VA 22202. Each quadrangle $2.00. An index map is available free from U.S.G.S. U.S.G.S. also provides aerial photos of specific areas (coordinates and desired season required) and satellite imagery—all in various sizes for various prices.

COUNTY MAPS

The following four maps are excerpted from the New York State Wall Map (see page 15) and show those parts of the 12 Adirondack Counties which lie within the Adirondack Park. The Park boundary is denoted by the quarter inch wide "tree line" on these maps.

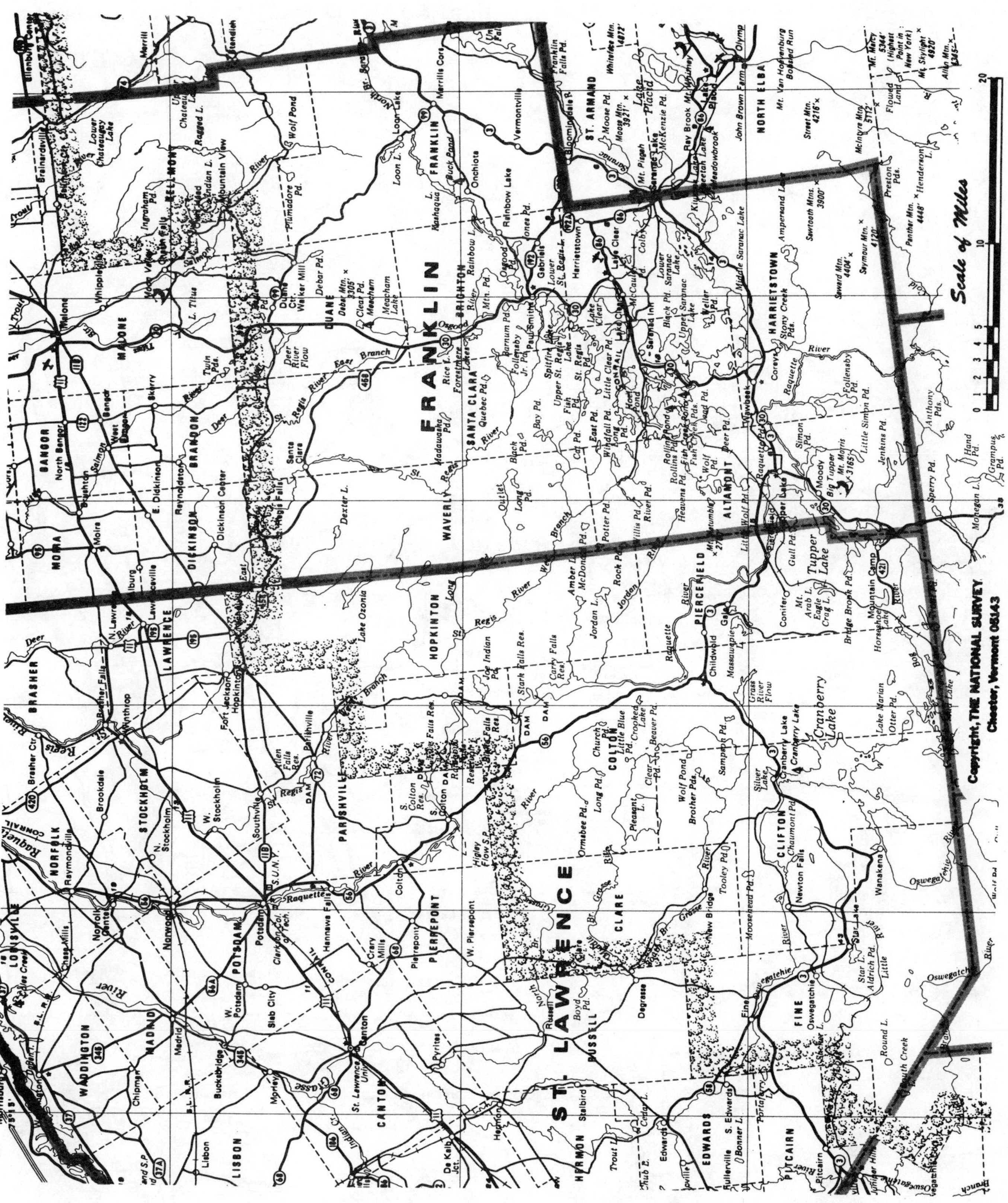

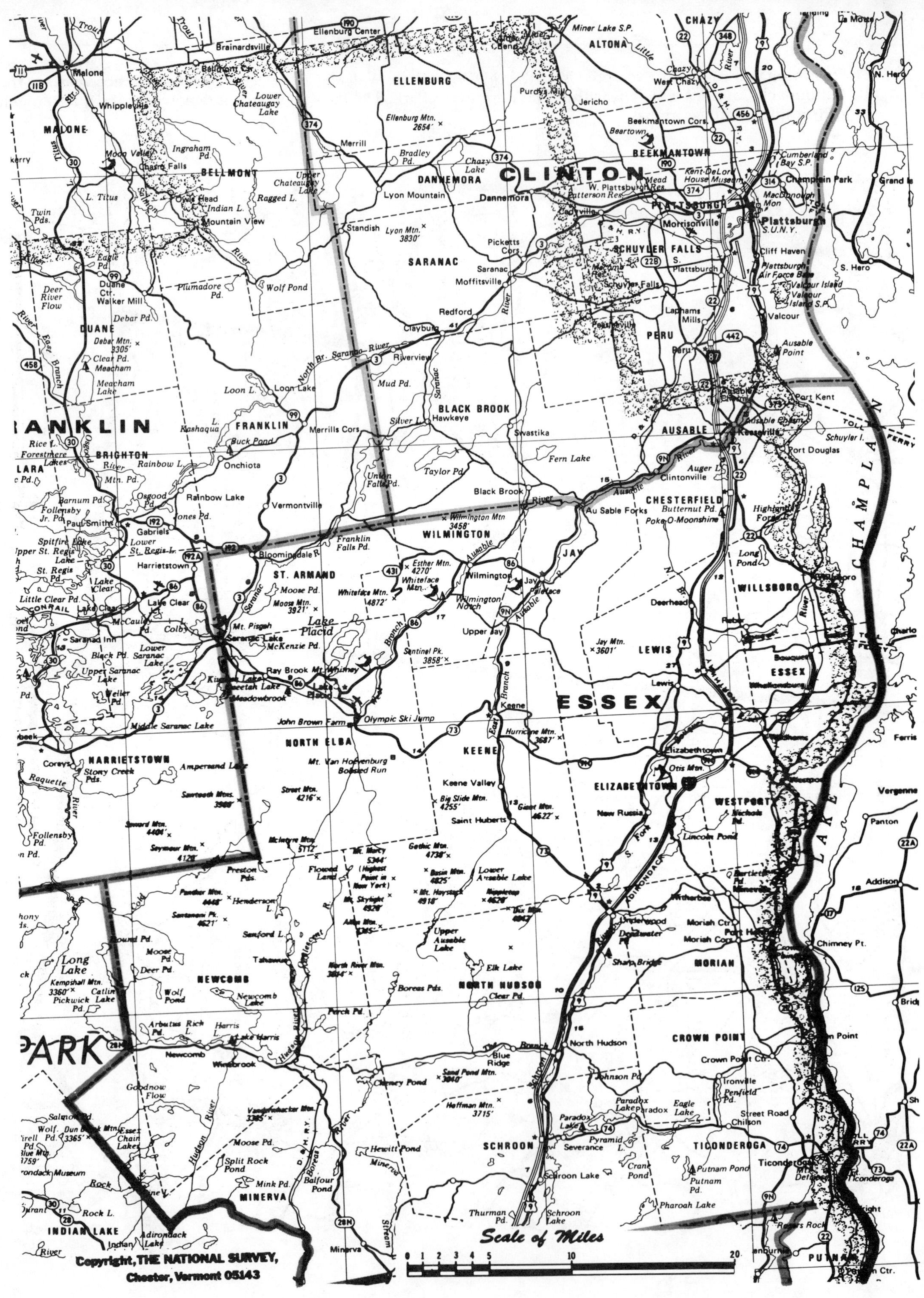
CLINTON
ESSEX
FRANKLIN
PARK
LAKE CHAMPLAIN
MALONE
BELLMONT
ELLENBURG
DANNEMORA
ALTONA
CHAZY
BEEKMANTOWN
SARANAC
SCHUYLER FALLS
PERU
BLACK BROOK
AUSABLE
DUANE
BRIGHTON
HARRIETSTOWN
ST. ARMAND
WILMINGTON
JAY
CHESTERFIELD
WILLSBORO
LEWIS
NORTH ELBA
KEENE
ELIZABETHTOWN
WESTPORT
NEWCOMB
NORTH HUDSON
MORIAH
CROWN POINT
SCHROON
TICONDEROGA
MINERVA
INDIAN LAKE
Malone
Plattsburgh
Saranac Lake
Lake Placid
Keene Valley
Elizabethtown
Ticonderoga
Newcomb
Lake Clear
Paul Smiths
Wilmington
Keeseville
Port Kent
Port Douglas
Westport
Olympic Ski Jump
John Brown Farm
Whiteface Mtn. 4872'
Mt. Marcy 5344' (Highest Point in New York)
Lyon Mtn. 3830'
Scale of Miles
0 1 2 3 4 5 10 20
Copyright, THE NATIONAL SURVEY,
Chester, Vermont 05143

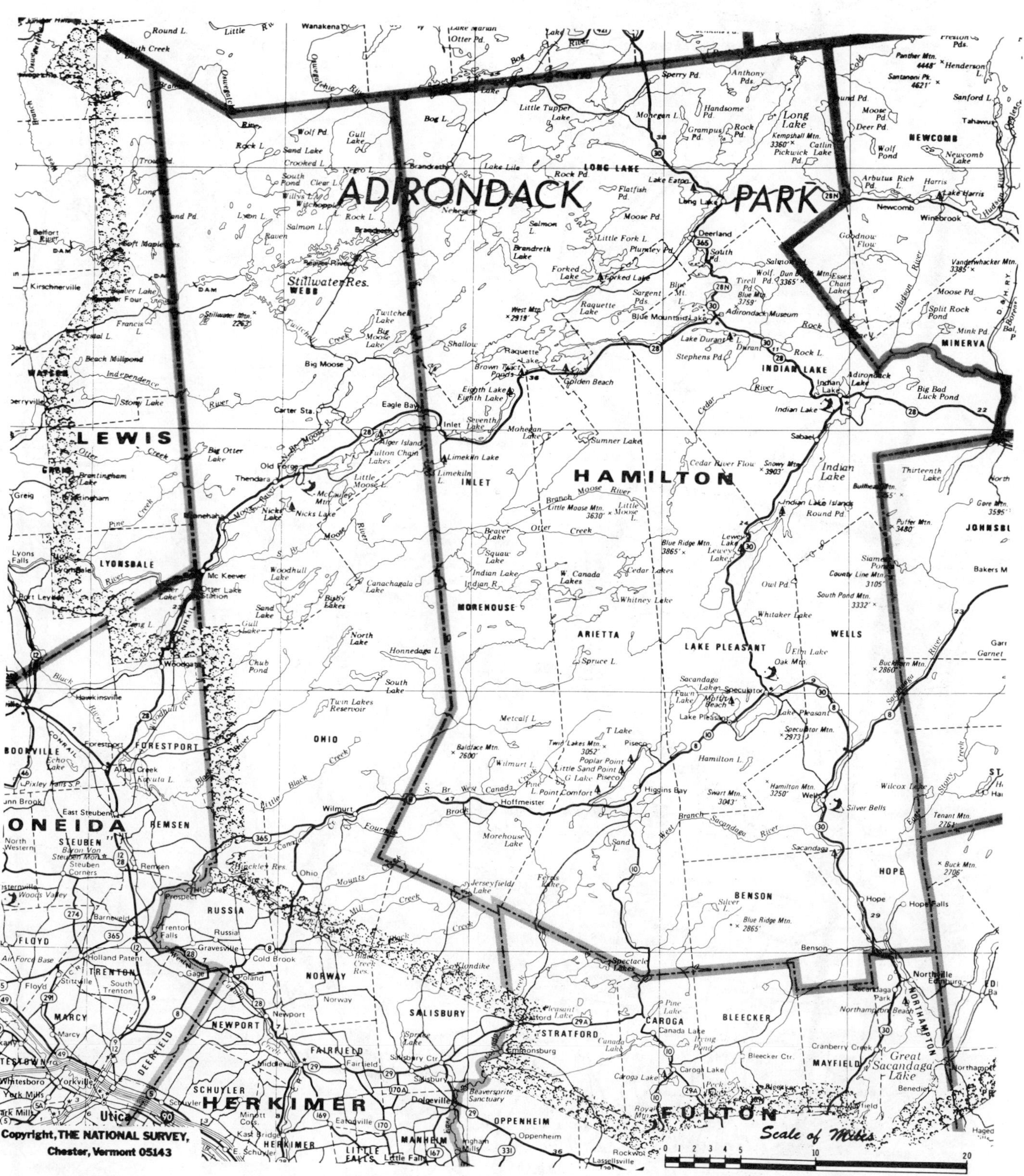

ADIRONDACK PARK
HAMILTON
LEWIS
ONEIDA
HERKIMER
FULTON
LONG LAKE
NEWCOMB
MINERVA
INDIAN LAKE
INLET
WEBB
MOREHOUSE
ARIETTA
LAKE PLEASANT
WELLS
HOPE
BENSON
OHIO
RUSSIA
NORWAY
SALISBURY
STRATFORD
CAROGA
BLEECKER
MAYFIELD
NORTHAMPTON
OPPENHEIM
MANHEIM
FAIRFIELD
NEWPORT
SCHUYLER
DEERFIELD
MARCY
TRENTON
FLOYD
REMSEN
STEUBEN
FORESTPORT
BOONVILLE
LYONSDALE
GREIG
JOHNSBURG
Stillwater Res.
Big Moose
Old Forge
Eagle Bay
Inlet
Raquette Lake
Blue Mountain Lake
Adirondack Museum
Indian Lake
Speculator
Lake Pleasant
Piseco
Wells
Hope
Northville
Great Sacandaga Lake
Dolgeville
Little Falls
Utica
Copyright, THE NATIONAL SURVEY, Chester, Vermont 05143
Scale of Miles
0 1 2 3 4 5 10 20

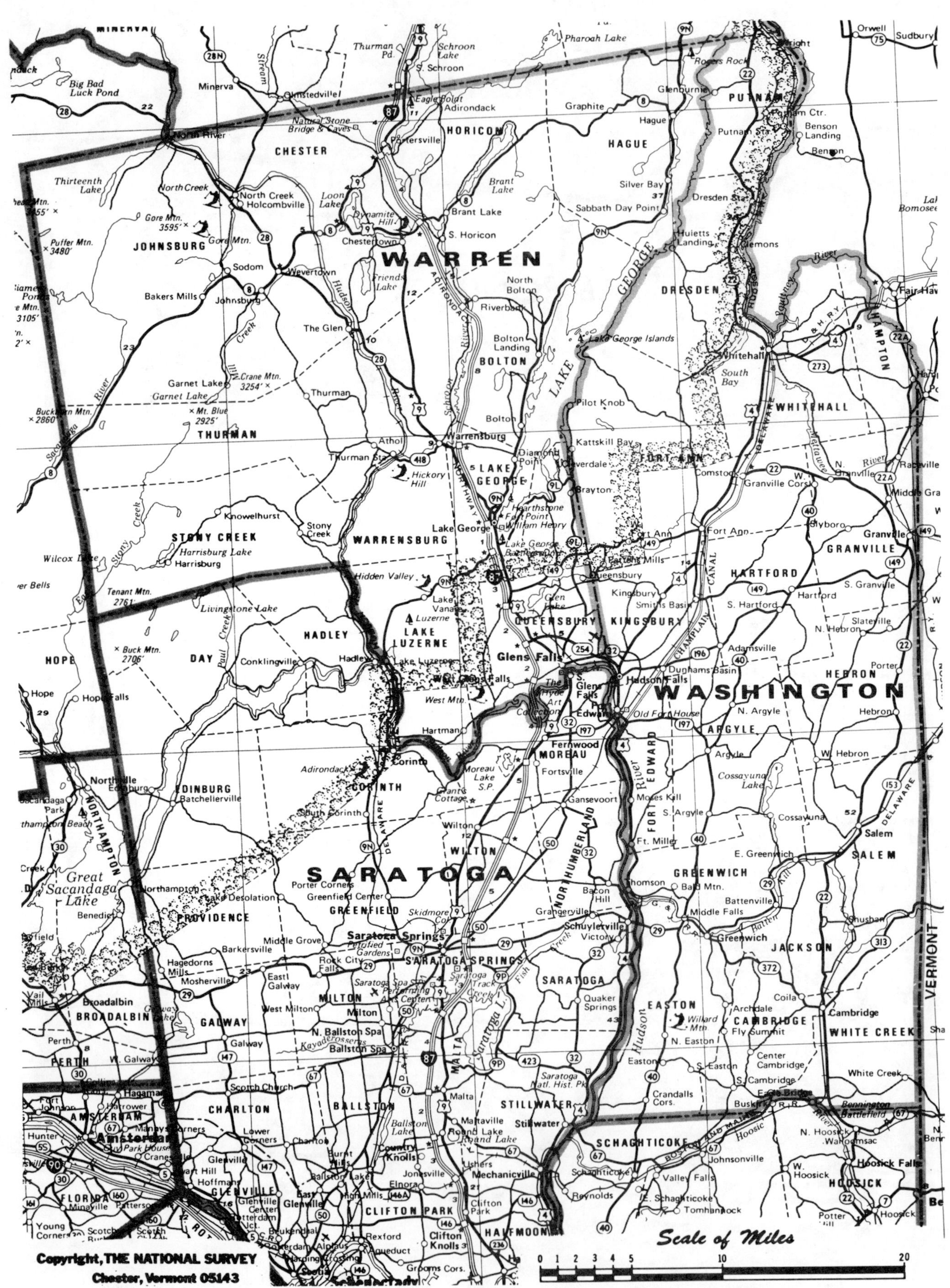
WARREN
WASHINGTON
SARATOGA
VERMONT
CHESTER
HORICON
HAGUE
PUTNAM
JOHNSBURG
DRESDEN
BOLTON
WHITEHALL
THURMAN
LAKE GEORGE
FORT ANN
STONY CREEK
WARRENSBURG
GRANVILLE
HARTFORD
HADLEY
LAKE LUZERNE
QUEENSBURY
KINGSBURY
HOPE
DAY
HEBRON
ARGYLE
MOREAU
FORT EDWARD
EDINBURG
CORINTH
NORTHAMPTON
WILTON
NORTHUMBERLAND
GREENWICH
SALEM
PROVIDENCE
GREENFIELD
JACKSON
SARATOGA SPRINGS
SARATOGA
BROADALBIN
GALWAY
MILTON
EASTON
CAMBRIDGE
WHITE CREEK
PERTH
CHARLTON
BALLSTON
MALTA
STILLWATER
AMSTERDAM
SCHAGHTICOKE
HOOSICK
FLORIDA
GLENVILLE
CLIFTON PARK
HALFMOON
LAKE GEORGE
CHAMPLAIN CANAL
Great Sacandaga Lake
Glens Falls
Saratoga Springs
Hudson Falls
Whitehall
Mechanicville
Ballston Spa
Schuylerville
Warrensburg
Ticonderoga
Schenectady
Scale of Miles
0 1 2 3 4 5 10 20
Copyright, THE NATIONAL SURVEY
Chester, Vermont 05143

(3)
POST OFFICES AND ZIP CODES

When a village or hamlet straddles two counties (e.g., AuSable Forks, Keeseville, Saranac Lake), it is listed under the county in which the post office building actually is located.

CLINTON COUNTY

Ausable Chasm	12911
Dannemora	12929
Ellenburg Center	12934
Lyon Mountain	12952
Redford	12978
Saranac	12981

ESSEX COUNTY

AuSable Forks*	12912
Bloomingdale	12913
Crown Point	12928
Elizabethtown	12932
Essex	12936
Jay	12941
Keene	12942
Keene Valley	12943
Keeseville	12944
Lake Placid	12946
Lewis	12950
Minerva	12851
Mineville	12956
Moriah	12960
New Russia	12964
Newcomb	12852
North Hudson	12855
Olmstedville	12857
Paradox	12858
Port Henry	12974
Port Kent	12975
Ray Brook	12977
Saranac Lake	12983
Schroon Lake	12870
Severance	12872
South Schroon	12877
Ticonderoga	12883
Upper Jay	12987
Wadhams	12990
Westport	12993
Whallonsburg	12994
Willsboro	12996
Wilmington	12997
Witherbee	12998

FRANKLIN COUNTY

Gabriels	12939
Lake Clear	12945
Onchiota	12968
Owls Head	12969
Paul Smiths	12970
Rainbow Lake	12976
St. Regis Falls	12980
Saranac Inn	12982
Saranac Lake	12983
Tupper Lake	12986
Vermontville	12989

FULTON COUNTY

Caroga Lake	12032
Mayfield	12117
Northville	12134
Statford	13470

HAMILTON COUNTY

Blue Mountain Lake	12812
Hoffmeister	13353
Indian Lake	12842
Inlet	13360
Lake Pleasant	12108
Long Lake	12847
Piseco	12139
Raquette Lake	13436
Sabael	12864
Speculator	12164
Wells	12190

HERKIMER COUNTY

Beaver River	13367
Eagle Bay	13331
Old Forge	13420
Thendara	13472

LEWIS COUNTY

Brantingham	13312

ONEIDA COUNTY

None within the Park

USE CORRECT ZIP CODE ®

ST. LAWRENCE COUNTY

Childwold	12922
Colton	13625
Cranberry Lake	12927
Fine	13639
Newton Falls	13666
Nicholville	12965
Oswegatchie	13670
Piercefield	12973
Star Lake	13690
Wanakena	13695

SARATOGA COUNTY

Corinth	12822
Edinburg	12134
Hadley	12835

WARREN COUNTY

Adirondack	12808
Athol	12810
Bakers Mills	12811
Bolton Landing	12814
Brant Lake	12815
Chestertown	12817
Cleverdale	12820
Diamond Point	12824
Hague	12836
Johnsburg	12843
Kattskill Bay	12844
Lake George	12845
Lake Luzerne	12846
North Creek	12853
North River	12856
Pottersville	12860
Silver Bay	12874
Stony Creek	12878
Warrensburg	12885
Wevertown	12886

WASHINGTON COUNTY

Clemons	12819
Pilot Knob	12844
Putnam Station	12861

* Throughout *The Guide* we have followed the general spelling practice of using "AuSable" for the hamlet and post office of AuSable Forks and the Town of AuSable and "Ausable" for Ausable River and Ausable Chasm.

(4)

LEGISLATIVE DISTRICTS AND REPRESENTATIVES

STATE OF NEW YORK

U.S. SENATORS FROM NEW YORK

Senator Alphonse D'Amato
Rm. SH-520
Washington, D.C. 20510

Senator Daniel P. Moynihan
Russell Senate Office Bldg.
Washington, D.C. 20510
(202) 224-4451

U.S. REPRESENTATIVES FROM UPSTATE NEW YORK

23rd District
Congressman Samuel S. Stratton
Rm. 2205 Rayburn House Office Bldg.
Washington, D.C. 20515
or
244 Guy Park Avenue
Amsterdam, NY 12010

24th District
Congressman Jerry Solomon
Rm. 227 Cannon House Office Bldg.
Washington, D.C. 20515
or
285 Broadway
Saratoga Springs, NY 12866

26th District
Congressman David O'B. Martin
Rm. 109 Cannon House Office Bldg.
Washington D.C. 20515
or
E.J. Noble Medical Bldg.
Main St.,
Canton, NY 13617
or
104 Federal Building,
Plattsburgh, NY 12901

27th District
Congressman George C. Wortley
Rm. 428 Cannon House Office Bldg.
Washington, D.C. 20515
or
1269 Federal Bldg.
Syracuse, NY 13260

29th District
Congressman Frank Horton
Rm. 2229 Rayburn House Office Bldg.
Washington, D.C. 20515
or
314 Federal Bldg.
Rochester, NY 14614

STATE ASSEMBLY DISTRICTS IN THE ADIRONDACK PARK

100th District
Assemblyman Neil W. Kellehe
Rm. 320 Legislative Office Bldg.
Albany, NY 12248
(518)455-5777

108th District
Assemblyman Robert A. D'Andrea
Rm. 325 Legislative Office Bldg.
Albany, NY 12248
(518)455-5404
or
285 Broadway, Gaslight Square,
Saratoga Springs, NY 12866
or
Additional Office: 21 Bay St.,
Glens Falls, NY 12801.

109th District
Assemblyman Glenn Harris
Rm. 521 Legislative Office Bldg.
Albany, NY 12248
(518)455-5565
or
100 West Main St.,
Johnstown, NY 12095

110th District
Assemblyman Andrew W. Ryan
Rm. 443 Legislative Office Bldg.
Albany, NY 12248
(518)445-5441
or
42 Clinton St.
Plattsburgh, NY 12901

112th District
Assemblyman John G.A. O'Neil
532 Legislative Office Bldg.
Albany, NY 12248
(518)455-5797
or
PO Box 1120
Potsdam, NY 13676
(315)265-8200

113th District
Assemblyman Anthony J. Casale
Rm. 533 Legislative Office Bldg.
Albany, NY 12248
(518)455-5783
or
246 North Main Street
Herkimer, NY 13350

114th District
Assemblyman H. Robert Nortz
Rm. 525 Legislative Office Bldg.
Albany, NY 12248
(518)455-5545
or
Box 48
Lowville, NY 13367

115th District
Assemblyman William R. Sears
Rm. 439 Legislative Office Bldg.
Albany, NY 12248
(518)455-5334
or
107 West Court St.
Rome, NY 13440

STATE SENATE DISTRICTS IN THE ADIRONDACK PARK

43rd District
Senator Joseph L. Bruno
Rm. 814 Legislative Office Bldg.
Albany, NY 12247
(518)455-2346
or
RD 3,Box 219A
Bulson Rd.
Troy NY 12180

44th District
Senator Hugh T. Farley
Rm. 903 Legislative Office Bldg.
Albany, NY 12247
(518)455-3171

45th District
Senator Ronald B. Stafford
Rm. 502 Capital
Albany, NY 12247
(518)455-2811
or
162 Margaret St.
Plattsburgh, NY 12901

47th District
Senator James H. Donovan
Rm 708 Legislative Office Bldg.
Albany, NY 12247
(518)455-2211
or
State Office Bldg.
207 Genesee St.
Utica, NY 13501
(315)793-2360

(5)
LAND USE AND ZONING

The regulations governing land use within the Adirondacks—for both public and private lands—are among the most stringent and geographically expansive zoning laws in the United States. These regulations, passed in 1972 (public lands)) and 1973 (private lands), are also the source of much controversy within the Adirondacks (see Section 10).

This section presents an overview of the various classifications of public and private land within the Adirondacks and some of the regulations pertaining to the use and development of these different classifications of land. For fuller descriptions of these topics, two publications are recommended: *Adirondack Park State Land Master Plan* and *A Citizens Guide to Adirondack Park Agency Land Use Regulations* (for private lands). Both are available at no cost from the Adirondack Park Agency, Box 99, Ray Brook, NY 12977. Phone: (518)891-4050. Almost all the material in this section is taken verbatim from these two publications.

THE STATE LAND MASTER PLAN

The approximately 2.3 million acres of state-owned land within the Adirondacks (38% of the Park's six million acres) are classified in nine basic categories:

Wilderness
Primitive
Canoe
Wild Forest
Intensive Use
Historic
State Administrative
Wild, Scenic and Recreational Rivers
Travel Corridors

Fundamental determinants in how a particular area of land is classified are:

(1) The physical characteristics of the land or water which have a direct bearing on the capacity of the land to accept human use

(2) Biological considerations such as wetlands, wildlife habitats, endangered species of plants and animals, etc.

(3) Intangible considerations having a social or psychological impact, such as sense of remoteness, degree of wilderness, particular views, etc.

(4) The established facilities on the land, the uses now being made by the public and the policies followed by the various administering agencies

(5) The uses being made of contiguous or nearby private lands.

Definitions of the nine classifications of public lands and waters are as follows:

Wilderness

A wilderness area, in contrast with those areas where man and his own works dominate the landscape, is an area where the earth and its community of life are untrammeled by man- where man himself is a visitor who does not remain. A wilderness area is further defined to mean an area of state land or water having a primeval character, without significant improvements or permanent human habitation, which is protected and managed so as to preserve, enhance and restore, where necessary, its natural conditions, and which (1) generally appears to have been affected primarily by the forces of nature, with the imprint of man's work substantially unnoticeable; (2) has outstanding opportunities for solitude or a primitive and unconfined type of recreation; (3) has at least ten thousand acres of land and water or is of sufficient size and character as to make practicable its preservation and use in an unimpaired condition; and (4) may also contain ecological, geological or other features of scientific, educational, scenic or historical value.

Primitive

A primitive area is an area of land or water that is either:

1. Essentially wilderness in character but, (a) contains structures, improvements, or uses that are inconsistent with wilderness, as defined, and whose removal, though a long term objective, cannot be provided for by fixed deadline, and/or, (b) contains, or is contiguous to, private lands that are of a size and influence to prevent wilderness designation; or

2. Of a size and character not meeting wilderness standards, but where the fragility of the resource or other factors require wilderness management.

Canoe

A canoe area is an area where the watercourses or the number and proximity of lakes and ponds make possible a remote and unconfined type of water-oriented recreation in an essentially wilderness setting.

(The terrain associated with parcels meeting the above definition is generally ideally suited to ski touring and snowshoeing in the winter months.)

Wild Forest

A wild forest area is an area where the resources permit a somewhat higher degree of human use than in wilderness, primitive or canoe areas, while retaining an essentially wild character. A wild forest area is further defined as an area that frequently lacks the sense of remoteness of wilderness, primitive or canoe areas and that permits a wide variety of outdoor recreation.

Intensive Use

An intensive use area is an area where the state provides facilities for intensive forms of outdoor recreation by the public. Two types of intensive use areas are defined by this plan: campgrounds and day use areas.

(These areas provide overnight accomodations or day use facilities for a significant number of visitors to the Park and often function as a base for use of wild forest, wilderness, primitive and canoe areas).

Historic

Historic areas are locations of buildings, structures or sites owned by the state (other than the Adirondack Forest Preserve itself) that are significant in the history, architecture, archeology or culture of the Adirondack Park, the state or the nation.

State Administrative Areas

State administrative areas are areas where the state provides facilities for a variety of specific state purposes that are not primarily designed to accommodate visitors to the Park.

Wild, Scenic and Recreational Rivers

(The Adirondack Park contains many rivers which, with their immediate environs, constitute an important and unusual resource. Classification of those portions of rivers that flow through state land is vital to the protection of existing free flowing streams. The classification system and the recommended guidelines specified below are designed to be consistent with and complementary to both the basic intent and structure of the legislation passed by the legislature in 1972 creating a wild, scenic and recreational rivers system on both state and private lands).

A wild river is a river or section of river that is free of diversions and impoundments, inaccessible to the general public except by water, foot or horse trail, and with a river area primitive in nature and free of any man-made development except foot bridges.

A scenic river is a river or section of a river that is free of diversions or impoundments except for log dams, with limited road access and with a river area largely primitive and undeveloped, or that is partially or predominantly used for agriculture, forest management and other dispersed human activities that do not substantially interfere with public use and enjoyment of the river and its shore.

A recreational river is a river or section of river that is readily accessible by road or railroad, that may have development in the river area and that may have undergone some diversion or impoundment in the past.

Travel Corridors

A travel corridor is that strip of land constituting the roadbed and right-of-way for state and interstate highways in the Adirondack Park, the Remsen to Lake Placid railroad right-of-way, and those state lands immediately adjacent to and visible from these facilities.

Special Management Guidelines

The nine previously described classifications reflect the minimum management constraints for the lands affected. Certain parcels of land often require special management to reflect unusual resource or public use factors. Examples of these include:

—Special interest areas deserving of public attention, such as: scenic areas, places of geological interest providing information on the formation of the Adirondacks or unusual mineral deposits or rock formations, designated historic areas;

—Nature preserves, such as habitats of rare, threatened or endangered species of plants or wildlife where protection to prevent overuse or destruction of a unique resource may be required; and

—Lakes and ponds whose size, character, inaccessibility, or fishery resources require special protective measures.

THE PRIVATE LAND USE AND DEVELOPMENT PLAN

The 3.7 million acres of privately owned land within the Adirondack Park (62% of the Park's six million acres) are classified in six categories:

Hamlet
Moderate Intensity Use
Low Intensity Use
Rural Use
Resource Management
Industrial Use

To a great extent, the classifications follow the original pattern of the way the land was being used before the Plan was adopted in 1973. Existing kinds of development, public services, relationship to the public lands, open space, scenic travel corridors and physical make-up such as slope, type of soil and wetland characteristics, were considered in determining the land use areas.

The Adirondack Park Act tries to channel much of the future growth in the Park around existing communities, where there already are roads and utilities and where services and supplies are available. The Moderate Intensity Use and the Low Intensity Use areas are intended to provide for and are capable of absorbing most of the new development in the Park.

The Act is more limiting in the extent and type of development allowed in the more remote areas and those areas that deserve special consideration because of natural characteristics, terrain or proximity to the public lands. These generally fall into the Rural Use and Resource Management areas.

To check on the land use classification of any parcel of land in the Adirondacks, one can write or call the Adirondack Park Agency (Ray Brook, NY 12977. (518) 891-4050. A copy of the Land Use and Development Map will be sent to you. Larger-scale maps can be viewed at the APA office or at the offices of the 12 Adirondack county clerks.

Descriptions of uses and regulations governing the six private land use areas follow. In addition to those mentioned, additional requirements exist regarding: properties within one-quarter mile of Wild, Scenic and Recreational Rivers; tree cutting along shore-lines; and critical environmental areas, such as wetlands and lands above 2,500 feet.

Hamlet

These are the growth and service centers of the Park. Hamlet boundaries usually go beyond established settlements to provide room for future expansion. Colored brown on APA map. No limit to number of buildings in this land use area. Minimum lot width on shorelines is 50 feet; minimum building setback is 50 feet. Minimum sewage setback is 100 feet for seepage pit or drainage field.

Moderate Intensity Use

Most uses are permitted, but relatively concentrated residential development is most appropriate. Colored red on APA map. Allowable building density is 500 principal buildings per mile, or average lot size of 1.3 acres. Miminum lot width on shorelines is 100 feet; minimum building setback is 50 feet. Minimum sewage setback is 100 feet.

Low Intensity Use

Most uses are permitted, but residential development at a lower intensity than above is appropriate. Colored orange on APA map. Allowable building density is 200 primary buildings per square mile, or average lot size of 3.2 acres. Minimum lot width on shorelines is 125 feet; minimum building setback is 75 feet. Minimum sewage setback is 100 feet.

Rural Use

Most uses are permitted, but rural uses and lower intensity development is most suitable. Colored yellow on APA map. Allowable building density is 75 primary buildings per square mile, or average lot size of 8.5 acres. Minimum lot width on shorelines is 150 feet; minimum building setback is 75 feet. Minimum sewage setback is 100 feet.

Resource Management

These areas include nearly two million acres (53% of private lands). Special care is taken to protect the natural open space character of these lands. The most suitable uses include agriculture, forestry and outdoor recreational pursuits. Colored green on APA map. Allowable building density is 15 buildings per square mile, or average lot size is 42.7 acres. Minimum lot width on shorelines is 200 feet; minimum building setback is 100 feet. Minimum sewage setback is 100 feet.

Industrial

This is where existing industrial uses are located and where future industrial development can be located. Colored purple on APA map. No limit to number of buildings in this land use area.

Blue Ridge Wilderness across Sagamore Lake

WILDERNESS AREAS

A wilderness area, in contrast with those areas where man and his own works dominate the landscape, is an area where the earth and its community of life are untrammeled by man—where man himself is a visitor who does not remain. A wilderness area is further defined to mean an area of state land or water having a primeval character, without significant improvements or permanent human habitation, which is protected and managed so as to preserve, enhance and restore, where necessary, its natural conditions, and which generally appears to have been affected primarily by the forces of nature, with the imprint of man's work substantially unnoticeable; has outstanding opportunities for solitude or a primitive and unconfined type of recreation; has at least ten thousand acres of land and water or is of sufficient size and character as to make practicable its preservation and use in an unimpaired condition; and may also contain ecological, geological or other features of scientific, educational, scenic or historical value.

BLUE RIDGE

This wilderness is located in the towns of Arietta, Lake Pleasant and Indian Lake in Hamilton County. It is roughly bounded on the north and northeast by Route 28; on the southeast by private lands immediately north and west of Cedar River Flow; and on the west by the Lake Kora and Sagamore Lake properties and the south Inlet of Raquette Lake.

State Lands	44,393 Acres
Bodies of Water (19)	455 Acres
Elevation (minimum)	1,700 Feet
(maximum)	3,744 Feet
Foot Trails	15.0 Miles
Lean-tos	3

DIX MOUNTAIN

This area is in the towns of Elizabethtown, Keene and North Hudson, Essex County. It is roughly bounded on the north by Route 73, on the east by the Adirondack Northway, on the south by Blue Ridge Road and on the west by Elk Lake and AuSable Club lands.

State Lands	50,190 Acres
Bodies of Water (12)	115 Acres
Elevation (minimum)	940 Feet
(maximum)	4,857 Feet
Foot Trails	36.5 Miles
Lean-tos	2
Non-conforming Uses	None

FIVE PONDS

This wilderness is located in the towns of Fine and Clifton in St. Lawrence County, the town of Webb in Herkimer County and the town of Long Lake in Hamilton County. It is bounded on the north by Cranberry Lake, a portion of the Oswegatchie River, the road leading to Inlet and private lands; on the east by the Colton town line and private lands in the vicinity of Gull Lake, a road leading to Gull Lake and the Remsen to Lake Placid railroad; on the south by Stillwater Reservoir; on the west by private lands and lands classified as wild forest in the former Schuler Tract.

State Lands	92,635 Acres
Private Inholdings (2)	350 Acres
Bodies of Water (95)	1,452 Acres
Elevation (minimum)	1,486 Feet
(maximum)	2,460 Feet
Foot Trails	100.1 Miles
Lean-tos	5
Non-conforming Uses:	None

GIANT MOUNTAIN

This area lies in Essex County, in the towns of Elizabethtown and Keene, and is roughly bounded by Route 9N on the north, by Route 73 on the west and south, and Route 9 on the east.

State Lands	22,104 Acres
Bodies of Water (2)	6 Acres
Elevation (minimum)	700 Feet
(maximum)	4,627 Feet
Foot Trails	12.5 Miles
Lean-tos	1
Non-conforming Uses:	None

HA-DE-RON-DAH

This area is located in the town of Webb, Herkimer County, and the Town of Greig, Lewis County. It is bounded on the north by private lands in the vicinity of North Pond, Hitchcock Pond, Moose Pond and the headwaters of the Independence River; on the east by private lands along the Remsen to Lake Placid railroad right-of-way; on the south by private lands along Route 28 and by the woods road leading to the Copper Lake property; and on the west by Pine Creek and a Department of Environmental Conservation maintained foot trail from Pine Creek to Pine Lake, East Pine Pond and Big Otter Lake.

State Lands	27,050 Acres
Bodies of Water (59)	610 Acres
Elevation (minimum)	1,440 Feet
(maximum)	2,340 Feet
Foot Trails	33.8 Miles
Lean-tos	7
Non-conforming Uses:	None

HIGH PEAKS

This is the largest wilderness area and is located in three counties and six towns: the town of Harrietstown in Franklin County, the towns of North Elba, Keene, North Hudson and Newcomb in Essex County and the town of Long Lake in Hamilton County. It is roughly bounded on the north by Route 3; the old Haybridge Road, which runs from Cold Brook to Averyville; the Adirondack Loj property at Heart Lake; the Mount Van Hoevenberg Winter Recreation Center; and Route 73 near the Cascade Lakes. Private land to the west of Route 73 forms the eastern boundary. The southern boundary is formed by privately owned lands, including the AuSable Club, Finch Pruyn, National Lead Company and the State University College of Environmental Science and Forestry's Huntington Wildlife Forest. This wilderness is bounded on the west by Long Lake and the Raquette River.

State Lands	226,435 Acres
Private Inholdings (10)	4,530 Acres
Bodies of Water (112)	1,392 Acres
Elevation (minimum)	1,040 Feet
(maximum)	5,344 Feet
Foot Trails	238.4 Miles
Horse Trails	52.3 Miles
Lean-tos	49
Impoundments	2
Non-conforming Uses:	
Ranger Cabins	2
Horse Barns	4
Telephone Lines	7.5 Miles
Lean-to Clusters	2
Roads (public)	1 Mile

HOFFMAN NOTCH

This area lies in the towns of Schroon, North Hudson and Minerva in Essex County. It is bounded on the north by private lands lying south of the Blue Ridge Road and the Sand Pond Mountain tract donated to the state by Finch, Pruyn and Company for fish and wildlife management and silvicultural research and experimentation purposes, on the east by the Adirondack Northway and private lands immediately west of the Northway, on the south by private lands lying north of Loch Muller Road, and on the west by the road and trail that extends from Irishtown along Minerva Stream northward to the Blue Ridge Road near Cheney Pond.

State Lands	36,045 Acres
Bodies of Water (8)	141 Acres
Elevation (minimum)	960 Feet
(maximum)	3,693 Feet
Foot Trails	30.0 Miles
Non-conforming Uses:	None

McKENZIE MOUNTAIN

This area is located in western Essex County in the towns of St. Armand, North Elba and Wilmington. In general, the Saranac River and Franklin Falls Reservoir border on the north, the Wilmington—Franklin Falls road, the Whiteface Mountain Memorial Highway and the west branch of the AuSable River form the eastern boundary, the Saranac Lake—Lake Placid Road, Route 86, forms the southern boundary, and the Saranac River forms the western boundary.

State Lands	35,298 Acres
Private Inholdings (3)	100 Acres
Bodies of Water (8)	22 Acres
Elevation (minimum)	1,463 Feet
(maximum)	4,869 Feet
Foot Trails	14.2 Feet
Horse Trails	4.0 Miles
Leantos	1
Non-conforming Uses:	
Vehicle Parking and Storage Area	1

PEPPERBOX

The Pepperbox Wilderness lies totally within the town of Webb in Herkimer County. Stillwater Reservoir and the Beaver River form the southern boundary, while the survey line between John Brown's tract and Watson's East Triangle generally forms the northern boundary. The western boundary is the county line, and the eastern boundary is partially the old jeep road to Raven Lake and partially the state land boundary.

State Land	14,600 Acres
Bodies of Water (40)	352 Acres
Elevation (minimum)	1,360 Feet
(maximum)	2,168 Feet
Foot Trails	2.0 Miles
Non-conforming Uses:	None

PHAROAH LAKE

The Pharoah Lake Wilderness straddles the Essex-Warren County Line in the towns of Ticonderoga, Hague, Horicon and Schroon. The county road along the east shore of Schroon Lake forms the western boundary; to the north, private land and Route 74 form the boundary. The state land boundary forms most of the remaining perimeter except for a stretch of Route 8 on the south. Pharoah Lake, an extremely attractive body of water, is one of the largest lakes in the Adirondack Park totally surrounded by forest preserve lands. Due to its configuration, it can provide a wilderness experience to relatively large numbers of people. In addition, the numerous and crystal-clear ponds, vistas resulting from rock outcroppings and severe fires, and intriguing geographic names such as Grizzle Ocean, Thunderbolt Mountain, Oxshoe Pond and Desolate Brook, make this one of the most appealing of all Adirondack areas.

State Lands	46,039 Acres
Private Inholdings (1)	117 Acres
Bodies of Water (39)	1,242 Acres
Elevation (minimum)	860 Feet
(maximum)	2,551 Feet
Foot Trails	48.0 Miles
Horse Trails	8.0 Miles
Lean-tos	15
Impoundments	1
Non-conforming Uses:	
Fire Towers (unmanned)	1
Observer Cabins	1
Horse Barns	1
Telephone Lines	3.0 Miles
Roads (public)	1 Mile

PIGEON LAKE

This area lies in the town of Webb, Herkimer County, and the towns of Long Lake and Inlet in Hamilton County. It is bounded on the north by Stillwater Reservoir and large blocks of private land in the vicinity of Rose Pond, Shingle Shanty Pond and Upper Sister Lake; on the east by a private road from Brandeth Lake to North Point and by Raquette Lake; on the south by private lands along the Uncas Road; and on the west by the Big Moose Road, private lands near Big Moose Lake, Thirsty Pond, Twitchell Lake, Razorback Pond, and the Remsen to Lake Placid railroad tracks.

State Lands	51,005 Acres
Bodies of Water (64)	1,499 Acres
Elevation (minimum)	1,700 Feet
(maximum)	2,900 Feet
Foot Trails	27.8 Miles
Lean-tos	4
Non-conforming Uses:	None

SENTINEL RANGE

This area is located in the towns of Wilmington, North Elba and Keene, Essex County. It is bounded by Route 86 on the north, Route 73 on the south, and private lands on the east and west. The Sentinal Range and its slopes dominate the area and 5 small ponds are situated near the northern and northwestern boundaries.

State Lands	23,137 Acres
Bodies of Water (5)	77 Acres
Elevation (minimum)	1,375 Feet
(maximum)	2,893 Feet
Foot Trails	13.8 Miles
Lean-tos	1
Non-conforming Uses:	
Jeep Trail	3.5 Miles

SIAMESE PONDS

The Siamese Ponds area is located in the towns of Lake Pleasant, Wells and Indian Lake in Hamilton County and the towns of Johnsburg and Thurman in Warren County. It is one of the largest wilderness areas, extending about 18 miles north to south and about 13 miles from east to west at its widest part. It is roughly bounded by Route 28 on the north; by private land tracts near Thirteenth Lake, Gore Mountain and Bakers Mills and by Route 8 on the east; by Route 8 on the south; and by Route 8, International Paper Company lands and Indian Lake on the west.

State Lands	108,503 Acres
Private Inholdings (1)	106 Acres
Bodies of Water (67)	1,090 Acres
Elevation (minimum)	1,280 Feet
(maximum)	3,472 Feet
Foot Trails	35.8 Miles
Lean-tos	4
Non-conforming Uses:	
Snowmobile Trails	2.5 Miles
Roads (public)	2.5 Miles

SILVER LAKE

This area is located in the towns of Lake Pleasant, Benson, Wells and Arietta in Hamilton County and is roughly bounded on the north by Route 8 and private lands near Piseco Lake, Oxbow Lake, Hamilton County, Sand Lake and Lake Pleasant; on the east by Route 30; on the south generally by the Hamilton County line; and on the west by Route 10, the West Branch of the Sacandaga and the Piseco Outlet.

State Lands	106,997 Acres
Private Inholdings (3)	1,450 Acres
Bodies of Water (48)	512 Acres
Elevation (minimum)	820 Feet
(maximum)	3,250 Feet
Foot Trails	26.5 Miles
Lean-tos	2
Non-conforming Uses:	None

WEST CANADA LAKE

This wilderness is located in the town of Ohio in Herkimer County and the towns of Morehouse, Arietta, Lake Pleasant and Indian Lake in Hamilton County. It is bounded on the north by the Moose River Plains area and private lands in the vicinity of Little Moose Lake, Squaw Brook, Snowy Mountain and Squaw Mountain; on the east by Route 30, lands of International Paper Company and the Spruce Lake—Piseco Lake Trail; on the south by private lands north of Route 8, the South Branch of West Canada Creek and an access road to private lands; on the west by West Canada Creek and private lands east of Honnedaga Lake.

State Lands	160,183 Acres
Private Inholdings (2)	1,630 Acres
Bodies of Water (168)	2,180 Acres
Elevation (minimum)	1,390 Feet
(maximum)	3,899 Feet
Foot Trails	67.1 Miles
Lean-tos	10
Impoundments	1
Non-conforming Uses:	
Snowmobile Trails	3.8 Miles
Ranger Cabins	1
Helicopter Platforms	1
Telephone Lines	7.5 Miles
Roads (public)	3.8 Miles

WILDERNESS STATISTICAL TOTALS

State Lands	1,034,935 Acres
Private Inholdings	8,380 Acres
Bodies of Water (755)	11,144 Acres
Foot Trails	701.5 Miles
Horse Trails	64.3 Miles
Lean-tos	94
Impoundments	4
Non-conforming Uses:	
Snowmobile Trails	6.3 Miles
Fire Towers: unmanned	1
Observer Cabins	1
Ranger Cabins	3
Helicopter Platforms	1
Horse Barns	5
Telephone Lines	18 Miles
Lean-to Clusters	2
Vehicle Parking and Storage Area	1
Roads (public)	8.3 Miles
Jeep Trail (abandoned public)	3.5 Miles

Source: *Adirondack Park State Land Master Plan* (Adirondack Park Agency, 1979).

Avalanche Lake, taken by Seneca Ray Stoddard

PRIMITIVE AREAS

A primitive area is an area of land or water that is either: (1) Essentially wilderness in character but, (a) contains structures, improvements, or uses that are inconsistent with wilderness, as defined, and whose removal, though a long term objective, cannot be provided for by a fixed deadline, and/or (b) contains, or is contiguous to, private lands that are of a size and influence to prevent wilderness designation, or (2) of a size and character not meeting wilderness standards, but where the fragility of the resource or other factors require wilderness management.

AMPERSAND

This area consists of a small belt of forest preserve between the Ampersand road and Ampersand Brook in the town of Harrietstown, Franklin County. It extends from the Ampersand Lake property westward to Stony Creek and thence northward to Stony Creek Ponds.

State Lands	700 Acres
Bodies of water (2)	13 Acres
Foot Trails	0.5 Miles
Non-conforming Uses:	
Road (Private)	3.5 Miles
Jeep Trails	0.8 Miles
Snowmobile Trails	3.5 Miles
Telephone Lines	3.5 Miles

BALD LEDGE

This area consists of an appendage from the Pharoah Lake Wilderness in the town of Ticonderoga, Essex County. It is severed from the wilderness by a road used periodically to harvest timber from an adjacent private parcel.

State Lands	500 Acres
Non-conforming Uses:	
Roads (private)	.5 Miles

BUCK POND

This area lies in the town of Fine, St. Lawrence County, and consists only of the private right-of-way following a very rough wood road providing access for all terrain vehicles to an inholding of private land at Buck Pond.

Non-conforming Uses:	
Jeep Trail	8.5 Miles

BUELL BROOK

This area is in the town of Indian Lake and Lake Pleasant, Hamilton County. It is bounded on the north by private lands south of the Cedar River; on the east by private lands along the Squaw Brook; on the south by an access road running from the Cedar River to the vicinity of Onion Hill along Little Squaw Brook; and on the west by the Cedar River Flow and private lands immediately east of the Cedar River.

State Lands	10,900 Acres
Private Inholdings (1)	10 Acres
Bodies of Water (1)	5 Acres
Elevation (minimum)	2,140 Feet
(maximum)	3,786 Feet
Non-conforming Uses:	
Roads (private)	4.5 Miles

CATHEAD MOUNTAIN

This area consists of one Great Lot (121) in the town of Benson, Fulton County, containing two rights of way to an inholding of private land as well as a telephone line to the state operated fire tower on Cathead Mountain lying within the inholding.

State Lands	206 Acres
Non-conforming Uses:	
Jeep Trails	1.0 Miles
Telephone Line	.5 Miles

CRANE POND

This area, in the town of Schroon, Essex County, consists of an existing town road right-of-way which provides access to the northern part of the Pharoah Lake Wilderness, one of the three most heavily used wilderness areas within the Park, due to accessibility and proximity to the Northway.

Non-conforming Uses	
Roads (public)	2.1 Miles
Snowmobile Trails	2.1 Miles
Telephone Lines	2.1 Miles

DUG MOUNTAIN

This is a small appendage of state land adjacent to the Siamese Ponds Wilderness area in the village of Speculator, Hamilton County. It is bounded on the north, west and south by private lands.

State Lands	60 Acres
Non-conforming Uses:	
Roads (private)	.2 Miles

FORT NOBLE MOUNTAIN

This area is in the town of Ohio, Herkimer County, and the town of Morehouse, Hamilton County. It consists of the state land west of the trail to the Fort Mountain fire tower, north of the South Branch of West Canada Creek, and south to the watershed divide between the South Branch and the North Branch of West Canada Creek.

State Lands	450 Acres
Foot Trails	1.5 Miles
Non-conforming Uses:	
Fire Towers	1
Observer Cabins	1
Telephone Lines	1.5 Miles

HUDSON GORGE

This primitive area is in the town of Minerva, Essex County, and the town of Indian Lake, Hamilton County. It encompasses the wildest and most remote section of the Hudson River, as well as a spectacular white water gorge.

State Lands	17,170 Acres
Private Inholdings (2)	2,900 Acres
Bodies of Water (13)	218 Acres
Elevation (minimum)	1,200 Feet
(maximum)	2,558 Feet
Foot Trails	13 Miles
Non-conforming Uses:	None

HURRICANE MOUNTAIN

This area is located in the towns of Elizabethtown, Jay, Keene and Lewis, Essex County. It is predominantly steep, rocky ground with thin soil. Hurricane Mountain, 3,694 feet in elevation, dominates this area.

State Lands	13,449 Acres
Bodies of Water (1)	10 Acres
Elevation (minimum)	1,400 Feet
(maximum)	3,694 Feet
Foot Trails	12.8 Miles
Lean-tos	2
Non-conforming Uses:	
Jeep Trails	1.7 Miles
Fire Towers	1
Observer Cabins	1
Telephone Lines	2.8 Miles
Roads (Public)	.2 Miles

JAY MOUNTAIN

This area lies within the towns of Jay and Lewis in Essex County. It is bounded by the Glen road on the south and private land boundaries elsewhere except where the road west of Mt. Fay severs an appendage of state land.

State Lands	7,100 Acres
Elevation (minimum)	1,435 Feet
(maximum)	3,600 Feet
Foot Trails	1.0 Miles
Non-conforming Uses:	None

JOHNS BROOK

This area is in the town of Keene in Essex County. It consists of the private right-of-way across state lands to several private parcels in the High Peaks Wilderness.

Non-conforming Uses:	
Roads (Private)	1.3 Miles
Ranger Cabin	1

LAKE LILA

This area lies in the town of Long Lake, Hamilton County. It is bounded on the west by the Remsen to Lake Placid railroad line and by a road leading to a private inholding encompassing Gull Lake, Deer Pond and Partlow Lake (an inholding that is scheduled to pass to state ownership in fifty years), which form the eastern boundaries of the Five Ponds Wilderness Area, and to the north, south and east by private lands.

State Lands	7,215 Acres
Bodies of Water (3)	1,414 Acres
Non-conforming Uses:	
Roads (private)	4.5 Miles
Railroad	2.0 Miles
Camp and associated outbuildings	

PILLSBURY LAKE

This area lies in the towns of Arietta and Lake Pleasant in Hamilton County. Until recently it consisted of a number of lots interspersed in a checkerboard arrangement with International Paper Company lots. In 1980 the voters approved an amendment to Article 14 permitting the state to negotiate with International Paper for an exchange of lands to form more manageable boundaries. The exchange is now completed, but the figures below represent the earlier situation and will need to be revised.

State Land	3,330 Acres
Private Inholdings (1)	5,620 Acres
Bodies of Water (5)	96 Acres
Elevation (minimum)	2,300 Feet
(maximum)	3,597 Feet
Foot Trails	7.8 Miles
Non-conforming Uses:	
State Truck Trails	4.1 Miles
Telephone Lines	1.8 Miles

SACANDAGA

This minor area is in the town of Wells in Hamilton County. It consists only of the Whitehouse road and its right-of-way in lots 362 and 382 of the Benson Tract.

Non-conforming Uses:	
Roads (public)	.7 Miles

VALCOUR ISLAND

This Lake Champlain island lies in the towns of Peru and Plattsburg in Clinton County.

State Lands	1,075 Acres
Private Inholdings (4)	25 Acres
Non-conforming Uses:	
Former Seaton House and Associated Outbuildings	1
Storage Sheds	2

WAKELY MOUNTAIN

This area is in the town of Lake Pleasant, Hamilton County. It consists of the state land south of the Wakely Mountain Trail.

State Lands	120 Acres
Foot Trails	1.0 Miles
Non-conforming Uses:	
Fire Towers	1
Observer Cabin	1
Telephone Lines	1.0 Miles

WEST CANADA MOUNTAIN

This area is in the Town of Morehouse in Hamilton County. It is surrounded by private lands on the north, east and west. The southern boundary is the access road to the Miller Camp.

State Lands	2,935 Acres
Elevation (minimum)	1,900 Feet
(maximum)	2,985 Feet
Non-conforming Uses:	
Roads (private access)	3.3 Miles

WILMURT CLUB ROAD

This area is in the town of Morehouse in Hamilton County.

Non-conforming Uses:	
Roads (private)	1.0 Miles

PRIMITIVE AREA STATISTICAL TOTALS:

State Lands	64,780 Acres
Private Inholdings	8,555 Acres
Bodies of Water(25)	1,765 Acres
Foot Trails	37.6 Miles
Lean-tos	2
Non-conforming Uses:	
State Truck Trails	4.1 Miles
Roads (public)	3.0 Miles
Roads (private)	22.5 Miles
Jeep Trails	12.0 Miles
Snowmobile Trails	.6 Miles
Fire Towers	3
Observer Cabins	3
Ranger Cabins	1
Telephone Lines	13.2 Miles
Railroad	4.5 Miles

Source: *Adirondack Park State Land Master Plan* (Adirondack Park Agency, 1979).

Upper AuSable Lake from Boreas Bay, taken by Seneca Ray Stoddard

(8)

15 WILD FOREST AREAS

A wild forest area is an area where the resources permit a somewhat higher degree of human use than in wilderness, primitive or canoe areas, while retaining an essentially wild character. A wild forest area is further defined as an area that frequently lacks the sense of remoteness of wilderness, primitive or canoe areas and that permits a wide variety of outdoor recreation.

BLACK RIVER
This area includes the state lands primarily in Herkimer County, south of Rt. 28, north of Rt. 8 and west of the Adirondack League Club holdings. The Black River flows in a generally east-west direction through the middle of the area.

BLUE MOUNTAIN
This area is located in Hamilton and western Essex counties. It is bounded by Rt. 30 on the west and south, the Hudson River on the east and Rt. 28N on the north.

CRANBERRY LAKE
This area is located in southern St. Lawrence County in the towns of Clifton, Colton and Fine.

DE BAR MOUNTAIN
This area is in the northern section of the Park primarily in the towns of Brighton and Duane, Franklin County. The summit of De Bar Mountain once permitted Verplanck Colvin to triangulate Lake Champlain and the St. Lawrence River. It also offers the broadest distant view in the Park of the High Peaks country to the south.

FERRIS LAKE
This area is located in the southwestern corner of the Park. It consists of those state lands south of Rt. 8 and west of Rt. 10.

HAMMOND POND
This area is located in the towns of Crown Point, Moriah, North Hudson and Schroon in Essex County. Bounded by Rt. 9 on the west and north, it extends south to Paradox Lake, and its eastern and southern boundaries border private lands.

INDEPENDENCE RIVER
This western Adirondack area lies in Lewis and Herkimer counties south of the Beaver River and north of Rt. 28.

JESSUP RIVER
This area is located in Hamilton Couty in the towns of Arietta and Lake Pleasant. Bounded on the north by the "saddle" of Indian Lake, this wild forest extends easterly to Sacandaga Lake and southerly to Piseco.

LAKE GEORGE
The wild forest tracts of land associated with this well-known section of the Park straddle the Warren-Washington county line. Mountains rising steeply on either side of the lake provide many views of rugged beauty. The area west of the lake is accessible by Rts. 9N and 73, while the forest preserve on the east side is accessible from the Pilot Knob and Hulett's Landing Roads.

MOOSE RIVER PLAINS
This area lies between Rt. 28 and West Canada Lakes Wilderness in Hamilton and Herkimer counties.

SARANAC LAKES
Easily accessible from Rt. 3 and 30, this southern Franklin County area offers a broad network of streams, lakes and ponds for water-oriented recreation.

SARGENT PONDS
Easterly of Raquette Lake, lying north of Rt. 28 and west of Rt. 30, lies a labyrinth of boreal swamp and forest. Much of this great spruce-balsam-white cedar tract borders the Raquette River, Marion River and Boulder Brook.

SHAKER MOUNTAIN
This area is located south of the Silver Lake Wilderness between Rts. 10 and 30 in Fulton County.

VANDERWHACKER MOUNTAIN
The Vanderwhacker tract lies both east and west of Rt. 28N in western Essex County. The three primary attractions of the area are the lakes and ponds, the Boreas River and Vanderwhacker Mountain. The latter, by virtue of its location, provides perhaps the best view of the High Peaks from the south in the Park.

WILCOX LAKE
This area lies south of Rt. 8 and east of Rt. 30 in the vicinty of the Hamilton-Warren-Saratoga county lines' convergence and is capable of withstanding considerably more use without destruction of the physical resource or the wild forest atmosphere.

Source: *Adirondack Park State Land Master Plan* (Adirondack Park Agency, 1979)

BUILDING PERMITS

In most of the rural areas of the Adirondacks, no municipal or county building permits are required (although it is best to check to be sure). However, three government agencies charged with managing development in the Park and protecting the public health and welfare often do require permits—the Adirondack Park Agency, the Department of Health and the Department of Environmental Conservation.

A "LEAD AGENCY" APPROACH

These three agencies have established a coordinated project review and permit system to eliminate duplication and speed up the review process. Under this system, a person applying for a permit deals only with the designated "lead agency" for a particular project. The lead agency coordinates its information requests, site inspections, etc. with the others. Following the review process, the lead agency transmits to the applicant, in a single package, the decisions of the agencies involved. Other federal, state or local regulations may also apply. The lead agency will be able to advise the applicant on this.

If yours is one of the following types of projects, and you need permits from more than one of these agencies, contact the "lead agency" indicated:

ADIRONDACK PARK AGENCY (APA)

Airports
Commercial seaplane bases
Forestry use structures
Golf courses
Industrial uses
Junk yards
Major public utility uses
Marinas, boat yards, boat launch sites
Mobile home courts
Multiple family dwellings other than new subdivisions
Municipal roads
New campgrounds
New group camps
New tourist accommodations
Private tourist attractions
Public and semi-public buildings (other than new medical)
Real property subdivisions
Sawmills
Single family dwellings
Ski centers
Special rivers systems permits
25 acre-plus clear-cut
Wetlands development

DEPARTMENT OF ENVIRONMENTAL CONSERVATION (DEC)

Commercial sand and gravel operations
Mineral extraction
Mineral extraction structures
Sewage treatment plants and collection systems
Shoreline development for public bathing beaches
Special flood hazard area building permits
Waste disposal area
Watershed management; stream protection and flood control

HEALTH DEPARTMENT (HD)

Modernization or expansion of:
  Campgrounds
  Group camps
  Tourist accommodations
  Mobile home courts
New medical facilities
Water treatment and distribution facilities
Commercial uses (restaurants, theatres, etc.)

PROJECT PERMIT CHECKLIST

The following checklist covers projects requiring a permit under the Adirondack Park Agency Act. If your project falls in any of the categories below, you should write, call or visit the APA office for a permit application, or an informal pre-application meeting. If your project is not subject to APA review, you can get a letter from the Agency to that effect.

Projects in Critical Environmental Areas

Critical Environmental Areas are sub-categories of the general land use areas. Critical Environmental Areas include wetlands, highways and state-owned lands. An APA permit is required in all land use areas for most development activities and subdivisions of land in:

—Wetlands—defined by the APA Act as "any land annually subject to periodic or continual inundation by water and commonly referred to as bog, swamp or marsh, and which are either one acre or more in size; or adjacent to a body of water with which there is a free interchange of water, in which case there is no size limit. For further information, including a site review by a staff member, please contact the Agency.

—An APA permit is required in all but hamlet areas for most development activities and subdivisions:

—At elevations over 2,500 feet.

—Within 1/4 mile of a "study river," including portions of the Oswegatchie, Osgood, Grasse, N. Branch Saranac, Middle and N. Branch Moose, East Stony Creek and Pleasant Lake Stream.

(A "study river" is a river being considered for inclusion in the state's Wild, Scenic and Recreational River System. Many other Adirondack rivers and streams are already classified in the system and are subject to its special regulations.)

—Within 1/8 mile of State Forest Preserve lands classified as Wilderness, Primitive or Canoe areas.

—Within 150 feet of state or federal highway rights-of-way (in rural use areas only).

—Within 300 feet of state or federal highway rights-of-way (in resource management areas only).

Subdivisions

An APA permit is often needed for subdivisions. These are broadly defined to include any division of land into two or more lots, parcels or building sites (including that portion retained by owner) for the purpose of sale, lease or any form of separate ownership or occupancy. An APA permit is needed for any subdivision in:

—A Critical Environmental Area (see above)

An APA permit is needed for any subdivision (regardless of lot sizes) that involves the following number of lots or residential units:

—100 or more lots in hamlet areas

—15 or more lots in moderate intensity use areas

—10 or more lots in low intensity use areas

—5 or more lots in rural use areas

—All subdivisions in resource management areas (two or more lots including portion retained by owner).

An APA permit is needed for any subdivision (regardless of the number of lots) having:

—A non-shoreline lot of less than 40,000 square feet in moderate intensity use areas (0.91 acres).

—A non-shoreline lot of less than 120,000 square feet in low intensity use areas (2.75 acres).

—A non-shoreline lot of less than 320,000 square feet in rural use areas (7.34 acres).

An APA permit is needed for any subdivision (regardless of the number of lots) having:

—A shoreline lot of less than 25,000 square feet in area or less than 100 feet in width in moderate intensity use areas (.57 acres).

—A shoreline lot of less than 50,000 square feet in area or less than 125 feet in width in low intensity use areas (1.14 acres).

—A shoreline lot of less than 80,000 square feet in area or less than 150 feet in width in rural use areas (1.83 acres).

A shoreline lot includes any lot partly or entirely within the minimum building setback distance from the water.

Single Family Dwellings

An APA permit is needed for single family dwellings and mobile homes in the following designated areas:

—resource management

—industrial use

—critical environmental areas

Other Projects

An APA permit is needed for:

—Any other project listed as a "regional project" in the APA Act, including structures over 40 feet high in all land use areas. (Contact the APA for further information.)

—Any new commercial or industrial use in all but hamlet areas.

—An expansion totaling 25 percent or more (whether such expansion is undertaken all at once or over an extended time) of an existing use or structure included on the list of "regional projects" in the APA Act.

Permits may also be required from other state agencies or local governments.

In areas governed by an Agency-approved local land use program, certain projects normally requiring an Agency permit will need only a local permit.

Shoreline restrictions apply along lakes, ponds, rivers and streams, irrespective of whether a project permit is needed.

Additional permit requirements apply within 1/4 mile of designated Wild, Scenic and Recreational Rivers.

Source: *A Citizen's Guide to Adirondack Park Agency Land Use Regulations*, published by the Adirondack Park Agency, undated.

(10)
ADIRONDACK CONTROVERSIES

MAJOR CONTROVERSIES

ACID RAIN. Although a minority of Adirondack lakes are affected (and a relatively small percentage of the entire lake acreage in the region), hundreds of Adirondack lakes are so acidic they no longer can support fish and plant life. Does industrial pollution from the Mid-West create this acidity which rains and snows on the Adirondacks and other areas? Does acid precipitation retard forest growth? What can be done to reduce "acid rain" and restore our lakes—eliminate pollution at its source, keep liming the lakes, develop acid-resistant fish? Industry says we don't know enough to start solving the problem. President Reagan agrees. Most scientists who have studied the problem and environmentalists say we do. Nationally the controversy centers on the Clean Air Act. Will it be gutted or strengthened? The future of the Adirondacks (and many parts of the nation) may hang in the balance. Believing that acid rain is analogous to the canaries that miners carried to warn them of life-threatening toxins in the air, a Coalition of Adirondackers to Neutralize Acid Rain (C.A.N.A.R.I.) has been formed to work on the problem. Information: C.A.N.A.R.I., c/o Trout Unlimited, Box 238, Paul Smiths, NY 12970.

ADIRONDACK PARK AGENCY. Created in 1972 by the NYS Legislature, the "APA" administers the strictest and most extensive rural zoning plan in the country (see Sections 5-9). From its start, the majority of Adirondack residents opposed the agency—complete with bumper stickers reading "Adirondack Park Agency—Another Word for Tyranny" and an unsuccessful attempt to burn down the APA headquarters in Ray Brook, NY. Most conservationists and a minority of local citizens defend the APA Act as reasonable long-range planning which still allows for economic development. In response to the controversy, the Legislature authorized the Adirondack Park Local Government Review Board (PO Box 818, Elizabethtown, NY 12932. (518)873-9286), a local, non-funded watchdog agency designed to monitor and evaluate APA activities. The controversy, while less heated than in the 1970's, continues today.

HISTORIC PRESERVATION. When the State purchased several "Adirondack Great Camps" (see Section 25) for the Forest Preserve in the 1970's, including the caretaking complex of buildings at historic "Camp Sagamore," the potential conflict between historic preservation and wilderness protection became apparent. While most environmentalists, preservationists, sporting groups and local organizations think that both historical and wilderness values can be preserved, the question is: how? Legislation, constitutional amendments, administrative solutions, using private sector solutions to avoid future problems, or a combination of these means have all been proposed. The editors believe that the eventual solution to this problem will involve: (1) completing the inventory of historic resources in the Adirondacks, (2) Private solutions for most future endangered historic properties, so they do not become part of the Forest Preserve, (3) the Sagamore Land Exchange Amendment (which may come before the voters in November 1983) authorizing the state to trade 10 acres and the endangered caretaking buildings to the non-profit organization which owns Camp Sagamore in return for 200 acres elsewhere in the Park, and (4) either an administrative solution for other historic properties in state ownership in the Forest Preserve or an amendment to Section 4 of Article 14 to extend the State Nature and Historical Preserve into the Adirondack and Catskill Parks on a limited number of acres.

TIMBER HARVESTING IN THE FOREST PRESERVE. Article 14 says of the Forest Preserve, "... nor shall the timber thereon be sold, removed or destroyed." Lumber companies, economic interests and many local residents who burn wood say this is wasteful and that good timber harvesting practices enhance a forest and encourage jobs and wildlife, especially deer. Environmentalists fear abuses, problems and costs of administration, and the threat to vulnerable natural areas and to Article 14. In its hundred year history, there have been dozens of attempts to introduce legislation to allow timber harvesting in the Forest Preserve. Such attempts have always been defeated. In recent years, however, they have gotten further along in the legislature than ever before. This will be a continuing source of controversy, especially if wood products become increasingly scarce or expensive.

OTHER CONTROVERSIES

ADIRONDACK RAILROAD. Should the tracks of the old Adirondack Division, which ran from Utica to Malone and to Lake Placid, be torn up and made a snowmobile/ski /hiking trail? Should the State try to facilitate the railroad's re-opening, either privately or publicly? Are both uses possible?

INSECT SPRAY. What types? Is it effective? Is it worth it? At what costs to the environment?

OVER-USED TRAILS. Should there be a hiking permit system? Should access to certain trails be limited, even closed for a period?

PREDATOR POLICY. Should coyotes continue to be protected as game animals, or should they be subject to unlimited hunting as predators destroying deer?

PRISONS. How many prisons can the Adirondacks handle? Are the Adirondacks becoming New York's Siberia, with urban prisoners sent far from their homes and families? Are the employment benefits of prisons irresistible?

STATE CAMPGROUNDS. How many are needed? How long should they be kept open?

WILDLIFE SANCTUARIES. Should certain areas in the Forest Preserve be set aside for wildlife refuges? Should local Board of Supervisor approval be necessary, as is now the case, or only DEC determination?

(11)
TERMINOLOGY

"Adirondack Park" — those 9,375 square miles or approximately 6,000,000 acres of northern New York State circumscribed by a boundary line established (and occasionally expanded) by the State Legislature. The Adirondack Park contains both private and state-owned lands.

"Blue Line"— the Adirondack Park boundary, nicknamed so because it was marked in blue on early maps. The Blue Line generally follows the edge of the foothills which rise from the surrounding Champlain, Mohawk, Black and St. Lawrence River Valleys.

"Forest Preserve Counties" — the 12 counties situated wholly or partly within the Adirondack Park or the four counties situated partly within the Catskill Park. The 12 Adirondack Forest Preserve Counties are: Clinton, Essex, Franklin, Fulton, Hamilton, Herkimer, Lewis, Oneida, St. Lawrence, Saratoga, Warren and Washington. Of these, only Essex and Hamilton are entirely within the Blue Line.

"New York State Forest Preserve" or just "The Forest Preserve" — all the state-owned land (except that in villages and in the towns of Altona and Dannemora) in the Forest Preserve Counties, whether within or beyond the Blue Line.

"Adirondack Forest Preserve" — the approximately 2,300,000 acres of Forest Preserve within the Adirondack Park, plus the approximately 12,000 acres of state-owned dry land in the Adirondack Forest Preserve Counties outside the Adirondack Park (in addition the state owns over 100,000 acres under Lake Champlain). The Adirondack Forest Preserve within the Blue Line is "forever wild," protected by Article 14 of the State Constitution (see Section 27).

"Adirondack Mountains" — sometimes used synonymously with "Adirondack Park" and other times used to connote the more mountainous sections of the Adirondack Park.

"The Adirondacks" — an abbreviated form of the "Adirondack Mountains".

"High Peaks" — the 46 mountains originally thought to be all over 4,000 feet and the highest in the Adirondacks (see Section 54).

"High Peaks Region" — that wilderness in Essex County where most of the Adirondack High Peaks are located.

"North Country" — usually used to describe the area spanning from approximately the Central Adirondacks to the Canadian border; although some users extend the boundary farther south.

HISTORY

(12)
IMPORTANT DATES IN ADIRONDACK HISTORY

PRE-EUROPEAN
Area used by Algonquins, Hurons, Mohawks and Oneidas for trapping, hunting and fishing.

16TH CENTURY
Commerce way stations set up by Iroquois on west shore of Lake Champlain.

1535
Standing atop Mount Royal (Montreal), Jacques Cartier and party are first Europeans to view the Adirondack Mountains.

1609
Samuel de Champlain is first white man to visit the Adirondacks; he earns the Iroquois Confederacy's enmity for the French.

1664
British Charles II, having gained control of area formerly held or claimed by Dutch, cedes it to his brother the Duke of York, creating the colony called "New York".

1731
French move south from Quebec, occupy Crown Point and build Fort St. Fredric. Three years later they begin constructing Fort Carillon at Ticonderoga.

1757
French General Montcalm beseiges Fort William Henry at the foot of Lake George. British surrender; fort is destroyed.

1759
British General Amhearst retakes Lake Champlain. Retreating French destroy Forts Carillon and St. Fredric. Fort Carillon reconstructed and renamed Ticonderoga. Crown Point fortifications also built, assuring British control.

1775
Patriots Ethan Allen and Benedict Arnold capture Ticonderoga and (the following day) Crown Point from the British. (May 30).

1776
First important naval battle of the Revolution takes place off Valcour Island in Lake Champlain.

1777
British General Burgoyne sails up Lake Champlain and recaptures Fort Ticonderoga from American troops. Later that year Burgoyne is defeated and surrenders at Saratoga.

1791
Alexander Macomb purchases 4 1/2 million acres of appropriated Oneida Nation lands—most of it in the Adirondacks—for eight cents an acre.

1814
Invading British fleet and army are turned back at Battle of Plattsburgh by American forces under Com. Thomas Macdonough.

1837
First ascent of Mt. Marcy by Ebenezer Emmons and party (August 5).

1849
John Brown arrives in North Elba to take charge of "Timbucto," a farming colony for ex-slaves.

1858
Philosphers' Camp. William James Stillman, Ralph Waldo Emerson, James Russel Lowell, Louis Agassiz and other New England luminaries, set up camp on Follensby Pond and later write and tell of wilderness experience.

1869
William H.H. Murray's *Adventures in the Wilderness* is published; influx of tourists to the Adirondacks begins.

1875
Verplanck Colvin measures height of Mt. Marcy at 5,402 feet (November 4).

1885
Adirondack Forest Preserve established by law.

1885
Dr. Edward L. Trudeau founds Trudeau Sanitarium.

1891
"Blue Line" is created, when the NYS Forest Commission submits a report with the proposed Adirondack Park outlined in blue (April 28).

1892
Adirondack Park established by law (May 20).

1892
Last spike driven on Mohawk and Malone Railroad (later the Adirondack Division of the NY Central) at Twitchell Creek (October 11).

1894
Article 7, Section 7, the "Forever Wild" provision of the NY State Constitution (later changed to Article 14) is passed and takes effect January 1, 1895.

1901
Association for the Protection of the Adirondacks holds its first meeting (December 12).

1922
Adirondack Mountain Club formed (April 27).

1932
Lake Placid hosts the Third Winter Olympic Games.

1935
Franklin Delano Roosevelt dedicates Whiteface Mt. Memorial Highway (September 13).

1957
Adirondack Museum opens.

1971
Temporary Study Commission on the Future of the Adirondack Park, formed in 1969, publishes its recommendations, many of which are adopted in the Adirondack Park Agency Act.

1973
Gov. Nelson Rockefeller signs Adirondack Park Agency Act into law (May 22).

1980
Lake Placid hosts the Thirteenth Winter Olympic Games.

(13)
IMPORTANT HISTORICAL FIGURES

This section includes those individuals who played a significant part in the history of the Adirondacks or whose presence in the Adirondacks has become an important part of the lore of the region. With a few exceptions, we have not included here the many famous people who visited or owned a camp in the Adirondacks or the many colorful hotel keepers who populated the mountains, as there would be no end to such a listing.

BROWN, JOHN (1800-1859)
Famous abolitionist, settled in North Elba to assist in Gerrit Smith's unsuccessful experiment of founding a Negro settlement. Following abortive attempt to start slave's rebellion and hanging at Harper's Ferry, body returned to celebrated gravesite in North Elba.

BRYERE, JOSEPH O.A. (1860-1941)
"An artist in rustic work," said Stoddard. Probably the most important builder of rustic furniture for Adirondack camps.

CHAMPLAIN, SAMUEL de (1567-1635)
First European to visit Adirondacks. His belligerence toward the Iroquois made them permanent enemies of the French, influencing North American and Adirondack history.

COLVIN, VERPLANCK (1847-1920)
Conducted early surveys of Adirondacks; made annual reports to State Legislature. Worked tirelessly for the creation of an Adirondack park and forest preserve.

COULTER, WILLIAM (1865-1907)
Saranac Lake-based architect who carried on Durant tradition of camp building; designed many of the Great Camps of the Adirondacks, especially in Saranac Lake region.

DEWEY, MELVIL (1851-1931)
Founded Lake Placid Club. Also invented Dewey Decimal Classification System. His son Godfrey was instrumental in the development of winter sports in Lake Placid.

DISTIN, WILLIAM G. (1884-1970)
Partner in architectural firm of Coulter and Distin; continued large Adirondack camp building tradition into the 1940s.

DUNNING, ALVAH (1816-1902)
One of the earliest settlers in the Raquette Lake area. One of the most famous Adirondack guides, hermits and all-around characters.

DURANT, FREDRIC CLARK (1853-1926)
Built Prospect House (1882)—major hotel in central Adirondacks, attracting large numbers of tourists and future estate owners to the area. Owned Camp Cedars.

DURANT, THOMAS CLARK (1820-1885)
Vice-President and General Manager of Union Pacific Railroad; spearheaded work on eastern portion of first transcontinental railroad. Built Adirondack Railroad (Saratoga Springs to North Creek), purchased enormous Adirondack holdings, and took first major steps to open up central Adirondacks to development.

DURANT, WILLIAM WEST (1850-1934)
Built transportation system that opened central Adirondacks to development. Built camps Pine Knot, Uncas, Sagamore and others; is considered father of Adirondack "Great Camp" architectural style.

EMMONS, EBENEZER (1800-1863)
Conducted earliest geographical survey of the Adirondacks (1837). Named the main range of mountains "The Adirondacks". Drew early attention of developers and sportsmen to Adirondacks. Made first ascent of Mt. Marcy.

FERNOW, BERNHARD EDUARD (1851-1923)
Brought scientific forestry to America. Founded State College of Forestry at Cornell. His unsuccessful attempts to introduce scientific forestry in the Adirondacks indirectly strengthened the recently-passed Article 14.

Verplank Colvin

Thomas Clark Durant

Orson Schofield Phelps

Edward Livingston Trudeau

FOSTER, NATHANIEL "NAT" (1767-1841)
Renowned North Country hunter and trapper and subject of famous 1834 murder trial. Possibly a partial model for Fenimore Cooper's "Natty Bumpo."

HENDERSON, DAVID (d.1845)
Manager and prime mover behind the McIntyre Adirondack Iron Works—one of major, early Adirondack industries.

HERRESHOFF, CHARLES FREDRIC (1763-1819)
Son-in-law of John Brown of Providence, RI. After Brown's unsuccessful attempt to develop the "Brown's Tract" in Herkimer and Hamilton Counties, Herreshoff moved to area, also failed at farming, sheep raising and mining, and committed suicide. Old Forge grew up around the site of his last failure.

HOCHSCHILD, HAROLD K. (1892-1981)
Founder of Adirondack Museum. Chairman of Temporary Study Commission on the Future of the Adirondacks, which led directly to passage of Adirondack Park Agency Act. Author of *Township 34.*

JESUP, MORRIS K. (1830-1908)
Railroader, philanthropist. Chairman of 1883 Forestry Committee; supporter of and activist for the creation of Adirondack Park.

JUDSON, EDWARD (1821-1886)
Pen name "Ned Buntine." Swashbuckling dime novel author and promoter of Buffalo Bill's Wild West Show. Resided in and attracted attention to Blue Mt. Lake area.

MACOMB, ALEXANDER (1748-1831)
Negotiated "Macomb's Purchase" in 1792 of 4.5 million acres of land, mostly in the Adirondacks, for other investors.

MARSHALL, LEWIS (dates unknown)
One of the major leaders in the fight to secure passage of "forever wild" constitutional protection in 1894 and to defend it over the following decades. Father of Robert Marshall.

MARSHALL, ROBERT (1901-1939)
Member of first party to climb all 46 Adirondack High Peaks. Went from Adirondacks to short but distinguished career as forester and conservationist, including founding of Wilderness Society.

MCINTYRE, ARCHIBALD (1772-1858)
Founder of Elba Iron Works (often called McIntyre Iron Works) and Adirondack Iron Works—one of the earliest major Adirondack industries.

MURRAY, HON. AMELIA M. (1795-1884)
Maid of honor to Queen Victoria. Wrote famous travelogue of her 1856 journey throughout America including a trip through the Adirondacks. Possibly first woman to make pleasure trip through the region.

MURRAY, WILLIAM H.H. (1840-1904)
Congregational minister; author of several Adirondack books including *Adventures in the Wilderness, or Camp Life in the Adirondacks* (1869), which hastened large-scale tourism in the Adirondacks. Nicknamed "Adirondack" Murray.

PHELPS, ORSON SCHOFIELD (1817-1905)
Nicknamed "Old Mountain" Phelps. Perhaps the most famous of the early Adirondack guides. Lived mostly in Keene Valley area.

RONDEAU, NOAH JOHN (1883-1967)
Most famous Adirondack hermit; spent about half a century in Cold River region of High Peaks.

RUSHTON, J. HENRY (1843-1906)
Famous canoe builder, with shop in Canton.

SABATTIS, MITCHELL (1816-1906)
One of the most famous Adirondack guides. Member of Abenaki tribe. Lived in Long Lake area.

SEARS, GEORGE WASHINGTON (1821-1890)
Pen-name "Nessmuk." His accounts of three cruises through the Adirondacks (and elsewhere) in light-weight Rushton canoes drew much attention of sportsmen to the region. Also author of *Woodcraft* (1884) a widely-read manual of the day.

SMITH, PAUL (1825-1912)
Built Paul Smith's Hotel. Pioneered development in northern Adirondack-St. Regis Lakes area. Heirs donated land for Paul Smith's College.

STODDARD, SENECA RAY (1844-1917)
Adirondack photographer, artist, guidebook writer and map maker, whose work informed and/or attracted tens of thousands of visitors in the late 1800s and early 1900s. Active in efforts to establish Adirondack Park.

TRUDEAU, EDWARD LIVINGSTON (1848-1915)
Founded Trudeau Sanitarium; made Saranac Lake region a haven for tuberculosis patients and, consequently, thousands of visitors to the Adirondacks.

VAN HOEVENBERG, HENRY (1849-1918)
Builder and founder of the Adirondack Lodge on Heart Lake. Pioneered in telegraph field. Developed and improved trail system in the High Peaks wilderness.

WEBB, WILLIAM SEWARD (b.1851)
Built Mohawk and Malone Railroad, later Adirondack Division of New York Central, hastening development of western and northern Adirondacks. Amassed 112,000 acre Nahasene Park.

WOODRUFF, TIMOTHY (1858-1913)
Lieutenant Governor of New York. First Chairman of Forest Preserve Board; later President of Forest, Fish and Game Commission and charter member of Association for Protection of the Adirondacks. Builder of original grand Kamp Kill Kare.

(14)

MUSEUMS

CLINTON COUNTY

CLINTON COUNTY HISTORICAL MUSEUM, City Hall, Plattsburgh, NY 12901. Various military items, documents, paintings and artifact exhibits relating to Clinton County's history. Admission fee. Open all year. Information: Mrs. Helen Allan, Director, PO Box 332, Plattsburgh, NY 12901. (518)561-0340.

ESSEX COUNTY

ADIRONDACK CENTER MUSEUM, Elizabethtown, NY 12932. The center's collection includes artifacts dealing with early settlement of the area, domestic and outdoor life, a doll collection, trade and crafts of the area, colonial garden, research library, and contemporary art exhibits by area artists. It also maintains the Crown Point Press, Inc., consisting of unique reprints of rare NY State history booklets, prints, maps and journals. Guided tours, film and lecture series offered. Admission fee. Open May 15-October 15. Directions: Exit 30 off I-87, proceed to Rt. 9 west and north. Information: (518)873-6466.

ADIRONDACK LOJ MUSEUM AND NATURE TRAIL, Heart Lake, Lake Placid, NY 12946. Adirondack nature museum with mineral, butterfly, bird and terrarium exhibits. Center for numerous natural history seminars and lectures. Open July-August. Information: (518)523-3441.

CROWN POINT, STATE HISTORIC SITE, Crown Point, NY 12928. Here are the preserved remains of Forts St. Frederic (1734) and Crown Point (1759), along with a modern Visitor Center which houses exhibits on the history and archeology of the Site as well as an introductory program. Free. Early June- late October, closed Monday & Tuesday, also open July 4th and Labor Day. November-May by appointment. Directions: just west of the Lake Champlain Bridge, off Rts. 9N/22. Information: R.D. #1, Box 219, Crown Point, NY 12928. (518)597-3666.

FORT TICONDEROGA MUSEUM, Ticonderoga, NY 12883. Guided tours take visitors through the restored Colonial and Revolutionary Fort containing a military museum. Admission fee. Open May-October. Directions: Exit 28 off the Northway (I-87) and then NYS 74. Information: (518)585-2821.

HANCOCK HOUSE, Ticonderoga, NY 12883. Reproduction of the Colonial Mansion built in Boston, 1737-1741, and occupied by John Hancock. Operated by Ticonderoga Historical Society as a research library and museum for local and Champlain Valley history. Open year round. Wednesday-Saturday, 10am-4pm. Open daily during July and August. No fee. Information: (518)585-7868.

HERITAGE MUSEUM AND GALLERY, Montcalm St., Ticonderoga, NY 12883. Artifacts displayed from aircraft carrier USS Ticonderoga of WWII and Apollo Missions. Information and picture display of USS Ticonderoga (CG-47) commissioned January 23, 1983. Open June-October, daily, 9-7 pm. Information: (518)585-6619.

JOHN BROWN FARM AND GRAVE, Lake Placid, NY 12946. State Historic Site. Self-guided tours enable visitors to see the 19th century farm, grave and home of John Brown, famous abolitionist. Open early May to late October (call for exact dates). Wednesday-Saturday 10-5pm, Sunday 1-5pm. Closed Monday and Tuesday. No fee. Directions: 2 miles south of Lake Placid, off Rt. 73. Information: Edwin Cotter, Jr., Director. (518)523-3900.

LAKE PLACID-NORTH ELBA HISTORICAL SOCIETY MUSEUM, Lake Placid, NY 12946. Located within the restored old Penn Central railroad station. Self-guided tours take visitors through a collection of artifacts and memorabilia telling Lake Placid's history, including the 1932 Winter Olympics exhibit. No fee. Open July-September. Directions: off Rt. 73 on Averyville Rd. Information: (518)523-3551.

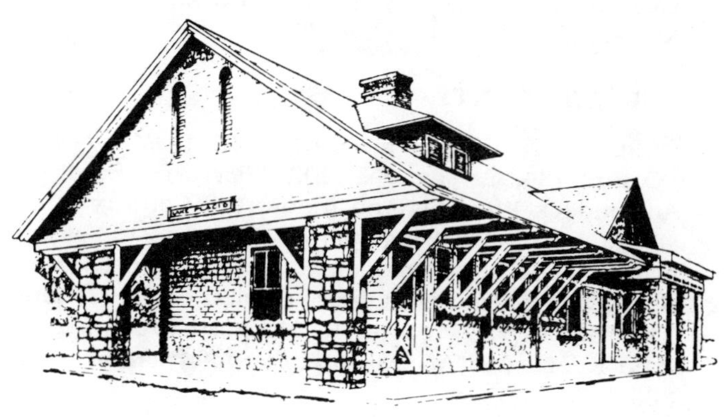

PENFIELD HOMESTEAD MUSEUM, Ironville, Crown Point, NY 12928. The museum contains home furnishings, paintings and other items of the Penfield Family and the mines of the Crown Point Iron Company. Self-guided walking tours around the Ironville ironwork ruins. Guided tours by appointment. The museum properties now total almost 500 acres. Reference library also available for use. No fee. Open May 15-October 15. Information: (518)597-3804.

ROBERT LOUIS STEVENSON MEMORIAL COTTAGE, Saranac Lake, NY 12983. A collection of Robert Louis Stevenson's personal memorabilia including original letters and first editions. Admission fee. Open July 1-September 15, Tuesday-Sunday. Directions: 11 Stevenson Lane. Information: (518)891-4480.

TOPRIDGE, The former Merriweather-Post Estate. Open for tours on weekends, Memorial Day-October 15. Admission fee. Information: Chamber of Commerce, Saranac Lake, NY 12983. (518)891-1990.

FRANKLIN COUNTY

CHARLES DICKERT MEMORIAL WILDLIFE MUSEUM, Saranac Lake, NY 12983. Located in the Saranac Lake Free Library. Collection consists of wide variety of mounted animals, birds and fish. Also exhibits in boat building, log tables and other regional art. Information: (518)891-4190.

FRANKLIN COUNTY HISTORICAL MUSEUM AND SOCIETY, 51 Milwaukee St., Malone, NY 12953. Display rooms with furnishings, tools, weaving and costumes of different periods in history. Donations. Open June 15-September 15, Tuesday-Saturday, 1-5pm; September 16-June 14, Saturday only 1-5 pm or by appointment. Information: (518)483-2750.

SIX NATIONS INDIAN MUSEUM, Onchiota, NY 12968. Iroquois relics, ancient and modern, displayed. Guided tours and lectures on the contributions of the Iroquois, including readings of beaded record belts. Admission fee. Open June-October daily. Information: (518)891-0769.

WILLIAM CHAPMAN WHITE MEMORIAL ADIRONDACK ROOM, Saranac Lake, NY 12983. Located in the Saranac Lake Free Library. Extensive collection of Adirondackana. No fee. Information: (518)891-4190.

FULTON COUNTY

CAROGA HISTORICAL MUSEUM, "THE HOMESTEAD," PO Box 434, Caroga, NY 12032. Recreates Southern Adirondack lifestyles and industries. Country store, school, farmhouse living quarters. Period costumes and artifacts. Special summer events. No fee. Open Tuesday-Sunday, 11-5. Tour groups please call ahead. Directions: Exit 28 from NYS Thruway, Rt. 30A North to Johnstown, then Rt. 29 west to Caroga Lake. Information: (518) 835-4400.

FULTON COUNTY MUSEUM, 237 Kingsboro Ave., Gloversville, NY 12078. Displays include glove making and tanning, the F.J. &G. Railroad, Sacandaga region, Indians of the area. No fee. July and August, Tuesday-Saturday, 10am-4pm, Sundays, noon-4pm. September-June, Tuesday-Saturday, noon-4pm. Tour groups please call ahead. Information: (518)725-2203.

HAMILTON COUNTY

THE ADIRONDACK MUSEUM, Blue Mt. Lake, NY 12812. Exhibits on Adirondack art, history, life, leisure and industry in 20 buildings. Major museum of the Adirondacks. Research library and off-season group tours open by arrangement. Open June 15-October 15, 10am-6pm daily. Adults $4.50, children (7-15) $2.75, under 7 free. Information: (518)352-7311.

PISECO LAKE MUSEUM, Piseco, NY 12139. Within a 19th century village tavern are Adirondack relics and antiques. Open late June through mid-October. Information: (518)548-6401.

SAGAMORE LODGE, Raquette Lake, NY 13436. A slide show on historic great camps, followed by a self-guided tour of the Sagamore buildings and grounds, former estate of the Alfred Vanderbilt family. Also bookstore and craft shop, dining room open for lunch. Open Saturdays and Sundays, 9:30-5pm, July and August (except 8/28/83) or by appointment for groups. Admission fee. Information: (315)354-5311.

HERKIMER COUNTY

FOREST INDUSTRIES EXHIBIT HALL, Old Forge, NY 13420. Dioramas and scale models of forest and wildlife management, veneer and plywood manufacturing. Some of the more than 5,000 different products of the forest industries on display. No fee. Open Memorial Day to Labor Day, closed Tuesdays. Directions: Rt. 28, 1 mile north of Old Forge. Information: (315)369-3078.

HERKIMER COUNTY HISTORICAL SOCIETY MUSEUM, 400 North Main St., Herkimer, NY 13350. New exhibit on the county's history; a resource center and offices are maintained within the 1884 Victorian house. No fee. Open Monday-Friday. Information: (315)866-6413.

LEWIS COUNTY

GOULD-HOUGH CULTURAL AND EDUCATIONAL CENTER, sponsored by the Lewis County Historical Society, PO Box 306, High St., Lyons Falls, NY 13368. Collection contains costumes, documents, farm equipment and other artifacts related to local history. Varied programs and services include guided tours, loan kits, lectures, musical programs and art classes. Minimal admission fee. Open May-October 15. Information: (315) 348-8089.

ONEIDA COUNTY

ONEIDA COUNTY MUSEUM, 318 Genesee St., Utica, NY 13502. Museum and library of local history located inside the Fountain Elms Building of the Munson-Williams-Proctor Inst. Open year-round. Tuesday-Saturday, 10-5pm. Information: (315)735-3642.

SARATOGA COUNTY

CORINTH MUSEUM, 604 Palmer Ave., Corinth, NY 12822. The collection contains displays and archives of local history. Tours available upon request. No fee.

SARATOGA COUNTY MUSEUM, Brookside, Ballston Spa, NY 12020. Exhibits on the history of everyday life in early Saratoga County. Admission fee. Open daily 1-5pm. Closed January-March. Information: (518)885-4000.

ST. LAWRENCE COUNTY

SILAS WRIGHT HOUSE MUSEUM, 3 E. Main St., PO Box 8, Canton, NY 13617. Sponsored by the St. Lawrence County Historical Association. Collection includes furniture, decorative arts, textiles, archival records, photographs and books all relating to St. Lawrence County history. No fee. Open Monday-Friday year round. Information: (315)386-2780.

WARREN COUNTY

CHAPMAN HISTORICAL MUSEUM, Glens Falls, NY 12801. A period home of the 1880's, with changing exhibits. Major collection of Seneca Ray Stoddard photos forms the nucleus of a 20,000-piece Adirondack photo library. Open Tuesday-Saturday, 2-5pm and by appointment; closed in January. No fee. Directions: Off I-87, exits 18, 19. Information: (518)793-2826.

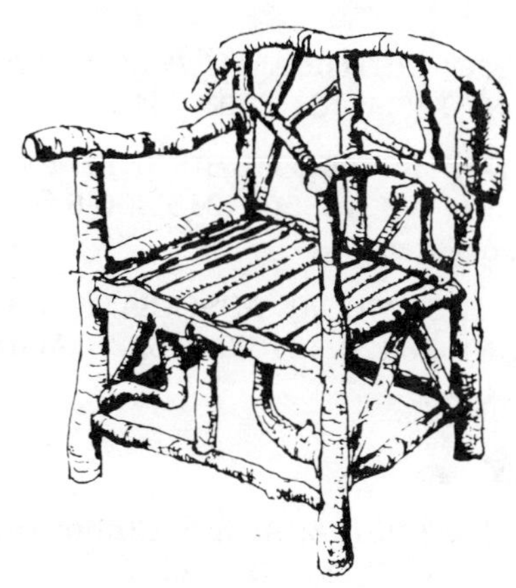

COURTHOUSE AND 19TH CENTURY JAIL CELLS, Lake George, NY 12845. Original cells and artifacts of 1800's. Sponsored by Lake George Historical Society. Directions: Exit 21 off I-87 to 9N, County Court House Building. Information: (518)668-5044.

FORT WILLIAM HENRY MUSEUM, Lake George, NY 12845. Unique tour with live demonstrations of various artillery of French and Indian War era. Guided tours available July-August. Admission fee. Open May to mid-October. Information: (518)668-5471.

HADLEY-LAKE LUZERNE HISTORICAL SOCIETY AND SCHOOL HOUSE MUSEUM, Lake Luzerne, NY 12846. Authentic one room schoolhouse with furnishings preserved. No fee. Directions: Exit 21 off I-87. Information: (518)696-2732.

HORICON HISTORICAL SOCIETY MUSEUM, Brant Lake, NY 12815. Early crafts, furniture and items from local residents are displayed in an old homestead. Guided tours, slide shows, lectures and craft exhibits offered to the public. No fee. Open late May through September. Directions: Exit 25 off I-87, Rt. 8. Information: (518) 494-2804.

LAKE GEORGE HISTORICAL ASSOCIATION, PO Box 472, Lake George, NY 12845. Collection includes relics and memorabilia of the region, photographs, and research library. Lecture series, slide programs and workshops offered. Admission fee. Open daily. Directions: Off I-87, Exits 21 or 22. Information: PO Box 472, Canada and Amhearst Sts., Lake George, NY 12845. (518)668-5044.

THE MARCELLA SEMBRICH MEMORIAL STUDIO, Bolton Landing, NY 12814. Collection consists of memorabilia relating to Marcella Sembrich, opera star. No fee. Open July-Labor Day. Directions: Rte. 9N, Lakeshore Dr. Information: (518)644-9836.

MUSEUM OF LOCAL HISTORY, Chestertown, NY 12817. Located on top floor of Town Hall. Collection includes common school, village store, dressmaker's shop, post office, photography exhibit and library. Guided tours during summer, research center maintained. No fee. Open July and August, Monday-Friday, 10-12, 1-3. Directions: Exit 25 off I-87. Information: (518)494-2711.

MUSEUM OF LOCAL HISTORY, Warrensburg, NY 12885. Artifacts, maps, books telling of the culture and industry of the area on display. Guided tours available June-August. No fee. Located: 47 Main St. Information: (518) 623-2928.

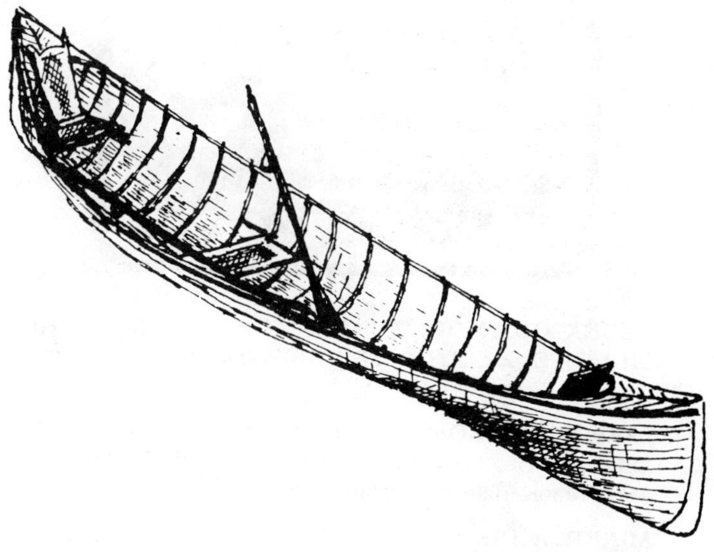

WARREN COUNTY HISTORIAN OFFICE, Warren County Municipal Center, Lake George, NY 12845. The office maintains geneology records, maps, history books, local literature, census records and information that relates to Warren County. Services include research assistance, tours for students, senior citizens, and geneology groups. Open Tuesdays and Thursdays. Information: (518) 761-6544.

WASHINGTON COUNTY

TUPPER'S EARLY AMERICAN AND FARM MUSEUM, W. Fort Ann, NY 12827. Park-like collection of early American buildings, wagons, utensils and memorabilia. Covered bridge, water wheel, nature trails. No fee. Open June-October, dawn to dusk daily. Located: Copeland Pond Road off Rt. 149 at West Fort Ann. Information: (518) 792-6058.

(15)

HISTORICAL SOCIETIES, ORGANIZATIONS AND COUNTY HISTORIANS

In addition to the groups and individuals listed below, towns and villages sometimes have designated historians

CLINTON COUNTY

CLINTON COUNTY HISTORIAN: Mrs. Addie L. Shields, Route 2, PO Box 40, Plattsburgh, NY 12901. (518) 563-7178.

CLINTON COUNTY HISTORICAL MUSEUM/ASSOCIATION, PO Box 332, Plattsburgh, NY 12901. (518) 561-0340. Mrs. Helen Allan, Director.

ESSEX COUNTY

ESSEX COUNTY HISTORIAN: Miriam W. Richard, Essex County Historical Society, Court St., Elizabethtown, NY 12932. (518)873-6466.

ESSEX COUNTY HISTORICAL SOCIETY, Court St., Elizabethtown, NY 12932. (518)873-6466. Miriam W. Richard, Director.

ESSEX COMMUNITY HERITAGE ORGANIZATION (ECHO), Essex, NY 12936. (518)963-7088. Mrs. Norma Jackson, President.

LAKE PLACID-NORTH ELBA HISTORICAL SOCIETY, 30 Lakeview St., Lake Placid, NY 12946. (518)523-3703. Mary MacKenzie, Historian.

MINERVA HISTORICAL SOCIETY, Olmstedville, NY 12857. (518)251-2718. Suzanne E. LaRocque, Director.

PENFIELD FOUNDATION, Ironville, Crown Point, NY 12982. (518)597-3804.

SCHROON-NORTH HUDSON HISTORICAL SOCIETY, Main St., Schroon Lake, NY 12870. (518) 532-7670. Charles W. Millard, President.

WESTPORT HISTORICAL SOCIETY, Westport Train Depot, Westport, NY 12993. (518)962-4449 (summer only). Mrs. Carol Buchanan, President.

TICONDEROGA HISTORICAL SOCIETY, Hancock House, Ticonderoga, NY 12883. (518)585-7868. Mrs. Elizabeth E. McCaughin, Curator.

FRANKLIN COUNTY

FRANKLIN COUNTY HISTORIAN: C. Walter Smallman, PO Box 35, Hermon, NY 13652. (Unofficial) (315)347-3221.

FRANKLIN COUNTY HISTORICAL SOCIETY, 51 Milwaukee St., Malone, NY 12953. (518)483-2750. Mr. John Hotchkiss, President.

FULTON COUNTY

FULTON COUNTY HISTORIAN: Dr. Robert M. Palmer, 401 North Main St., Gloversville, NY 12078. (518) 725-3073.

CAROGA HISTORICAL ASSOCIATION, PO Box 434, Caroga Lake, NY 12032.

HAMILTON COUNTY

HAMILTON COUNTY HISTORIAN: Ted Aber, PO Box 3, Indian Lake, NY 12842. (518)648-5329.

ADIRONDACK HISTORICAL ASSOCIATION, Adirondack Museum, Blue Mt. Lake, NY 12812. (518)352-7311.

HERKIMER COUNTY

HERKIMER COUNTY HISTORIAN: H. Paul Draheim, PO Box 7, Herkimer, NY 13350. (315)866-2413.

HERKIMER COUNTY HISTORICAL SOCIETY, 400 North Main St., Herkimer, NY 13350. (315)866-6413. Mrs. James E. Spellman, Director.

TOWN OF WEBB HISTORICAL ASSOCIATION, Crosby Blvd., Old Forge, NY 13420. (315)369-6338. Marion G. Holmes, Director.

LEWIS COUNTY

LEWIS COUNTY HISTORIAN: Arthur Einhorn, Courthouse, Lowville, NY 13367. (315)376-2812.

LEWIS COUNTY HISTORICAL SOCIETY, High St., PO Box 306, Lyons Falls, NY 13368. (315)348-8089. Arlene S. Hall, Director.

ONEIDA COUNTY

ONEIDA COUNTY HISTORIAN: Mrs. Christopher Kelly, Main St., Holland Patent, NY 13354. (315)865-8350.

ONEIDA COUNTY HISTORICAL SOCIETY, 318 Genesee St., Utica, NY 13502. (315)735-3642. Douglas M. Preston, Director.

ST. LAWRENCE COUNTY

ST. LAWRENCE COUNTY HISTORIAN (unofficial): Mary H. Smallman, RFD 1, Box 171B, Hermon,NY 13652. (315)347-3221.

SARATOGA COUNTY

SARATOGA COUNTY HISTORIAN: Violet R. Dunn, 31 Woodlawn Ave., Saratoga Springs, NY 12866. (518) .

SARATOGA COUNTY HISTORICAL SOCIETY, Brookside, Ballston Spa, NY 12020. (518)885-4000. Field Horne, Director.

WARREN COUNTY

WARREN COUNTY HISTORIAN: Pamela Vogel, County Office Building, Rt. 9, Lake George, NY 12845. (518) 761-6544.

BOLTON HISTORICAL SOCIETY, Bolton Landing, NY 12814.

HADLEY-LAKE LUZERNE HISTORICAL SOCIETY, Kinnear Museum of Local History, Main St., Lake Luzerne, NY 12846. (518)696-3202.

HAGUE HISTORICAL SOCIETY, Hague, NY 12836. Clifton West, Historian.

HISTORICAL SOCIETY OF THE TOWN OF CHESTER, INC., Chestertown, NY 12817. (518)494-2711.

HORICON HISTORICAL SOCIETY, Brant Lake, NY 12815. (518)494-2804. Isabel Carpenter, Director.

JOHN THRUMAN HISTORICAL SOCIETY, INC., Athol, NY 12810. Leona Walker, President.

LAKE GEORGE HISTORICAL ASSOCIATION, PO Box 472, Lake George, NY 12845. (518)668-5044.

STONY CREEK HISTORICAL ASSOCIATION, Lanfear Rd., Stony Creek, NY 12878. Meta Sayre, President.

WASHINGTON COUNTY

WASHINGTON COUNTY HISTORIAN: Mildred E. Southard, Upper Broadway, Fort Edward, NY 12828.

OUTSIDE THE ADIRONDACK PARK

ADIRONDACK RESEARCH CENTER, Schaffer Library, Union College, Schenectady, NY 12308. (518)370-6278. Ellen Fladger, Archivist.

Source: Original source: Folwell, B.(Ed.) *Cultural Resources in New York's North Country*. (Blue Mt. Lake: Adirondack Museum, 1980). Additional material added. Each entry verified.

(16)
NATIONAL REGISTER OF HISTORIC PLACES: ADIRONDACK LISTINGS

Dates in parentheses refer to when the property was listed on the National Register.

ADIRONDACK FOREST PRESERVE. Entire Forest Preserve is an historic district.

ADIRONDACK IRON AND STEEL COMPANY, UPPER WORKS. North of Tahawus at Henderson Lake. (10-5-77)

BLUE MOUNTAIN LAKE HOUSE ANNEX, "Log Hotel," Blue Mountain, NY Rt. 30, Blue Mt. Lake. (12-7-77)

CAMP SAGAMORE, Raquette Lake vicinity, off Rte. 28 at west end of Sagamore Lake. (1-11-76)

CHESTERTOWN HISTORIC DISTRICT, Chestertown, Canada Dr. (US 9). (8-22-77)

CHURCH OF NAZARENE, Essex vicinity, west bank of Essex on NY 22. (6-19-73)

CHURCH OF THE TRANSFIGURATION, Blue Mountain Lake vicinity, north of Blue Mountain on NY 30. (7-26-77)

ELKANAH WATSON HOUSE, Port Kent, 3 miles east of US 9. (10-15-66)

ESSEX VILLAGE HISTORIC DISTRICT, Essex and vicinity, Town of Essex and surroundings on west bank of Lake Champlain. (5-28-75)

FORT CROWN POINT, Crown Point vicinity, Crown Point Reservation, south-west of Lake Champlain Bridge and NY 8. (11-24-68)

FORT ST. FREDERIC, Crown Point, Jct. of NY 8 and 9N. (10-15-66)

FORT TICONDEROGA, Ticonderoga vicinity, 2.5 miles south of Ticonderoga on NY 22. (10-15-66)

HAND-HALE HISTORIC DISTRICT, Elizabethtown, River and Maple Sts. (3-5-79)

IRONVILLE HISTORIC DISTRICT, Ironville. (12-27-74)

JOHN BROWN'S FARM, Lake Placid, (North Elba), John Brown Road. (6-19-72)

JOSHUA'S ROCK, OWL'S NEST (EDWARD EGGLESTON ESTATE), Lake George, NY 9L. (11-11-71)

NORTH CREEK RAILROAD STATION COMPLEX, Ncrth Creek, Railroad Pl. (8-27-76)

OCTAGONAL SCHOOLHOUSE, Essex vicinity, on Rt. 22 in Bouquet. (1-17-73).

OLD WARREN COUNTY COURTHOUSE COMPLEX, Lake George, Canada and Amherst Sts. (6-19-73)

PAUL SMITH'S HOTEL STORE, Paul Smiths. (12-3-80)

SILVER BAY ASSOCIATION COMPLEX, Silver Bay, NY 9N. (3-20-80)

WARRENSBURG MILLS HISTORIC DISTRICT, Warrensburg, roughly bounded by the Osborne and Woolen Hill bridges, Schroon River, and the railroad right of way. (9-18-75)

ROADSIDE HISTORIC MARKERS

The New York State Education Department, prior to 1960, erected numerous roadside historic markers to commemorate events, people or places of historic significance to New York State. Those pre-1960 markers within the Adirondacks are listed below. They are excerpted from statewide, unpublished listings at the Education Department. Included is the exact text which appears on the marker and, in parentheses, the marker's location.

CLINTON COUNTY

TURNPIKE - PORT KENT TO HOPKINTON - BUILT 1829-32. VIA AUSABLE FORKS, BLACK BROOK, FRANKLIN FALLS, LOON LAKE, ST. REGIS FALLS, HOPKINTON (On NYS 9N at Clintonville; on county road at Black Brook; on county road at Union Falls)

UNDERGROUND RAILROAD STATION WHERE NEGRO SLAVES WERE AIDED TO ESCAPE TO CANADA (In front of Green Apple Inn on Rt. 9 at Keeseville)

ESSEX COUNTY

Town of Chesterfield

TURNPIKE - PORT KENT TO HOPKINTON - BUILT 1829-32. VIA AUSABLE FORKS, BLACK BROOK, FRANKLIN FALLS, LOON LAKE, ST. REGIS FALLS, HOPKINTON (On NYS 9N at Clintonville; on NYS 373 about 2 miles from Port Kent)

Town of Crown Point

RUINS OF PRE-REVOLUTIONARY VILLAGE AND TRADING POST (On Crown Point Reservation at Champlain Bridge)

GRENADIER FORT - ONE OF SECONDARY DEFENSES OF CROWN POINT - BUILT BY GENERAL AMHEARST 1759 (On Crown Point Reservation at Champlain Bridge)

LIGHT INFANTRY FORT - ONE OF THE SECONDARY DEFENSES OF CROWN POINT - BUILT BY GENERAL AMHEARST 1759 (On NYS 8 at Crown Point Reservation)

COLONIAL AND REVOLUTIONARY MILITARY ROAD - CROWN POINT TO TICONDEROGA (On NYS 8 about 2 miles south of Champlain Bridge)

Town of Elizabethtown

STATE ARSENAL - ERECTED BY STATE OF NEW YORK IN 1811 - USED DURING WAR OF 1812 - SOLD IN 1848 (On US 9 at Elizabethtown)

NORTHWEST BAY ROAD - BEGUN PRIOR TO 1810 - FROM WESTPORT VIA ELIZABETHTOWN, LAKE PLACID, SARANAC LAKE, SANTA CLARA, HOPKINTON (On NYS 9N at Elizabethtown)

ELIZABETHTOWN - FORMED FEBRUARY 12, 1798 - NAMED IN HONOR OF ELIZABETH, WIFE OF WILLIAM GILLILAND - PATANTEE MANOR OF WILLSBORO-COUNTY SEAT ESSEX COUNTY (On US 9 at Elizabethtown)

Town of Essex

SPLIT ROCK - CALLED ROCHE REGIO BY INDIANS - BOUNDARY BETWEEN MOHAWKS AND ALGONQUINS - BY TREATY OF UTRECHT CONCEDED AS LIMIT OF ENGLISH DOMINIONS (On county road about 3 miles south of Essex)

COON MOUNTAIN - NEAR THE NORTHERN BASE OF THIS MOUNTAIN - WILLIAM GILLILAND - EARLY PIONEER OF CHAMPLAIN VALLEY, MET HIS TRAGIC DEATH IN 1796 (On NYS 22 about 1 mile north of Wadhams)

SITE OF WILLSBOROUGH BLOCKHOUSE - ERECTED 1797 AS A PROTECTION AGAINST INDIANS - USED FROM 1799-1807 AS ESSEX COUNTY COURTHOUSE (On NYS 22 at Essex)

Town of Minerva

THEODORE ROOSEVELT, SEPT 14TH 1901 - STOPPED AT AIDEN LAIR TO CHANGE HORSES IN NIGHT RIDE ON BUCKBOARD FROM MT. MARCY TO NORTH CREEK TO TAKE OATH OF PRESIDENT AT BUFFALO, NY (On NYS 28N about 6 miles north of Minerva)

Town of Moriah

MEACHAM HOUSE - BUILT IN 1818 BY CAPT. WILLIAM MEACHAM (On NYS 9N and NYS 22 at Port Henry)

THIS BUILDING ERECTED IN 1850 ON SOUTH MAIN STREET AS SECOND SCHOOLHOUSE IN PORT HENRY (On Broad St. at Port Henry)

CHAMPLAIN ACADEMY - SITE OF PORT HENRY'S FIRST TAVERN 1826 - THIS BUILDING ERECTED AS PEASE HOUSE 1850 (On NYS 9N and NYS 22 at Port Henry)

HUBBARD HOUSE - BUILT IN 1802 (On Broad Street at Port Henry)

SHORE LINE OF BUTTERFIELD'S BAY - BOATS WERE MOORED ALONG NORTH MAIN ST. BEFORE BUILDING OF RAILROAD THROUGH HERE (On NYS 9N and NYS 22, Port Henry)

GUILFORD HOUSE - FIRST POST OFFICE IN PORT HENRY LOCATED IN THIS BUILDING (On NYS 9N and NYS 22, Port Henry)

TRAINING GROUND - PRIOR TO 1850 MILITIA OF SOUTHERN ESSEX COUNTY, HELD JUNE TRAINING HERE (On NYS 9N and NYS 22, Port Henry)

DALLIBA HOUSE - BUILT 1824 BY MAJOR JAMES DALLIBA - WHO NAMED PORT HENRY IN 1827 FOR HENRY HUNTINGTON OF ROME, NY (On NYS 9N and NYS 22, Port Henry)

SITE OF FIRST BLAST FURNACE - ERECTED IN 1824 BY MAJOR JAMES DALLIBA - CONVERTED INTO STOVE WORKS IN 1827 (On NYS 9N and NYS 22, Port Henry)

SITE OF PORTER'S AND LEWIS'S MILLS - BUILT 1766 -SUPPLIED LUMBER FOR FORT CROWN POINT AND ARNOLD'S FLEET - ENTIRE VALLEY DEPENDENT ON GRIST MILL (On NYS 9N and NYS 22, Port Henry)

MORIAH PLANK ROAD - HORSE DRAWN WAGONS HAULED IRON ORE FROM MINES TO PORT HENRY OVER THIS ROAD UNTIL 1869 (On Broad Street at Port Henry; on county road between Port Henry and Moriah; on county road at Moriah; on county road between Mineville and Moriah Center)

MILLER HOUSE - BUILT 1839 BY HENRY MILLER, PORT HENRY'S FIRST WHEELWRIGHT (On Broad Street at Port Henry)

Town of North Elba

NORTHWEST BAY ROAD - BEGUN PRIOR TO 1810 - FROM WESTPORT VIA ELIZABETHTOWN, LAKE PLACID, SARANAC LAKE, SANTA CLARA, HOPKINTON (On NYS 73 about 2 miles south of Lake Placid, near Intervales Ski Jumps)

JOHN BROWN OCCUPIED HOUSE ON THIS SITE IN 1848-1850 WHILE CLEARING THE LAND NOW KNOWN AS JOHN BROWN'S FARM (On NYS 73 about 1 1/2 miles south of Lake Placid)

Town of Ticonderoga

A BATTERY OF GUNS PLACED ON MOUNT DEFIANCE BY BRITISH ARTILLERY OFFICERS IN JULY 1777 FORCED EVACUATION OF FORT TICONDEROGA BY GENERAL ST. CLAIR (On the portage at Ticonderoga)

ON THIS SPOT IN 1756 FRENCH ENGINEERS BUILT A REDOUBT TO GUARD THE BRIDGE AND LANDING PLACE AT THE HEAD OF THE PORTAGE (On Black Point at Ticonderoga)

GARRISON CEMETERY - HERE ARE BURIED SEVERAL HUNDRED OFFICERS AND MEN OF THE AMERICAN ARMY - CHIEFLY NEW YORK, NEW JERSEY AND PENNSYLVANIA MILITIA 1775-1777 (On Fort Ticonderoga Reservation at Ticonderoga)

NEAR HERE ON JULY 30, 1609 SAMUEL DE CHAMPLAIN AIDED BY TWO FRENCHMEN AND HURON AND MONTAGNAIS ALLIES DEFEATED A BAND OF IROQUOIS WARRIORS (On Fort Ticonderoga Reservation at Ticonderoga)

NEAR HERE ON JULY 6, 1758 LORD HOWE WAS KILLED IN A SKIRMISH WITH A FRENCH ADVANCE GUARD UNDER LANGY AND TREPEZEC (On Alexandria Ave., southwest of Ticonderoga)

THESE DEFENSES WERE BUILT BY AMERICAN TROOPS IN 1776 AND OCCUPIED BY GENERAL BURGOYNE IN 1777 CONTROLLING THE PORTAGE AND LOWER LANDING PLACE (On Mt. Hope at Ticonderoga)

NEAR HERE MARCH 13, 1758 ROGERS' RANGERS FOUGHT THE SNOWSHOE BATTLE AND WERE DEFEATED BY FRENCH AND INDIANS UNDER DURANTAYE AND LANGY (On Ticonderoga Golf Course south of Ticonderoga)

HERE STOOD THE KING'S STORE - A STONE BUILDING ERECTED BY THE FRENCH IN 1756, AND IN USE FOR ABOUT 100 YEARS (On Ft. Ticonderoga Reservation at Ticonderoga)

ALONG THIS STREET RAN THE OLD MILITARY ROAD - FORTIFIED IN 1759 BY GENERAL AMHEARST PRIOR TO HIS SEIGE OF FORT TICONDEROGA (On the portage at Ticonderoga)

ON THIS POINT IN 1759 - STOOD A BLOCKHOUSE - THE SOUTHERLY OUTPOST OF THE FORT - HERE LANDED ROGERS' RANGERS AS THE VANGUARD OF GENERAL AMHEARST'S ARMY (On Black Point Rd. south of Ticonderoga)

ON THE EAST SHORE OPPOSITE THIS PLACE - WERE ERECTED TWO BLOCKHOUSES TO GUARD THE NARROWS AND LANDING PLACE 1759 (On Black Point Rd. south of Ticonderoga)

FATHER JOGUES, RENE GOUPIL AND GUILLAUME COURTE IN 1642 WERE THE FIRST WHITE MEN TO SEE THESE WATERS, NAMED LAC DU ST. SACREMENT BY JOGUES IN 1646 (On Black Point Rd. south of Ticonderoga)

OPPOSITE THIS SPOT ON THE WEST BANK OF THE OUTLET OF LAKE GEORGE STOOD A BLOCKHOUSE AND FRENCH DEFENSES TO COVER THE BRIDGE AND LANDING PLACE (On Baldwin Road south of Ticonderoga)

REDOUBT LOTBINIERE - BUILT BY THE FRENCH IN 1756 - CALLED BY THE BRITISH AND AMERICAN ARMIES THE GRENADIERS' BATTERY (On Ft. Ticonderoga Reservation at Ticonderoga)

COLONIAL AND REVOLUTIONARY MILITARY ROAD - CROWN POINT TO TICONDEROGA (On NYS 8 and NYS 9N and NYS 22 about 3½ miles north of Ticonderoga)

HUT SITES - WITHIN A RADIUS OF ONE-HALF MILE WERE 150 HUTS OCCUPIED BY AMERICAN TROOPS 1776 (On Fort Ticonderoga Reservation at Ticonderoga)

THE FRENCH LINES - BUILT BY TROOPS UNDER MONTCALM JULY 6-7, 1758 - REPAIRED BY AMERICAN TROOPS 1776 (On Ft. Ticonderoga Reservation at Ticonderoga)

SCENE OF ROGER'S BATTLE ON SNOWSHOES - PREVIOUS TO HIS REPUTED GLIDE OFF ROGERS' ROCK 1758 (On NYS 8 and NYS 9N about 1 mile south of Ticonderoga)

MOUNT HOPE BATTERY - OCCUPIED BY GENERAL BURGOYNE, 1777 (On Mt. Hope Ave. at Ticonderoga)

Town of Westport

NORTHWEST BAY ROAD - BEGUN PRIOR TO 1810 - FROM WESTPORT VIA ELIZABETHTOWN, LAKE PLACID, SARANAC LAKE, SANTA CLARA, HOPKINTON (On NYS 9N about 1 mile west of Westport)

HERE STOOD THE FIRST TAVERN AT NORTHWEST BAY BUILT BY JOHN HALSTEAD ABOUT 1800 (On NYS 9N and NYS 22 about 3 miles south of Westport)

FIRST SAWMILL IN TOWN OF WESTPORT STOOD HERE - BUILT IN 1770 - BOARDS FROM MILL USED IN BUILDING BARRACKS AT CROWN POINT AND TICONDEROGA (On NYS 9N and NYS 22 about 3 miles south of Westport)

Town of Willsboro

BOUQUET RIVER - BURGOYNE'S ENCAMPMENT - JUNE 20, 1777 - TREATY WITH THE INDIANS MADE AND PROCLAMATION ISSUED (On NYS 22 at Willsboro)

NEAR HERE - EBENEZER ALLEN CAPTURED BRITISH SOLDIERS AND MILITARY STORES AFTER SURRENDER AT SARATOGA (On NYS 22 about 1/2 mile north of Essex)

SITE OF FIRST HOUSE BUILT BY WILLIAM GILLILAND IN 1765 (On NYS 22 at Willsboro)

MASONIC HALL - ESSEX LODGE NO. 152 - CHARTERED FEBRUARY 14, 1806 - DISCONTINUED IN 1826 (On NYS 22 about 2½ miles south of Willsboro)

LAKEVIEW CEMETERY - FIRST BURIAL 1791 - CONTAINS GRAVE OF WILLIAM GILLILAND - FOUNDER OF TOWN OF WILLSBORO (On NYS 22 about 2½ miles south of Willsboro)

MEMORIAL CEMETERY - FIRST BURIAL 1793 - CONTAINS GRAVE OF MARTIN AIKEN - LEADER OF AIKEN'S VOLUNTEERS AT BATTLE OF PLATTSBURGH (On NYS 22 about 1/2 mile south of Willsboro)

WILLSBORO - FOUNDED IN 1765 BY WILLIAM GILLILAND - TOWN FORMED 1788 - COUNTY SEAT OF ESSEX COUNTY 1797-1807 (On NYS 22 at Willsboro)

FRANKLIN COUNTY

ON THIS SITE WAS BUILT IN 1874 THE WORLD'S LARGEST CATALAN FORGE ABANDONED IN 1893 (On NYS 374 about 1 mile south of Brainardsville)

NORTHWEST BAY ROAD - BEGUN PRIOR TO 1810 - FROM WESTPORT VIA ELIZABETHTOWN, LAKE PLACID, SARANAC LAKE, SANTA CLARA, HOPKINTOWN (On NYS 192 at Gabriels; on NYS 72 about 3 miles north of McColloms; on NYS 86 at north end of Saranac Lake village; on NYS 72 at Santa Clara)

OLDEST BUILDING - TOWN OF SANTA CLARA - FORMER RAILROAD STATION - BUILT BY JOHN HURD WHO BUILT RAILROAD IN 1889 (On NYS 72 at Santa Clara)

JENNINGS ROAD - USED BY US TROOPS - WAR OF 1812 - MARCHING WEST FROM LAKE CHAMPLAIN TO LAKE ONTARIO (On NYS 72 about 6 miles southeast of Santa Clara)

TURNPIKE - PORT KENT TO HOPKINTON - BUILT IN 1829-32 - VIA AUSABLE FORKS, BLACK BROOK, FRANKLIN FALLS, LOON LAKE, ST. REGIS FALLS, HOPKINTON (On county road, about 1 mile north of St. Regis Falls)

FULTON COUNTY

FRENCHMANS CREEK - IN 1810 DUNCAN McMARTIN ON THIS CREEK BUILT A SAW, GRIST AND WOOLEN MILL - HE WAS SURVEYOR, LAWYER, JUDGE COURT COMMON PLEAS 1813 - LATER ELECTED STATE SENATOR (On county road at North Broadalbin)

RICE HOMESTEAD - BUILT ABOUT 1790 BY OLIVER RICE - A SOLDIER OF THE AMERICAN REVOLUTION SERVING UNDER GENERAL WASHINGTON (On NYS 148 at Riceville)

SITE OF ROMEYN'S MILL - ERECTED 1773 BY SIR WILLIAM JOHNSON - REBUILT BY COLONIAL ABRAHAM ROMEYN - COMMANDER MONTGOMERY COUNTY MILITIA (On NYS 30 at Mayfield)

ICEVILLE CEMETERY - HERE ARE BURIED JONATHAN FISK - OLIVER RICE - WILLIAM WOODWORTH - SAMUEL WOODWORTH - JESSE FOOTE - ISAAC BEMIS - JONATHAN CANFIELD - SOLDIERS OF THE REVOLUTION (On NYS 148 at Riceville)

BURYING GROUND OF MAJOR HARMON AND FRANCIS VAN BUREN SEVENTH ALBANY COUNTY REGIMENT -REVOLUTIONARY WAR - SETTLERS ON THIS LAND (On town road about 2 miles southeast of Mayfield)

KING CEMETERY - HENRY KING AND SON JOHN SETTLED ON THIS SITE AND ARE BURIED HERE - GRAVES OF REVOLUTIONARY SOLDIERS AND PIONEERS OF 1788-1815 (On NYS 148 about 1½ miles southwest of Northville)

BAPTIST CHURCH OF MAYFIELD AND BROADILBIN ORGANIZED HERE IN 1792 - THEN THE HOME OF CALEB WOODWORTH - SOLDIER OF REVOLUTION - FIRST SETTLER (On NYS 148 about 4 miles northeast of Gloversville)

BURYING GROUND GRAVES OF CAPTAIN GERSHOM WOODWORTH - FRENCH AND INDIAN AND REVOLUTIONARY WARS - AND SERGEANT SELAH WOODWORTH OF REVOLUTION - MAYFIELD PIONEER (On town road 1/4 mile west of Mayfield)

SITE OF DUTCH REFORMED CHURCH OF MAYFIELD, 1793-1826 CHURCHYARD CONTAINING REMAINS OF MANY PIONEERS OF THIS SECTION (On NYS 30 at Mayfield)

WOODWORTH FARM - CONVEYED BY COMMISSIONERS OF FORFIETURE TO WILLIAM G. WOODWORTH IN 1786 - SERVED IN REVOLUTION - PASSED TO HIRAM WOODWORTH 1810-1910 (On county road about 1½ miles west of Mayfield)

INDIAN RAID - JACOB DUNHAM AND SAMUEL, HIS SON, KILLED HERE APRIL 1779 - OTHERS OF THE FAMILY ESCAPED BY HIDING IN THE WOODS - SITE OF THEIR HOME (On NYS 30 about 3/4 mile north of Mayfield)

GODFREY SHREW - FIRST SETTLER FISH HOUSE - UNDER SIR WILLIAM JOHNSON - 1762 - SONS, JOHN, STEPHEN, JACOB CAPTURED IN TORY AND INDIAN RAID JUNE 3, 1778. TAKEN TO CANADA (On county road at Hampton)

"FISH HOUSE" OF SIR WILLIAM JOHNSON 1500 FEET NORTHEAST OF THIS MARKER BUILT 1762 - VILLAGE DERIVED NAME FROM LODGE - BURNED BY TORIES AND INDIANS - 1781 (On county road at Northampton)

COVERED BRIDGE - ERECTED 1818 BY STATE - AT FISH HOUSE OVER SACANDAGA RIVER - D. STEWART, BUILDER - JACOB SHEW - ASSEMBLYMAN - TORN DOWN 1930 - 2000 FT. NORTH (On county road at Northampton)

MARVIN HOUSE - BUILT 1815 - SITE SIR WILLIAM JOHNSON'S FISH HOUSE BY DAVID MARVIN, CONNECTICUT REVOLUTIONARY SOLDIER - HIS SON, DR. L.I. MARVIN ASSEMBLYMAN 1840 FROM FULTON COUNTY - HOUSE MOVED 1929 (On county road at Northampton)

SHEW HOUSE - BUILT 1784 BY GODFREY SHEW AND HIS SONS JOHN, STEPHEN, AND JACOB AFTER THEIR RETURN FROM CANADA AS PRISONERS OF COLONEL ROSS ON JUNE 3, 1778 (On county road at Northampton)

ST. JOHN HOUSE - BUILT 1795 BY ALEX ST. JOHN ON CONFISCATED LANDS OF COLONEL GUY JOHNSON - NEPHEW OF SIR WILLIAM JOHNSON (On county road at Northampton)

HAMILTON COUNTY

The State Education Department lists no markers for this county. One of our reviewers states that there is a marker in Sabattis commemorating the burning of Long Lake West, September 27, 1903. Reviewer states actual date was September 27, 1908.

HERKIMER COUNTY

WOOD HOME - WHEELOCK WOOD (1794-1887) AND WIFE - HANNAH SOUTHWICK COMSTOCK (1797-1892) OF MASSACHUSETTS LOCATED HERE IN 1829 AND BUILT THIS HOUSE (On county road about 4 miles east of Gray)

WARREN COUNTY

DIAMOND ISLAND - IN CENTER OF LAKE - MILITARY DEPOT OF BURGOYNE'S ARMY - ATTACKED SEPTEMBER 1777 - BY AMERICANS UNDER COLONEL BROWN - LATER ABANDONED BY ENEMY (On Diamond Island in Lake George)

THROUGH THIS PASS TO TROUT BROOK WAS AN INDIAN TRAIL USED BY ROBERT ROGERS AFTER BATTLE ON SNOWSHOES - 1758 - ON RETREAT TO FT. WILLIAM HENRY (On NYS 8 and NYS 9N about 1 mile north of Hague)

FORT WILLIAM HENRY - 1755 BUILT BY SIR WILLIAM JOHNSON - 1757 - AFTER A GALLANT DEFENSE COLONEL MONROE IN COMMAND SURRENDERED TO THE FRENCH UNDER GENERAL MONTCALM (On lake front, Lake George Village)

THE HOSPITAL - AT BATTLE OF LAKE GEORGE - MANY WOUNDED SOLDIERS AND SOME WITH SMALLPOX WERE CRUELLY MURDERED BY INDIANS OF MONTCALM'S ARMY (On state reservation at Lake George Village)

MONTCALM'S CAMP - 1757 - ON THESE GROUNDS MONTCALM'S ARMY CAMPED DURING THE SEIGE OF FT. WILLIAM HENRY AUGUST 6-9TH 1757 (On US 9 at Lake George Village)

JAMES CAMERON - PIONEER WOODSMAN FARMER -JUSTICE OF THE PEACE - SETTLED IN THIS VALLEY IN 1773 (On county road about 5 miles west of Warrensburg)

LEWIS, ONEIDA, ST. LAWRENCE, SARATOGA and WASHINGTON COUNTIES have none in the Adirondack Park.

Beginning in 1960, the State Education Department began creating larger, cast aluminum markers that describe the importance of entire counties or regions. The following are located in the Adirondack Park.

THE ADIRONDACKS

The Adirondack Mountains, consisting of rocky peaks, sheer cliffs and narrow valleys, also have wooded slopes and sparkling lakes. Forty-three mountains have elevations 4000 feet or higher, Mount Marcy, with an altitude of 5,344 feet, is the highest. Near Marcy's summit is Lake Tear-of-the-Clouds, the source of the Hudson River.

Iroquois Indians derisively gave the name Adirondack (meaning "tree-eater") to some of the Algonkians, their enemies. Used as Indian hunting territory, the vast wilderness was not penetrated by white men until the late 18th century. Mining began at the end of that century, and Adirondack mines have yielded such ores as iron, zinc, titanium, talc and garnet. The great wealth of the Adirondack forests supplied demands for timber in the 19th century and first decades of the 20th. Alarmed over the denuding of this natural treasure, New York set up the Forest Preserve in 1885. The Adirondack Park now consists of more than two million State-owned acres.

Railroad construction after 1871 turned remote forest retreats into popular summer resorts. The opening of automobile highways in the 20th century made the area accessible for all to enjoy the rugged beauty of the Adirondack Mountains. (Route 28, east of McKeever; Route 30, north of Wells; Route 28, north side, 1 1/2 miles east of Blue Mountain Lake.

FORT TICONDEROGA

During the 18th century, when nations fought to control the strategic route between the St. Lawrence River in Canada and the Hudson River to the south, the fortification overlooking the outlet of Lake George into Lake Champlain was called "the key to a continent." The French constructed here in 1755 the stronghold they named Carillon, and made it a base to attack their English rivals. In 1758, Carillon, under Marquis de Montcalm, withstood assualt by superior British forces. The next year Jeffery Amhearst's troops catured Carillon and forced the French to retreat from Lake Champlain. The British renamed the fortress Fort Ticonderoga.

During the American Revolution, Ethan Allen and his Green Mountain Boys captured Ticonderoga in a surprise attack, May 10, 1775. Cannons hauled from Ticonderoga to Boston helped George Washington drive the British from that city. In July, 1777, General Burgoyne's invading army overwhelmed the American fort and Ticonderoga again became British. Americans unsuccessfully attacked the fort in September, 1777; later the British abandoned it. In 1816, William Ferris Pell acquired the fort. His descendents began its restoration and in 1909 opened Ticonderoga to the public. Now the Fort Ticonderoga Association maintains the historic fort and its military museum. (Fort Ticonderoga, Ticonderoga, NY)

LAKE GEORGE

The natural route by water and portage between the St. Lawrence River and the Hudson River traversed Lake George. Christened Lac du Saint Sacrement in 1646 by the Jesuit missionary, Isaac Jogues, it was renamed in 1755 by Sir William Johnson to honor King George II.

Above the outlet of Lake George, overlooking Lake Champlain, the French in 1755 built Fort Carillon (Ticonderoga), which became a military objective during the colonial conflicts between the English and the French. Fort William Henry, built at the southern end of Lake George to check the French, was destroyed by French and Indians in 1757. In 1758 General James Abercomby led a large force northward to attack the French at Ticonderoga and was repulsed, but General Jeffery Amhearst was successful the following year. With the outbreak of the American Revolution, Ethan Allen and Benedict Arnold took Fort Ticonderoga. Abandoned in 1777 to General John Burgoyne's invading army, it remained in British hands until 1782.

From earliest times, the singular beauty of this forest-bound lake has charmed visitors. Sportsmen, artists, and nature-lovers have been drawn to its shores. Boating and fishing have made it a popular recreation area. State-owned campsites and beaches today preserve some of its pristine charm. (Route 9N, south of Sabbath Day Point; Interstate 87, West of Lake George Village)

SCHROON LAKE

Schroon Lake, approximately 9 miles long with a maximum width of 1 1/2 miles, was formed by glacial rubble damming an ancient valley. The lake is a wide part of the Schroon River which flows from the Adirondacks to join the Hudson at Warrensburg. The name's origin is hidden in local legends. Several attribute it to Indian words, and one claims it was inspired by Madame Scarron, a beautiful French widow, who became the wife of Louis XIV.

Settlers from New England came into the mountain-rimmed region in 1797. Impressed by the grandeur of massive pine trees, they thought it "a most wonderful lumbering country." Log drivers originated on the Schroon River in 1813, and great stands of timber were floated down the Schroon and Hudson to mills at Glens Falls and Hudson Falls. Local mills and tanneries exploited the vast forest. Lumbering reached its peak in the 1870's. Iron works used mountain ores.

The semi-wilderness was a popular vacation retreat in the 19th century. Visitors traveled by railroad, stagecoach and steamboat to stay at spacious hostelries near the lake shore. Mountains, lakes and ponds still make the Schroon Lake region a paradise for pleasure seekers. (Interstate 87, northbound, near Schroon Lake)

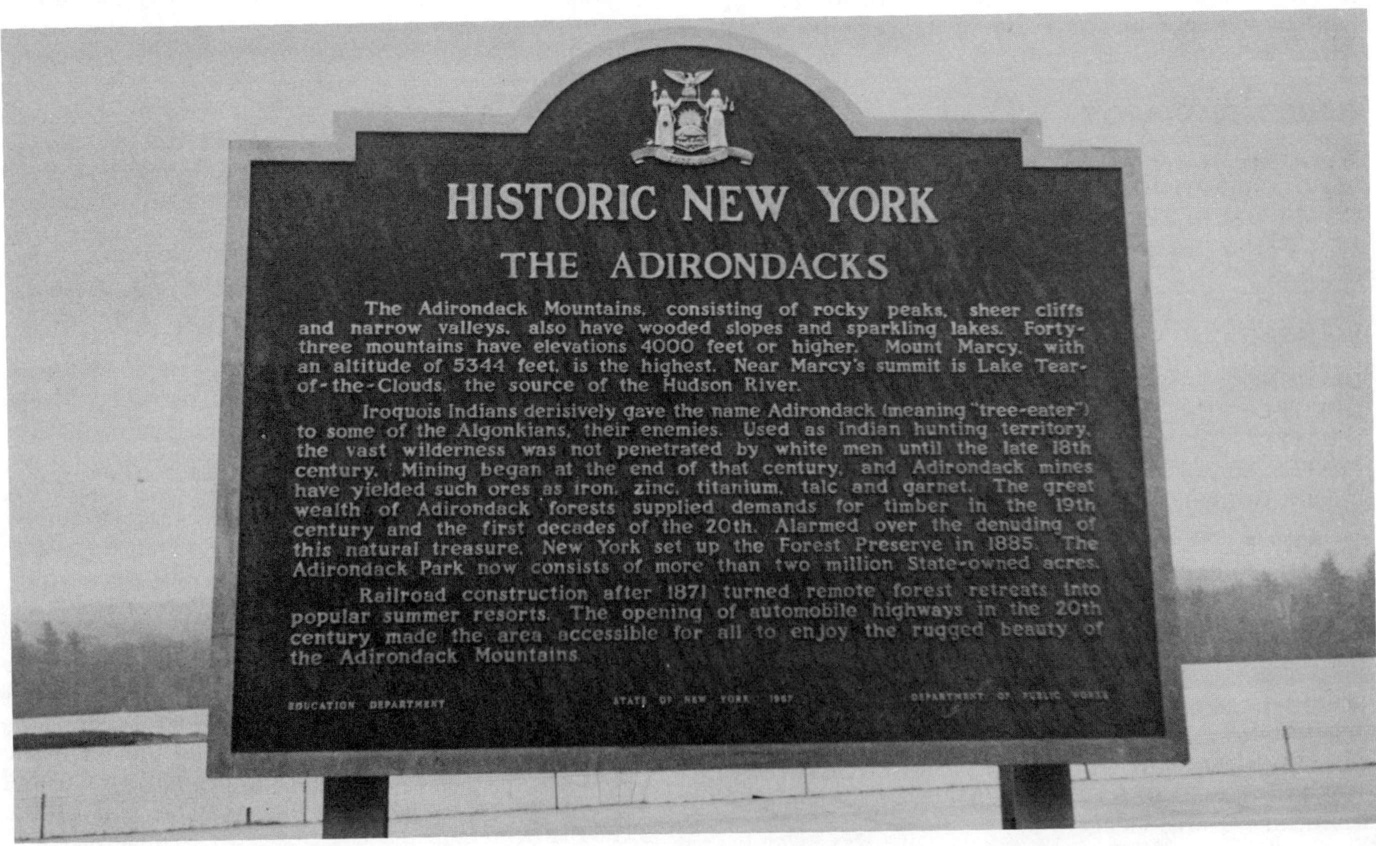

(18)

ORIGINS OF ADIRONDACK PLACE NAMES

To identify the origins of most Adirondack place names would take many volumes. To fully explore the etiology of even single names, in many cases, would take an essay for each name. The word "Adirondack," for example, which is discussed briefly in Section 19, is a good case in point. This section can only whet the reader's appetite with a limited number of names and a brief derivation for each. Three sources to consult for more extensive material on this topic are Donaldson's *History of the Adirondacks* (see Section 29), M. Beauchamp's "Aboriginal Place Names of New York (Bulletin 108 of the New York State Museum, 1907) and Grace Hudowalski's (Ed.) *The Adirondack High Peaks* (Adirondack, NY: Adirondack Forty-Sixers, 1970). Even these just scratch the surface of a major professional discipline.

Adirondack names come from many sources—Native American words, individuals' names (often the first European to visit that place or someone with whom the first visitor wished to curry favor by naming a lake or mountain after him), the physical characteristics of the named object (e.g., Mt. Haystack, Forked Lake), and often the names of animals. In a February 12, 1924 article in the *Saturday Evening Post* entitled "1746 Lakes and Ponds in Adirondack Preserve," Robert and George Marshall listed the following bodies of water bearing duplicate names of wildlife: deer 13, moose 12, wolf, 12, bear 10, gull 8, beaver 7, buck 7, trout 7, chub 6, fish 6, loon 5 and salmon 5. And they probably missed some at that.

Here, then, is a selection of short derivations for the names of several mountains, lakes, towns and other locations in the Adirondack Park.

MT. DONALDSON. Long nameless, this mountain was called North Seward when Robert and George Marshall climbed it in 1921. That year, after laboring in ill health for 10 years at his home in Saranac Lake, Alfred Donaldson completed his monumental history of the Adirondacks. Upon petition of the Marshalls and others, the mountain was renamed in Donaldson's honor in 1924.

RAQUETTE LAKE. In the Mohawk Valley, the son of Sir William Johnson, Sir John, had inherited his father's vast estate, manor house, and loyalties to King George III. In 1776, to fight another day for his king, Sir John and one hundred and seventy of his tenants and their families fled the Mohawk Valley, guided northward through the Adirondacks by three Mohawk warriors. Although it was May, tradition states that they entered the mountains prepared to encounter snow, bringing snowshoes—or "raquettes" as they were known in those days—with them. When they realized these would not be necessary, they abandoned them at a lake and continued their journey by boat. Thereafter the lake was referred to as the "Raquette Lake."

WILLSBORO and ELIZABETHTOWN. Two towns in Essex County, named after William Gilliland and his wife Elizabeth, early settlers.

TAHAWUS. Early name of Mt. Marcy. Indian word meaning "he splits the sky."

COUCHSACHRAGA MT. From the Indian word meaning "dismal wilderness." Other historians have said the word means "winter," "the beaver hunting grounds," "at the place of beaver dams," and other meanings.

AUSABLE. Name of river, lakes, town, chasm. Derived from two French words "au sable," meaning "of sand," "to the sand" or "sandy."

OLD FORGE. Site of Charles Frederick Herreshoff's (1763-1819) unsuccessful mining operation in Herkimer County. The cluster of buildings around his "old forge" gradually assumed that name.

VERMONTVILLE. Many settlers from Vermont moved to this area north of Saranac Lake, possibly because it reminded them of the more rolling Vermont countryside set close to the larger mountains.

SANTANONI. Indian pronounciation of the French Saint Anthony.

FULTON CHAIN. After Robert Fulton, inventor of the steamboat, who in 1811 surveyed the chain of lakes from Old Forge Pond to Eighth Lake for possible inclusion in a canal navigation system.

AMPERSAND. Name of mountain, lake, brook and early hotel. Donaldson's best theory is that the name is a corruption of "amber sand." Less favored is the theory that the brook was so twisty it reminded an early settler of the ampersand ("&").

ESTHER MOUNTAIN. In 1839 Esther McComb was climbing Whiteface Mt., lost her way and spent the night on the nearby nameless peak. She is credited with being first to climb the mountain which bears her name.

AXTON. This location just south of Upper Saranac Lake is the site of a former logging camp (Axe-town) and, at the turn of the century, the Cornell School of Forestry.

ALUMINUM POND. A small pond in the northern corner of the Town of Lake Pleasant, Hamilton County, where Dr. Arpad Gerster was said to have given his friend William West Durant a set of aluminum cooking utensils.

ROGERS' ROCK. Site on Lake George where, on March 13, 1758, Robert Rogers and a number of his Rangers, who survived a terrible defeat by the French in what was known as "The Battle on Snowshoes," were reported to have escaped from their pursuers by using their snowshoes as skis and sliding off the huge rock onto the frozen lake.

DUANE and HARRIETSTOWN. Two towns in Franklin County, named after James Duane and his wife, the former Harriet Constable, early settlers.

MT. JO. In 1877 Henry Van Hoevenberg and his fiance Miss Josephine Scofield visited the Adirondacks and fell under their spell. Donaldson says, "They decided to climb the highest mountain and from its summit select the most beautiful sight as a location for a future home." They climbed Mt. Marcy and selected their spot, on the shore of a lovely heart-shaped lake in the distance. One of the mountains rising from the lake Van Hoevenberg named Mt. Jo. That year Miss Scofield died. The following summer, the bereaved Van Hoevenberg returned to the Adirondacks and purchased 640 acres around the lake, including Mt. Jo. He named the lake Heart Lake and on its shores built the original Adirondack Lodge.

ONCHIOTA. A hamlet in Franklin County, after an Indian word meaning "rainbow." Interestingly, Rainbow Lake is just a few miles away.

PISECO LAKE. An 1824 publication called this large Hamilton County lake "Pezeebo Lake," after an Indian hermit who lived upon its shores. In publications in 1836 and 1842, the name changed to *Pisceo* Lake and then to *Piseco*. Various sources say it was named after an Indian chief, or the word *pisco* or "fish", or an Indian word meaning "miry places."

ST. HUBERT'S. The hamlet and inn in Keene Valley was named for St. Hubert, the patron saint of hunted deer. Formerly a wild and reckless youth, one Good Friday, when hunting, Hubert was surprised by a beautiful stag with a crucifix shining between its antlers. "The astounded young man," relates Donaldson, "then heard a voice reprimanding the ruthless hunter and preaching compassion for the hunted. He was frightened into conversion on the spot, and became so ardent a game protector that he was ultimately sainted." When the Adirondack Mountain Reserve Club bought thousands of acres in 1890, they named their clubhouse "St. Hubert's Inn," with the goal of protecting the game in the area and caring for the surrounding forests.

(19)
NATIVE AMERICANS IN THE ADIRONDACKS

The Adirondacks played a dramatic role in the history of the Iroquois Indians. The Iroquois were a widespread linguistic group that included Hurons (in what is now Ontario) and Susquehannas (along the river which bears their name). But five of the Iroquois nations, sometime between 1200 and 1570 A.D., formed a confederacy which stretched westward from the northern Hudson Valley into western New York. These five nations, from east to west, were the Mohawks, the Oneidas, the Onondagas, the Cayugas, and the Senecas. In 1722, a sixth nation, the Tuscaroras of North Carolina, who were also an Iroquoian people, moved northward and took refuge with the confederacy, which then became known as the Six Nations. That confederacy continues to the present day, its traditional capital at Onondaga (near present-day Syracuse) hosting the meetings of the Grand Council of chiefs.

Iroquois longhouse.

While the Mohawk Iroquois dominated the eastern half of the Adirondack region, the western half was controlled by another Iroquois nation, the Oneidas.

"Adirondacks" is a Mohawk word and was one of the earliest (1684) Iroquoian pronounciations of the region's name. However, there were many variations in the different Mohawk Iroquoian dialects and in the various Iroquoian languages. One of the most preferred was *Hatiron taks*. The Oneida's pronounciation was *La-dee-loon-dacks* (spelled phonetically). Other variations were: *Adirondacs, Adirontak, Adisonks, Adnondecks, Arundacs, Honanduk, Iroondocks, Orondacks, Rarondaks, Ratiruntaks, Rondaxe* (1656) and many more.

"Adirondacks" meant "tree eaters" or "they are eating trees." The term may refer to the bark-eating beavers who once lived in dense colonies among the mountain lakes. But oral tradition among some Iroquois notes that the word may refer to the Algonquin Indian nation who lived in the mountains at one time and were at war with the Iroquois who claimed the same territory. Oral tradition states that when the Iroquois warriors were finally victorious over these Algonquins, the defeated Indians were so desperate that they were reduced to eating the bark off the trees and the Iroquois derisively called them "tree eaters."

The Adirondacks' northern reaches along the St. Lawrence was an important corridor long before Indians and Europeans used it in the fur trade. Sometime before 1600, columns of Iroquois refugees—men, women, and children—made their way westward along the river valley from western Quebec, fleeing triumphant Algonquin Indians who forced them off their lands. Some of these refugees moved southwesterly through and around the Adirondacks to join Iroquois already living in the Mohawk Valley and in central New York.

The great retreat described above perhaps was responsible for the creation of what today may be the most important Indian site in the Adirondack region, still being carefully studied by archeologists: a huge, palisaded Indian town or fortress protected by massive vertical log walls. Its precise location on the perimeter of the Adirondacks, while known to archeologists and other specialists, cannot be made public at this time because the site might be subjected to looting by greedy "pot hunters"—thieves who prey on Indian sites throughout the Americas to make a profit selling artifacts, despite the fact that such "digging" is as illegal as stealing a painting from a museum.

In 1609, Samuel de Champlain, two other Frenchmen, and a war party of sixty Algonquin and Huron warriors made their way south to attack the Mohawk Iroquois along the Mohawk Valley. At the juncture of Lake Champlain and Lake George, they encountered a larger Mohawk Iroquois war party which had been moving north to attack the Algonquins in Canada. The Mohawks were wearing armor made of a quilted material, perhaps cotton traded from the south, reinforced with wooden staves—an adequate defense against arrows. But Champlain and his two men had muskets, weapons never seen before by the Mohawks, and these large-bore muskets (arquebuses) carried the day. "When I saw them making a move to fire at us, I rested my musket against my cheek," Champlain later wrote, "and aimed directly at one of the three chiefs. With the same shot, two fell to the ground." The Mohawks, after firing a volley of arrows, finally broke for the forest when one of Champlain's men also fired his musket. Although Champlain won the battle for the French and their Canadian Indian allies, he forced the Iroquois to seek allies among the Dutch and later among the English. One hundred and fifty years after Champlain's battle with the Iroquois, the Iroquois and the English drove the French government from Canada, forever.

If 1609 was a turning point in human history in the Adirondacks, the year 1640 was a turning point for the environment; for by this year the beavers in the Adirondacks had been nearly exterminated by Indians. The Dutch and French, greedy for the pelts of fur-bearing animals, offered more and more trade goods to their Indian allies (the Dutch traded with the Iroquois, the French with the Canadian Algonguins and Hurons). The Indians integrated these European goods into their own economies to such an extent that their economies, and hence their societies, became dependent in part on these goods. To obtain more European goods, the Indians killed more beavers, and the more beavers the Indians killed the more the Europeans encouraged them. Finally, by 1640, the Iroquois could no longer find enough beavers in the Adirondacks to meet their needs, and they were forced to expand their hunting grounds into other Indians' territories to the west in the Great Lakes region.

In 1755 William Johnson won himself the title of baronet for his victory at Lake George against the French and Indian forces under a German mercenary general, Baron Dieskau, but at the cost of the life of one of the great Mohawk Iroquois leaders of the eighteenth century. Hendrick, a good friend of Johnson's, had as a young man visited London and the court of Queen Anne as part of an Iroquois delegation in 1710. On the morning of the battle, Johnson ordered Hendrick to take one thousand men to scout out the enemy's location. Hendrick knew that this was too many men to move quietly through the forest, yet not enough men to fight a battle. He said to Johnson: "If they are to fight, they are too few; if they are to die, they are too many." Johnson overruled his friend, and Hendrick obediently led his warriors and Johnson's soldiers forward — even though he was seventy-five years old and was so plump he had to be hoisted upon his horse. The French ambushed the Iroquois-English "morning scout" but most escaped. Hendrick did not. Shot off his horse, he was bayoneted to death by a French soldier. Later that day, Johnson decisively defeated the French.

In 1757, the central incident in James Fenimore Cooper's *The Last of the Mohicans* (1826) took place at Fort William Henry on the shores of Lake George. The English garrison had surrendered to the French forces under the Marquis de Montcalm and were marching, unarmed, from inside the fort when Montcalm's Catholic Indian allies from missions along the St. Lawrence suddenly attacked the helpless Englishmen, killing at least fifty. Montcalm and his fellow Frenchmen never overcame their shame for being unable to stop their Indian allies, especially since these Indians were converts to the French faith. After the slaughter, some of the Indians went into the fort and looted blankets that the English had left behind. But the English had left these behind for good reason: they were in the smallpox hospital, and the Indians who thought they had blankets of value discovered too late that they had instead looted shrouds of death, as the smallpox spread into their own villages, killing their families.

During the entire American Revolution, between 1775 and 1783, the Adirondacks provided the setting for lonely but dangerous work, as Mohawk Iroquois spies working for the British traveled back and forth between New York and Canada with messages and intelligence reports hidden in their hair ornaments and elsewhere in their clothing.

In the Mohawk Valley, the son of Sir William Johnson, Sir John, had inherited his father's vast estate, manor house, and loyalties to King George III. In 1776, to fight another day for his king, Sir John and one hundred and seventy of his tenants and their families fled the Mohawk Valley, guided northward through the Adirondacks by three Mohawk warriors. Although it was May, tradition states that they entered the mountains prepared to encounter snow, bringing snowshoes—or "raquettes" as they were known in those days—with them. When they realized these would not be necessary, they abandoned them at a lake and continued their journey by boat. Thereafter the lake was referred to as the "Raquette Lake."

In 1777, General John Burgoyne led a combined army of British, German, and Iroquois southward toward Albany to deal a deathblow to the Patriot cause; but on July 27 near Fort Edward a young loyalist, Jane McCrea, was killed as she was being escorted by some of Burgoyne's Indian scouts into the British lines. The Indians claimed she had been killed by a Patriot bullet fired at them as they evaded a Patriot scouting party. The Patriots claimed that some Canadian Indians had killed her. Whatever the truth of the incident, the impact counted more: the Patriots believed that the Indians had killed her, and if Burgoyne's Canadian Indian allies were willing to kill their allies the loyalists, the Patriots' imaginations soared with regard to their own lives. They thronged to the Patriot banner and defeated Burgoyne, forcing him to surrender at Saratoga. During the fighting, Mohawk Iroquois served on the side of the British, while Oneida and Tuscarora Iroquois fought on the side of the Patriots.

Much of the Adirondacks was part of a 4½ million acre track of land claimed by the Oneida Iroquois. The Patriots, eager to have Indian support during the War of Independence, promised the Oneida that, if they sided with the revolutionaries, this land would remain theirs for as long as the grass grew and the waters flowed. After the victory, however, the State of New York repaid its allies by appropriating their lands and paying them less than one cent per acre in compensation. Three years later, in 1792, the State resold the same land to a British investment company, represented by speculator Alexander Macomb, for ten times that amount. References to "Macomb's Survey" appear in many Adirondack property deeds until this day.

Indian Point on Raquette Lake was the site of an Indian encampment.

During the nineteenth century, Mohawk and other Indians served as guides in the Adirondacks for sportsmen and surveyors. Between 1840 and 1860, white men began to predominate in this role. The tradition of the Adirondack guide continues into the twentieth century.

On May 13, 1974, Mohawk and other Indian activists took possession of an abandoned girls' camp at Moss Lake (Eagle Bay), determined to rebuild Iroquois culture and force New York State to recognize their claim that the Adirondacks had never been legally transferred by treaty from the Iroquois to the state. Exactly three years later, on May 13, 1977, both sides agred to postpone the treaty issue when Mario Cuomo, then Secretary of State, negotiated a settlement which exchanged the Eagle Bay land for some lands near Plattsburgh which the Indians agreed to occupy instead. The three-year occupation focused the attention of many New Yorkers on the issues facing today's American Indians, including the challenge of continuing their religion and culture.

Ray Fadden operates the Six Nations Indian Museum in Onchiota—an excellent resource on Iroquois history and culture. (See Section 14 for details.)

This section was written by Robert Venables, former education curator of the Museum of the American Indian and consultant on Native American history.

(20)
FAMOUS ADIRONDACK GUIDES

The Adirondack guide, from whom this book derives its name, was a fixture throughout the Adirondack Mountains in the later half of the nineteenth and in the early twentieth centuries. In 1891, the Adirondack Guides Association was formed to promote the guides' services, to provide a social and economic support network and to lobby for common interests. The tradition of the Adirondack guide continues today (See Section 86), with hundreds of guides licensed by the State of New York.

During the late 1800s and early 1900s there were hundreds of guides. The following listing includes those who were among the most popular, longest-lasting and notorious guides in their respective regions.

Adirondack French Louie (c.1825-1915), West Canada Lakes
Ed Arnold (1829-1906), Fulton Chain.
Sal Benham (1844-1905), Saranac Region.
Julia Burton (1896-1969), Piseco Lake area
Reuben Cary (1845-1933), Long Lake & Brandreth Lake
John, Cheney (1800-1887), Tahawus
Warren Cole (1854-1922), Long Lake
Herb Clark (1870-1940), Saranac Lake
Earl Covey (1876-1952), Big Moose area
Henry Davis (1856-1920), Saranac Lake area
Sam Dunakin (c.1835-1907), Fulton Lake Chain
Alvah Dunning (1816-1902), Raquette Lake
Indian Dan Emmet (1870-1951), Saranac Lakes
Nat Foster (1767-1841), Fulton Chain
Henry Dwight Grant (1833-1911), Bonneville
Les Hathaway (1862-1952), Saranac Lakes
James Higby (1842-1913), Big Moose
Chauncey Hathorn (1826-1891), Blue Mt. & Raquette Lake area
Harvey Holt (1808-1893), Keene Valley
Monroe Holt (1845-1921), Keene Valley
Noah LaCasse (1864-1951), Tahawus-Newcomb area
Henry Martin (1860-1915), St. Regis area
Harvey Moody (1808-1880), Saranac Lakes
Gort Moody (1822-1902), Saranac Lakes
Mart Moody (1833-1910), Saranac Lakes
William B. Nye (1816-1893), High Peaks area
Pete O' Malley (1855-early 1930's), Saranac Lake area
Ellsworth Petty (1863-1956), Saranac Lake area
Tom Peacock (1853-1942), Saranac Lake area
Orson S. ("Old Mountain") Phelps (1817-1905), Keene Valley
John ("Honest John") Plumbley (1827-1900), Long Lake region
Mitchell Sabattis (1816-1906), Long Lake area
Jack Sheppard (c.1837-1921), Fulton Chain
Nick Stoner (c.1762-1850), Southern Adirondacks
Mel Trumbell (1849-1927), Keene Valley

Alvah Dunning

(21)
ADIRONDACK HERMITS

Ebenezer Bowen, Long Lake (1798-1888)
Moses Follensby, Follensby Pond (d.c. 1840)
Harney, Long Lake (1835-c.1902)
Ferd Jansen, Tupper Lake area (1859-1947)
Atwell Martin, North Lake, dates unknown
Archie "Bobcat" Ranney, Bakers Mills, dates unknown
Walter Channing Rice, "The Hermit of Ampersand Mt." (1852- 1924)
Noah John Rondeau, " Mayor of Cold River" (1883-1967)
"French Louie" Seymour, West Canada Lake (c.1825-1915)
Bill Smith, Bloomingdale (1827-c.1910)
Dave Smith, Smith's Lake, dates unknown

Noah John Rondeau, "Mayor of Cold River"

(22)
ADIRONDACK GUIDE-BOAT BUILDERS

The "guide-boat" was one of the major means of transportation throughout the Adirondacks in the nineteenth and early twentieth centuries. This indigenous craft has attracted much attention in recent years. The Adirondack Museum has an excellent display of early guide-boats and sponsored the definitive work on this subject—Kenneth and Helen Durant's *The Adirondack Guide-Boat* (1980).

The present listing includes many of the more important, famous and/or prolific guide-boat builders. It was compiled from the displays at the Museum and from historical works, then augmented from the much more complete and detailed listing in the aforementioned work, and finally revised to include reviewers' input. The second group of names includes a number of guide-boat builders living and working today in the Adirondacks to maintain and revive this rich native tradition and craft.

MOST FAMOUS GUIDE-BOAT BUILDERS

Merlin Austin (c.1875-c.1951) Long Lake
Albert Henry Billings (1853-1903) Lake Placid
John Blanchard (1878-1948) Raquette Lake
Reuben Carey (1845-1933) Long Lake
Caleb J. Chase (1830-1911) Newcomb
Warren Cole (1854-1922) Long Lake
Wallace Emerson (1874-1953) Long Lake
H. Dwight Grant (1833-1911) Boonville
& son Lewis Grant (1878-1960) Boonville
Theodore Hanmer (1860-1927) Saranac Lake
& son Willard Hanmer (1902-1962) Saranac Lake
William Kerst (1874-1950) Sabael
William Allen Martin (1849-1907) Saranac Lake
Luther Owen (b.1853) & son, Tupper Lake
Cyrus H. Palmer (1845-1897) Long Lake
Riley Parsons (1839-1904) Old Forge
& son Ben Parsons (1868-1945) Old Forge
Fred W. Rice (1852-1934) Saranac Lake
J.H. Rushton (1843-1906) Canton
George W. Smith (1866-1926) Long Lake
Henry Stanton (c.1844-1881) Long Lake
William Vassar (1866-1951) and son, Bloomingdale

CURRENT BUILDERS

Austin, Harold, Long Lake
Bailey's Boats, Keene
Burns, Fred, Long Lake
Hathaway, Carl, Saranac Lake
Hornbeck Boats, Olmstedville
Morrow, Ralph, Saranac Lake
Outcalt, George, Saranac Lake
Pezzulo,Tony, Walden, NY
Smith, Everett, Parishville (just outside of Park)

Warren Cole, guide-boat builder

(23)

FAMOUS HOTELS

The following hotels were among the major hotels in the Adirondacks at the turn of the century—the height of the Adirondack's popularity as a tourist area. Accommodations for at least 100 guests is a criterion for inclusion (with a few exceptions) and/or frequent mention in the guidebooks and travelogues of that period. Numbers in parentheses indicate the capacity of the hotel, as given in Seneca Ray Stoddard's *The Adirondacks Illustrated*, 1898 edition, or in a few cases from other sources.

Adirondack House, The, Keene Valley (200)
Adirondack Inn, Schroon Lake (100)
Algonquin, The, Lower Saranac Lake (150)
Altamount, Hotel, Tupper Lake
Ampersand, Hotel, Lower Saranac Lake (300)
Anibal House, Piseco
Antlers, The, Raquette Lake
Bald Mountain House, Third Lake (100)
Berkley Hotel, The, Saranac Lake (100)
Burleigh Hotel, Ticonderoga (100)
Cascade Lake House, Cascade Lakes (100)
Champlain, Hotel, Bluff Point (500)
Chateaugay, The, Chateaugay Lake
Chester House, The (150)
Childwold, Hotel, Massawepie Lake (300)
Cliff House, Fourth Lake (100)
DelMonte, Hotel, Saranac Lake (125)
Eagle Bay Hotel, Eagle Bay (150)
Fenton House, Beaver Lake (160)
Forge House, The, Old Forge (200)
Fort William Henry Hotel, Lake George
Grand View House, Lake Placid (350)
Grove Point House, The, Schroon Lake (100)
Hemlocks, The, Raquette Lake (80)
Higby's, Big Moose (200)
Holland's Blue Mountain Lake House, Blue Mountain Lake (400)
Hundred Island House, Lake George (100)
Interlaken, The, Auger Lake (100)
Lake Clear Hotel, Clear Pond (125)
Lake Placid House, The, Lake Placid (80)
Lake Pleasant Inn, Lake Pleasant (150)
Leland House, The, Schroon Lake (225)
Long Lake House, Long Lake
Loon Lake House, Loon Lake (325)
Mansion House, The, Elizabethtown (150)
Marion House, Lake George (400)
Martin's or Miller House, Lower Saranac Lake (300)
Merwin's Blue Mountain House, Blue Mountain Lake (80)
Ondawa, The, Schroon Lake (100)
Paul Smith's Hotel, Lower St. Regis (500)
Pond View House, Catamount Pond (100)
Prospect House, Blue Mountain Lake (500)
Pyramid Lake House, Paradox (100)
Ralph's, Chateaugay Lake (125)
Risiup House, Chestertown (100)
River View Hotel, Luzerne (100)
Rockwell's Hotel, Luzerne (150)
Rocky Point Inn, Old Forge (125)
Ruisseaumont, The, Lake Placid (250)
Sagamore Hotel, The, Long Lake (250)
Saranac Inn, Upper Saranac Lake (350)
Stevens House, Lake Placid (400)
St. Hubert's Inn, Keene Valley (300)
Tahawus House, The, Keene Valley (150)
Taylor House, Schroon Lake (175)
Undercliff, Lake Placid (100)
Watch Rock Hotel, Schroon Lake (125)
Wawbeek Hotel, Upper Saranac Lake (200)
Wayside, The, Luzerne (200)
Westport Inn, Westport (150)
Whiteface Inn & Cottages, Lake Placid (250)
Whiteface Mountain House, Wilmington (60)
Windsor, The, Elizabethtown (250)

Loon Lake House

(24)

ADIRONDACK RAILROADS AND PRIVATE RAILROAD CARS

The following is a partial list of railroads operating in the Adirondacks around the turn of the century.

The Adirondack Railroad
Adirondack Railway Company (became Blue Line and Canada Southern Line).
Carthage and Adirondack Railway
Chateaugay Railroad Company
Delaware and Hudson Railroad
Fulton Chain Railway Company
Grasse River Railroad Corporation
Keeseville, Ausable Chasm, Lake Champlain Railroad Company
Mohawk and Malone Railroad
Northern Adirondack Extension Company (became Northern and Adirondack Railroad; became Northern New York Railroad;became New York and Ottawa Railroad).
The Ogdensburg and Lake Champlain Railroad
Raquette Lake Railway
Raquette Lake Transportation Company
Saranac and Lake Placid Railroad Company
St. Lawrence and Adirondack Railway Company

During this period a number of wealthy land owners visited their Adirondack estates in their private railroad cars. These included:

Anthony N. Brady- "Adventurer"
Collis P. Huntington- "Genesta"
Alfred G. Vanderbilt- "Wayfarer"
William C. Whitney- "Wanderer"

June 22, 1896

(25)
29 GREAT CAMPS

What is an Adirondack "Great Camp"? Architect Paul Malo has said:

"An Adirondack Great Camp is more than an historic building; it is more even than a complex of buildings. It is rather like a small village, with large residences, cabins, dining buildings, game rooms, staff quarters, blacksmith shop, carpentry shop, stables, barns, greenhouses and more. It represents a unique way of life relating man to the wilderness, motivated by the challenge of self-sufficiency in a sometimes hostile environment. Such a Great Camp not only was characteristically remote, but built with the materials at hand. Paradoxically, the architectural style, while rustic, was also elegant, with characteristics often borrowed from the Japanese, Swiss and other influences, combined gracefully with the native Adirondack log building style."

Adirondack Museum Director Craig Gilborn has suggested the term "grand camp" to describe those complexes built with similar themes but with fewer buildings than a Great Camp. Still another term, "Adirondack Lodge," might describe a single impressive building of characteristic Adirondack style—rustic materials, log beams, some wainscoted walls or ceilings, large living room with fieldstone fireplace, and assorted decorative touches such as animal heads on walls, log railings indoors or out, rustic furnishings, etc., usually built on the shore of and overlooking a lake.

Definitions vary; but whether a Great Camp, grand camp or Adirondack Lodge, a particular building or a set of buildings may be equally impressive and, especially to its owners and guests, equally wonderful woodland retreats. The following listing, then, includes not necessarily the 29 *greatest* camps in the Adirondacks, but the 29 most significant "Great Camps" known to the editors.

Some final qualifications. We have not included former Great Camps, no longer in existance due to fire or removal. There are other Great Camps hidden in the Adirondack woods whose privacy the owners have protected for generations. In a few cases, upon the request of the owners, we have not listed their camps.

The dates given represent the year(s) in which the major building campaigns began. In many cases, the camps would continue to be expanded over several decades. The names given are those people most closely associated with the building and/or early history of the camps.

GREAT CAMPS

BLUFF POINT, Raquette Lake. 1877. Frank Stott, Robert Collier. Private.

CAMP CAROLINA, Lake Placid. 1913. Caesar Cone. Private.

DURYEA CAMP, Blue Mt. Lake. 1880. Gen. Hiram Duryea. Guest Lodge, ("The Hedges").

EAGLE ISLAND CAMP, Upper Saranac Lake. 1898. Vice-Pres./Gov. Levi P. Morton. Girl Scout Camp.

EAGLE NEST, Blue Mt. Lake. 1900. W.W. Durant, Hochschild family. Private.

ECHO CAMP, Raquette Lake. 1883. Gov. Phineas Lounsbury. Summer camp for girls.

INDIAN POINT CAMP ("DAY CAMP"), Upper Saranac Lake. Early 1920's. Private.

CAMP KATIA, Upper St. Regis Lake. 1890. George Earle. Private.

Nehasane, Lake Lila

KAMP KILL KARE, Raquette Lake. Originally W.W. Durant hunting camp. 1898. Timothy Woodruff. 1915. Garvan family. Private.

KILDARE CLUB, near Tupper Lake. William Seward Webb, Fredrick Vanderbilt, etc. 1906. Friedman family. Private.

KNOLLWOOD CLUB, Lower Saranac Lake. 1899. Marshall, Guggenheim, Ashiel, Blumenthal, Stein, Nathan. Private.

LEWISOHN CAMP, Upper Saranac Lake. 1903. Adolph Lewisohn. Young Life conference center.

MARKAM POINT CAMP, Upper Saranac Lake. 1920's. Private.

MEIGS CAMP, Big Wolf Lake, near Tupper Lake. 1916. Ferris Meigs. Private.

CAMP MINNOWBROOK, Blue Mt. Lake. 1948. R.M. Hollingshead. Syracuse University Conference Center.

NEHASANE, Lake Lila, near Sabattis. 1893. William Seward Webb. NY State Forest Preserve; lodge scheduled for demolition.

CAMP PINEBROOK AND MOSS LEDGE, Upper Saranac Lake. Levi Morton and Isabel Ballantine; Loeb; Syracuse University. Private.

CAMP PINE KNOT, Raquette Lake. 1876. William West Durant, Collis P. Huntington. SUNY Cortland outdoor education center.

READ CAMP, Little Simon Pond. 1897. William A. Read. Private.

CAMP SAGAMORE, Raquette Lake. 1897. William West Durant. 1903 Alfred Vanderbilt. Lodge and Conference Center. Public tours on summer weekends.

CAMP SANTANONI, Newcomb. 1888. Robert Pruyn, Melvin family. Part of NY State Forest Preserve; future uncertain.

SEKON LODGE, Upper Saranac Lake. Isaac Seligman. Subdivided; private camps.

STOKES CAMP, Upper St. Regis Lake. 1885. Stokes family. Private.

CAMP TOPRIDGE, Upper St. Regis Lake. 1923. Marjorie Merriweather Post. State of NY conference center; public tours on summer weekends.

CAMP UNCAS, Raquette Lake. 1893. William West Durant, J. Pierpont Morgan. Private and summer camp.

WELLSCROFT LODGE, Upper Jay. Private.

WENONAH LODGE, Upper Saranac Lake. About 1915. Jules Bache. Guest lodge (spelled Winonah).

CAMP WILDAIR, Upper St. Regis Lake. 1882, 1917. Whitelaw Reid. Private.

CAMP WONUNDRA, Upper Saranac Lake. 1930. William Rockefeller. Guest lodge ("The Point").

Camp Sagamore, Raquette Lake

OTHER ARCHITECTURALLY SIGNIFICANT ESTATES

Listed here are a few additional properties, of Great Camp proportions, but of a style different from the Adirondack rustic style of the Great Camp.

CAMP COBBLESTONE, Spitfire Lake. George Earle, Jr. Cobblestone construction. Private.

PINE TREE POINT, Upper St. Regis Lake. H.M. Twombley. Japanese style reconstruction 1902. Fredrick Vanderbilt family. Private.

LITCHFIELD CHATEAU, south of Tupper Lake. 1911. Edward Litchfield and family. Massive stone French chateau. Private.

Sources: H. Kaiser, *Great Camps of the Adirondacks* (Boston: David Godine, 1982); C. Gilborn. *Durant* (Sylvan Beach, NY: North Country Books, 1981); editors' personal knowledge of Adirondack Great Camps.

(26)

THE FOUNDING OF AN ADIRONDACK COUNTY

Adirondack counties and their townships were organized relatively late in New York State history. For example, Essex County was set off from Clinton County in 1799. The 18 townships in Essex County were established in the following years:

1786	Crown Point
1788	Willsboro
1798	Jay
	Elizabethtown
1802	Chesterfield
1804	Schroon
	Ticonderoga
1805	Essex
	Lewis
1808	Moriah
	Keene
1815	Westport
1817	Minerva
1821	Wilmington
1828	Newcomb
1844	St. Armand
1848	North Hudson
1849	North Elba

Source: Essex County Historical Society; other material added.

(27)

ARTICLE 14 CHRONOLOGY

Article 14, the "forever wild" provision of the New York State Constitution, is considered one of the earliest significant pieces of environmental conservation legislation in history. Even today, friends and foes alike of Article 14 would agree that it remains one of the strongest examples of such legislation in existance.

Since its adoption in 1894, there have been approximately 150 pieces of legislation introduced in the New York State Legislature to amend this constitutional provision. Only a relative handful of these amendments have been successful, each having to pass two successive sessions of the State Legislature, with a general election intervening, and then pass a statewide public referendum. Following is a chronology showing the original legislation and the subsequent amendments to this provision throughout its ninety year history.

1894
Passage of Article 7, Section 7 of the New York State Constitution, the original text as follows:

he lands of the state, now owned or hereafter acquired, constituting the forest preserve as now fixed by law, shall be forever kept as wild forest lands. They shall not be leased, sold or exchanged, or be taken by any corporation, public or private, nor shall the timber thereon be sold, removed or destroyed.

1913
Permitting the use of up to 3% of the total Forest Preserve acreage for municipal water supply reservoirs, state canals, and for regulation of the flow of streams.

1918
Permitting the construction of a state highway from Saranac Lake in Franklin County to Long Lake in Hamilton County and thence to Old Forge in Herkimer County by way of Blue Mt. Lake and Raquette Lake.

1927
Permitting the construction of a state highway in Essex County from Wilmington to the top of Whiteface Mountain.

1931
Providing an annual appropriation of funds to purchase lands outside the Adirondack and Catskill Parks for reforestation purposes (the "Reforestation Amendment").

1932
Permitting the construction of a state highway in Hamilton County from Indian Lake to the village of Speculator.

1938
Constitutional Convention renumbered Article 7 to Article 14 and re-arranged its various sections: Section 1 with "forever wild" provision and previously authorized highways; Section 2 with previous reservoir/canal amendment; Section 3 with previous Reforestation Amendment and a declaration that wildlife conservation and reforestation be the policies of the State; and Section 4 providing remedies for violation of Article 14.

1941
Permitting the construction and maintenance of up to 20 miles of ski trails, thirty to eighty feet wide, on the north, east and northwest slopes of Whiteface Mountain in Essex County.

1947
Permitting the construction and maintenance of up to 20 miles of ski trails on Belleayre Mountain in Ulster and Delaware counties and up to 30 miles of ski trails on Gore, South and Pete Gay Mountains in Warren County—both thirty to eighty feet wide, with appurtenances.

1953
Eliminating the use of the forest preserve "to regulate the flow of streams"—a deletion from Article 14, Section 2.

1957
Permitting the sale, exchange or use for other State purposes of Forest Preserve parcels of ten contiguous acres or less outside the Adirondack or Catskill Parks.

1957
Permitting the use of up to 400 acres of Forest Preserve for relocating, reconstructing and maintaining not more than 50 miles of existing State highways to eliminate dangerous curves and grades.

1959
Permitting the use of up to 300 acres of Forest Preserve in the construction of the Adirondack Northway on the west side of Schroon Lake.

1963
Permitting the State to convey 10 acres of Forest Preserve land to the Village of Saranac Lake, for the purpose of refuse disposal, in exchange for 30 acres of "true forest land" owned by the Village of Saranac Lake.

1965
Permitting the State to convey 28 acres of Forest Preserve land to the Town of Arietta, for the purpose of expanding the Piseco airport, in exchange for 30 acres of land owned by the Town of Arietta.

1969
Authorizing acquisition of lands outside the Forest Preserve counties as the State Nature and Historical Preserve. This became the new Section 4 of Article 14, and the previous Section 4 on legal remedies became Section 5.

1973
Raising to 100 acres the limitation on sales and exchanges of Forest Preserve outside the Adirondack and Catskill Parks authorized in the 1957 amendment.

1980
Permitting the State to convey approximately 8,500 acres of land to International Paper Company, for the purpose of consolidating adjoining tracts of land having difficult-to—administer boundary lines, in exchange for an approximately equal number of acres owned by International Paper Company. (Actually the State conveyed 7,133 acres and received 10,344.)

1983
An amendment which probably will be placed before the voters in November 1983 will, if passed, permit the State to convey 10 acres and buildings in the Town of Long Lake, Hamilton County to Sagamore Institute, a non-profit organization, for the purpose of historic preservation, in exchange for approximately 200 acres of land owned by Sagamore Institute within the Adirondack Park.

The most complete work on the history of Article 14, through 1968, is Norman VanValkenburgh's *The Adirondack Forest Preserve* (Blue Mt. Lake: The Adirondack Museum, 1979).

LAKE PLACID OLYMPIC WINTER GAMES 1932 and 1980: A COMPARISON

NUMBER OF EVENTS AND NEW EVENTS

Winter Olympic events increased from 14 in 1932 to 38 in 1980. The 1932 Winter Olympics did not include: Alpine Skiing, which was added in 1948; Biathalon, which was added in 1960; Men's Figure Skating, which was added in 1948; Ice Dance, which was added in 1976; Luge which was added in 1964; various cross-country events, which were added after 1952; 90-meter Ski Jump, which was added in 1976; and Women's Speed Skating, which was added in 1960.

NUMBER OF SPECTATORS

The total number of spectators at the 1932 Winter Olympics, which was held in the depths of the Depression, is an indefinite figure, but probably did not exceed 50,000 maximum for all events. In 1980, the total number of spectators was in the range of 450,000 to 500,000, (Environmental constraints imposed by the Federal Funding Program restricted ticket sales to a maximum of 51,000 on any given day.)

COST OF GAMES

Total cost of the 1932 games probably did not exceed one million dollars, taking into consideration the many areas of governmental support that were not calculated as an expense of the 1932 Winter Olympics. The total cost of the 1980 Winter Olympics has been projected at 168,688,812.00 (see detailed breakdown of 1980 Olympic figures below, taken from the official final report).

NUMBER OF PARTICIPANTS

In 1932, there were 17 countries participating, with over 300 competitors, 32 of whom were women. In 1980, there were 37 countries competing with over 1,600 competitors, over 300 of whom were women.

SNOW CONDITIONS

The snow conditions in 1932 were marked by limited snow and warm weather. The only outdoor events in 1932 included Speed Skating, Hockey, Ski Jumping, Cross-Country and Bob-Sledding. The only refrigerated facility in 1932 was the Olympic Arena, which was constructed for the Figure Skating and Ice Hockey. The weather, again, in 1980 was a problem, because of the lack of snow and multiplicity of events that were held outdoors. The Speed Skating, Luge, and Bob-sledding events were held on artificially refrigerated surfaces. Massive artificial snow-making equipment made it possible for the Alpine Ski, Cross-Country and Ski-Jumping events to be held under ideal snow conditions in spite of the lack of natural snow.

UNITED STATES GOLD MEDALS

In 1932, the United States won 6 Gold Medals out of 14 events—2 in Bob-sledding and 4 in Speed Skating. In 1980, the United States won 6 Gold Medals out of 38 events—one in Hockey and 5 in Speed Skating (all of which were won by Eric Heiden). In 1980, two countries earned more Gold Medals than the United States—Russia, with 10 Gold Medals (primarily in Speed Skating and Cross-Country and Figure Skating) and East Germany (GDR) (primarily in Nordic Skiing, Luge and Speed Skating). As an aside, it is interesting to note that the United States has never won Olympic Winter Gold Medals in Men's Alpine Skiing, Ice Dance, Figure Skating Pairs, Men's or Women's Luge, Biathalon, Cross-Country Skiing events, Ski-Jumping events or 1,000- and 3000-meter Womens's Speed Skating events.

GENERAL CHANGES

In addition to the increase in competitors, number of competitors' events and number of spectators, the major contrast between 1932 and 1980 was the massive scope of a modern Olympic Winter Games, where literally thousands of support personnel were required to conduct the events, and special transportation systems numbering 400 to 500 busses were required to transport the spectators and officials. The world-wide audience of the Olympic Winter Games was another major difference. It was estimated over a billion people world-wide viewed the 1980 Winter Olympics via television. There were probably fewer than 250 accredited media representatives in 1932; this number swelled to over 2,500 in 1980. The logistics of providing transportation and support facilities for the media alone far surpassed the total organization problems of the 1932 Olympics. The security forces required to conduct a modern Olympics are both expensive (estimated at $8,000,000 for 1980) and almost mind-boggling in scope, involving Federal, State and local law enforcement agencies, including 900 New York State Police, who were in residence in the area to assist with security and traffic arrangements. It is estimated that there were 11 Federal and 15 State security agencies involved in the 1980 Winter Olympics security arrangements.

Stevens Brothers, gold medal winners, 1932

Bobsledding, 1980

OLYMPIC INDEBTEDNESS

It is reported that the 1932 Winter Olympics ended with a profit of approximately $250,000. There was a bonded indebtedness of $300,000 incurred in the construction of the 1932 Olympic Arena. It is further reported that the North Elba Town Board elected not to reduce the Olympic Arena bonded indebedtness with the profits from the 1932 Winter Olympics, and after several extensions of the bond issue (which was amortized at the rate of approximately $30,000 a year) the 1932 Olympic Arena bonded indebtedness was paid off in the early 1960's. The reported 1980 Winter Olympics indebtedness has been estimated at $6,500,000. In 1981, the State of New York provided funds to pay off this indebtedness in exchange for which, the Lake Placid 1980 Olympic Committee and the Town of North Elba leased or transferred to a State-created Olympic Regional Development Authority the right to use, maintain and operate the 4 ice sheet Olympic Arena figure skating and hockey facility, the refrigerated speed skating oval, the 70 and 90-meter ski jump complex and the refrigerated luge facility. The construction cost of these facilities transferred to the Olympic Regional Development Authority was in excess of $40,000,000. The Olympic Regional Development Authority has also taken over the use, operation and maintenance of the Mt. Van Hoevenberg Complex, including the bob-sled run, cross-country trails and biathalon range and trails, as well as Whiteface Mountain Ski Center and its alpine facilities.

BUDGET: 1980

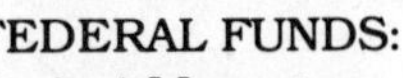

FEDERAL FUNDS:	
Project Management	7,076,763
New Field House	14,281,673
Existing Arena Renovations	2,560,019
Athlete Housing	22,692,771
Administration Center	640,999
70-90 Meter Ski Jumps	5,371,302
Luge Run	5,290,450
Parking Facilities	513,763
Increased Electric Power	2,417,296
Sanitary and Potable Water	267,172
Temporary-Miscellaneous	3,206,059
Dept. of Defense Grant	7,000,000
Bureau of Outdoor Recreation	3,200,000
Highway Administration	4,800,000
Aviation Administration	1,100,000
Department of Energy	708,000
EDA-Railroad Project	1,600,000
Total Federal Funds	82,726,267
NEW YORK STATE:	
Whiteface Mountain Alpine Facilities	11,300,000
Mt. Van Hoevenberg Cross Country, Bobsled Run Biathalon Range and Trails	7,900,000
Support Housing	4,600,000
State Police Headquarters	3,800,000
Road, Airport, Railroad Improvements	4,800,000
Total State Funds 32,400,000	
LAKE PLACID OLYMPIC ORGANIZING COMMITTEE:	
Project Management	734,237
New Field House	73,327
Existing Arena Renovations	1,177,981
Broadcast and Press Centers	3,450,000
Administration	48,127,000
Total LPOOC Funds	53,562,545
TOTAL ALL FUNDS	168,688,812

This section was contributed by Norman Hess, attorney for the Lake Placid Olympic Organizing Committee.

LITERATURE

(29)
BASIC ADIRONDACK LIBRARY: NON-FICTION

This section answers the question: "If you were to recommend ten non-fiction works that would help me really understand and appreciate the Adirondacks, what would those ten choices be?" Leaving off trail and field guides (see Sections 80 and 57), the following annotated listing contains our nominations. They are not necessarily the 10 best books on the Adirondacks (though all are at least very good); but taken together they do, indeed, comprise a basic Adirondack non-fiction library. They are listed here chronologically.

Alfred L. Donaldson, *A History of the Adirondacks.* 2 volumes (New York: Appleton-Century-Crofts, 1921). Facsimile reprint.

Although outdated and marred by factual errors, this remains the basic historical reference work on the Adirondacks.

Russel M.L. Carson, *Peaks and People of the Adirondacks* (Garden City, NY: Doubleday, Doran & Co., 1927; reprinted by Adirondack Mountain Club, 1973).

This classic book relates the documented history and the many anecdotes surrounding the discovery, first ascent, and naming of the Adirondack High Peaks. Of greatest interest to those somewhat familiar with the High Peaks, the book also conveys an important sense of Adirondack lore and history for non-climbers as well, especially as the High Peaks have been almost synonomous with the feeling of wilderness and adventure for generations of Adirondack residents and visitors.

Harold K. Hochschild, *Township 34: A History, with Digressions, of an Adirondack Township in Hamilton County in the State of New York* (Privately Printed, 1952).

This rare book (600 copies printed) is a collectors' item available only in libraries and a few private collections. However, revised sections totalling over 400 of the original 600 pages have been reprinted by the Adirondack Museum in a boxed set of seven books. Both the original volume and the revised extracts, by focusing in depth on one locality, give a vivid portrait of Adirondack history, especially during the latter 19th century. Filled with numerous facts, anecdotes and early photographs, this work truly captures the flavor of the Adirondack past.

William Chapman White, *Adirondack Country* (New York: Alfred Knopf, 1954; revised and updated, 1967).

A lyrical history and often moving interpretation of the Adirondacks. White captures the spirit of the region as well as any writer before or since. Paul Jamieson called the work "the most comprehensive book on the region since Donaldson's History."

Temporary Study Commission on the Future of the Adirondacks, *The Future of the Adirondacks,* 2 volumes (Blue Mountain Lake: Adirondack Museum, 1971).

These two volumes—the first containing 181 recommendations and the second consisting of lengthy technical documentation to support the recommendations—led directly to the passage of the Adirondack Park Agency Act and much subsequent legislation and policy. The first volume, especially, is fascinating reading (with beautiful color photographs) and, more than any other work, conveys the sense of the Adirondacks as a "Park," in actuality and in its potential.

Lincoln Barnett, *The Ancient Adirondacks* (New York: Time-Life Books, 1974).

While this book, Part of Time-Life's series on The American Wilderness, adds little new information, it does provide an excellent profile of the Adirondacks and a magnificent collection of color and black and white photographs. The motif is the author's journey around the Adirondacks and the discoveries he makes. The book definitely contributes to one's appreciation of the region.

Frank Graham, Jr., *The Adirondack Park: A Political History* (New York: Alfred Knopf, 1978).

A well-written history of "the century-long struggle to create and protect the vast wilderness Park in New York State's Adirondack Mountains—and how that struggle has influenced the fate of America's great land resources." This volume updates and covers the political history of the Park in more depth than previous works.

Kenneth and Helen Durant, *The Adirondack Guide-Boat* (Camden, Maine: International, Marine Publishing Co. in association with the Adirondack Museum, 1980).

Guides are central figures in Adirondack history, and their lovely boats are key artifacts of the era when the Adirondacks truly were the "Great Northern Wilderness." The definitive study of guide-boats, their builders, and their role in opening the Adirondacks to travel, this volume is a social as well as technical history. Its lavish illustrations include portraits of many guides and builders, scenes, and a complete set of patterns for a Grant guide-boat and equipment.

Craig Gilborn, *Durant: The Fortunes and Woodland Camps of a Family in the Adirondacks* (Sylvan Beach, NY: North Country Books, 1981) and/or Harvey Kaiser, *Great Camps of the Adirondacks* (Boston: David Godine, 1982).

In recent years, we have increasingly come to appreciate the unique architectural and cultural heritage associated with the "Adirondack Great Camps." These two books cover different, sometimes overlapping aspects of this subject, and have different merits. *Durant* is historically impeccable and provides an in-depth look at Durant and the origins of the Great Camps, excellent coverage of Durant's major camps, and excellent historic black and white photos. *Great Camps* tackles a broader subject, covering 26 Great Camps, is often inaccurate in minor details, has fine color and black and white photographs and has a contemporary perspective. Price tags of $20 and $60, respectively, are also a factor to consider.

Paul Jamieson, *The Adirondack Reader* (Macmillan, 1964; Second Edition, Adirondack Mt. Club, 1983).

Both the first and second editions of *The Reader* are lengthy, extraordinary and different collections of essays, short stories, historical reports, autobiography and more. Warder Cadbury calls this book "the best single introduction to the region's life and letters."

(30)
BASIC ADIRONDACK LIBRARY: LITERATURE

The variety of Adirondack literature is rich enough for every taste. Some titles are hard to find, some quite easy. Perhaps the earliest novel was *The Forest* (Redfield, 1852), with hunting and fishing at Lewey Lake and Lake Pleasant as background. The author was Jedidiah Vincent Huntington, brother of the painter Daniel Huntington who was the president of the National Academy of Design for many years. A recent convert to Catholicism, Huntington's romance is a mixture of the spiritual and secular—and something of a collector's item. More recently there has appeared: Ian Fleming, *The Spy Who Loved Me* (James Bond at Lake George-Viking, 1962); John D. McDonald, *The Quick Red Fox* (Travis McGee at Speculator- Fawcett, 1964); Joyce Carol Oates, *Childwold* (Vanguard, 1971) and *Bellefleur* (Dutton, 1980); and F.C. Doctorow, *Loon Lake* (Random House, 1980).

The best single introduction to the region's life and letters are the two quite different editions of Paul Jamieson's *The Adirondack Reader.* Originally published by Macmillan in 1964 and now out of print, a new anthology with quite different selections has been published by the Adirondack Mountain Club (1983) in paperback and cloth.

The most famous volume in the Adirondack literature was William H.H. Murray's *Adventures in the Wilderness* (1869). A centennial reprint edition of 1970 by Syracuse University Press and the Adirondack Museum has a long historical introduction about the author and his book, as well as an interesting map of a century ago. Murray's stories are a light-hearted mixture of adventure and reflection deftly done. Success spoiled Murray's style for his later books on trapper John Norton in the Adirondacks are cloying and didactic.

At the same time one should read Charles Dudley Warner's *In the Wilderness* (Houghton), which first appeared in 1878. It has long been out of print, but is not a rare book, and still likely to be found on local public library shelves. Unlike Murray, Warner was not a sportsman; he preferred the more genteel cottage life in Keene Valley. With urbane irony and understated humor, his stories sometimes made fun of the hunter and fisherman. And his profile of Old Mountain Phelps reveals the uneasy admiration of a city sophisticate for the character of a remarkable Adirondack guide.

In *The Ruling Passion* (Scribners, 1901) by Henry Van Dyke, "A Lover of Music" is a sympathetic portrait of a lumberjack and his violin.

More sombre are the powerful short stories by Philander Deming about the life of hardscrabble pioneers on the northern edge of the wilderness towards the St. Lawrence. These were collected in three small volumes (all Houghton-Mifflin) around the turn of the century: *Adirondack Stories* (1880), *Tompkins and Other Folks* (1885), and *Story of a Pathfinder* (1907). All have been reprinted in the recent past, or your local library could get copies on loan.

The best known Adirondack story is Theodore Dreiser's *An American Tragedy* (Horace Liveright, Inc., 1925), a tale of the murder at Big Moose of a poor and pregnant factory girl by a capitalist playboy. If you enjoy it, then look at Eleanor Franz's article, "The Tragedy of the 'North Woods'", in the *New York Folklore Quarterly* (Summer, 1948, pp. 85-97) which gives the real names and places involved in the true story of Grace Brown's death by tennis racket blow and drowning.

In a quite different vein is Harvey Dunham's *Adirondack French Louie* (author, 1952; also North Country Books), a trapper and hermit in the West Canada Lake country. The book has been reprinted a number of times and has become a minor classic. Edward Livingston Trudeau's *Autobiography* (Lea and Febiger, 1916) is the moving story of his triumph over tuberculosis and his enlistment of help from friends to build his sanitarium at Saranac Lake. Another important and interesting Adirondack figure was the artist Rockwell Kent. In *This is My Own* (Duell, Sloan & Pearce, 1940) he narrates his encounters with Adirondack winters, dairy farming, the railroad and local politics at AuSable Forks.

As a further guide one should learn how to explore the two volumes of the *Adirondack Bibliography* (Adirondack Mountain Club, 1958 and Adirondack Museum, 1973). Each has an introduction with a survey and further suggestions for the interested reader. It is fun to scan the index for references to your favorite place or person or historical event.

Finally, there are currently two book dealers who specialize in the literature of the Adirondacks: Breck Turner at With Pipe and Book (117 Main St., Lake Placid, NY 12946) and Ted Comstock at Wildwood (Old Forge, NY 13420). Each welcomes browsers, mails out lists of books for sale, and is happy to respond to your inquiries.

This section was written by Warder H. Cadbury, Professor of Humanities, State University of New York at Albany.

(31)
PERIODICALS

ADIRONDAC. The major hiking, outdoor and conservationist magazine for the Adirondack region. 8 1/2 x 11, black on white format; advertising; 10x/year; circulation 8000; founded 1936. Subscription: a benefit of Adirondack Mountain Club membership or $10/year, foreign $15/year, $1.50 single copy. Barbara McMartin, Editor. Published by Adirondack Mountain Club, Inc., 172 Ridge St., Glens Falls, NY 12801. (518)793-7737.

ADIRONDACK BITS N' PIECES. A new publication consisting of stories, articles and photographs with an emphasis on the history of the area. Advertising directory. $2.95 a copy. 8 1/2 x 11, black on white glossy format. Published semi-annually by Banister Publications, Box 63, Port Henry, NY 12974.

ADIRONDACK LIFE. Major general readership magazine for Adirondack region, covering all subjects. 8 1/2 x 11, full color glossy format; advertising; 6x/year; circulation 37,000; founded 1970. Subscription: $12/year, $20/2 years; $2.25 single copy. Information: Editor, *Adirondack Life*, 420 E. Genesee St., Syracuse, NY 13202.

BARKEATER, THE. The fishing and hunting magazine of the Adirondacks; fiction and non-fiction articles; 8 1/2 x 11, black on white glossy format; advertising; 4x/year; circulation 10,000; founded 1982. Subscription: 4 issues /$7.00, 8 issues/$13.50, $1.95 single copy. Information: *The Barkeater*, Box 547, Lake George, NY 12845.

BLUELINE. Literary magazine of poetry about the Adirondacks. 5 1/2 x 8 1/2 black on white with sketches; no advertising; 2x/year; circulation 600; founded 1979. Subscription: $4/year; $2.25 single issue. Alice Gilborn, Editor. *Blueline*, Blue Mountain Lake, NY 12812.

CENTER FOR ADIRONDACK STUDIES *NEWSLETTER.* Quarterly newsletter of the Center for Humanities and Adirondack Studies at the North Country Community College. Includes North Country Calendar, review of recent projects and events at the center, other articles. 8 1/2 x 11, black on white format; no advertising; 2x/year; circulation 800; founded 1978. Subscription: $5/year. Information: Murray Heller, Director, Center for Humanities and Adirondack Studies, North Country Community College, 120 Winona Ave., Saranac Lake, NY 12983.

THE NORTHERN LOGGER AND TIMBER PROCESSOR. The only logging and timber processing journal serving the Northern U.S. 8 1/2 x 11, black on white format; advertising; 12x/year; circulation 10,600; founded 1952. Subscription: $6/year, $11/2 years, add $2 for foreign subscriptions. Information: *The Northern Logger*, Circulation Department, Old Forge, NY 13420.

(32)

NEWSPAPERS

ADIRONDACK DAILY ENTERPRISE, 61 Broadway, Saranac Lake, NY 12983. Daily, Monday-Friday. (518)891-2600.

ADIRONDACK ECHO, PO Box 188, Old Forge, NY 13420. Weekly. (315)369-3747.

ADIRONDACK RECORD POST, Main St., AuSable Forks, NY 12912. Weekly. (518)647-8195.

ADIRONDACK TOURIST, PO Box 672, Old Forge, NY 13420. Weekly. (315)369-6664.

CHATEAUGAY RECORD, Chateaugay, NY 12920. Weekly. (518)497-6142.

CHRONICLE, THE, PO Box 159, Glens Falls, NY 12801. Bi-weekly. (518)792-1126.

ESSEX COUNTY REPUBLICAN, Keeseville, NY 12944. Weekly. (518)834-2001.

HAMILTON COUNTY NEWS, Speculator, NY 12164. Weekly. (518)548-4593.

LAKE GEORGE GUIDE, 526 Canada St., Lake George, NY 12845. (518)668-4887.

LAKE PLACID NEWS, Mill Hill, Lake Placid, NY 12946. (518)523-4401.

NORTH CREEK NEWS ENTERPRISE, PO Box 85, North Creek, NY 12853. (518)251-3012.

POST-STAR, THE, Lawrence and Cooper Sts., Glens Falls, NY 12801. Daily. (518)792-3131.

TIMES OF TI, THE, 26 1/2 Father Joques Place, Ticonderoga, NY 12883. Weekly. (518)585-6204.

TUPPER LAKE FREE PRESS, 136 Park, Tupper Lake, NY 12986. Weekly. (518)359-2166.

PLATTSBURGH PRESS REPUBLICAN, 170 Margaret St., Plattsburgh, NY 12901. (518)561-2300. Daily. Adirondack Bureau Offices at: Main St., Lake Placid, NY 12946, (518)523-1559; 73 Main St., Saranac Lake, NY 12983, (518)891-2001; 160 Montcalm, Ticonderoga NY 12883, (518)585-4070.

VALLEY NEWS, Elizabethtown, NY 12932. Weekly. (518)873-6368.

WARRENSBURG-LAKE GEORGE NEWS, 159 Main St., Warrensburg, NY 12885. Weekly. (518)623-3411.

WATERTOWN DAILY TIMES, Star Route 2, Tupper Lake, NY 12986. Daily. (518)359-3603. Adirondack Bureau Office.

In addition to the daily or weekly newspapers there are several promotional newspapers that are printed monthly, quarterly, or seasonally.

BIG TUPPER SKI REPORT, PO Box 820, Tupper Lake, NY 12986. (518)359-3651.

NORTH COUNTRY LIVING, Plattsburgh.NY 12901. (518)873-6368.

ON THE TRAIL, PO Box 456, East Syracuse, NY 13057. (315)437-9296.

TRAVEL TIMES, WTLB, Inc., Utica, NY 13503. (315)797-1330.

UPSTATE TRAVELER, and *UPSTATE SNOW TRAVELER*, WADR, PO Box 1480-UT, Remsen, NY 13438. (315)831-3941.

ECONOMICS

(33)
EMPLOYMENT AND INCOME STATISTICS

CLINTON COUNTY

Population, 1980 80,750
Employment, July 1982 30,900
Unemployment Rate, July 1982 .... 9.8%
Total Personal Income, 1980 .... $543 million
Per Capita Income,1980 .... $6,706

ESSEX COUNTY

Population, 1980 36,176
Employment, July 1982 17,500
Unemployment Rate, July 1982 .... 11.7%
Total Personal Income, 1980 .... $251 million
Per Capita Income, 1980 .... $6,929

FRANKLIN COUNTY

Population, 1980 44,929
Employment, July 1982 17,600
Unemployment Rate, July 1982 .... 10.4%
Total Personal Income, 1980 .... $286 million
Per Capita Income, 1980 .... $6,353

FULTON COUNTY

Population, 1980 55,153
Employment, July 1982 23,900
Unemployment Rate, July 1982 ....12%
Total Personal Income, 1980 .... $396 million
Per Capita Income, 1980 .... $7,167

HAMILTON COUNTY

Population, 1980 5,034
Employment, July 1982 2,500
Unemployment Rate, July 1982 .... 7.1%
Total Personal Income, 1980 ....$34 million
Per Capita Income, 1980 .... $6,665

HERKIMER COUNTY

Population, 1980 66,714
Employment, July 1982 26,900
Unemployment Rate, July 1982 ....11%
Total Personal Income, 1980 .... $521 million
Per Capita Income, 1980 .... $7,786

LEWIS COUNTY

Population, 1980 25,035
Employment, Sept. 1982 10,000
Unemployment Rate, Sept. 1982 .... 11.2%
Total Personal Income, 1980 .... $158 million
Per Capita Income, 1980 .... $6,316

ONEIDA COUNTY

Population, 1980 253,466
Employment, July 1982 102,100
Unemployment Rate, July 1982 .... 8.6%
Total Personal Income, 1980 ....$2,076 million
Per Capita Income, 1980 .... $8,173

ST. LAWRENCE COUNTY

Population, 1980 114,254
Employment, July 1982 38,000
Unemployment Rate, July 1982 .... 9.9%
Total Personal Income, 1980 .... $751 million
Per Capita Income, 1980 .... $6,558

SARATOGA COUNTY

Population, 1980 153,759
Employment, July 1982 69,400
Unemployment Rate, July 1982 .... 6.1%
Total Personal Income, 1980 ....$1,252 million
Per Capita Income, 1980 .... $8,124

WARREN COUNTY

Population, 1980 54,854
Employment, July 1982 24,300
Unemployment Rate, July 1982 .... 7.6%
Total Personal Income, 1980 .... $448 million
Per Capita Income, 1980 .... $8,140

WASHINGTON COUNTY

Population, 1980 54,795
Employment, July 1982 24,200
Unemployment Rate, July 1982 .... 8.5%
Total Personal Income, 1980 .... $382 million
Per Capita Income, 1980 .... $6,959

Source: New York State Department of Commerce, Division of Economic Research and Statistics.

(34)

ECONOMIC PROFILES

CLINTON COUNTY, in the extreme northeast corner of the state, is bounded by Canada on the north and Lake Champlain on the east. The southwest portion is part of the Adirondack Park. The county is a large dairy and apple producer, and its industries include several paper mills.

ESSEX COUNTY, the second largest county in the State in area, is sparsely populated, with all of its land area within the Adirondack Park. Among its noted attractions are Lake Placid and Whiteface Mountain, scene of the 1980 Winter Olympics. Resort industries and logging are important sources of employment. Chief manufacturing employers are producers of paper, sanitary products and lumber. Titanium is mined at Tahawus and wollastonite and garnet at Willsboro.

FRANKLIN COUNTY extends from the Adirondack Mountain region north to Canada. The county has much of its land area within the Adirondack Park and is a popular vacationland, with the resorts of Saranac Lake and Tupper Lake. Although the service industries and retail trade together account for over half of the county's employment, manufacturing is important in some of the villages. Manufactured products include wood products, footwear and dresses. Agriculture is also important to the county, and three quarters of its farm production is dairy products.

FULTON COUNTY, in the Mohawk Valley, with its northern portion in the Adirondack Park, is the center of leather dress-glove manufacturing in the United States. The glove industry, concentrated mainly in Gloversville and Johnstown, is the principle source of manufacturing employment in the county. The industry is characterized by a large number of small firms, many of which are engaged in the production of leather, knitted and fabric gloves, while others tan and prepare leather or supply knitted or fur linings.

HAMILTON COUNTY is the most sparsely populated of all counties of New York State. Lying entirely within the boundaries of the Adirondack Park, the county's territory, largely State-owned, consists of mountains, forests, 77 lakes, and numerous rivers, ponds and streams. The area has expanded its resort facilities to provide a year-round vacation industry that is an important source of income to residents. The chief sources of employment are logging, the manufacture of lumber and wood products, and the hotels and recreational facilities in the resort areas.

HERKIMER COUNTY is a county of physical contrasts. The northern part is mountainous and heavily forested, while the southern portion lies in the fertile Mohawk Valley, which is also highly industrialized. The Mohawk River, the Barge Canal and water-level highways and railways have long given this section excellent transportation facilities. Major industries produce footwear, clothing, food products, agricultural and shop tools, fluid-food-handling machinery, library equipment, sporting firearms and other sporting goods, data-processing equipment, and pneumatic hydraulic tools. The northern two-thirds of the county, lying within the Adirondack Park, provides timber resources and is popular for hunting, fishing, snowmobiling and other recreation.

LEWIS COUNTY, its eastern portion lying within the Adirondack Park, attracts vacationers with its rugged country and many lakes and rivers. The part of the county in the western foothills of the Adirondacks is largely devoted to agriculture, with specialization in dairy farming. Milk is shipped to large metropolitan markets or sold to local cheese factories. Lowville, the county seat and major population and trading center, is known for its cheese manufacturing.

ONEIDA COUNTY, with just its northeast corner in the Adirondack Park, is one of the most industrialized counties in upstate New York. Its factories produce furniture, copper wiring, tubing and utensils, cutlery and tableware, metal stampings and forgings, electronic equipment, corrugated boxes, knitware, construction equipment, heating and cooling equipment, beer and ale, and apparel. Utica is best known for the production of electronic equipment and aircraft parts. Rome is famous for copper and brass works, and for Griffis Air Force Base located nearby. Sherrill is known for silver work, silverware and silver plate. The county also contains exceptionally fertile farm lands. It ranks sixth among the counties in the state in the production of dairy products.

ST. LAWRENCE COUNTY, the state's largest county in area, is bordered on the northwest by the St. Lawrence River, and its southeast portion lies in the Adirondack Park. The county's proximity to the huge hydroelectric capacity of the St. Lawrence Power Project and its location on the St. Lawrence Seaway provide major sources of employment. The Thousand Islands region is a major tourist and vacation area. Massena is the aluminum center of the state, and extensive pulp and paper-mill operation in the county attest to the importance of the lumber and pulpwood industry as well. The largest talc mines in the world are found in the county, along with a wide variety of minerals, including iron ore, zinc and lead. Ogdensburg has a variety of industries and is the region's leading harbor, handling domestic, overseas and Canadian cargo.

SARATOGA COUNTY, with its northwestern corner in the Adirondack Park, has been noted for its mineral springs and horse racing for well over a hundred years. Major industrial products include paper and pulp, brass fittings, shirts, dresses, underwear, cotton and wool hose, knit fabrics and other textiles, cartons and other containers, tissues and napkins, silicones, electrical equipment and bottled mineral water. General Electric operates facilities devoted to research and production of silicones near the village of Waterford. The New York State Energy Research and Development Authority's Saratoga Research and Development Center is the site of the Malta Test Station. In the county is the world-famous resort of Saratoga Springs, which attracts thousands of visitors each year to its healthful mineral springs and to its racing events. The state-owned Spa has beautifully appointed facilities for recreation and entertainment. Within the Spa is the Saratoga Performing Arts Center, summer home of the Philadelphia Orchestra and New York City Ballet.

WARREN COUNTY, lying almost entirely within the Adirondack Park, offers a large choice of recreational opportunities to vacationers. Numerous cottages, camps and hotels are found along the shore line of Lake George, one of the best-known lakes in the country and the largest lake entirely within the Adirondack Park. Other popular resort lakes in the county include Schroon, Friends, Brant, Loon, and Luzerne. The county also attracts many winter sports enthusiasts to its ski slopes. North Creek is an important center of garnet mining. The largest community in the county is Glens Falls, which is an insurance center and has a variety of manufacturing industries producing such items as pigment colors, paper, pulp, lace, chemicals, cement, apparel, catheters and textiles.

WASHINGTON COUNTY, on the east bank of the Hudson River, with only its northwestern corner in the Adirondack Park, is known for its paper-making industry, with mills located in several communities. Paper-making and other industrial machinery are produced in Hudson Falls. The manufacture of capacitors is an important source of employment in the county. Also manufactured in the county are metal tubes, catheters, furniture and coated materials. Much of the county is farmland, with dairy farming accounting for almost four-fifths of farm revenue.

Source: New York State Department of Commerce.

(35)
FARMERS' MARKETS

This section includes farmers' markets and farms which sell their produce to the public—within the Blue Line. It was compiled from information provided by the New York State Department of Agriculture and Markets and by county chambers of commerce.

ESSEX COUNTY

BOARDMAN'S GREENHOUSE & MARKET GARDEN, Middle Rd., Willsboro, NY 12996. (1.5 miles south of village.) May-October, roadside market and pick your own, various vegetables, maple syrup, honey, herbs and crafts. (518) 963-8925.

FROG ALLEY FARM, Main St., Keene Valley, NY 12943. (Rt. 73, Frog Alley Farm.) April-July, maple syrup. (518) 576-9835.

GRAYDON DENSMORE, Rt. 9, Schroon Lake, NY 12870. (1/2 mile south of village.) May-October, roadside market, various produce, cider, eggs, honey, maple syrup.

JOHNSON ORCHARDS, Johnson Farm Rd., Ticonderoga, NY 12883. (2 miles north of village, just west of Rt. 9N via Street Rd.) Roadside market, apples, honey, maple syrup. (518)585-2565.

KELLY'S FRUITS AND VEGETABLES, Rt. 22, Essex, NY 12936. (2.5 miles south of village.) May-September, roadside market, various produce. (518) 963-4167.

LAWRENCE SAYWARD, Middle Rd., Willsboro, NY 12996. (2 miles south of village.) July-October, roadside market, vegetables, honey. (518)963-4189.

THOMPSON ORCHARDS, Street Rd., Ticonderoga, NY 12883. (2 miles north of village at Street Rd.) September-November, roadside market and pick your own, apples.

VALLEY VIEW FARMS, Rt. 9N, Ticonderoga, NY 12883. (4 miles south of Village.) May-October, roadside market and pick your own, various produce, maple syrup, honey. (518)585-7517.

WOOD'S GREENHOUSE, Russell St., Crown Point, NY 12928. (west off Rts. 9N and 22.) Year-round, roadside market, melons, strawberries, various vegetables and plants. (518) 597-3478.

FRANKLIN COUNTY

GILLISES FARM MARKET, "The Market Place," Tupper-Saranac Highway, Tupper Lake, NY 12986. (Intersection of Rts. 3 and 30.) May-December, roadside market, various produce, greenhouse, vegetable bedding plants, honey, maple syrup. (518) 359-9500.

FULTON COUNTY

TIMBERLANE BLUEBERRY FARM, INC., Mussey Rd., Caroga Lake, NY 12032. (2 miles south of Caroga Lake between Beeckridge Rd. and Rt. 10.) July-mid October, pick your own and roadside, wholesale and retail, raspberries, vegetables, crafts, blueberries. (518) 835-6335 or 762-9128.

WARREN COUNTY

JAMES A. FARRAR, Farrar Rd., Warrensburg, NY 12885. (Rt. 87 to Exit 23, right on Truesdale Hill Rd. to end of Farrar Rd.) March-April, roadside market, tours, maple syrup and cream. (518) 623-9449.

WARRENSBURG FRUIT, 44 Main St., Warrensburg, NY 12885. (Across street from Historical Society Museum.) May-October, roadside market, various produce, cider, plants. (518) 623-9449.

WASHINGTON COUNTY

GOOD MANOR FARM, West Ft. Ann, NY 12827. (Rt. 149 onto Goodman Rd.) Open 4-6:30pm. Dairy. (518) 639-5504.

CHAMBERS OF COMMERCE

COUNTY CHAMBERS OF COMMERCE

CLINTON COUNTY AND PLATTSBURGH CHAMBER OF COMMERCE,
135 Margaret St.,
PO Box 310,
Plattsburgh, NY 12901.
(518) 563-1000.

ESSEX COUNTY DEPARTMENT OF TOURISM,
Elizabethtown, NY 12932.
(518) 873-6301.

FRANKLIN COUNTY TOURISM,
Court House,
63 West Main St.,
Malone, NY 12953.
(518) 483-6767 ext. 230.

FULTON COUNTY CHAMBER OF COMMERCE
40 North Main St.,
Gloversville, NY 12078
(518) 725-0641
or
County Office Building,
Johnstown, NY 12095.
(518) 762-4128.

HAMILTON COUNTY PUBLICITY BUREAU,
Long Lake, NY 12847.
(518) 624-4151.

HERKIMER COUNTY CHAMBER OF COMMERCE,
9 W. Main St.,
PO Box 129
Mohawk, NY 13407.
(315) 866-7820.

LEWIS COUNTY CHAMBER OF COMMERCE,
Lowville, NY 13367.
(315) 376-2213.

ONEIDA COUNTY CHAMBER OF COMMERCE,
209 Elizabeth St.,
Utica, NY 13501.
(315) 724-3151.

ST. LAWRENCE COUNTY CHAMBER OF COMMERCE,
Drawer A,
Canton, NY 13617.
(315) 386-4000.

SARATOGA COUNTY CHAMBER OF COMMERCE,
494 Broadway,
Saratoga Springs, NY 12866.
(518) 584-3255.

WARREN COUNTY DEPARTMENT OF TOURISM,
Municipal Center,
Dept. 567,
Lake George, NY 12845.
(518) 761-6366.

WASHINGTON COUNTY PLANNING BOARD,
Washington County Bldg.,
Ft. Edward, NY 12828.

LOCAL CHAMBERS OF COMMERCE

ADIRONDACK LAKES CHAMBER OF COMMERCE,
Chestertown, NY 12817.
(518) 494-2722.
Serving Chestertown, Pottersville and Brant Lake.

AUSABLE VALLEY CHAMBER OF COMMERCE,
PO Box 300,
AuSable Forks, NY 12912.

BOLTON LANDING CHAMBER OF COMMERCE,
Bolton Landing, NY 12814.
(518) 644-3831 or 644-3311.

CRANBERRY LAKE CHAMBER OF COMMERCE,
Cranberry Lake, NY 12977.
(315) 848-2900.

ELIZABETHTOWN CHAMBER OF COMMERCE
Essex County Historical Society,
Adirondack Center Museum,
Elizabethtown, NY 12932.
(518) 873-6466
Also serving Keene, Lewis, Minerva, Moriah, Newcomb, St. Armand.

HAGUE ON LAKE GEORGE CHAMBER OF COMMERCE,
Hague, NY 12936.
(518) 543-6353.

INDIAN LAKE CHAMBER OF COMMERCE,
PO Box 18,
Indian Lake, NY 12842.
(518) 648-5112.

INLET CHAMBER OF COMMERCE,
Inlet, NY 13360.
(315) 357-5501.

LAKE GEORGE CHAMBER OF COMMERCE,
PO Box 272,
Lake George, NY 12845.
(518) 668-5755.

LAKE LUZERNE CHAMBER OF COMMERCE,
PO Box 222,
Lake Luzerne, NY 12846.
(518) 696-3500.

LAKE PLACID CHAMBER OF COMMERCE,
Olympic Arena,
Lake Placid, NY 12946.
(800) 342-9561 in NYS, (800) 833-2521 outside NYS, or
(518) 523-2445.

LONG LAKE,
Alice Scivally,
Publicity Director,
Long Lake, NY 12847.
(518) 624-4151.
Serving Town of Long Lake.

NORTH CREEK CHAMBER OF COMMERCE,
Town of Johnsburg,
North Creek, NY 12853.
(518) 251-2612.
Also serving the Greater Gore Mt. Area.

NORTH HUDSON VACATION ASSOCIATION,
PO Box 501,
North Hudson, NY 12855.
(518) 532-7863.

OLD FORGE TOURIST INFORMATION CENTER,
Rt. 28,
PO Box 129,
Old Forge, NY 13420.
(315) 369-6983 or 357-5000.

SARANAC LAKE AREA CHAMBER OF COMMERCE,
30 Main St.,
Saranac Lake, NY 12983.
(518) 891-1990.

SCHROON LAKE CHAMBER OF COMMERCE,
Schroon Lake, NY 12870.
(518) 532-7675.

SPECULATOR CHAMBER OF COMMERCE,
Speculator, NY 12164.
(518) 548-4521
Also the address for the Office of Tourism and Community Development, serving Lake Pleasant and Piseco.

STONY CREEK CHAMBER OF COMMERCE,
PO Box 135,
Stony Creek, NY 12878.
(518) 696-2395.

TICONDEROGA AREA CHAMBER OF COMMERCE,
PO Box 70,
Ticonderoga, NY 12883.
(518) 585-6619. Also serving Crown Point.

THURMAN, TOWN OF,
CHAMBER OF COMMERCE,
Athol, NY 12810.
(518) 623-9649.

TUPPER LAKE AND TOWN OF ALTAMONT, INC.,
55 Park St.,
Tupper Lake, NY 12986.
(518) 359-3328.

WARRENSBURG CHAMBER OF COMMERCE,
Main St.,
PO Box 382
Warrensburg, NY 12885.
(518) 623-2161 summer, 623-5611 winter.

WESTPORT CHAMBER OF COMMERCE,
Westport, NY 12993.
(518) 962-8211.

WHITEFACE MT. CHAMBER OF COMMERCE,
PO Box 277,
Wilmington, NY 12997.
(518) 946-2255. Also serving Jay and Wilmington.

WILLSBORO CHAMBER OF COMMERCE,
PO Box 124,
Willsboro, NY 12996.
(518) 963-8668. Also serving Essex.

EDUCATION

(37)
COLLEGES AND UNIVERSITIES

Only two colleges have their main campus within the Adirondack Park. Another has an Adirondack field campus where it offers a complete degree program. Many other colleges have conference centers and field campuses within the Adirondacks; these are listed in section 41.

NORTH COUNTRY COMMUNITY COLLEGE, Saranac Lake, NY 12983. Two-year programs in Liberal Arts and Science, Allied Health, Business, Secretarial and Human Services. Includes a Center for Adirondack Studies, Murray Heller, Director. Founded 1968. Information: (518) 891-2915.

PAUL SMITH'S COLLEGE, Paul Smiths, NY 12970. Associate Degree programs in Hotel Management, Forestry, Surveying, Environmental Technology and Chef Training. Founded 1937. Information: (518) 327-6211.

WANAKENA CAMPUS, School of Forestry, College of Environmental Science and Forestry, State University of New York, Wanekena, NY 13695. Forest Technician Program. Information: (315) 848-2566.

Other colleges and universities on the perimeter of the Adirondacks are:

ADIRONDACK COMMUNITY COLLEGE, Bay Rd., Glens Falls, NY 12801. (518) 793-4491.

CLARKSON INSTITUTE OF TECHNOLOGY, Potsdam, NY 13676. (315) 268-6480.

CLINTON COMMUNITY COLLEGE, Bluff Point, NY 12901. (518) 561-6650.

EMPIRE STATE COLLEGE, 2 Union Ave., Saratoga Springs, NY 12866. (518) 587-2100.

FULTON-MONTGOMERY COMMUNITY COLLEGE, Rt. 67, Johnstown, NY 12095. (518) 762-4651 or (518) 829-7321.

HAMILTON COLLEGE, Clinton, NY 13323. (315) 859-4421.

HERKIMER COUNTY COMMUNITY COLLEGE, Reservoir Rd., Herkimer, NY 13350. (315) 866-0300.

MATER DEI COLLEGE, Riverside Dr., Ogdensburg, NY 13669. (315) 393-5930.

MOHAWK VALLEY COMMUNITY COLLEGE, 1101 Sherman Drive, Utica, NY 13501. (315) 797-9530.

SKIDMORE COLLEGE, North Broadway, Saratoga Springs, NY 12866. (518) 584-5000.

ST. LAWRENCE UNIVERSITY, Canton, NY 13617. (315) 379-5011.

UTICA COLLEGE OF SYRACUSE UNIVERSITY, Utica, NY 13502. (315) 792-3006.

STATE UNIVERSITY OF NEW YORK (SUNY) at Plattsburgh, NY 12901. (518) 564-2000.

STATE UNIVERSITY OF NEW YORK (SUNY) at Potsdam, Potsdam, NY 13502. (315) 267-2180.

STATE UNIVERSITY OF NEW YORK (SUNY), College of Technology at Utica-Rome, 811 Court St., Utica, NY 13502. (315) 792-3300.

WADHAMS HALL SEMINARY, Riverside Dr., Ogdensburg, NY 13669. (315) 393-4231.

(38)
PRIVATE SCHOOLS

HOLY GHOST ACADEMY, Marion Ave., Tupper Lake, NY 12986. Grades K-6, day, 221 boys and girls. Teaching Order—Daughters of the Holy Spirit. Established 1903. Information: (518) 359-2203.

KINDERWOOD PROGRAM, Old Forge Community Arts Center, Rt. 28, Old Forge, NY 13420. Early childhood education program. Ages 3-4, day, 28 boys and girls. Established 1969. Miriam Kashiwa, Director. Information: (315) 369-6411.

THE MOUNTAIN HOUSE SCHOOL, 11 Maple St., Lake Placid, NY 12946. College preparatory and athletic training school. Grades 9-12, boarding and day, 35 boys and girls. Established 1977. Information: Robert L. Zimmerman, Jr., Headmaster. (518) 523-3460.

NORTH COUNTRY SCHOOL, Lake Placid, NY 12946. Grades 4-8, boarding and day, 90 boys and girls. Established 1938. Information: (518) 523-9329.

NORTHWOOD SCHOOL, Lake Placid, NY 12946. Grades 8-12, boarding and day, 150 boys and girls. Established 1905. Information: (518) 523-3357.

ST. AGNES SCHOOL, Lake Placid, NY 12946. Grades K-8, day, 110 boys and girls. Established 1958. Information: (518) 523-3771 or 3202.

ST. BERNARD'S SCHOOL, 32 River St., Saranac Lake, NY 12983. Grades K-6, day, 156 boys and girls. Established 1922. Information: (518) 891-2830.

(39)
LIBRARIES

Listed first are library systems serving several of the Adirondack counties. Following are individual libraries, listed by county.

CLINTON, ESSEX, FRANKLIN LIBRARY SYSTEM, 17 Oak St., Plattsburgh, NY 12901. (518) 563-5190.

SOUTHERN ADIRONDACK LIBRARY SYSTEM. Serving Hamilton, Saratoga, Warren, and Washington counties. 22 Whitney Pl., Saratoga Springs, NY 12866. Bookmobile service, film orders. Information: (518) 584-7300, 792-3343 and 885-1073.

CLINTON COUNTY

DANNEMORA FREE LIBRARY, PO Box 326, Dannemora, NY 12929. (518) 492-7005.

ESSEX COUNTY

AUSABLE FORKS FREE LIBRARY, West Church St., AuSable Forks, NY 12912. (518) 647-5596.

BELDEN NOBLE MEMORIAL LIBRARY, Main St., Essex, NY 12936.

BLACK WATCH MEMORIAL LIBRARY, Montcalm St., Ticonderoga, NY 12883. (518) 585-7380.

BREWSTER MEMORIAL LIBRARY, Essex County Historical Society, Court St., Elizabethtown, NY 12932. (518) 873-6466.

ELIZABETHTOWN LIBRARY ASSOCIATION, River St., Elizabethtown, NY 12932. (518) 873-2690.

GEORGE AND MARGARET GEY LIBRARY, W. Alton Jones Cell Science Center, Old Barn Rd., Lake Placid, NY 12946. By appointment. (518) 523-2427.

HAMMOND PUBLIC LIBRARY, Main St. Crown Point, NY 12928. (518) 597-3285.

HANCOCK HOUSE RESEARCH LIBRARY, Ticonderoga Historical Society, Moses Circle, Ticonderoga, NY 12883. (518) 585-7868.

KEENE VALLEY LIBRARY, Loomis Room, Main St., Keene Valley, NY 12942. (518) 576-4335.

KEENE PUBLIC LIBRARY, Keene, NY 12942. (518) 576-2200.

KEESEVILLE FREE LIBRARY, Keeseville, NY 12944. (518) 834-9054.

LAKE PLACID PUBLIC LIBRARY, 67 Main St., Lake Placid, NY 12946. (518) 523-3200.

MINERVA PUBLIC LIBRARY, Rt. 28N, South of Minerva, NY 12851.

NETTIE MARIE JONES FINE ARTS LIBRARY, Center for Music, Drama, and Art, Saranac Ave., Lake Placid, NY 12946. (518) 523-2512.

PAINE MEMORIAL FREE LIBRARY, Willsboro, NY 12996. (518) 963-4478.

SCHROON LAKE LIBRARY, Box 1, Schroon Lake, NY 12870. (518) 532-7737.

SHERMAN FREE LIBRARY, Church St., Port Henry, NY 12974.

WADHAMS FREE LIBRARY, Wadhams, NY 12990. (518) 962-4514.

WELLS MEMORIAL LIBRARY, PO Box 57, Upper Jay, NY 12987. (518) 946-2644.

WESTPORT LIBRARY ASSOCIATION, Westport, NY 12993. (518) 962-8219.

FRANKLIN COUNTY

FRANK L. CUBLEY LIBRARY, Paul Smith's College, Paul Smiths, NY 12970. (518) 327-6313.

GOFF-NELSON MEMORIAL LIBRARY, 41 Lake St., Tupper Lake, NY 12986. (518) 359-9421.

SARANAC LAKE FREE LIBRARY, 100 Main St., Saranac Lake, NY 12983. (518) 891-4190.

HAMILTON COUNTY

ADIRONDACK MUSEUM LIBRARY, Blue Mt. Lake, NY 12812. By appointment. (518) 352-7311.

RAQUETTE LAKE FREE LIBRARY, Raquette Lake, NY 13436.

TOWN OF INDIAN LAKE PUBLIC LIBRARY, Indian Lake, NY 12842. (518) 648-5444.

HERKIMER COUNTY

OLD FORGE LIBRARY, PO Box 128, Crosby Blvd., Old Forge, NY 13420. (315) 369-6008.

SARATOGA COUNTY

CORINTH FREE LIBRARY, 89 Main St., Corinth, NY 12822. (518) 654-6913.

WARREN COUNTY

BOLTON FREE LIBRARY, PO Box 398, Main St., Bolton Landing, NY 12814. (518) 644-2233.

CALDWELL-LAKE GEORGE LIBRARY, 340 Canada St., Lake George, NY 12845. (518) 668-2528.

RICHARDS LIBRARY, 36/38 Elm St., Warrensburg, NY 12885. (518) 623-5611.

Fulton, Lewis, Oneida, St. Lawrence, and Washington counties have no public libraries in the Adirondack Park.

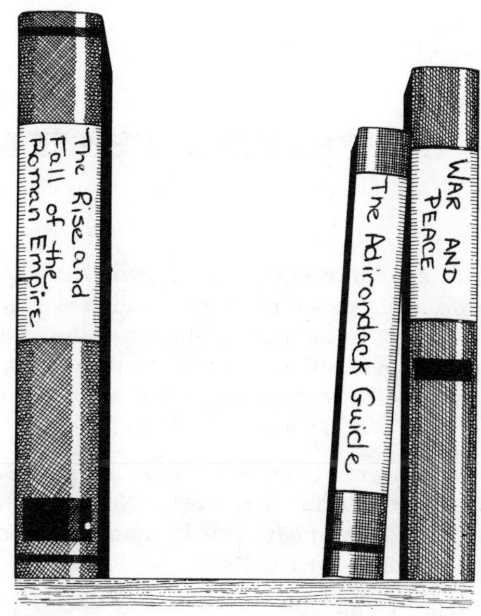

(40)
SCIENTIFIC RESEARCH CENTERS

ATMOSPHERIC SCIENCES RESEARCH CENTER, S.U.N.Y. Albany, Whiteface Mountain Field Station, Wilmington, NY 12997. Facility for atmospheric research conducted at Whiteface Mountain. Activities also include educational/environmental programs and tours for school, university and special interest groups in meteorological and atmospheric sciences. Incidental public visitation area for self-guided tours at Field Station (Marble Lodge) possible during business hours. Information: Douglas Wolfe, Director. (518)946-7191.

W. ALTON JONES CELL SCIENCE CENTER, Old Barn Rd., Lake Placid, NY 12946. A non-profit research and teaching institute dedicated to developing and passing on knowledge of cell growth, differentiation, aging, and malignancy. Information: Dr. Gordon H. Sato, Director. (518)523-2427.

HUNTINGTON WILDLIFE FOREST AND ADIRONDACK ECOLOGICAL CENTER, Newcomb Campus, College of Environmental Science and Forestry, State University of New York, Newcomb, NY 12852. Wildlife studies and silviculture research. (518)582-4551.

LAMONT DOHERTY GEOLOGICAL OBSERVATORY OF COLUMBIA UNIVERSITY, Palisades, NY 10964. Seismic field stations in vicinity of Blue Mt. Lake are monitored year-round at the Palisades facility.

TRUDEAU INSTITUTE BIOMEDICAL RESEARCH LABORATORY, PO Box 59, Saranac Lake, NY 12983. A non-profit institute dedicated to the study of immunity to infectious diseases and cancer. Items of historical interest on grounds. Tours by appointment. Information: Mr. David Kirstein. (518)891-3080.

UIHLEIN-CORNELL BLACKFLY RESEARCH LABORATORY, Bear Cub Rd., Lake Placid, NY 12946. A field station to study the biology and control of blackfly species in the Adirondacks. Information: Dr. E.W. Cupp. (607) 256-6570.

UIHLEIN FARM OF CORNELL UNIVERSITY, Lake Placid, NY 12946. The official foundation seed potato farm in New York State. On this well-isolated 317 acre farm, disease-free nuclear seed stocks are developed each year by meristem tissue culture for New York's seed potato industry. Plantlets are thoroughly screened for microorganisms using serology and recombinant DNA technology.

(41)
CONFERENCE CENTERS AND COLLEGE FIELD CAMPUSES

Listed below are conference centers owned and operated by non-profit organizations. Each publishes a listing of its programs and/or facilities available to individuals or outside groups. A number of privately owned hotels and resorts, principally in the Lake Placid and Lake George areas, also host conferences at their facilities.

LAND'S END, Saranac Lake, NY 12983. On Upper Saranac Lake. United Presbyterian Synod of the Northeast. Newton Fink, Director. Programs include human relations training and personal growth. (518)891-4034.

SAGAMORE LODGE AND CONFERENCE CENTER, Sagamore Rd., Raquette Lake, NY 13436. On Sagamore Lake. Sagamore Institute. Dr. Howard Kirschenbaum, Director. Programs include: Adirondack Bound Outdoor Education and Recreation Program, Effective Schools Institute, Management Training Program, Personal Development Workshops, Museum Program and Historical Tours, and Public Schools Program. Brochures available. (315)354-5311.

SILVER BAY ASSOCIATION, Silver Bay, NY 12874. On Lake George. YMCA. Walt Jacoby, Director. Programs on religious studies, family recreation, human relations training, arts and literature, etc. (518)543-8833.

WORD OF LIFE, Schroon Lake, NY 12870. On Schroon Lake. Auspices: Word of Life Fellowship, Inc. Jack Wyrtzen, Director. Programs on religious studies and renewal. (518)532-7111.

YOUNG LIFE-SARANAC VILLAGE, Box QQ, Tupper Lake, NY 12986. On Upper Saranac Lake. Tom Johnson, Director. Programs on religious studies and renewal. (518)891-3010.

The following entries are conference centers or field campuses of colleges and universities whose main campuses are outside the Adirondack Park. Some are used for their own college-sponsored programs; others are available for use by outside groups.

ANTLERS CAMP, Raquette Lake, NY 13436. State University of New York at Cortland. Jay Cummings, Director. (315)354-4631.

COLGATE UNIVERSITY CAMP, Saranac Inn, NY 12983. (518)891-3090.

CRANBERRY LAKE CAMPUS, College of Environmental Science and Forestry, State University of New York, Cranberry Lake, NY 12972.

HUNTINGTON MEMORIAL CAMP, Raquette Lake, NY 13436. State University of New York at Cortland. Outdoor education center (Camp Pine Knot). Dr. George Fuge, Director. (315)354-4784.

MINNOWBROOK CONFERENCE CENTER, Blue Mt. Lake, NY 12812. Syracuse University. (518)352-7322 or 352-9766.

NEWCOMB CAMPUS, College of Environmental Science and Forestry, State University of New York, Newcomb, NY 12852. Includes Archer and Anna Huntington Wildlife Forest and Adirondack Ecological Center. (518)582-4551.

ST. LAWRENCE CONFERENCE CENTER, Star Route, Box 44, Saranac Lake, NY 12983. St. Lawrence University. Dr. Ron Hoffman, Director. (518)891-4111, June-August. (315)379-5883, September-May.

STAR LAKE CAMPUS, Potsdam College, Star Lake, NY 13690. (315)848-3486.

WARRENSBURG CAMPUS, College of Environmental Science and Forestry, State University of New York, Warrensburg, NY 12885. Includes Charles Lathrop Pack Demonstration Forest and Summer Field Program.

(42)
OTHER EDUCATIONAL RESOURCES AND ORGANIZATIONS

ADIRONDACK ADVENTURES, Inlet, NY 13360. Daytime activities and evening lectures offered during the summer, autumn, and winter. All programs open to the public, free of charge, are designed to develop understanding of the land, the wildlife and the people of the Adirondacks. Information: (315)357-3598.

ADIRONDACK EDUCATIONAL CENTER, Board of Cooperative Educational Services (BOCES), Route 3, Bloomingdale Rd., Box 630, Saranac Lake, NY 12983. Serving Franklin, Essex and Hamilton Counties. Adult education courses in auto mechanics, carpentry, bookkeeping, typing, small engine repair, shorthand and others. Both evening and day courses. Information: (518)891-1330.

ADIRONDACK RESEARCH CENTER, at Schaffer Library, Union College, Schenectady, NY 12308. Includes standard reference works, plus unique photos and files of the late John S. Apperson, and over 80 volumes of Archives of the Assn. for the Protection of the Adirondacks. A research collection of materials on the Adirondacks available for use by the general public. Also sponsors various symposia and programs on the Adirondacks. Ellen Fladger, Archivist. Information: (518)370-6278.

ADIRONDACK YESTERYEARS, Saranac Lake, NY 12983. Provides slide shows on various Adirondack topics, such as hermits, logging, Colvin, the Saranacs, Keene Valley, Lake Placid, Lake George, early hotels, Adirondack guides, etc. Also sells out-of-print Adirondack books, as well as their own publications. Information: Maitland DeSormo, President, Adirondack Yesteryears, Lower Lake—Drawer 209, Saranac Lake, NY 12983. (518)891-3206.

ATMOSPHERIC SCIENCES RESEARCH CENTER, S.U.N.Y. Albany, Whiteface Mountain, Wilmington, NY 12997. Workshops for teachers and environmental groups, tours for school groups and summer lecture series on environmental topics. Open to the public. Information: (518)946-7191.

BOARDS OF COOPERATIVE EDUCATIONAL SERVICES. These boards are consortia of various public school districts around N.Y. State, usually but not always organized by counties, providing vocational, educational and training services beyond the financial or administrative capacities of the individual school districts. Not all Adirondack counties or school districts are served by "B.O.C.E.S." Four B.O.C.E.S. which do serve some sections of the Adirondacks are:

SARATOGA-WARREN COUNTIES B.O.C.E.S.
Byron F. Evans, Superintendent
112 Spring St.,
Saratoga Springs, NY 12866
(518) 584-3239.

WASHINGTON-WARREN-HAMILTON-ESSEX COUNTIES B.O.C.E.S.
Edward F. Huntington, Superintendent
Washington Co. Bldg. Annex,
Hudson Falls, NY 12839
(518) 793-7721

CLINTON-ESSEX-WARREN-WASHINGTON COUNTIES B.O.C.E.S
John W. Harrold Educational Center
P.O. Box 455,
Plattsburgh, NY 12901
(518) 561-0100

FRANKLIN-ESSEX-HAMILTON COUNTIES B.O.C.E.S.
Robert R. Whitman, District Superintendent
Box 28
West Main St. Road
Malone, NY 12953
(518) 483-6420

DEPARTMENT OF ADIRONDACK STUDIES, North Country Community College, Saranac Lake, NY 12983. Courses in guideboat building, log building and other Adirondack-oriented topics. Publication of a newsletter listing Adirondack events, departmental activities, and other information. Murray Heller, Director. Information: (518)891-2915.

FISH HATCHERIES. The following hatcheries raise various species to stock Adirondack waters. The public can visit and view fish. School groups can arrange for guided tours during certain seasons and should make reservations in advance.

Adirondack Hatchery (Franklin County) Star Route 113, Box 1, Saranac Lake, NY 12983. State operated.

Crown Point Hatchery (Essex County), Box 268, Crown Point, NY 12928. (518)597-3844. County operated.

Warren County Fish Hatchery, (Warren County), Warrensburg, NY 12827. (518) 623-2877. County operated.

GOOD MANOR FARM, West Ft. Ann, NY 12827. Public is invited to observe modern dairy operations, daily 4-6pm. Rt. 149 onto Goodman Rd. Information: (518)639-5504.

HERONWOOD OUTDOOR CENTER, PO Box 188, Warrensburg, NY 12885. The off season operation of Camp Echo Lake. Sports facilities, lodging, outdoor education, group programming, conferences. Blanche McSherry, Director. Information: (518)623-2385 or 623-9635.

MEADOWMOUNT SCHOOL OF MUSIC, Wadhams-Lewis Rd., Westport, NY 12993. Students of violin, viola and cello come from all over the world to live, study and practice for eight weeks during July and August. Ivan Galamian, Founder. Information: (518)873-2063.

PARSONS SCHOOL OF DESIGN, Lake Placid Center for Music, Drama and Art. Credit or non-credit summer workshops offered in the following areas: clay, metals, fibers, surface design, printmaking, papermaking, and photography. One and two week sessions. Information: Office of Special Programs, Parsons School of Design, 66 Fifth Ave., New York, NY 10011. (212)741-8975.

POK-O-MACCREADY OUTDOOR EDUCATION CENTER, Willsboro, NY 12996. Day and overnight programs designed to encourage individuals to develop their awareness and appreciation for nature. Environmental Studies, Outdoor Living Skills. Information: (518)936-7967.

TRUDEAU INSTITUTE BIOMEDICAL RESEARCH LABORATORIES, PO Box 59, Saranac Lake, NY 12983. Guided tours and lectures available to the public on the research being done. Information: (518)891-3080.

UIHLEIN CORNELL SUGAR PROJECT, Heaven Hill Farm, Bear Cub Road, Lake Placid, NY 12946. Guided tours through the research facilities and demonstrations of modern maple syrup operations and production techniques. Information: (518)523-9337.

WILDERNESS WORKSHOP OF S.U.N.Y. POTSDAM. Annual courses offered in August, including English, history and astronomy while backpacking in Adirondack High Peaks or canoeing in St. Regis canoe area. Information: Wilderness Workshop, State University College of Arts and Science, Potsdam, NY 13676. Information: (315) 267-2005.

ANNUAL EDUCATIONAL EVENTS CALENDAR

Note: See also Annual Entertainment Events Calendar (Section 79) and Annual Recreational Events Calendar (Section 101).

LECTURE SERIES

ADIRONDACK ADVENTURES, Inlet Town Hall, Inlet, NY 13360. Joan Payne, Director. (315)357-3598. Evening lectures on Adirondack wildlife, recreation, and cultural heritage. Also daytime outings. All activities free. Summer, autumn and winter seasons.

ADIRONDACK CENTER MUSEUM, Court St., Elizabethtown, NY 12932. Miriam Richards, Director. (518)873-6466. Topics related to North Country history and environment. Winter lecture series. Sunday afternoons, late February and March.

ADIRONDACK ECOLOGICAL CENTER, State University College of Environmental Science and Forestry, Newcomb, NY 12852. William F. Porter, Director. (518)582-4551. Lectures about wildlife, nature and the Adirondacks; designed to interest expert and layperson alike. Free of charge. Every other Thursday night, 8 pm, July and August.

ADIRONDACK MUSEUM, Blue Mountain Lake, NY 12812. Craig Gilborn, Director. (518)352-7311. "Mondays at the Museum", Monday evenings, 8 pm, July and August. Lectures on history, art, literature and folklife of the Adirondacks; occasional concerts. Admission fee varies. Traditional Adirondack craft demonstrations in August.

ADIRONDAK LOJ, Lake Placid, NY 12946. John Gorman, Director. (518)523-3441. Lectures on Adirondack nature and environmental topics. Sponsored by Adirondack Mountain Club. Wednesday and Sunday evenings, 8pm, July and August.

ATMOSPHERIC SCIENCES RESEARCH CENTER, (S.U.N.Y. Albany), Whiteface Mountain, Wilmington, NY 12997. Douglas Wolfe, Director. (518)946-7191. Lecture topics include general science, environmental, energy, etc. Tuesday nights, 8:30pm, July and August.

COMMUNITY ARTS CENTER, Old Forge, NY 13420. Lorraine Stripp, Director. (315)369-6411. Audubon Series, slideshow and talks by ornithology scholars, Wednesday evenings and Thursday early-morning bird watching sessions. Slides and films. Art lecture series on art in the Adirondacks, Thursday nights. Both series run during the summer months and require a registration fee.

LAKE GEORGE HISTORICAL ASSOCIATION, P.O. Box 472, Lake George, NY 12845. Donald Fangboner, Director. (518)668-5044. Varied topics from U.F.O.'s to railroading in the North Country. Monday nights, 8 pm, July and August.

OTHER EDUCATIONAL EVENTS

May

ADIRONDACK FOLK SINGING AND STORY TELLING FESTIVAL, Sagamore Lodge and Conference Center, Raquette Lake, NY 13436. Forth annual festival in 1984. Variety of performances, workshops, swap sessions and informal happenings. Information: (315)354-5311.

June

ADIRONDACK CONFERENCE, St. Lawrence University Conference Center, Upper Saranac Lake. Oldest annual Adirondack conference. Free of charge. Organized by Environmental Studies Program and North Country Research Center at St. Lawrence University, Canton, NY 13617. Information: (315)376-5207 or (315)379-5814.

July

ANNUAL SUMMER INSTITUTUE, Center for Humanities and Adirondack Studies, North Country Community College, Saranac Lake, NY 12983. Week-long workshop on Mountain Rhythms, with workshops in traditional Adirondack music, song and dance. Information: Murray Heller, (518)891-2915.

August

ADIRONDACK GREAT ESTATES TOUR AND VACATION ADVENTURE, Sagamore Lodge and Conference Center, Raquette Lake, NY 13436. Tours of five or more Adirondack Great Camps, visits to scenic locations, boat tours, lectures, movies, slide shows, discussions, opportunities for hiking, canoeing, arts and crafts shopping. Accommodations at Sagamore. Usually last week of July or first week of August. Information: (315)354-5311.

September

ADIRONDACK GREAT CAMPS WEEKEND, Sagamore Lodge and Conference Center, Raquette Lake, NY 13436. Tours of three outstanding camp/estates; lectures, slideshows, movies on history, architecture, environment; discussions of contemporary legal and preservation issues. Accommodations at Sagamore. Last weekend in September. Information: (315)354-5311.

October

TEACHING ABOUT THE ADIRONDACKS, sponsored by Board of Cooperative Educational Services (B.O.C.E.S.). Early October, Friday-Saturday conference with many workshop sessions offered. Location varies around the Adirondacks. Information: Dr. Ted Huntington, Washington, Warren, Hamilton and Essex Counties BOCES, Hudson Falls, NY 12839. (518)793-7721.

ORGANIZATIONS AND AGENCIES

(44)
ADIRONDACK ORGANIZATIONS

ADIRONDACK-WIDE ORGANIZATIONS

ADIRONDACK NORTH COUNTRY ASSOCIATION. Founded 1954. Formerly named the Adirondack Association and the Adirondack Park Association. Concerned about the economy and welfare of the Adirondacks and making the region "a finer place in which to live, vacation, work and bring up families." The functions of the Association are: "to provide region-wide representation. . . to the NYS Administration" and to cooperate with similar organizations in other regions. Membership is $15 for individuals, $50 for institutions and chambers of commerce and $100 for businesses. Members can attend meetings and vote; they receive a newsletter and invitations to workshops and legislators' luncheon. Information: Adirondack North Country Association, Adirondack, NY 12808. (518)494-2515.

ADIRONDACK CONSERVANCY. Founded 1971. An operating committee of the Nature Conservancy, this organization seeks to protect critical natural areas in the Park. It does this by purchasing and receiving tracts and reselling or giving them to New York State for the Forest Preserve; by obtaining conservation easements restricting future development; and by owning and maintaining a few tracts of particular interest to the public. Dues are $10/year. Annual membership meeting is held in summer at locations around the Park. Information: Tim Barnett, Exec. Dir., Adirondack Conservancy, The Hand Building, Box 188, Elizabethtown, NY 12932. (518)873-2610.

ADIRONDACK CONSERVATION COUNCIL. Founded in 1947. The organization represents sportmen's interests in the 13 counties of the Adirondack Region. Activities include monitoring fish, wildlife and forest conservation practices in cooperation with the Department of Environmental Conservation. Concerns include environmental and conservation issues, education, wise use of Forest Preserve and maintenance of natural resources. Represents local organized sportsmen's clubs and County Federations. Individual membership is through local club organizations and/or direct membership in the Council. Information: Mr. Gerry Pendas, President, Adirondack Conservation Council, PO Box 548, Saranac Lake, NY 12983.

ADIRONDACK COUNCIL. Founded 1975. A coalition of the National Audubon Society, Wilderness Society, Natural Resources Defense Council, Association for the Protection of the Adirondacks, and other concerned organizations and individuals. The Council is the major Adirondack organization engaged in lobbying and litigation on behalf of Article 14. The Council also engages in other advocacy and public education activities to protect and enhance appreciation of the Adirondack Park. Basic dues are $15/year. Members receive a quarterly newsletter. Annual membership meeting is held in summer at locations around the Park. Information: Gary Randorf, Exec. Dir., Adirondack Council, Box D-2, Elizabethtown, NY 12932. (518) 873-2240.

ADIRONDACK HISTORICAL ASSOCIATION. Founded 1952. The governing body for the Adirondack Museum. One-time, life membership of $500 carries certain Museum benefits, e.g., free pass, discount on publications, etc. The Association meets annually in the summer at the Museum. Information: Adirondack Historical Association, Adirondack Museum, Blue Mt. Lake, NY 12812.

ADIRONDACK FORTY-SIXERS. Founded 1948. Members have climbed the 46 Adirondack High Peaks. The club maintains records of climbing activities and works on behalf of the Adirondack wilderness through a litter bag program, volunteer trail work and annual wilderness workshop. Their newsletter is called "Adirondack Peeks." Information: Grace Leach Hudowalski, Adirondack 46ers, The Boulder, Adirondack, NY 12808.

ADIRONDACK MOUNTAIN CLUB. Founded 1922. With over 8,000 members, "ADK" focuses on hiking, climbing and trail maintenance around the Park and lobbying on behalf of Article 14 and outdoor recreation in the Adirondacks. The Club publishes and sells an excellent collection of trail and field guides, publishes the magazine *Adirondac*, runs workshops, maintains trail markers and conducts clean-up campaigns on a number of Adirondack trails, and operates the Adirondak Loj and Johns Brook Lodge in the High Peaks region. Organized into 27 local chapters (e.g., Glens Falls, Albany, Lake Placid, etc.). Dues are $20/year. Information: Adirondack Mt. Club, 172 Ridge St., Glens Falls, NY 12801. (518)793-7737.

ASSOCIATION FOR THE PROTECTION OF THE ADIRONDACKS. Founded 1901. The oldest Adirondack conservation organization, founded to protect the new "Forever Wild" provision in the Constitution and still serving that purpose today. Engages in lobbying activities and public education. Membership is $25/year. Members receive annual report and can attend annual meeting. Information: Association for Protection of Adirondacks, P.O. Box 951, Schenectady, NY 12301.

ALSO

NORTHEASTERN LOGGERS ASSOCIATION. Based in the Adirondacks but not necessarily or exclusively Adirondack focused. Membership of 2,400 "open to all those interested in the conservation and wise use of the forests of this area for the many benefits they can provide." Association maintains the Forest Industries Exhibit Hall in Old Forge (see Section 14) and publishes monthly magazine *The Northern Logger and Timber Processor* with worldwide circulation of some 11,000. Conducts annual Northeastern Loggers' Congress at localities throughout the Northeast and provides training and consulting services for its members. Dues are $10/year. Information: Northeastern Loggers Association, Old Forge, NY 13420.

LOCAL ORGANIZATIONS

There are local organizations throughout the Park—such as parent/teacher associations, fish and game clubs, garden clubs, etc.—that are too numerous to include here. The following listing contains basic information only, as available, for those local or regional organizations which appeared to be relatively unique and did not have counterparts in many other communities. This is one listing we are sure could be greatly enhanced and invite readers to send in additional information on other local organizations for future editions.

ADIRONDACK TRAIL IMPROVEMENT SOCIETY, Ausable Club, Keene Valley, NY 12943. Maintains trails in St. Huberts area.

CENTRAL ADIRONDACK ASSOCIATION, Old Forge, NY 13420. Promotes recreational, commercial, industrial and civic development.

HIGH PEAKS AUDUBON SOCIETY, INC., Discovery Farm, RD 1, Elizabethtown, NY 12932.

LAKE CHAMPLAIN COMMITTEE, 14 South Williams St., Burlington, VT 05401. (802)658-1414. Volunteer citizens conservation organization.

NORTHERN ADIRONDACK AUDUBON SOCIETY, c/o Susan A. Millar, 66 Oak St., Plattsburgh, NY 12901.

NORTHLAND ROCK AND MINERAL CLUB, Lake Placid, NY 12946. (518)523-3810.

TRI-LAKES HUMANE SOCIETY, 11 Mills Ave., Saranac Lake, NY 12983.

(45)

GOVERNMENT AGENCIES

Dozens of federal, state and county agencies that typically are found in every part of New York State naturally also operate within the Adirondacks—for example, departments of motor vehicles, New York State Police, unemployment insurance offices, etc. Rather than list every government agency in existence, this section describes only those agencies whose function in the Adirondacks is unique to this region or whose work in this region is, at least in part, somewhat different than it would be elsewhere in the state.

ADIRONDACK HIGHWAY COUNCIL. An agency formed—not by legislative mandate, but by inter-agency agreement—to coordinate highway planning activities in the Adirondacks. Consists of representatives from Adirondack Park Agency, Department of Environmental Conservation, Department of Transportation, Public Service Commission, local government, and citizens. The Council is working on: developing a roadside corridor management plan for the Park, making the roadside corridors more "park-like," park interpretation and visitors' centers. Information: Commissioner of Transportation, Department of Transportation, State Office Campus, Albany, NY 12232. (518)457-4422.

ADIRONDACK PARK AGENCY. Created by the State Legislature in 1971 to plan and regulate land use and development in the Adirondack Park, the "APA" has jurisdiction over development activities on both the public and the private lands throughout the Park. With a State Land Master Plan for public lands and a Land Use and Development Plan for private lands, the Agency reviews projects, issues permits and tries to balance the difficult tasks of protecting the natural beauty and resources of the Park while providing for ample economic growth and development. The Agency also engages in various educational activities to enhance residents' and visitors' appreciation of the Adirondack Park and its many natural resources. Information: Adirondack Park Agency, Box 99, Ray Brook, NY 12977. (518)891-4050.

ADIRONDACK PARK LOCAL GOVERNMENT REVIEW BOARD. A non-funded "watchdog" agency created by the legislature to monitor the activities of the Adirondack Park Agency and make recommendations for improvement of the Agency's work. Consisting of the Agency's work. Consisting of representatives from the Adirondack counties, the APLGRB has always been critical of the APA (see Section 10 on Adirondack Controversies) and contributes to efforts to abolish the Agency. Information: Robert R. Purdy, Exec. Dir., APLGRB, Box 818, Elizabethtown, NY 12932. (518)873-9286.

DEPARTMENT OF COMMERCE. A state-wide agency charged with enhancing business and industry throughout New York, "DOC's" influence in the Adirondacks is mostly felt through its efforts to promote tourism in the region. The Department's "I Love New York" promotional campaign has an active office in Lake Placid which promotes travel, recreation, special events, and numerous attractions and places in the Adirondacks of interest to millions of visitors. Information: Betsy Boyd, Director, "I Love New York" Regional Tourism Office, Department of Commerce, 90 Main St., Lake Placid, NY 12946. (518)523-2412.

DEPARTMENT OF ENVIRONMENTAL CONSERVATION. Operating throughout New York State, the manifold duties of "DEC" within the Adirondacks include: management of the Forest Preserve; hunting and fishing regulations; forest management on private lands; forest protection and forest fire control; forest insect and disease control; regulations on horse and snowmobile trails; construction and operation of campsites and boat landings; operation of the Fish Hatchery at Saranac Inn; reclaiming and restocking of lakes, ponds, and streams; acquisition of land; operation of Saranac River locks; fish and wildlife management; enforcement of the Environmental Conservation Laws; freshwater, wetlands and stream protection; air, water, and solid waste management; and much more. Statewide headquarters of DEC are located at 50 Wolf Rd., Albany, NY 12205. Regional headquarters of the Department, within and serving the Adirondacks, are located in Ray Brook, Warrensburg, Utica and Watertown. Complete addresses and phone numbers for these regional offices can be found in the "For More Information" section (Section 116).

DEPARTMENT OF HEALTH. This agency is charged with protecting the public health and safety in public accommodations and facilities throughout the state. In the Adirondacks, the department's activities center primarily around regulating and approving: modernization or expansion of campgrounds, group camps, tourist accommodations and mobile home courts; medical facilities; water treatment and distribution facilities; sewage disposal; and commercial uses such as restaurants, swimming pools, etc. Statewide headquarters are located at Tower Building, Empire State Plaza, Albany, NY 12237. (518) 474-3968. The main regional headquarters is: Dept. of Health, Bldg. 7A, State Office Campus, Albany, NY 12226. (518) 457-7150. District Health Offices are located at 31 Bay Street, Glens Falls, NY 12801, (518) 793-3893 and 11-15 St. Bernard Street, Saranac Lake, NY 12893, (518) 891-1800.

NEW YORK STATE OFFICE OF PARKS, RECREATION AND HISTORIC PRESERVATION. While "OPRHP" has primary responsibility for operating the state parks throughout New York State, in the Adirondack and Catskill Parks this responsibility is vested in the Department of Environmental Conservation. In the Adirondacks, OPRHP's responsibilities are primarily in the area of historic preservation—maintaining the State and National Register of Historic Places and operating two historic sites in the Adirondacks, i.e., John Brown's Farm and the Crown Point Battleground. Their headquarters are at: Empire State Plaza, Albany, NY 12238. (518) 474-0456.

DEPARTMENT OF TRANSPORTATION. As elsewhere in the state, "DOT" is responsible for building and maintaining state highways and roads, landscaping and providing scenic overlooks, and regulating the placement of signs along state highways. They do all this within the Adirondack Park, in particular, enforcing the "Adirondack sign law" which has been instrumental in maintaining the open space character and beauty of the region. Information: DOT, Office of Public Affairs, State Office Campus, Albany, NY 12232. (518) 457-6400.

For information on permit requirements of the Adirondack Park Agency, the Department of Environmental Conservation and the Department of Health, see Section 9.

(46)
LANDOWNING CLUBS

Because of its remote location and difficult climate, the Adirondacks remained largely untouched by real estate development until the late nineteenth century. In the late 1800s enormous parcels of land were still available at relatively low cost. As tourism came to the mountains in the last quarter of the century, wealthy sportsmen were attracted to the area and recognized a good real estate deal when they saw one.

Thus begun the era of the Adirondack "landowning clubs"—associations of businessmen/sportsmen who purchased large tracts of Adirondack land for private parks, game preserves and, eventually, sites for their own camps, often clustered around a common clubhouse. In 1890, for example, the Adirondack League Club bought 104,000 acres of forest land, including 25 lakes, in the southwestern Adirondacks for $4.75 an acre. The Adirondack Museum estimates that, by 1900, there were almost 50 landowning clubs in the Adirondacks.

The five best known such clubs today are:

THE ADIRONDACK LEAGUE CLUB, Herkimer County

THE AUSABLE CLUB (ADIRONDACK MOUNTAIN RESERVE), Essex County

THE NORTHWOODS CLUB, Essex County

THE TAHAWUS CLUB, Essex County

BEAR POND CLUB, Hamilton County

For general interest and to better understand contemporary land use and ownership patterns in the Adirondacks, *The Adirondack Guide* is commencing a survey on this topic, eventually to be published. As this information is not readily available to the public, we must rely on club members and other knowledgable persons to provide this information. The next edition of *The Adirondack Guide* will include a listing of private landowning clubs of at least 640 acres (one square mile). Ideally each listing will include:

—the name of the club
—the county or counties in which the club is located
—the year the club was founded
—the club's current acreage
—the number of members

ENVIRONMENT

(47)
SCENIC ATTRACTIONS

VIEWS

PROSPECT MOUNTAIN. Overlooks Lake George, Warren County. 2021 feet at summit. 5.5miles on 4-lane highway to parking lot, then take "viewmobiles" to summit. Picnic area. Open: May-October, 7 days, weather permitting. Fee.

WHITEFACE MOUNTAIN. Town of Wilmington, Essex County. Whiteface Memorial Highway, an 8.2 mile toll road to the summit of Whiteface Mountain, 4,682 feet high. New York's fifth highest mountain. Open: Memorial Day Weekend- Columbus Day Weekend. Cost: $2.00 for Adults, $1.00 for Juniors, maximum $6.00 per car. Includes tunnel, elevator, castle with restaurant. Overlooks Lake Placid, High Peaks, Canada, and Vermont.

CHAIR LIFTS/GONDOLAS

BIG TUPPER CHAIRLIFT, Rt. 30, Tupper Lake. Open daily, 9am-4:30pm. June-September 1. Information: Big Tupper Ski Center Area, Box 820, Tupper Lake, NY 12986. (518)359-3651.

GORE MOUNTAIN GONDOLA, Gore Mt. Ski Center, North Creek. Previously operated on fall weekends. Department of Environmental Conservation is uncertain as to whether gondola will be operating in the fall of 1983 and 1984.

MCCAULEY MOUNTAIN CHAIRLIFT, off Rt. 28, Old Forge. Open daily July-September 1st. Open weekends spring and fall. Picnic area. Information: McCauley Mt. Ski Center, Old Forge, NY 13420. (315)369-6983.

WHITEFACE MOUNTAIN AERIAL CHAIRLIFT, Rt. 86, Wilmington. Open daily, 9am-4pm. July-early September. Information: Chamber of Commerce, Wilmington, NY 12997.

BOAT CRUISES

BLUE MOUNTAIN LAKE LIVERY, INC. This two-hour scenic boat tour goes through three lakes: Blue Mt. Lake, Eagle Lake, Utowana Lake, just as tourists did in yesteryear. Ride on the "Neenykin", leaving at 2pm daily. Information: Blue Mt. Lake Livery, Blue Mt. Lake, NY 12812. (518)352-7351.

HISTORIC LAKE CRUISES, Old Forge. Ride the "Uncas" or the "Clearwater" double decker tour boats on a 28-mile narrated tour of the Fulton Chain of Lakes. Daily cruises leaving 3-4 times a day; options include showboat cruise and moonlight cruise. Snack bar, restrooms, souvenir shop. Special rates available for groups and children. Information: Captain Don Lawson, PO Box 72, Old Forge, NY 13420. (315)369-6473 or 369-3773.

HOLIDAY HARBOR BOAT TOURS, Lake Placid. A narrated cruise on beautiful Lake Placid. The daily trips last about an hour, leaving three to five times per day. Twilight cruises available. Season: Mid-June to mid-October. Information: Holiday Harbor Scenic Cruises. (518)523-8155.

LAKE GEORGE STEAMBOAT COMPANY, Steel Pier, Lake George. "Cruise ships on Lake George since 1817." Includes: MOHICAN—75 mile day-cruise. Departs from Lake George Village through Paradise Bay on to Ticonderoga and returns. Captain narrates. Snack bar and cocktail lounge. TICONDEROGA—35 miles of lakefront scenery including islands of the Narrows. Captain narrates. Luncheonette and cocktail lounge. Dinner jazz cruises and moonlight cruises also available. STEAMBOAT MINNE-HA-HA—one hour day-cruises and moonlight jazz cruises. In 1986 the 190 foot SAINT SACREMENT will be added to the Steamboat Company's fleet of passenger vessels. The Saint Sacrement will be operated from the time the ice is out until it freezes again in January. Holding 1500 passengers and seating 800 in one room, this vessel will serve both as a tourist attraction and mini-convention facility. Schedules and rates vary according to season. Private charters and group rates available on all boats. Information: The Lake George Steamboat Co., Steel Pier, Lake George, NY 12845. (518) 668-5777.

SHORELINE CRUISE, Lake George, 12845. Historic SHORELINE CRUISE travels into many of the historic bays with full narration by the captain on the battlegrounds, mansions and historic sites. One hour cruise. Fare: adults $4.00, children (11 and under) $2.00, 3 and under free. ISLAND CRUISE travels through narrows to Black Mountain Point and into Paradise Bay, with a brief stay on one of the islands to walk around or take a quick swim. Bring snack and drink. Fare: adults $6.75, children (4-11) $3.50, under 4 free. Open seven days a week. Free parking for passengers. Capacity: 50 passengers. Marine toilet and cocktail bar. Boat Cruise Season: May 1-October 24. Frequent departures: June 26th-September 6th. Group outings, packages available. Information: Shoreline Cruise, Beach Rd. and Canada St., Lake George, NY 12845. (518) 668-4644.

NATURAL WONDERS

AUSABLE CHASM. South of Plattsburgh, Essex County. Great sandstone cliffs cut by a fast-flowing prehistoric river display massive stone formations at this geological wonder. Open to the public since 1870, it includes a walking tour, boat ride, picnic grounds and gift shop. Open: Mid-May to early October. 9am to 4pm. Admission fee. Group rates available. Information: Ausable Chasm Co., Ausable Chasm, NY 12911. (518)834-7454.

BARTON MINES. North Creek, Warren County. Off Rt. 28, take Gore Mt. Road to the mines. 93% of the world's industrial garnet comes from this mine. Giant red garnets, meta anorthosite, charnockite and metagabbro are the main rock types. Open: July and August. Monday-Saturday 9am-5pm, Sunday 10am-5pm. Rock Museum, mineral shop, open pit mine tour, collecting and slide presentation. Admission fee. Information: (518)251-2706 or 251-2296.

HIGH FALLS GORGE. Rt. 86, Wilmington, Essex County. Impressive views as the Ausable River plunges over waterfalls in the High Falls Gorge. Entrance building with Rock Shop, cafeteria, picnic tables. Open: Memorial Day weekend until mid-October. Hours generally 8:30am-5:30pm. Information: (518)946-2278.

NATURAL STONE BRIDGE AND CAVES. Pottersville, Warren County. Exit 26 off I-87. Natural wonder of rock carved from Grenville marble by rushing water; see falls, caves, overhanging ledges. Self-guided tours in English and French, rock cutting demonstrations, exhibition swims, mineral and gift shop. Picnic area. One admission good for entire season. Group rates. Open: Memorial Day-Columbus Day, 8am-dark. Information: (518)494-2283.

(48)
SCENIC VISTAS

In many cases, the following roadside vistas are enhanced by pull-off areas for automobiles. Whether such pull-offs exist or not, caution should be observed while slowing down and pulling off to appreciate these magnificent Adirondack vistas.

TOWN	**LOCATION**
Altamont	At intersection of road east of Sunmount State School and State Routes 3 and 30
Altamont	Approximately 1.5 miles west of Faust on State Route 3
Bellmont	1 mile west of Owl's Head
Bolton	Two on Federal Hill Road
Bolton	One on Coolidge Hill Road
Corinth	Approximately 0.5 miles east of Daly Creek Road and 0.1 miles north of West Mountain Road
Dannemora	0.5 miles west of Village of Dannemora on State Route 374
Dannemora	0.25 miles east of Merrill Road
Dannemora	2.75 miles northeast of Village of Dannemora on French Settlement Road
Dannemora	1 mile northeast of hamlet of Standish on road from Standish to Lyon Mountain
Ellenburg	Approximately 6.5 miles north of Upper Chateaugay Lake and approximately 1/4 mile west of West Hill School
Essex	1.5 miles northeast of Whallonsburg on Christian Road
Essex	0.75 miles southwest of Whallon Bay (Lake Champlain) on Lake Shore Road
Fine	Two vistas approximately 1.25 miles south of hamlet of Fine

Harrietstown	Approximately 0.5 miles north of intersection of State Routes 86 and 192-A
Hopkinton	Whites Hill
Indian Lake	On State Route 30 overlooking Lake Abanakee
Indian Lake	2.5 miles east of Lake Abanakee overlooking Lake Snow, on Rt. 28
Inlet	Approximately 3.5 miles east of hamlet of Inlet, across Seventh Lake, on Rt. 28
Jay	.25 miles east of Rts. 9N and 86 intersection. 1857 covered bridge and beautiful waterfall.
Johnsburg	3 miles south of hamlet of North Creek
Johnsburg	3 miles south of North River on Barton Mine Road
Johnsburg	1 mile east of Chatiemac Lake south of Gore Mountain by 2 miles
Keene	Intersection of Route 73 and 9N
Keene	Chapel Pond and cliffs across pond*
Keene	Lower Cascade Lake, Route 73*
Lake Pleasant	On southeast shore of Lake Pleasant
Long Lake	From town beach, Route 30
Newcomb	3 miles east of hamlet of Newcomb on State Route 28N
North Elba	0.5 miles east of Village of Lake Placid on State Route 86
North Elba	Near intersection of State Route 73 and Heart Lake Road in North Elba
North Hudson	Blue Ridge Road, approximately 5.5 miles west of intersection with I-87.
Ohio	Intersection of West Canada Creek Road and State Route 8 at hamlet of Nobleboro
Santa Clara	Two miles west of Keese Mill on Keese Mills Road
Santa Clara	On State Route 30 at Pelky Bay on Upper Saranac Lake
Saranac	3.25 miles east of Picketts Corners near Hardscrabble Road
Saranac	2 miles southeast of hamlet of Saranac on Burnt Hill Road
Saranac	At intersection of Chazy Lake Road and Chateaugay Branch of the Delaware and Hudson Railroad
Saranac	Two miles northwest of Clayburg on Clayburg to Standish Road
Willsboro	1.5 miles south of Willsboro on County Route 22-M
Willsboro	4.5 miles northeast of Willsboro on County Route 27 on Willsboro Point
Wilmington	2.5 miles north of hamlet of Wilmington
Westport	4.0 miles north of Westport

*Based on submissions to *Adirondack Life*, Chapel Pond is the most photographed pond in the Adirondacks, with Lower Cascade Lake a close second.

Source: Adirondack Park Agency listing; editors' choice

(49)
SCENIC AUTO TOURS

Every Adirondack lover has his or her favorite highway or stretch of back-country road. There's a back-road, for example, that goes from Ausable Forks to Jay, in Essex County—past the Rockwell Kent Farm, down the Ausable Valley, and across the covered bridge at Jay—that has this editor's vote for the most scenic seven-mile drive in the Adirondacks. But that road will not be described here, and possibly, neither will be your favorite. Rather this section describes a dozen or so of the more accessible, easier-to-find routes and tours that rarely fail to excite the motorist with their beauty and grandeur. Come to think of it, you wouldn't want many cars on your favorite back-road anyway. Enjoy the views—and drive carefully.

LAKE GEORGE TO KEESEVILLE, VIA THE ADIRONDACK NORTHWAY, I-87. This is a beautiful 90 mile stretch of highway passing numerous mountain, valley and lake views. For years, a sign stood on the northbound side of I-87, just north of Lake George at the 55th milepost, stating: "America's Most Scenic Highway. Next 23 miles. 1966-67 Award." Well and Good. For the 1980 Winter Olympics, however, some public officials saw fit to replace this sign with a new one reading: "America's Most Scenic Highway. Next 84 Miles." Beautiful it is; America's most scenic highway it is not. Instead of a source of legitimate pride, this sign is now a source of embarrassment to Adirondackers and Adirondack lovers. Let's bring truth-in-packaging back to the Adirondack Northway.

TOP O' THE WORLD, Warren County. Exit 21 off I-87, Northway. Drive 6 miles northeast off Rt. 9 on Rt. 9L to sign; steep drive to summit. Magnificent views overlooking Lake George and beyond. Time: 30 minutes, one way.

LAKE GEORGE VILLAGE TO HAGUE, Warren County. Exit 22 off I-87 Northway. Drive north along shoreline of Lake George on Rt. 9N through villages of Lake George, Diamond Point and Bolton Landing, then over Tongue Mountain to Silver Bay and Hague. Excellent overlooks and views. Time: 1 hour, one way.

WARRENSBURG TO INDIAN LAKE, Warren County. Exit 23 off I-87, Northway. Drive through Warrensburg to junction of Rt. 9 and Rt. 28. Proceed west 16 miles to North Creek, 5 miles to North River, and 10 miles to Indian Lake. Magnificent river and mountain country. Time: 1 hour, one way.

BRANT LAKE TO HAGUE, Warren County. Exit 25 off I-87, Northway. Drive east on Rt. 8 to Rt. 9N and Hague through Pharaoh Lake Wilderness Region and Dixon Forest. Great scenic overlooks. Time: 1 hour, one way.

BELFREY HILL FIRE TOWER, Essex County. New Russia area toward Port Henry. Drive south on Rt. 9 to New Russia; turn left. At the river is the site of ancient sawmill and iron forge. On top of Simond's Hill, turn right. Giant Mountain and Rocky Peak Ridge are seen to the west. Cross Lincoln Pond and continue climbing. On top of the ridge are views of mountains and Lake Champlain. (Belfrey Hill Fire Tower is on right.) Ahead is Mineville, and Moriah, and other towns originating in the late 1700's when Republic Steel began mining operations here. Roads lead to the left (east) to Port Henry on Rts. 9N and 22.

OLMSTEADVILLE TO MINERVA, VIA BROOK ROAD, Essex County. Begin at Sullivan's Store in Olmsteadville and inquire for the Trout Brook Road to Schroon Lake. When you reach the 4th bridge, turn left and go through Hoffman. On this Hoffman Road, turn right at the old Church-School Combination (incorporated 1843). After turning right, continue on this road until you reach an old hotel, now called Sky Notch. Magnificent view of the pass to Blue Ridge. Retrace your route about 2 miles and turn right at the forks. Continue on this road to the next right turn. You will reach Oliver Pond on the right with a camp ground on the north end and another on the south end. Follow road to Irishtown (old school and St. Mary's Church built in 1847, now abandoned). Straight ahead takes you back to Olmsteadville. Or turn right at church and go to Minerva on Rt. 28N. Before reaching Minerva there is a public beach, with cottages and campsites on Minerva Lake.

ELIZABETHTOWN TO LAKE PLACID, Essex County. Drive west from Elizabethtown on Rt. 9N, crossing the ridge between Giant and Hurricane Mountains with breathtaking views of the High Peaks to the west. Descend into the Keene Valley; turn right and north on Rt. 9N to Keene. Take left fork in Keene and Rt. 73 past the Cascade Lakes. Before entering Lake Placid, enjoy more outstanding views of the High Peaks to your left (south). Time: 45 minutes.

JAY TO LAKE PLACID, VIA WILMINGTON, Essex County. Off Rt. 9N, take Rt. 86 west over the ridge, with magnificent views of the Whiteface and Sentinel Ranges to the west and south. Pass through Wilmington, cross the Ausable River West Branch twice, pass by Whiteface Mt. Ski Center, and then negotiate one of the curviest, most exciting roads in the Adirondacks—the "Wilmington Notch", which follows right alongside the raging Ausable River West Branch through a steep notch between the Whiteface and Sentinel Ranges. As you enter Lake Placid, the view south (left) across the Lake Placid Club golf course is considered by many to be the finest road-side view in the Adirondacks. Time: 45 minutes.

WHITEFACE MOUNTAIN, Essex County. Beginning at the Whiteface Mt. toll road in Wilmington, on Rt. 86 north of Lake Placid, one begins the eight mile ascent to the summit—the highest spot to which a motor vehicle may be driven in New York State. Cars climb to within 700 feet of the top. The remainder of the climb can be done by foot or by elevator. Whiteface Mt. is 4,867 feet high, offering a grand view of surrounding High Peaks, Lake Placid, and the St. Lawrence River as far as Montreal. Note: The toll gate is shut on many days when the peak is lost in clouds (and from mid-fall to mid-spring).

NORTH HUDSON TO NEWCOMB AND LONG LAKE, Essex and Hamilton Counties. From Exit 29 of I-87 (Frontiertown), drive west on County Route 2B (Blue Ridge Road). Perhaps one of the loneliest stretches of highway in the Park, this road passes only half-dozen houses in the (approx.) 20 miles to Newcomb. Sweeping vistas of Hoffman Notch Wilderness Area to the south, crossing Boreas River and, at Newcomb, the infant Hudson. Time: One hour, one way. Consider side trips by car or foot to Elk Lake Lodge, Tahawus, Goodnow Mountain fire tower, Huntington research station, and Santanoni Preserve.

LONG LAKE TO TUPPER LAKE, Hamilton and Franklin Counties. This 20 mile stretch of Rt. 30 passes many beautiful lake and mountain views, beginning with the view down Long Lake to the High Peaks and including many views across Tupper Lake and Simon's Pond. Time: 30 minutes.

EAGLE BAY TO LOWVILLE, VIA STILLWATER ROAD, Herkimer County. Turn off Rt. 28 at Eagle Bay north onto the Big Moose Rd. Passes Moss Lake (2 minute walk from parking area) and swings to the left, and after a total drive of 8 miles ends at Big Moose R.R. Station, highest point on the Adirondack Division of the New York Central System. Continue on the Stillwater Road—a poor, dirt, unmarked road. This scenic drive passes Twitchell Creek and Stillwater Reservoir. From Stillwater Village, proceed to Number Four (a crossroads settlement), then to Lowville (on Rt. 12), a total of 26 miles. Abundant wildlife along the way. Time: 1 hour, 15 minutes.

Source: Adirondack Park Agency listing and editors' choice.

(50)
GEOLOGICAL FACTS

On February 9, 1876, at Saranac Lake, the first written record was taken of an earthquake in the Adirondacks. It was recorded by Verplanck Colvin, Superintendent of the Adirondack Survey. While specific earthquakes have continued to be recorded, overall seismic activity in the Park remains rather minor.

Some of the best rhodolite garnet in the world has been found at Gore Mountain in Warren County. Niney-three percent of the world's industrial garnet is produced there, at the Barton Garnet Mines. Garnet is the official gem of New York State.

Titanium, used as the principal white pigment in paint, paper, and ceramics and used in high-strength alloys, is mined at NL Industries' Tahawus Mine. Located near Newcomb, it is a world-wide major supplier of titanium.

Whiteface Mountain acquired its name due to a tremendous landslip in 1816, exposing the anorthosite rock. The nature of this kind of rock with the hard regular surfaces made it easy for mudslides to start. Other mountains with these "bald spots" are found throughout the park, including Blue Mountain and Bald Mountain.

Wollastonite is an important mineral found in the Adirondacks. Used in ceramics production and in insulation, it is a white asbestos-like mineral. It is mined near Willsboro and at Natural Bridge.

Many of the largest lakes in the area occupy fault zones that were dammed by glacial debris. Examples of such lakes are Lake George, Indian Lake, Long Lake, Cascade Lakes, and the Ausable Lakes.

Measurements show that the Adirondacks are rising at a rate of 3 mm per year, which is greater than the average rate of erosion and considered one of the highest growth rates among the mountains of the world.

Although the Adirondack Mountains are often called some of the oldest mountains in the world, it is actually the rocks and minerals which are some of the oldest. The mountain formation happened in stages and the most widely accepted view is that the present land formations were created by uplift of the land which occurred relatively recently, about 5 million years ago. The Adirondack Mountains were further shaped by glaciation which occurred over the past 2 million years and most recently about 20,000 years ago.

One theory of geology, which is still in dispute, explains the formation of the Ancestoral Adirondacks. It is proposed that mountains higher than the present day Himalayas were formed over one billion years ago. These were then eroded down to sea level 600 million years ago. For millions of years the Adirondacks were a low lying land mass receiving sediments from the Appalacians to the east. This sediment eroded and the rocks and mineral below began heaving up some 5 million years ago (see above). This hypothesis suggests that the present Adirondack Mountains are the exposed roots of the Ancestoral Mountains.

Potsdam sandstone is the first example in the Adirondacks of sedimentary rock.

Three kinds of feldspar—labradorite, sunstone and moonstone—are all used as semiprecious gemstones and are mined in the Adirondacks.

Common rocks in the Adirondacks include:
- metanorthosite, the most erosion-resistant of the major Adirondack rocks.
- metagabbro, the only igneous (volcanic) type rock in the Adirondacks.
- marble, a metamorphosed sedimentary limestone.
- charnokite, a green gneiss.
- granite gneiss, commonly pink rock, widely distributed.
- garnet-biotite gneiss, metamorphosed shale, originally in the form of "marine mud".

Scientists estimate that at least three mountain glaciers, with the headwalls of their cirques almost back to back, once encircled the summit of Whiteface Mountain, creating its conical shape.

Geologists theorize that in pre-glacial times the Ausable River was part of the Hudson River drainage, but due to the effects of the ice age the Ausable River changed to its present course. Ausable Chasm was formed when the river's new course cut through layers of sandstone, eroding away the least resistant layers. Also it is well-established that Blue Mt. Lake formerly drained into the Hudson River; it now drains westerly and then northerly to the St. Lawrence. Another feature left from the ice age is the flat plains formed by retreating "glacial lakes." The "Plains of Abraham" located north and east of Lake Placid is an example of these plains.

GEOLOGIC HISTORY OF NORTHERN NEW YORK STATE (ADIRONDACK MOUNTAIN REGION)

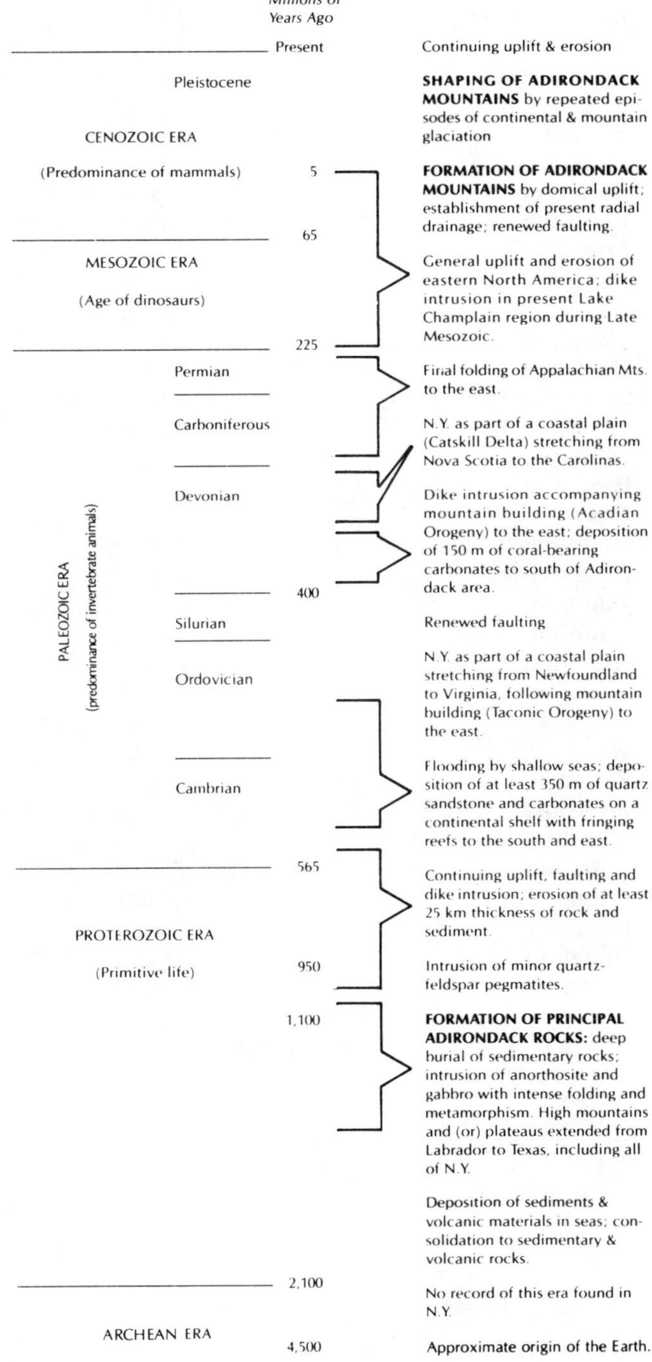

The High Peaks region is composed mostly of anorthosite. It is a relatively uncommon rock on Earth, but one of the major constituents of the highlands of the moon.

For rockhounds interested in an excellent listing of rocks and sites throughout the Adirondacks, write to: The Adirondack Gem and Rock Shop, PO Box 668, Saranac Lake, NY 12983. (518)891-3390. This list gives types of rocks, location and directions.

(51)

34 LARGEST LAKES

COUNTY	NAME OF WATER	NO. OF ACRES
Essex-Clinton	Lake Champlain*	281,600
Warren	Lake George	28,100
Fulton-Saratoga	Great Sacandaga Lake*	26,656
St. Lawrence	Cranberry Lake	6,976
St. Lawrence	Carry Falls Reservoir	6,458
Franklin	Tupper Lake	6,240
Herkimer	Stillwater Reservoir	6,195
Hamilton	Raquette Lake	5,274
Franklin	Upper Saranac Lake	5,056
Hamilton	Indian Lake	4,365
Essex	Schroon Lake	4,128
Hamilton	Long Lake	4,090
Hamilton	Piseco Lake	2,848
Essex Lake	Lake Placid	2,803
Herkimer	Hinckley Reservoir*	2,784
Clinton	Upper Chateaugay Lake	2,605
Hamilton	Little Tupper Lake	2,381
Franklin	Lower Saranac Lake	2,285
Herkimer	Fourth Lake (Fulton Chain)	2,138
Clinton	Chazy Lake	1,606
Hamilton	Sacandaga Lake	1,600
Hamilton	Lake Pleasant	1,440
Hamilton	Lake Lila	1,424
Franklin	Middle Saranac Lake	1,376
Franklin	Union Falls Flow	1,376
Warren	Brant Lake	1,376
Fulton	Peck Lake	1,370
Herkimer	Big Moose Lake	1,286
Hamilton	Blue Mountain Lake	1,261
Hamilton	Forked Lake	1,248
Franklin	Meacham Lake	1,203
Herkimer	Woodhull Lake	1,158
Hamilton	Abanakee Lake	1,018
Franklin	Lake Clear	1,000

*parts of these lakes lie outside the Adirondack Park. Source: Adirondack Park Agency listing; other material added.

(52)

RIVERS

In 1972 the state legislature created a wild, scenic and recreational rivers system on both state and private lands.

A wild river is a river or section of river that is free of diversions and improvements, inaccessible to the general public except by water, foot or horse trail, and with a river area primitive in nature and free of any man-made development except footbridges.

A scenic river is a river or section of a river that is free of diversions or impoundments except for log dams, with limited road access, and with a river area largely primitive and undeveloped, or that is partially or predominantly used for agriculture, forest management and other dispersed human activities that do not substantially interfere with public use and enjoyment of the river and its shore.

A recreational river is a river or section of a river that is readily accessible by road or railroad, that may have development in the river area that may have undergone some diversion or impoundment in the past.

RIVER	WILD	SCENIC	RECREATIONAL
Ampersand Brook		8.0 miles	
Ausable-Main Branch			22.0
Ausable-East Branch		9.0	28.3
Ausable-West Branch			34.5
Black		7.8	
Bog		7.3	
Boreas		11.5	
Bouquet			47.7
Bouquet-North Fork		6.0	
Bouquet-South Fork		5.5	
Blue Mt. Stream		9.0	
Cedar	14.3	15.0	11.0
Cold	14.0		
Deer		6.2	
East Canada Creek		20.9	
Grasse-Middle Branch		14.5	
Grasse-North Branch		25.4	
Grasse-South Branch		38.9	5.2
Hudson	10.5	13.0	58.6
Independence		26.0	0.5
Indian (Tributary of Hudson R.)			8.3
Indian (Tributary of Moose R., S. Branch)	13.0		
Jordan		18.0	
Kunjamuk	8.0	10.4	
Long Pond Outlet		16.0	
Marion		5.0	
Moose-Main Branch		15.8	
Moose-South Branch		38.9	
Opalescent	11.0		
Oswegatchie-Main Branch	18.5		
Oswegatchie-Middle Branch	14.5	23.4	
Oswegatchie-West Branch		7.0	6.1
Otter Brook		10.0	
Ouluska Pass Brook	3.0		
Piseco Outlet	4.2		
Raquette		33.8	39.0
Red		9.7	
Rock		6.9	1.2
Round Lake Outlet		2.7	
St. Regis-East Branch		14.5	6.1
St. Regis-Main Branch		15.5	25.0
St. Regis-West Branch		35.0	5.5
Sacandaga-East Branch	11.5		14.0
Sacandaga-Main Branch			31.0
Sacandaga-West Branch	18.7		17.8
Salmon			12.3
Saranac			60.4
Schroon			66.7
West Canada Creek	8.0	17.0	11.0
West Canada Creek-S. Branch	5.9		9.7
West Stony Creek		7.7	8.7
TOTALS	155.1	511.3	539.5
TOTAL MILES CLASSIFIED	1205.9		

Source: Adirondack Park State Land Master Plan, published by the Adirondack Park Agency, 1979.

WATERFALLS

WATERFALLS	OWNERSHIP **	NOTES	COUNTY	TOWN	15' QUAD
T- Lake Falls	S	Dangerous, very steep; (approx. 200' drop)	Hamilton	Arietta	Piseco Lake
Hulls Falls	P	Falls and Gorge	Essex	Keene	Mt. Marcy
Augur Falls	S	Falls, flume, and whirl-pool; Sacandaga River	Hamilton	Wells	Harrisburg
Falls Brook	S	Falls, flume; 2 miles west of Irishtown, 1 mile from road	Essex	Minerva	Schroon Lake
Buttermilk Falls	S	Steep rapids; Raquette River from Deerlands	Hamilton	Arietta	Blue Mountain
Bog River Falls	S	South end of Tupper Lake	St. Lawrence	Piercefield	Tupper Lake
Rocky Falls	S	Falls and gorge; Indian Pass Brook	Essex	North Elba	Mt. Marcy
Hanging Spear Falls	S	High vertical drop; Opalescent River	Essex	Newcomb	Mt. Marcy
Wanika Falls	S	Chubb River	Essex	North Elba	Santanoni
High Falls	S	Oswegatchie River	St. Lawrence	Fine	Cranberry Lake
Bushnell Falls	S	Johns Brook	Essex	Keene	Mt. Marcy
Indian Falls	S	Marcy Brook	Essex	Keene	Mt. Marcy
Raquette Falls	P	Raquette River	Franklin	Harrietstown	Long Lake
Sliding Falls	S	Six Mile Creek	St. Lawrence	Clifton	Cranberry Lake
Millers Falls	S	Cold River	Essex	Newcomb	Santanoni
Cascade Falls	S	Cascade Pond Outlet	Hamilton	Indian Lake	Blue Mountain
Twitchell Creek Falls	S	Falls and gorge	Herkimer	Webb	Big Moose
Gleasman's Falls	S	Independence River	Lewis	Watson	No. Four
Rainbow Falls	P	Middle branch Grass River	St. Lawrence	Clare	Stark
Roaring Brook Falls	P	Drops over 100'	Essex	Keene	Mt. Marcy
Clifford Falls	P	Clifford Brook	Essex	Keene	Lake Placid
O.K. Slip Falls	P	On Hudson below Blue Ledge	Hamilton	Indian Lake	Newcomb
Ohio Gorge	P	Horseshoe falls and canyon	Herkimer	Ohio	Ohio
East Canada Falls	S	Above Brayhouse Creek confluence	Hamilton	Arietta	Piseco Lake
Split Rock Falls	P	Upper Bouquet River	Essex	Elizabethtown	Elizabethtown
High Falls	P	Waterfalls and gorge	Clinton	Saranac	Lyon Mountain
Lampson Falls	P	Grass River; 60' drop	St. Lawrence	Clare	W. Pierrpont* Russell
Basford Falls	P	(Low Key) So. Br. Grass River	St. Lawrence	Clare	De Grasse* Russell
Sinclair Falls	P	Vertical tack and fault; So. Branch Grass River	St. Lawrence	Clare	De Grasse* Russell
Twin Falls	P	S. Br. Grass River	St. Lawrence	Clare	De Grasse* Russell
Luzerne Falls	P	Hudson River	Warren	Hadley-Luzerne	Lake Luzerne
Copper Rock Falls	P	S. Br. Grass River	St. Lawrence	Clare	Tooley Pd.* Stark
(No Name) Falls	P	30'; Middle Br. Grass River	St. Lawrence	Clare	De Grasse* Russell
(No Name) Falls	P	(divided) Middle Br. Grass River	St. Lawrence	Clare	W. Pierrpont* Russell
Harpers Falls	P	30'; No. Br. Grass River	St. Lawrence	Clare	W. Pierrpont* Russell
Pelkey Falls	P	N. Branch Grass River	St. Lawrence	Clare	W. Pierrpont* Russell
Gleason's Falls	P	N. Branch Grass River	St. Lawrence	Clare	Albert Marsh* Stark
Rainbow Falls	P	Off Lower Ausable Lake	Essex	Keene	Mt. Marcy
Jenny Creek Falls	P	Split falls; 60' drop	St. Lawrence	Pitcairn	Harrison
Beaver Meadow Falls	P	1.2 m. N.E. Lower Ausable Lake	Essex	Keene	Mt. Marcy

Compiled by Greenleaf Chase, APA

**Indicates 7 1/2' quad.*
***Private or State owned*

Beaver Meadow Falls.

(54)

100 HIGHEST PEAKS

Different criteria have been used to determine the Adirondack's highest peaks. The original listing of the 46 highest peaks (originally presumed to all be over 4000 feet), still used by the Adirondack Mountain Club, employed elevation above sea level as its only criterion for placement on the list. A subsequent listing of the 100 highest peaks by Robert Collin and Lee Barry (*Adirondac*, August 1982) and the Adirondack Mountain Club's listing of 47th-to-100th highest added the criteria that the mountain must have at least a 300 foot elevation rise from the highest part of the base to the summit and must be at least three fourths of a mile from the next listed summit. In other words, they wanted each peak listed to be a distinct peak and not merely a knoll near the top of another mountain.

In the listing below, we have combined both the Adirondack Mountain Club's traditional list of the 46 highest peaks (see *Guide to Adirondack Trails*, referenced in Section 80) and the Collin-Barry list; so that peaks number 47 to 100 meet the 300 foot-3/4 mile criteria, while numbers 1-46 do not necessarily meet these criteria. The most recently surveyed elevation figures availble are employed. Where a peak is nameless, its UTM coordinates on the USGS topographical map and a reference to a nearby landmark are provided in lieu of name. Finally, as newer editions of the USGS maps have been released, there are some descrepancies between which maps are used to locate a given peak. To minimize confusion, the date of the particular map is given.

NAME	ELEVATION	MAP
1 Mt. Marcy	5344	Mt. Marcy (1979)
2 Algonquin	5115	Keene Valley (1979)
3 Mt.Haystack	4961	Mt. Marcy (1979)
4 Mt. Skylight	4924	Mt. Marcy (1979)
5 Whiteface Mt.	4866	Lake Placid (1979)
6 Dix Mt.	4839	Mt. Marcy (1979)
7 Gray Peak	4830	Mt. Marcy (1953)
8 Iroquois Peak	4830	Mt. Marcy (1953)
9 Basin Mt.	4826	Mt. Marcy (1979)
10 Gothics	4734	Keene Valley (1979)
11 Mt. Golden	4715	Keene Valley (1979)
12 Giant Mt.	4626	Elizabethtown (1978)
13 Nippletop	4610	Mt. Marcy (1953)
14 Santanoni Peak	4606	Santanoni (1979)
15 Mt. Redfield	4606	Mt. Marcy (1953)
16 Wright Peak	4580	Mt. Marcy (1953)
17 Saddleback Mt.	4528	Keene Valley (1979)
18 Panther Peak	4442	Santanoni (1953)
19 Table Top Mt.	4413	Keene Valley (1979)
20 Rocky Peak Ridge	4410	Elizabethtown (1978)
21 Hough Peak	4409	Mt. Marcy (1979)
22 Macomb Mt.	4390	Mt. Marcy (1979)
23 Armstrong Mt.	4390	Mt. Marcy (1953)
24 Mt. Marshall	4380	Ampersand (1978)
25 Seward Mt.	4347	Ampersand (9178)
26 Allen Mt.	4347	Mt. Marcy (1979)
27 Big Slide Mt.	4249	Keene Valley (1979)
28 Esther Mt.	4239	Wilmington (1978)
29 Upper Wolf Jaw Mt.	4185	Mt. Marcy (1953)
30 Lower Wolf Jaw Mt.	4173	Keene Valley (1979)
31 Phelps Mt.	4161	Mt. Marcy (1953)
32 Street Mt.	4150	Ampersand (1978)
33 Sawteeth Mt.	4150	Mt. Marcy (1979)
34 Mt. Donaldson	4140	Santanoni (1953)
35 Cascade Mt.	4098	Keene Valley (1979)
36 Seymour Mt.	4091	Ampersand (1978)
37 Porter Mt.	4085	Keene Valley (1979)
38 Mt. Colvin	4085	Mt. Marcy (1979)
39 South Dix	4060	Mt. Marcy (1953)
40 Mt. Emmons	4040	Santanoni (1953)

	NAME	ELEVATION	MAP
41	Dial Mt.	4020	Mt. Marcy (1953)
42	East Dix	4006	Mt. Marcy (1979)
43	Blake Peak	3986*	Mt. Marcy (1979)
44	Cliff	3944*	Mt. Marcy (1979)
45	Nye	3895*	Santanoni (1953)
46	Couchsachraga	3820*	Santanoni (1953)
47	McNaughton	3983	Ampersand (1978)
48	Green	3960	Elizabethtown (1978)
49	Snowy	3899	Indian Lake (1954)
50	Moose	3898	Saranac Lake (1979)
51	5/77.2 x 48/90.3 (Lost Pond)	3891	Ampersand (1978)
52	Kilburn Mt.	3881	Lake Placid (1979)
53	5/81.5 x 48/76.1 (North River Mts.)	3878	Mt. Marcy (1979)
54	Blue Ridge	3870	Indian Lake (1954)
55	Panther Mt.	3865	Indian Lake (1954)
56	Sentinel Mt.	3858	Lake Placid (1979)
57	5/70.2 x 48/93.0 (Sawtooth Mts.)	3855	Ampersand (1978)
58	McKensie Mt.	3832	Saranac Lake (1979)
59	Lyon Mt. (NE Peak)	3830	Moffitsville (1968)
60	5/85.1 x 48/88.2 (Indian Falls)	3822	Keene Valley
61	Avalanche Mt.	3816	Keene Valley (1979)
62	Averill Peak	3803	Lyon Mountain (1968)
63	5/68.9 x 48/93.4 (Sawtooth Mts.)	3789	Ampersand (1978)
64	Buell Mt.	3786	Indian Lake (1954)
65	Boreas Mt.	3776	Mt. Marcy (1979)
66	Wakely Mt.	3770	West Canada Lakes(1954)
67	Blue Mt.	3759	Blue Mt. (1954)
68	Lewey Mt.	3742	Indian Lake (1954)
69	Wallface Mt.	3727	Ampersand (1978)
70	Henderson Mt.	3724	Santanoni (1979)

GIANT
KEENE VALLEY
1928

NAME	ELEVATION	MAP
71 5/71.3 x 48/91.1 (Sawtooth Mts.)	3694	Ampersand (1978)
72 Hoffman Mt.	3693	Schroon Lake (1953)
73 Cheney Cobble	3684	Mt. Marcy (1979)
74 Hurricane Mt.	3678	Elizabethtown (1978)
75 Little Moose Mt.	3630	West Canada Lakes(1954)
76 Calamity Mt.	3625	Santanoni (1979)
77 Sunrise Mt.	3619	Mt. Marcy (1979)
78 Saddleback Mt.	3616	Lewis (1978)
79 Stewart Mt.	3616	Lake Placid (1979)
80 Pillsbury	3597	West Canada Lakes (1954)
81 Jay Mts.	3592	Lewis (1978)
82 Slide Mt.	3592	Lake Placid (1979)
83 Dun Brook Mt.	3590	Blue Mt. (1954)
84 Gore Mt.	3583	Thirteenth Lake (1954)
85 Nonnmark Mt.	3556	Keene Valley (1979)
86 Fishing Brook Mt.	3550	Blue Mt. (1954)
87 Mt. Adams	3520	Santanoni (1979)
88 Little Santanoni Mt.	3504	Santanoni (1979)
89 Blue Ridge	3497	Blue Mt. (1954)
90 Pitchoff	3497	Keene Valley (1979)
91 5/54.6 x 48/62.8 (Fishing Brook Range)	3490	Blue Mt. (1954)
92 Puffer Mt.	3472	Thirteenth Lake (1954)
93 Wolf Pond Mt.	3470	Schroon Lake (1953)
94 5/69.2 x 48/91.6 (Sawtooth Mts.)	3461	Ampersand (1978)
95 Morgan Mt.	3458	Wilmington (1978)
96 Wilmington Range	3458	Wilmington (1978)
97 Blue Ridge Mt.	3450	Schroon Lake (1953)
98 Cellar Mt.	3447	West Canada Lakes (1954)
99 Blue Ridge	3436	Raquette Lake (1954)
100 Blue Ridge, West	3430	Schroon Lake (1953)
Spur or Bullhead Mt.	3430	Thirteenth Lake (1954)

* As these peaks are among the original 46 peaks thought to be over 4000 feet, they appear here in traditional order; although later surveys would properly place them further down the list.

(55)
WEATHER STATISTICS

Several weather field stations are located in the Adirondacks. Data in this section is derived almost exclusively from three sites: Sunmount Field Station (SM) at Tupper Lake, elevation 1680 feet, for the period 1951-80; Lake Placid Field Station (LP), elevation 1864 feet, for the period 1925-1954; and Whiteface Mountain Field Station (WF), elevation 4866 feet, for the period 1964-1982. Although the figures given for these three locations during the periods covered give a good picture of weather in the Adirondacks, more extreme figures for all the categories can be found periodically in other parts of the Adirondacks and for other years not covered by these statistics.

YEAR-ROUND TEMPERATURES

Average annual temperatures are 40.7 (SM), 40.4 (LP) and 42.1 (WF). (All temperatures are on the Fahrenheit scale).

Average daily maximum temperatures are 51.5 (SM), 51.8 (LP) and 50.1 (WF).

Average daily minimum temperatures are 29.8 (SM), 28.9 (LP) and 34.0 (WF).

SUMMER TEMPERATURES

June-August mean temperatures are 62.9 (SM) and 62.57 (LP).

Summer afternoon maximum temperatures average 70-80 (SM & LP).

Hottest days on record were 98 on July 31, 1975 (SM) and 97 in July 1973 (LP). However, days with readings of 90 or more are somewhat rare, with many summers having none (SM).

The hottest day of the year averages 90 (SM).

Nights are usually cool in summer, with many lows of 50-55 (SM) and most nights in the 40s and 50s (LP).

WINTER TEMPERATURES

Winter temperatures average 16.2 (SM) and 17.0 (LP).

The coldest winters on record averaged 11.5 in 1958-59 and again in 1976-77 (SM). The mildest winter averaged 23 in 1952-53 (SM).

The average winter low mark is -29 (SM).

Record lows at the field stations were -38 on February 18, 1979 (SM) and -37 in 1943 (LP).

The coldest temperature in New York State history was recorded at Stillwater, Herkimer County on February 9, 1934: -52 degrees.

The average date of the first zero of winter is December 6, with the last occurance averaging March 18. The earliest zero was recorded November 21, the latest April 7 (SM).

The temperature never rises above 32 an average of 77 days per year (SM) and 79 days (LP).

The temperature drops to 32 or below an average of 190 days per year (SM) and 194 days (LP).

The temperature drops to 0 or below 39 days per year (SM & LP).

RAINFALL

Average precipitation is 38.6 inches (SM & LP) and 39.24 inches (WF).

The greatest daily rainfalls were 3.12 inches in September 1979 (SM) and 3.58 inches in 1945 (LP).

Days with .01 inch or more of precipitation (including snowfall) average 177 per year (SM).

Days with .1 inch or more of precipitation (1" snow = .1" precipitation) average 97 (SM) and 106 (LP).

Days with 1.0 inch or more of precipitation (10" snow = 1" of precipitation) average 5 per year, with counts ranging from 2 to 9 days per year (SM).

Thunder is heard on an average of about 29 days per year (SM).

SNOWFALL

Annual snowfalls have ranged from a low of 53.1 inches in 1979-80 to 164.3 inches in 1970-71 (SM) and from 68 inches to 167 inches (WF).

Averages for annual snowfall are 101.7 inches (SM), 122.3 inches (LP) and 112 inches (WF).

The frequency of snowfalls of one inch or more a day averages 35 per season. Snowfalls of two inches or more average 19 per season. Falls of four inches or more average 7 per season. Falls of 8 inches or more average one per season (SM).

The greatest daily snowfall was 26 inches in January 1925 (LP) and 21 inches in March 1971 (SM).

The longest continuous snowcover of one inch or more depth averages 105 days, and has varied from 31 to 152 days' duration (SM).

The average seasonal maximum snow depth is 30 inches, at a date averaging February 9. The maximum depth ever recorded was 84 inches in March 1963 (SM).

There is little difference in monthly snowfall amounts from December through March (LP).

WIND

Average wind speed at Whiteface Mt. Field Station is 6.1 mph.

GROWING SEASON

Although specific values of possible sunshine are not available, interpolated values based on other records in the state indicate that the area can expect to have sunshine around 40% of the possible hours in January and about 60% in July (LP).

The "growing season," or period free of any 32 degree or lower temperature to which tender vegetation is susceptible, averages 108 days (SM) and 100 days (LP).

The average date of the last spring freeze is May 30 and the first fall freeze averages September 15. While there is variation from season to season, the dates fall within about 12 days from the average in two-thirds of the cases.

The last spring freeze has varied from May 2 to June 27. The first fall freeze has ranged from August 17 to October 6 (SM).

The low, marshy areas have shorter seasons, while favored slopes and urban centers have a longer season. Hardier vegetation may not be affected by a 32 degree freeze. For a 28 degree freeze the season averages 137 days, from May 14 to September 28. At the 24 degree level the season is 169 days, from April 25 to October 11. At the 20 degree level the season averages 195 days, from April 17 to October 29. For a 16 degree freeze, the season is lengthened to 213 days, from April 10 to November 11 (SM).

(56)
NATURAL DISASTERS

1816
Year without a summer. Throughout the summer the north wind blew in snow and ice across the Adirondacks. Few crops were left to harvest in the fall. Many towns were abandoned by early settlers.

1845
Great Windfall of 1845. In mid-afternoon on September 20, the only major tornado to strike the Adirondacks swept through Jefferson, St. Lawrence and Essex Counties. No lives were lost, but extensive property damage occurred. Immediately after the tornado a hailstorm occurred.

1850
Ausable Valley Flood

1884
Great Burned Tract, on the road to Indian Lake. This occurred just before the Forest Preserve was created.

1903
464,189 acres of forest burned, scorching over Mts. Noonmark, South Dix and Giant, destroying the original Adirondack Lodge, and burning many other areas to the west and north.

1908
346,953 acres of forest burned.

1950
Blowdown. On November 25, 100 mile an hour winds destroyed 1/2 million acres of timber in High Peaks region. It took special legislation and eight years to clear the debris.

1952
May 6th, a small tornado occurred at Lake Placid, the only storm of the kind to be reported in the Lake Placid area since the beginning of the record in 1897 (through 1954).

1963
On June 29, Giant Mountain, Essex County, received 6 inches of rain in 1½ hours. The deluge loosened the thin clay layer covering over the rock base, and trees, rocks and boulders slid down the mountain. Sections of Rt. 73 were scattered with debris 10-15 ft. deep. Today exposed rock slides are visible on the west slopes of Giant Mountain.

(57)
FIELD GUIDES

Beehler, Bruce McP., *Birdlife of the Adirondack Park* (Glens Falls, NY: Adirondack Mountain Club, 1978).

Betters, Francis, *Fishing the Adirondacks* (Wilmington, NY: Adirondack Sports Publication, 1982).

Carleton, Jeffrey, *Birds of Essex County, New York* (Elizabethtown, NY: High Peaks Audubon Society, 1980).

DiNuzio, Michael, *Adirondack Wild Guide: A Natural History of the Adirondack Park* (Elizabethtown, NY: Adirondack Conservancy and Adirondack Council, in press, summer 1983). Illustrations by Anne Lacy.

Ketchledge, E.H., *Trees of the Adirondack High Peak Region* (Glens Falls, NY: Adirondack Mountain Club, 1979).

McGrath, Anne and J. Treffs, *Wildflowers of the Adirondacks* (Sylvan Beach, NY: North Country Books, 1981).

Wyckoff, Jerome, *The Adirondack Landscape* (Glens Falls, NY: Adirondack Mountain Club, 1979). Hiker's guide to geology and common landforms.

LIFE ZONES

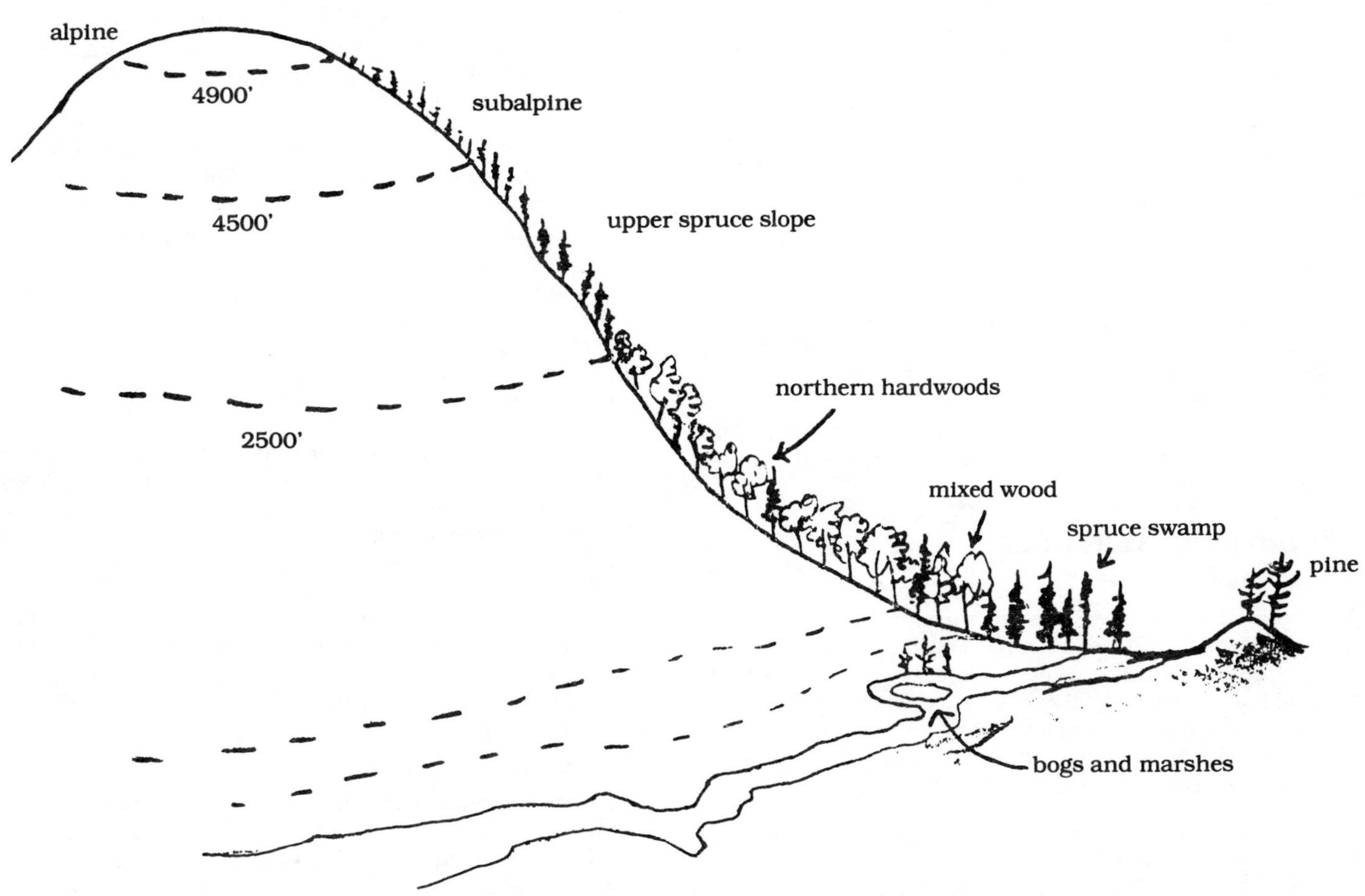

BOGS AND MARSHES

The majority of Adirondack bogs and marshes are the result of shallow ponds which have filled in with vegetation over the years. This is an intermediate step in the natural succession from open water to a dry land forest. A "bog" is characterized as stagnant acidic water with low oxygen content and very slow decomposition rates, covered by a mat of sphagnum moss that may support a few shrubs. A "marsh" is characterized by cattails, sedges or rushes anchored in moist ground that is periodically inundated with water. Once tree species appear in either, a bog or a marsh site is referred to as "swamp."

Besides sphagnum, bogs generally contain plants such as leather-leaf, bog rosemary, and the insect-eating pitcher plant and sundew as well as orchids. This watery zone supports abundant insect life and serves as the breeding ground for many notorious biting insects as well as birds that feed on insects. Small mammals make frequent use of the bog habitat in their life cycles. The bog lemming, a rare small mammal, is found only in the bog habitat. Abundant fresh water, with high nutrient levels, makes marshes the most productive sites.

SPRUCE SWAMP

Spruce swamps occupy the lowlands where water remains standing following snowmelt and rain because of poor drainage and soil saturation. The wettest portions of this zone are dominated by black spruce and tamarack. These areas often border bogs. The more common spruce swamp association is composed of red spruce and balsam fir; paper and yellow birch, red maple, elm, and white cedar are infrequent associates, with tamarack and alders on the fringes.

Animal life typical of this zone includes the Canada jay and the spruce grouse. These areas are used as the primary winter "yards" of the white-tail deer. Though the deer food production is poor here, the forest canopy provides the necessary shelter from snow and biting winter winds. The high water table of spruce swamp areas removes the need for the tree species to sink their roots deeply, and trees are particularly susceptible to windthrow.

Ground cover is sparse as the dense canopy keeps the forest floor heavily shaded. A deep mat of spruce and fir needles often builds up, further reducing the opportunity for smaller plants to seed in.

MIXED WOOD

The moist lower slopes above the spruce swamp provide a transition zone between the conifers and the hardwoods. Conifers become fewer with increased elevation and better drainage. Conversely, the percentage of red maple and yellow birch increases. Although red spruce continues, in lesser abundance, into the next zone, the balsam fir gradually disappears and is replaced by hemlock. Scattered individual white pine trees occur in the mixed wood zone, towering above the forest.

Ground cover is profuse. Witch-hobble seems to be everywhere just waiting to trip the hiker. Clintonia, bunchberry, goldthread, and ferns are common. Bird life becomes extremely varied. Deer tracks are frequently observed. Here the complexity of plant and animal life contrasts vividly with the dark, deep, and desolate spruce swamp.

NORTHERN HARDWOOD

The better-drained slopes up to an elevation of approximately 2500 feet are forested with a mixture of sugar maple and beech. Yellow birch is common, while lesser amounts of white ash, hemlock, white pine, ironwood, and black cherry are also associated with this site. This forest type is found on rich well-drained soils. This is by far the most common site type in the Adirondacks, occupying over fifty percent of the forested land.

The percentage of beech in the forest is higher now than before man entered the Adirondacks. For years, beech was uneconomical to log; so when an area was cut, most of the beech remained. With this headstart, the proportion of beech increased with each cutting. The benefactors were the deer, bear, and smaller mammals that feast on beechnuts during the fall months. (The serious beech blight of recent years is changing this pattern.)

The ground cover is less complex than in the mixed woods. It is commonly composed of leaf litter, maple and beech seedlings, and scattered herbs. Warblers and other birds are common.

UPPER SPRUCE SLOPE

At approximately 2500 feet, a marked change takes place in the forest cover, with a return to conifers. The elevational change varies, depending on the direction the slope faces, occurring at about 2300 feet on north and east slopes and in the vicinity of 2800 feet on south and west slopes. Climatic conditions at these elevations cause the hardwoods to become stunted, to grow slowly, and, as a result, to be replaced by the boreal conifers—red spruce and balsam fir. This progression from spruce swamp to mixed woods to northern hardwoods and then to spruce and fir indicates that hardwoods need the better sites. Conifers cannot compete with the more vigorous hardwoods for sunlight and space on the best sites. But as harsher conditions prevail, the conifers' niche is found.

The upper spruce slope is nearly pure spruce and fir, though occasional paper birch, yellow birch, and mountain ash are found. Ground cover is sparse, again due to a lack of sunlight reaching the forest floor; but club mosses are common.

Animal life here is indicative of northern latitudes; crossbills, three-toed woodpeckers, and various northern warblers live in this zone. Many of these same species can also be found in the bog and spruce swamp zones. The pine marten, a furbearing carnivore, made its last stand here and in the subalpine zone. (Once found throughout the Adirondacks, the species seems to be making a comeback.)

SUBALPINE

Tree line is the point beyond which climatic conditions become so harsh that trees cannot survive. Trees are stunted; boles, or tree trunks, taper rapidly (giving an inverted ice cream cone appearance), and forests grow in patches interspersed with open areas of low plants. In the Adirondacks, the subalpine zone is generally found at elevations between 4300 and 4900 feet. At the higher elevations, trees are found only in depressions where they are protected from the harsh winds; their tops are killed back as they poke above the snow shelter, so they grow in a prostrate form.

Balsam fir is the primary tree species in this zone, almost to the exclusion of all others except a few red spruce. At the upper fringe of this belt, however, the balsam becomes rare and the red spruce vanishes. In their place, in the most extreme climatic conditions, comes black spruce in a dwarf condition. At first glance it seems strange that the only black spruce one encounters in the Adirondacks is at two elevational extremes, spruce swamp and subalpine. Yet it is at these two extremes that growing conditions are most severe, competition from other species least, and moisture most abundant. These site similarities exhibit themselves in the ground vegetation also; the open areas support shrubs such as Labrador tea and bog laurel, previously found only in the bog and swamp areas.

Ground cover under these stunted balsam forests, or Krummholz (German for "elfin forests"), is as sparse as under the upper spruce slope forests. However, in the open areas, lichens, mosses, and numerous herbs and sedges abound. These will be described in more detail in the next zone. The subalpine is basically a transitional zone between the true forest and the alpine. Marten, pine siskins, crosbills, boreal chickadees, and red squirrels are frequently seen here.

ALPINE

The existence of an alpine life zone is one of the lures of the Adirondacks. Limited as it is to the summits of only ten peaks, and a total of only 80 acres, it retains an aura of mystery to the amateur naturalist as well as to the scientist. Though species composition is not complex, the species themselves are so rare that little is known of them. (The mystery extends to animal life; The alpine peaks are the principal Adirondack habitat of the yellow-nosed or rock vole, a mountain relative of the meadow mouse.) The zone is generally found above 4900 feet, although in several instances it is located at elevations as low as 4500 feet. Lichens and mosses are common, but of particular interest are the "cushion" plants. These miniature or bonsai-like plants strike one as tiny reproductions of the herbs and flowers of our gardens. In many cases this is exactly what they are.

Winds on these mountain summits would dessicate plants which survive at lower elevations. Natural selection favored species that could cope with this drying factor. The resultant cushion plants, nicknamed for their fat, cushion-like leaves and stems, are small enough to be sheltered by pebbles or topographic irregularities. Their thick leaves minimize their leaf surface area to volume ratio. The alpine zone in mid-June reminds one of a miniature but extensive flower garden. The limited growing season demands that flowers appear soon after the season begins. Thus the alpine carpet blooms almost as a unit. Because of wind and cooler temperatures, there are fewer black flies here than at lower elevations, making a hike to the high country in June well worthwhile.

PINE

The previously described land life zones and site types are primarily dependent upon elevation. The pine site depends almost strictly upon soil, although it is not found in the upper elevations. This site type is characterized by dry sandy soils where the more demanding hardwoods cannot get the foothold necessary to crowd out the pine. Thus it is found on sand plains and eskers. Though eskers are scattered throughout the Adirondacks, the sand plains are most common in the southeastern quadrant and on the western fringes of the Park.

White pine is the most common pine, though some red pine is found in the pine zone. Generally the white pine will crowd out red pine and become a climax species. On the lower elevations in the southeastern region, pitch pine is occasionally found. Pine stands are often evenly aged, seeding in after a natural or man-caused catastrophe such as fire, clearcutting, or windthrow. Lake shores which burn more frequently than other areas because of heavy human use, often exhibit this forest type. Undergrowth is limited to a few ferns, herbs, and berry-producing plants.

Source: George Davis, "Man and the Adirondack Environment" (1971) and *An Environmental Education Resource Manual for Adirondack Schools* (1979), produced jointly by the Department of Environmental Conservation and the Adirondack Park Agency.

(59)
TREES

10 MOST COMMON LARGER TREES

SUGAR MAPLE: perhaps most common Adirondack tree
--long lived, 200 to 350 years old is common
--70 feet to 90 feet high
--long platey bark
--very shade tolerant
--products: hardwood dimension lumber, mainly for furniture; maple syrup
--deer browse on twigs, buds
--demands rich soil

AMERICAN BEECH: stately in all seasons
--Long-lived, up to 200+ years
--70 to 90 feet in height
--smooth, light gray bark ("elephant leg")
--very shade tolerant
--products: paper pulp and hardwood pallets, furniture turnings, etc.
--often sends up "root suckers" to begin new trees
--beech nuts occasionally heavy and eaten by most wildlife
--threatened by "scale fungus" and rapidly declining

YELLOW BIRCH: found on a variety of sites
--fast growing and quite long-lived (200 years+)
--70 to 100 feet in height
--bark-thin, yellowish, with paper-thin curls, platey when old
--mid-tolerant to shade
--products: paneling, dimension lumber for furniture and trim
--twigs with distinct wintergreen taste
--often grows on "stilts" after seeds germinate on rotting— stumps or logs
--grows on rich soils with good moisture

HEMLOCK: our longest-lived Adirondack tree
--up to 600+ years old
--70 to 80 feet in height
--bark is rough, with reddish purple bands inside
--very shade tolerant
--products: construction lumber, timbers
--shallow root system, moisture needed
--scattered in hardwoods, but often found in groves
--excellent winter deer shelter

RED SPRUCE: characterizes Adirondack region
--up to 350 years
--70 to 80 feet in height
--bark: small, flakey plates
--very shade tolerant
--products: construction lumber, musical instruments, — pulp
--scattered, but common on "higher" swamps and upper mountain slopes, shallow rooted

WHITE PINE: tallest Adirondack tree
--up to 200+ years
--up to 125 feet tall
--bark is rough and platey when old; smooth when young
--mid-tolerant to shade
--products: siding, timbers, dimension boards
--often found on sandy eskers and outwash soils
--our only "five needle" pine

BALSAM FIR: typical Adirondack Christmas tree
--up to 90 years
--height: 60 feet maximum
--bark: smooth with numerous horizontal resin blisters
--needs abundant moisture and can withstand severe cold and ice to timberline
--needles very aromatic, soft to touch

RED MAPLE: leaves scarlet in September
--up to 100 years
--height: 70 feet maximum
--bark: platey to shreddy, smooth when young
--mid-tolerant to shade
--products: dimension lumber, pulp
--most often found in swamps, bottomlands and severe sites
--usually the first tree to "turn" in autumn
--buds are excellent winter deer food

WHITE BIRCH: often found as a result of fire
--up to 80 years
--60 to 70 feet tall
--bark: white with papery curls
--low shade tolerance
--products: pulp, furniture, turnings, firewood
--pure stands common where severe forest fires have occurred, and near timberline
--also called "paper birch"

ASPEN: better known as "poplar" or "popple"
--up to 60 years, fast growing
--50 to 60 feet tall
--bark light yellowish-green, smooth, rough tan ridges when old
--very low tolerance to shade
--products: few, pulp
--usually the first tree to re-populate a highly disturbed site—a "pioneer"
--spreads by light windblown seeds and vegetative— "cloning"
--buds eaten by grouse, bark by beaver
--two species: quaking and bigtooth

ADIRONDACK TREE SPECIES TOLERANCE RATINGS

Tolerance normally refers to a plant's ability to live in shade. That is, all plants need sunlight to manufacture food, but some can continue to produce even at very low levels of light. Most grasses and open field perennials need full sunlight to prosper. At the other end of the scale, Christmas fern, wintergreen nd partridgeberry are forest ground-cover plants which tolerate extremely low levels of light and compete well with other non-woody plants. Varying degrees of tolerance are shown on the following chart, with degrees of tolerance from top to bottom.

TOLERANT

Hemlock
Red spruce
Balsam fir
American beech
Sugar maple

MID-TOLERANT

Hop hornbeam
Northern white cedar
White spruce
Basswood
Red maple
Black spruce
Yellow birch
Red oak
American elm
White pine

INTOLERANT

Serviceberry
White ash
Black cherry
Mountain ash
Paper birch
Red pine
Pitch pine
Balsam poplar
Pin cherry
Gray birch
Bigtooth aspen
Quaking aspen
Jack pine
Tamarack

Sources: George Davis, "Man and the Adirondack Environment" (1971) and An Environmental Education Resource Manual for Adirondack Schools (1979) produced jointly by the Department of Environmental Conservation and the Adirondack Park Agency.

(60)
WILDFLOWERS

A DOZEN ROADSIDE ATTRACTIONS

The twelve flowers sketched below are commonly seen when driving through the Adirondacks. They are also the most frequently picked Adirondack wildflowers. Actually most are not native to the region, having been brought to America from Europe. Nevertheless, they add much to the color and beauty of the Adirondacks every year.

GOLDENROD
July-October

ST. JOHNSWORT
June-September

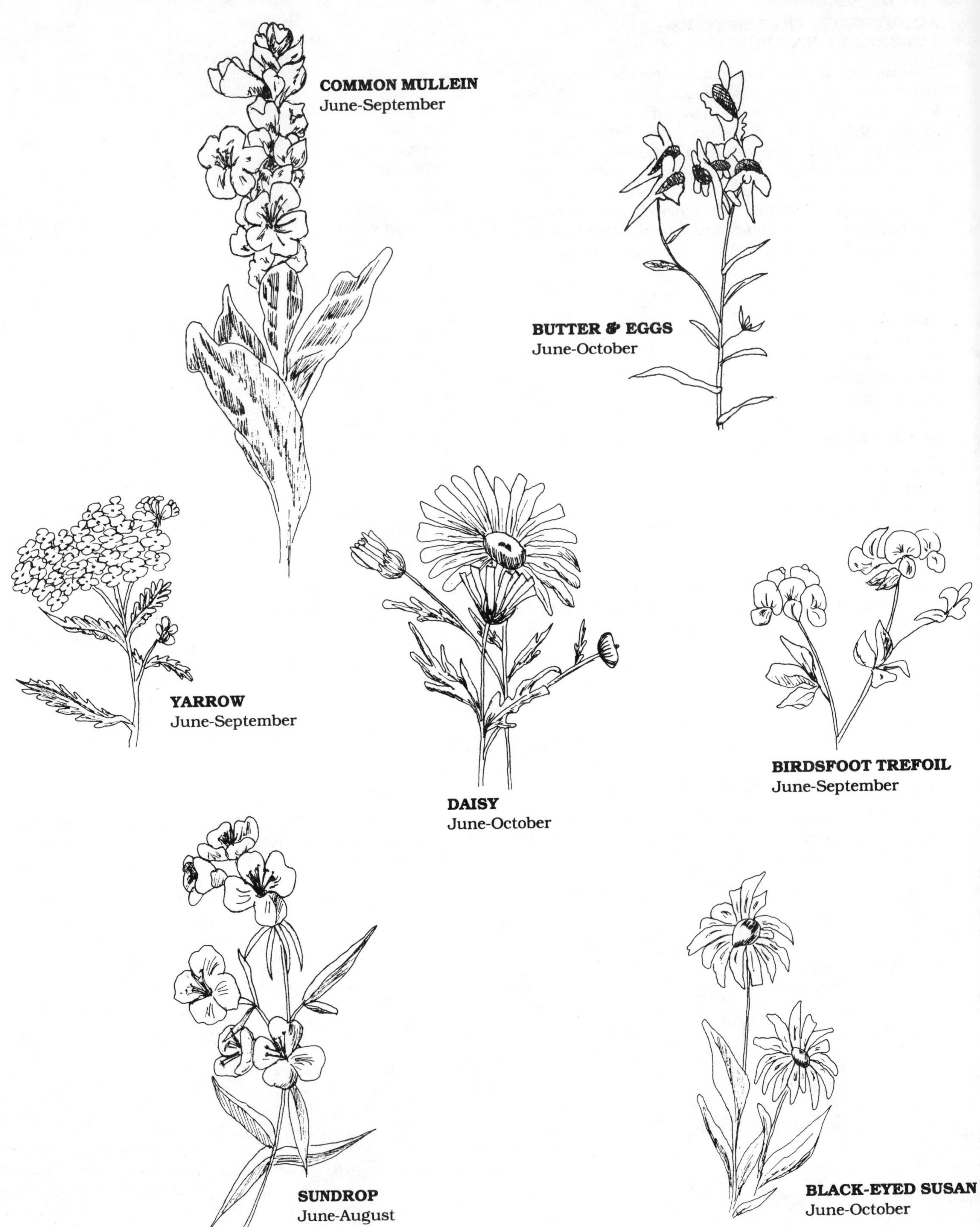
COMMON MULLEIN
June-September
BUTTER & EGGS
June-October
YARROW
June-September
DAISY
June-October
BIRDSFOOT TREFOIL
June-September
SUNDROP
June-August
BLACK-EYED SUSAN
June-October

ORANGE HAWKWEED
June-September

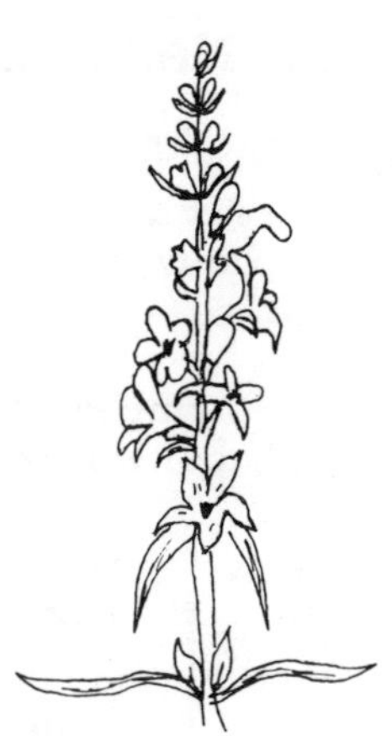

PURPLE LOOSESTRIFE
June-September

FIREWEED
July-September

COMMON WILDFLOWERS

The following are some of the common wildflower families and species within these families found in the Adirondacks.

Buttercup Family
Goldthread, also called Canker Root
Canada Anemone
White Baneberry
Wood Anemone
Tall Meadow Rue
Virgins' Bower, also called Old Man's Beard
Marsh Marigold

Ginseng Family
Wild Sarsaparilla
Dwarf Ginseng

Lily Family
Bluebeard Lily, also called Clintonia Lily
Yellow Pond Lily, also called Bullhead or Cow Lily
Trout Lily, also called Fawn Lily or Adder's Tongue
Large-flowered Trillium, also called White Trillium
Red Trillium, also called Wake-Robin
Painted Trillium
Solomon's Seal
Hairy Solomon's Seal
False Solomon's Seal
Canada Hayflower
Rose Twisted Stalk, also called Rosybells and Pink or Rose Mandarin
Wild Oats
Indian Cucumber Root

Orchid Family
Large Purple Fringed Orchid
Purple Fringeless Orchid
Small Purple Fringed Orchid
Stemless Orchid, also called Pink Lady's Slipper or Mocassin Flower

Poppy Family
Bloodroot
Dutchman's Breeches

Rose Family
Meadowsweet
Steeplebush
Purple-flowering Raspberry
Barren Strawberry
Rough-fruited Cinquefoil
Wild Strawberry
Canadian Burnet
Pasture Rose

Sunflower Family
Spotted Joe-Pye Weed
Spotted Knapweed
Coltsfoot
Yellow Goatsbeard
Black-Eyed Susan
Green-Headed Coneflower
Goldenrod
Orange Hawkweed
Chicory
New York Aster
Common Fleabane, also called Philadelphia Fleabane
Bonset, also called Thoroughwart
Pearly Everlasting
Flat-topped White Aster

Wildflower sketches by Heidi Miller. Source: Anne McGrath and Joanne Treffs, *Wildflowers of the Adirondacks* (1981). This is an excellent introduction to the subject for the non-botonist and is widely available in bookstores or from the publisher, North Country Books, Sylvan Beach, NY 13157.

(61)

PROTECTED NATIVE PLANTS

Effective September 1, 1974, no one may knowingly pick, pluck, sever, remove or carry away, without the consent of the owner thereof, any protected plants. Violations of the law are punishable by fines of up to $25 each (Environmental Conservation Law 9-1503). The following are native plants which are protected pursuant to the above law and state regulation (NYCRR 193.3). This list applies statewide.

Incidentally, the rarest of known Adirondack plants is a tiny orchid, the auricled twayblade (Listera auriculata). The only know extant population in New York State, one of perhaps five in the nation, is located in Warren County (Source: Tim Barnett, Adirondack Conservancy).

COMMON NAME*	SCIENTIFIC NAME
Green-dragon (Dragonroot)	*Arisaema dracontium*
Butterfly-weed (Chigger-flower; Orange Milkweed; Pleurisy-root)	*Asclepias tuberosa*
Bluebell-of-Scotland (Harebell)	*Campanula rotundifolia*
American Bittersweet (Waxwork)	*Celastrus scandens*
Pipsissewa (Prince's-pine; Wax-flower) Spotted Evergreen (Spotted Wintergreen)	*Chimaphila spp.*
Flowering Dogwood	*Cornus florida*
Sundew (Daily-dew; Dewthread)	*Drosera spp.*
Trailing Arbutus (Groud Laurel; Mayflower)	*Epigaea repens*
Burning-bush (Wahoo) Strawberry-bush (Bursting-heart)	*Euonymus spp. (Native)*
All ferns, including: Adder's tongue, Azolla, Buckhorn, Cliff Brake, Curly-grass, Fiddleheads, Hart's-tongue, Maidenhair, Moonwort, Polypody, Rock Brake, Salvinia, Spleenwort, Walking-leaf, Wall-rue, Water-spangle, Woodsia. But excluding Braken (Pteridium aquilinum); Hay-scented Fern (Dennstaedtia punctilobula); Sensitive Fern (Onoclea sensibilis), which are not protected.	*Filices (Filicinae: Ophioglossales and Filicales) (Native)*
Ague-weed, Blue-bottles, Gentian (Gall-of-the-earth)	*Gentiana spp.*
Golden Seal (Orange-root; Yellow Puccoon)	*Hydrastis canadensis*
Holly (Hulver); Inkberry (Bitter Gallberry); Winterberry (Black Alder)	*Ilex spp. (Native)*
Laurel, Spoonwood (Calico-bush) Wicky (Lambkill)	*Kalmia spp.*
Lily, Turk's-cap	*Lilium spp. (Native)*
Cardinal-flower (Red Lobelia)	*Lobelia cardinalis*
All Clubmosses, including: Bear's-bed (Christmas-green, Running Evergreen; (Trailing Evergreen; Ground Pine); Bunch Evergreen; Festoon Pine (Coral Evergreen; Buckhorn; Staghorn Evergreen; Wolf's-claws); Ground Cedar (Creeping Jenny); Ground Fir; Heath Cypress	*Lycopodium spp.*
Bluebell (Roanoke-bells; Tree Lungwort; Virginia Bluebell; Virginia Lungwort; Virginia Cowslip)	*Mertensia virginica*

COMMON NAME	SCIENTIFIC NAME
American Bee-balm; Oswego Tea (Indian-heads; Scarlet Bee-balm)	*Monarda didyma*
Bayberry (Candleberry)	*Myrica pensilvanica*
Lotus (Lotus Lily; Nelumbo; Pond-nuts; Water Chinquapin; Wonkapin; Yellow Lotus)	*Nelumbo lutea*
Prickly Pear (Wild Cactus; Indian Fig)	*Opuntia humifusa (O. compressa, p.p.)*
All Native Orchids, including: Adder's-mouth (Malaxis); Arethusa (Dragon's-mouth; Swamp-pink;) Bog-candle (Scent-bottle); Calopogon (Grass-pink; Swamp-pink); Calypso (Fairy-slipper); Coral-root; Cypripedium (Lady's-slipper; Moccasin-flower; nerve root); Goodyera (Lattice-leaf; Rattlesnake-plantain); Kirtle-pink; Ladies'-tresses (Pearl-twist; Screw-auger); Orange-plume; Orchis; Pogonia (Beard-flower; Snake-mouth); Putty-root (Adam-and-Eve); Soldier's-plume; Three-birds; Twayblade; Whipporwill-shoe	*Orchidaceae*
Golden-club	*Orontium aquaticum*
Ginseng (Sang)	*Banax quinquefolius*
Wild Crabapple	*Pyrus coronaria*
Azalea; Great Laurel (White Laurel); Honeysuckle; Pinxter (Election-pink; Pinxter-bloom); Rhododendron (Rosebay); Rhodora	*Rhododendron spp. (Native)*
Bitterbloom (Marsh-pink; Rose-pink; Sabatia; Sea-pink)	*Sabatia spp.*
Bloodroot (Puccoon-root; Red Puccoon)	*Sanguinaria*
Pitcher-plant (Huntsman's-cup; Sidesaddle-flower)	*Sarracenia purpurea*
Wild Pink	*Silene caroliniana*
Bethroot (Birthroot; Squawroot; Stinking Benjamin; Wake-robin); Toadshade, Trillium	*Trillium spp.*
Globe-flower (Trollius)	*Trollius laxus*
Bird's-foot Violet	*Viola pedata*

*NOTE: In this list above, common names are not included if they repeat the generic common name with a modifier (e.g. "Trillium" is understood to include "Painted Trillium," "White Trillium", "Nodding Trillium" and all others.) Names appearing within parentheses are less familiar synonyms for the principal common names of each species listed.

(62)
BLACK FLY FACTS

Approximately 26 species of black flies exist in the Adirondacks, with two species doing the most damage: Prosimulium mixtum (mid-May-early June) and Simulium venustum (end of May-early July).

Black flies have stout black bodies 1/6 inch long, short legs, and a humpbacked stance.

Only in the mature adult stage do black flies bite humans and animals, and then only the females take blood. The blood is needed as a protein source so eggs can be produced.

Eggs are laid on or just below the surface of water. One female is capable of laying between 300-500 eggs in just a few minutes.

At Death Brook near Raquette Lake, counts were made and approximately 800 larvae per square foot found. Over 100 larvae were discovered on a dead leaf floating on a stream near Old Forge.

At Twitchell Lake dam a record concentration was once discovered, with one rock alone yielding 2800 individuals in a mat half an inch thick and several inches wide.

Females use colors, silhouette, odor and CO2 (carbon dioxide) emission as clues for finding hosts.

Flies are least attracted to bright orange, yellow, and green, and are attracted to blues, purples and purple-reds.

Black Fly Life Cycle: egg,larvae, pupa for 2-4 weeks, adult males for 1 week and adult females for 2-3 weeks.

Female Simulium Vittatum *taking a meal of human blood.*

The Adirondack region is particularly a black fly haven due to the numerous clean, pristine streams for larvae development and large number of mammals available as hosts for adult females.

Aerial spraying can provide temporary relief; stream spraying is more effective but may cause ecological side-effects.

Visitors to the Adirondack region, from mid-May through early July in some locations, should wear repellents and be forewarned.

Sources: Dr. E.W. Cupp, Dept. of Biology, Cornell University; Dr. Anne LaBastille, "The Black Fly," *Adirondack Life*, Summer 1974.

(63)
BIRDS

Species of Adirondack birds vary within the different natural environments found throughout the region—from Lake Champlain to the High Peaks, from spruce bog to abandoned farm field. Species may also be categorized as "breeding" or "non-breeding." The following listing includes relatively common and/or significant "breeding" birds, i.e., those which breed in the Adirondacks. The list is further differentiated by the following coding system: P=Permanent, Tr=Transient, S=Summer, W=Winter, V=Visitant, Ab=Abundant, C=Common, FC=Fairly Common, Unc=Uncommon, Occ=Occasional, R=Rare, L=Local, Irr=Irregular. For example, SR-Unc, Tr-FC would mean that it would be rare to uncommon for this bird to stay in this area for the whole summer (S), but it is fairly common for the bird to be a transient visitor, i.e., to spend a brief time here while passing through.

10 BIRDS OF THE OPEN MARSH AND LAKESHORE

Great Blue Heron - SR-Unc, Tr-FC
Mallard - Tr-Unc
Black Duck - SR-FC, Tr-C
Killdeer - SR-FC
Spotted Sandpiper - SR, Tr-C
Alder Flycatcher - SR-C
Tree Swallow - SR, Tr-C
Common Yellowthroat - SR-Ab to C
Red Winged Blackbird - SR-C, Tr-Ab, WV-Occ
Song Sparrows - SR, Tr-C, WR-Occ

10 BREEDING SPECIES OF THE NORTHERN HARDWOOD FOREST

Yellow-bellied Sapsucker - SR-C
Downy Woodpecker - PR-C
Least Flycatcher - SR-Ab
Black-capped Chickadee - PR-Ab
Veery - SR-C
Red-eyed Vireo- SR-Ab
Ovenbird - SR-Ab
American Redstart - SR-Ab
Rose-breasted Grosbeak - SR-FC
White-throated Sparrow - SR, Tr-Ab, WR-Occ

10 BREEDING BIRDS OF THE BOREAL/MONTANE FOREST

Black-capped Chickadee - PR-Ab
Blue Jay - PR-C
Red-breasted Nuthatch - PR-C
Golden-crowned Kinglet - SR-FC, WR-Occ
Swainson's Thrush - SR, Tr-C
Black-throated Green Warbler - SR, Tr-C
Yellow-rumped Warbler - SR-FC
Dark-eyed Junco - SR-C, Tr-Ab, WR-Occ
White-throated Sparrow - SR, Tr-Ab, WR-Occ
Boreal Chickadee - PR-C

10 BREEDING BIRDS OF THE SPRUCE/TAMARACK BOG

Yellow-bellied Flycatcher - SR-FC, Tr-Unc
Olive-sided Flycatcher - SR, Tr-FC
Boreal Chickadee - PR-FC
Hermit Thrush - SR-FC
Black-capped Chickadee - PR-Ab
Golden-crowned Kinglet - SR-FC, WR-Occ
Nashville Warbler - SR-C
Swamp Sparrow - SR-FC
Lincoln's Sparrow - SR, Tr-Unc
American Spruce Grouse - PR-R

10 BIRDS OF ABANDONED FIELDS AND AGRICULTURAL HABITATS

Eastern Kingbird - SR, Tr-FC
Tree Swallow - SR, Tr-C
Common Crow - PR-C
American Robin - SR-C, WR-Occ
Cedar Waxwing - SR-C, WR-Occ
Chestnut-sided Warbler - SR, Tr-C
Common Yellowthroat - SR-Ab
Red-winged Blackbird - SR-C, Tr-Ab, WV-Occ
American Goldfinch - SR-C, WV-FC
Song Sparrow - SR, Tr-C, WR-Occ

Sources: Bruce McP. Beehler, *Birdlife of the Adirondack Park* (Glens Falls, NY: Adirondack Mountain Club, 1978) and *"Birds of the Central Adirondacks,"* Chamber of Commerce, 30 Main St., Saranac Lake, NY 12983. Thanks also to John M.C. Peterson of the High Peaks Audubon Society and Ronnie Renoni for their assistance.

(64)
FISH

The following is a list of the most significant game and non-game fish species found in the Adirondack zone. G = Game Fish. NG = Non-Game Fish. N = Native. I = Introduced. Some of the introduced species were native to some waters but then introduced to others.

FAMILY ANGUILLIDAE (Freshwater Eels)
American Eel (Anguilla rostrata). NG, N

FAMILY CLUPEIDAE (Herrings)
Alewife (Alosa Pseudoharengus). NG, I

FAMILY SALMONIDAE (Trouts)
Round whitefish (Prosopium Cylindraceum). NG, N
Sockeye salmon (Oncorhynchus nerka). G, I
Rainbow trout (Salmo gairdneri). G, I
Atlantic salmon (Salmo salar). G, I
Brown trout (Salmo trutta). G, I
Brook trout (Salvelinus fointinalis). G, N
Lake trout (Salvelinus namaycush). G, N
Splake (Hybrid) (S. namaycush x S. fontinalis). G, I

FAMILY OSMERIDAE (Smelts)
Rainbow smelt (Osmerus mordax). NG, I

FAMILY ESOCIDAE (Pikes)
Northern pike (Esox lucius). G, I
Hybrid muskellunge (E. masquinongy x E. lucius). G, I

FAMILY CYPRINIDAE (Minnows)
Golden shiner (Notropis crysoleuces). NG, N
Common shiner (Notropis cornucus). NG, N

FAMILY CATOSTOMIDAE (Suckers)
White sucker (Catostomus commersoni). NG, N

FAMILY ICTALURIDAE (Freshwater catfishes)
Brown bullhead (Ictalurus nebulosus). NG, N

FAMILY CENTRARCHIDAE (Sunfishes)
Rock bass (Ambloplites rupestris). NG, I
Pumpkinseed (Lepomis gibbosus). NG, N
Smallmouth bass (Micropterus dolomieui). G, I
Largemouth bass (Micropterus salmoides). G, I

FAMILY PERCHIDAE (Perches)
Yellow perch (Perca flavescens). NG, I
Walleye (Stizostedion vitreum). G, I

Source: Department of Environmental Conservation.

Lake Trout

Yellow Perch

Pumpkinseed

MAMMALS

BEAVER

The largest member of the rodent family in North America, the beaver is the New York State mammal. Adult beavers are 3 to 4 feet long and weigh 40 to 50 pounds, sometimes more. Ponds and watershed areas created by beaver dams range in size from one to 200 acres. In the 1920's trapping seasons were instituted. The annual harvest is now around 6,000 beavers. They continue to be common and abundant in the Adirondacks.

Beavers feed both on bark and aquatic vegetation. Their preferred foods include aspen (poplar), alder and willow, but several other types of trees and aquatic plants are also used. Winter food stores are composed of quantities of branches lodged in the bottom of the pond. Beavers must continually gnaw, or their teeth grow back into their skulls. Beaver ponds often provide breeding grounds for other mammals including muskrats, otters and minks.

Beavers breed January to March. Young are born 128 days later, with a litter size of 1 to 8.

BLACK BEAR

New York State has one of the largest bear populations in the eastern United States. It is estimated that the Adirondack population is around 3,600. 400 to 675 bears are taken by hunters annually from northern NY.

The size of their home range is determined by such factors as age and sex of the animal, season and the capability of a certain area to meet the bear population's needs. The adult male black bear averages 300 pounds, with the female about half that size. Cubs are born blind and weigh less than one pound. Bears are omnivores and will eat almost anything.

Contrary to common folklore, bears are not true hibernators but "den up" for most of the winter. They seldom use caves but dig holes under tree roots or pile boulders and seal themselves in with leaves and twigs. During the summer and early fall they will often make "nests" by tearing off limbs of beech and cherry trees and piling them in the crotch of trees.

BOBCAT

The bobcat has a small but stable population in the Adirondacks. Annual harvests from hunting and trapping average 100-200 bobcats statewide. Looking much like an overgrown short-tailed house cat, a bobcat can reach 36" long and up to 45 pounds. Its home territory, often dense forest lands, ranges from .5 to 200 square kilometers, tending to be larger areas in the Adirondacks than in the Catskills. The bobcat typically feeds on small mammals and birds. It hunts by stealth, never chasing anything too far, but rather sneaking up and pouncing on its prey. It occasionally eats larger animals like beaver or deer, which are hunted by stalking.

COYOTE

Studies suggest that the great differences in territory range size are relative to the sex and age of the coyotes. A yearling male can easily have a 15 to 68 square kilometer home range, while a female may stay within a 10 to 36 square kilometer range. Typically coyotes eat rodents, rabbits and large animal carrion, or they are vegetarians when meat is scarce. Coyotes in northern New York are larger than their western counterpart, and sometimes as large as the Eastern Timber Wolf. Due to interbreeding, it can be difficult to distinguish coyotes and "coydogs" by physical appearance.

DEER

The populations of white-tailed deer that are commonly seen throughout the Adirondacks fluctuate in size depending on winter food, ground cover and weather. Figures from the 1981 harvest indicate 58,959 deer taken from the Southeastern Region in New York; 97,245 from the Central-Western Region; and only 9,599 from the Northern Region. As reported in the Department of Environmental Conservation's "Deer Management Update, 1982," the Northern Region's 1981 deer harvest was as follows:

County	Total Take
Clinton	233
Essex	772
Franklin	667
Fulton	173
Hamilton	918
Herkimer	948
Lewis	687
Oneida	863
St. Lawrence	1,852
Saratoga	463
Warren	403
Washington	948

FISHER

The fisher is a large mammal of the weasel family. Its coloring varies from black to dark brown, with gray-tipped hairs all over its body. Males are 34-40 inches in length, including a 13-15 inch tail, and weigh 7-12 pounds. Females are about one third smaller and tend to weigh about half as much. The fisher is an omnivore and has varied habitats, but seems to prefer heavily forested regions. Fishers are agile and active predators. As a species they have an estimated range of 10,000 square miles, mostly in Northern New York. Due to regulated trapping, the harvest has varied from 684 (1982) to 2049 (1979) fishers in recent years. The population is abundant in the Adirondacks.

FOX

The red fox is distinguishable by its yellowish red fur and white-tipped tail. Reaching lengths of 42 inches, it rarely exceeds 15 pounds in weight. Its bushy tail is about three-fifths as long as its body. This nocturnal carnivore is generally limited to the Adirondack foothills, prefering open forests and fields.

In contrast, the gray fox is found throughout the Adirondacks in swamps, cut over areas and overgrown fields. It is the only member of the canine family that can climb trees.

While both red and gray foxes are common in the Adirondacks, their population densities are lower here than in southern NY.

OTTER

The primary otter range, of about 20,000 square miles, is located in northern New York's watersheds. Due to regulated trapping, an average of 513 otters were harvested annually from 1972-1982.

The otter, with an average weight of 12 pounds, is a large member of the weasel family. Otters have been known to weigh up to 25 pounds with coats ranging in color from light brown to black. Their total length ranges from 38-47 inches; a strong, muscular tail generally making up one-third their length, is 12-17 inches long. Their webbed feet are unique in the weasel family, as otters inhabit lakes, rivers and streams, playing in mud and snow slides, resting in hollow logs and abandoned beaver homes. They are carnivorous, with fish and other animals as their main food source. Young are born in April and May, with an average litter size of 1 to 5.

PINE MARTEN

While male martens average 16-17 inches in length and generally weigh less than 3 pounds, female martens average 22 inches in length and weigh about 2 pounds. The marten's most distinguishing feature is the buff or yellow-orange fur on the underside of its throat, with the rest of the body light to dark brown fur. It is a member of the weasel family. Young are born in late March or early April, with litters of 1 to 5.

The pine marten's habitat varies, but it prefers heavily forested areas. It is an agile and active predator, spending much time in tree tops. Having semi-retractable claws the marten is well-adapted for its forested habitats. It eats small mammals, insects and fruits, depending on availability. The pine marten is also known as the American Sable.

SMALLER MAMMALS

The following is a list of smaller wild mammals often seen throughout the Adirondacks. (We have omitted humans from this section on mammals, as they are well represented elsewhere in *The Guide.)*

- Bat
  - Little Brown Bat
- Chipmunk
- Mink
- Mole
  - Hairy-tailed Mole
- Mouse
- Deer Mouse
  - Meadow Jumping Mouse
  - White-footed Mouse
  - Woodland Mouse
- Muskrat
- Porcupine
- Rabbit
  - Snowshoe Rabbit
  - Varying Hare
- Raccoon
- Shrew
  - Masked Shrew
  - Pigmy Shrew
  - Short-tailed Shrew
- Squirrel
  - Flying Squirrel
  - Red Squirrel
- Vole
  - Boreal Redback Vole
  - Meadow Vole
- Weasel
  - Long-tailed Weasel
  - Short-tailed Weasel

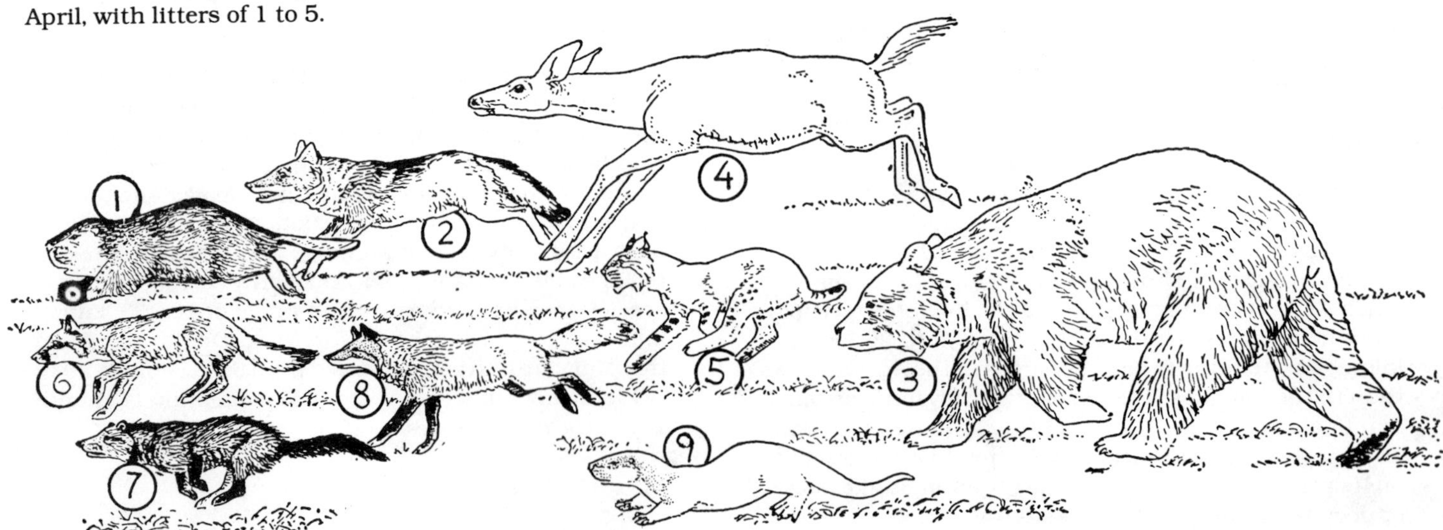

1. Beaver 2. Coyote 3. Black Bear 4. White-tailed deer 5. Bobcat 6. Gray Fox 7. Fisher 8. Red Fox 9. Otter

ENDANGERED WILDLIFE

Species may exist in varying degrees of danger, which are sometimes categorized as "endangered", "threatened" and "special concern". Endangered wildlife are in danger of becoming extirpated (eliminated from one area but not extinct) from one or more of their habitats. Threatened wildlife are likely to become endangered within the foreseeable future. Endangered and threatened wildlife are legally protected. Species of special concern may border on the threatened status or may be listed because more data is necessary to clarify their true status. They may or may not be legally protected.

The cougar and wolf, which are extirpated from New York, are listed as endangered because they are federally listed as endangered, and they once occurred in this state. A brief summary of the recent status of the moose is included, although it is not officially listed in any of these categories. It is, however, legally protected.

BALD EAGLE

(Haliaeetus leucocephalus)

The bald eagle is federally listed as "endangered". Prior to the 1940's, as many as 70 pairs of nesting bald eagles were scattered throughout the state. Currently, there are two active nests in New York State--in Livingston and Jefferson counties. Pesticide contamination, shooting and habitat loss all played a role in this fish-eating bird's decline. Recent work at restoring the species through hacking of young birds obtained from other areas and manipulation of existing nests bodes well for the return of this raptor to the state. Beginning in 1983 the D.E.C. anticipates releasing bald eagles in southern Franklin County. (Endangered)

BLUE-SPOTTED SALAMANDER

(Ambystoma laterale)

The blue-spotted salamander is a large fossorial amphibian which inhabits moist mixed deciduous woodlands with temporary pools for breeding. Often confused with the Jefferson salamander, this species tends to be more southern in distribution. Iowa, Ohio and New Jersey all list this species as "endangered". (Special concern)

COMMON LOON

(Gavia immer)

The common loon is a species that breeds in lakes and rivers throughout Northern forested areas of North America. Within New York it nests on Adirondack lakes and, to a lesser degree, along the St. Lawrence River. It winters along Long Island and more southerly Atlantic coastlines. A Department of Environmental Conservation breeding loon survey conducted between 1977 and 1980 yielded 124 pairs of loons on 96 of 420 lakes visited. (Special concern)

COMMON NIGHTHAWK

(Chordeiles minor)

The common nighthawk is found breeding statewide. Formerly, nighthawks nested in bare open areas of rock or soil. In forested areas, burns provided an unobstructed substrate for nests. In the recent past, nighthawks have moved from natural areas to towns and cities where they nest on flat gravel rooftops. Although concern for this species has been expressed by birders in New York, there is little data available regarding possible causes of decline. (Special concern)

COMMON RAVEN

(Corvus corax)

The raven was once widely distributed over the state before the virgin forests were cut . The now uncommon species has increased in recent years, but the total number of nesting pairs is still relatively low, with less than two dozen cliff nests in the Adirondacks believed to exist in 1978. (Special concern) (More recent findings indicate the raven's comeback appears to be accelerating. Eds.)

COUGAR

(Felis concolor)

The cougar was once distributed throughout much of Central and North America, but due to conflicts with encroaching civilization, it has subsequently been restricted to only remote or inaccessible regions. Within New York State, the cougar was eliminated by the 1890's and Florida now harbors the last population in the eastern United States. Eastern populations are federally listed as "endangered". Although there have been unconfirmed reports of cougar sightings in the Adirondacks, because of the ever increasing human population and the resulting demands on the remaining wildlands of New York, it is uncertain whether the cougar could ever again survive in this state. (Endangered)

GOLDEN EAGLE

(Aquila chrysaetos)

Although more common in the west, the golden eagle is extremely rare as a breeder in the eastern United States. This large raptor prefers open areas such as bogs, old burns, and wet areas for hunting. Never common in this state, the last young eagle was produced in the Adirondacks in 1970 in Hamilton County. As recently as 1979, there were signs of activity at this site with an adult seen in an incubating posture; however, no young were produced. Although an analysis of habitat at some of the historical sites showed a decline in the open types of habitat necessary for hunting, there appears to be suitable habitat left in some areas and the reason for the species' failure to nest are unclear. (Endangered)

GRAY WOLF

(Canis lupus)

The gray wolf once inhabited most of North America, including all of New York State. It is now restricted mainly to Canada, Alaska and Northern Minnesota. It has been federally listed as "endangered" in the contiguous United States, with the exception of Minnesota, where it is listed as "threatened". The wolf was extirpated from New York by 1910, probably because of expanding civilization and the resulting conflicts. It is uncertain whether subsequent changes in human activities and land use will ever allow this wide-ranging species to re-inhabit the Adirondacks. (Endangered)

MOOSE

(Alces alces)

Moose were once native to New York State but were extirpated by 1861 probably as a result of changing land use patterns and human activities. Between 1935, when the next moose entered the state (other than released animals), and 1980 at least 17 and perhaps as many as 23 different moose came into New York from populations in Canada and/or New England. Never more than three individuals were seen in any one year. The most recent sighting of one individual was in Franklin County on February 19, 1981. Two moose are known to have died. Necropsies failed to reveal any evidence of brain worm (Parelaphostronglus tenuis) infection. Presently, five moose are believed to be alive in the Adirondack region.

OSPREY

(Pandion haliaetus)

The osprey is a fish-eating species and therefore is intimately tied to lakes, ponds and rivers. In New York, two main populations occur: one on Long Island and one in the Adirondacks. Although in recent years the population on Long Island has increased and it is reasonable to be optimistic about its future, there is still some concern about the upstate population. It has been determined that 0.79 young per active nest are needed to maintain population stability. This has been reached consistently since 1976 by the Long Island osprey population, but has not been recorded in the Adirondacks recently. For this reason, additional information clarifying the factors affecting the Adirondack population is necessary. (Threatened)

PEREGRINE FALCON

(Falco peregrinus)

This species is federally listed as "endangered". It once nested throughout the eastern United States with approximately 300 pairs in residence east of the Mississippi River. Due to the eggshell thinning effects of the pesticide DDT, by the late 1950's not a single nesting pair remained in New York State, where at least 75 cliff eyries were known to have existed. A program to restore this species to the state involving the release of captive-bred birds has been underway since 1974. A total of 25 peregrines were released at two sites in the Adirondacks in the last two years, and more such releases are expected. (Endangered)

ROUND WHITEFISH

(Prosopium cylindraceum)

The round whitefish was once abundant in many deep, cool lakes in the central Adirondacks. Today, it is believed to be confined to fourteen lakes, with only two supporting modest populations. Populations in the remaining waters are either low or unknown. Efforts to establish the round whitefish in other suitable Adirondack lakes are underway and have met with some success. The continuing acid precipitation problem is, however, reducing the potential of this effort as well as threatening the well-being of existing populations. (Endangered)

SPOTTED SALAMANDER

(Ambystoma maculatum)

The spotted salamander inhabits moist deciduous mixed forests, travelling to temporary pools in spring to lay eggs. Although statewide in distribution they are somewhat local and rarely seen, except during spring concentrations. The spotted salamander has been listed as "threatened" in Wisconsin, "local" in Massachusetts, and "declining" in New Jersey. Habitat destruction has been responsible for losses of populations in heavily urbanized or agricultural sections of the state. However, acid precipitation has invaded the salamander's remaining habitats, killing eggs and developing larvae. (Special concern)

SPRUCE GROUSE

(Dendragapus canadensis)

In New York State, this species is found only in the lowland conifer forests of the Adirondacks, usually associated with tamarack and black spruce swamps and bogs. The number of occupied sites has declined in recent years to approximately 20, representing a population estimated at 200 individuals. While there appears to be unoccupied spruce grouse habitat available in the Adirondacks, the ability of the species to repopulate such sites at the existing low population levels is questionable. Potential habitats, especially those located between occupied population centers, must be preserved in order to minimize necessary dispersal distances. Possible causes of current declines include logging activities and human disturbance. (Threatened)

TIMBER RATTLESNAKE

(Crotalus horridus)

This large viviparous pit viper inhabits wooded, mountainous areas of New York. Although it once ranged throughout hilly areas in most of the state, exclusive of the higher elevations in the Adirondacks, the species is now restricted to southeastern New York, with isolated populations in western New York, and the highlands of Lake George and Lake Champlain. The status of the species is listed as "endangered" in New Jersey and "undetermined" in Pennsylvania. Collecting by humans has been one of the major threats to this species, although some den sites have been destroyed as well. (Threatened)

(67)

ADIRONDACK CONSERVANCY PROJECTS AND PROPERTIES

The Adirondack Conservancy is an operating committee of the national organization The Nature Conservancy. It is a publicly supported, non-profit organization directed toward the conservation of ecologically and environmentally significant tracts of land. The Adirondack Conservancy has three major means for achieving this goal:

1. Land acquired by the Conservancy is repurchased by New York State and incorporated into the Forest Preserve.
2. The Conservancy acquires, rather than fee title, an easement by which existing private ownership is retained, but the development rights are owned by the Conservancy, protecting the land against misuse in the future.
3. Where circumstances warrant, a tract may be held by the Conservancy and administered by it either because its uniqueness merits special protection or because it can serve as a focus for environmental, educational and research activities in conjunction with area schools and colleges.

Since its founding in 1971, the Adirondack Conservancy has completed the following projects in the Adirondack Park:

1972	Santanoni. 12,500 acres. Transferred to NY State
1972	Pack Forest. 12 acres. Transferred to CESFSNY
1972	Dunham Bay Wetlands. 1400 acres. Transferred to NY State
1973	Cherry Patch Pond. 375 acres. Transferred to NY State
1973	Shelving Rock Falls. 250 acres. Transferred to NY State
1974	Everton Falls. 529 acres. A.C. Preserve (purchased)
1974	Monty Bay Wetlands. 200 acres. Transferred to NY State
1974	Seton, Valcour Island. 129 acres. Transferred to NY State
1975	Silver Lake Camp Preserve. 52.8 acres. A.C. Preserve (gift)
1975	Big Simon's Pond Preserve. 5 acres. A.C. Preserve (gift)
1975	Big Simon's Easement. 50 acres. Land retained by owner
1975	Pack Forest addition. 3 acres. Transferred to CESFSNY
1976	Riparius Canoe access. 1 acre. Transferred to NY State
1976	Silver Lake addition. 8 acres. A.C. Preserve (gift)
1977	Camp Riverdale. 89 acres. Transferred to NY State
1977	A.G. Paine Preserve. 17 acres. A.C. Preserve (gift)
1977	A.G. Paine Easement. 470 acres. Land retained by owner
1978	Ne Ha Sa Ne Park. 14,600 acres. Transferred to NY State
1978	Ne Ha Sa Ne Easement. 10,000 acres. Land retained by owner
1978	Otterbrook Preserve. 50 acres. A.C. Preserve
1978	Otterbrook Easement. 4,756 acres. Land retained by owner
1978	Brandon Easement. 27,124 acres. Land retained by owner
1979	Headlands Preserve. 4.5 acres. A.C. Preserve (gift)
1979	Headlands Easement. 545 acres. Land retained by owner
1979	Bay Pond Easement. 21,383 acres. Land retained by owner
1980	Alder Brook Park. 2735 acres (gift). Land to be transferred to NY State
1981	Four Brothers Islands. 17.8 acres. A.C. Preserve
1982	Orton Easement. 24.5 acres. Land retained by owner.
1982	Alder Brook Park Easement 1200 acres. Land retained by owner

There are three properties retained as nature preserves by the Adirondack Conservancy which are open for the public to visit and enjoy. These are:

EVERTON FALLS PRESERVE. 529.9 acres in Santa Clara, Franklin County. Located on the Red Tavern Road (Route 99), 8 miles west of Duane Corners on Route 30 and 7 miles east of St. Regis Falls. The preserve protects one and a half miles of the St. Regis River, including the impressive 18 foot Everton Falls. The range in elevation on the tract, which includes slopes of Conger Mountain and Mutton Ridge, is 350 feet. Deer are occasionally sighted on sandbars; signs of their presence are everywhere. Beaver actively dam the brooks. A guide to two trails through the heavily wooded preserve is available from the Adirondack Conservancy.

SILVER LAKE CAMP PRESERVE. 62.8 acres near Hawkeye, Clinton County. Located on the Union Falls Rd. between Hawkeye and Rt. 3. From AuSable Forks on Rt. 9N, take the Silver Lake Rd. to Hawkeye, then west on the Union Falls Rd. about one mile to the Silver Lake Camp Road. The preserve encompasses ten distinctive vegitational communities with a minimum of 182 vascular plant species in 43 families. By walking the property line, more or less, one passes through an outstanding spruce bog, a hardwood forest, and eventually comes to a bluff with white and red pines overlooking Silver Lake and an excellent view. The bog is best viewed from the Conservancy's 600 foot boardwalk which can be reached from a parking area clearly marked along Silver Lake Camp Rd. A map and more detailed description are available from the Adirondack Conservancy.

BIG SIMON'S POND PRESERVE. 5 acres near Tupper Lake, Franklin County. To visit the Conservancy's 5 acre island at the easterly end of Big Simon's Pond, launch a canoe or boat at the New York State launch site, just south of the Simon's Pond outlet on Route 30, south of Tupper Lake. The island contains a conifers stand. Along the shore of Simon's Pond, the Conservancy also holds an easement on 75 acres, including 5,800 feet of unspoiled shoreline with mature northern hardwoods and some conifers. A beautiful canoe ride and great picnic spot, but no fires or camping on the island. A map and more details are available from the Adirondack Conservancy.

For more information on the Adirondack Conservancy and any of the three preserves open to the public, write Tim Barnett, Executive Director, Adirondack Conservancy, Box 188, Elizabethtown, NY 12932.

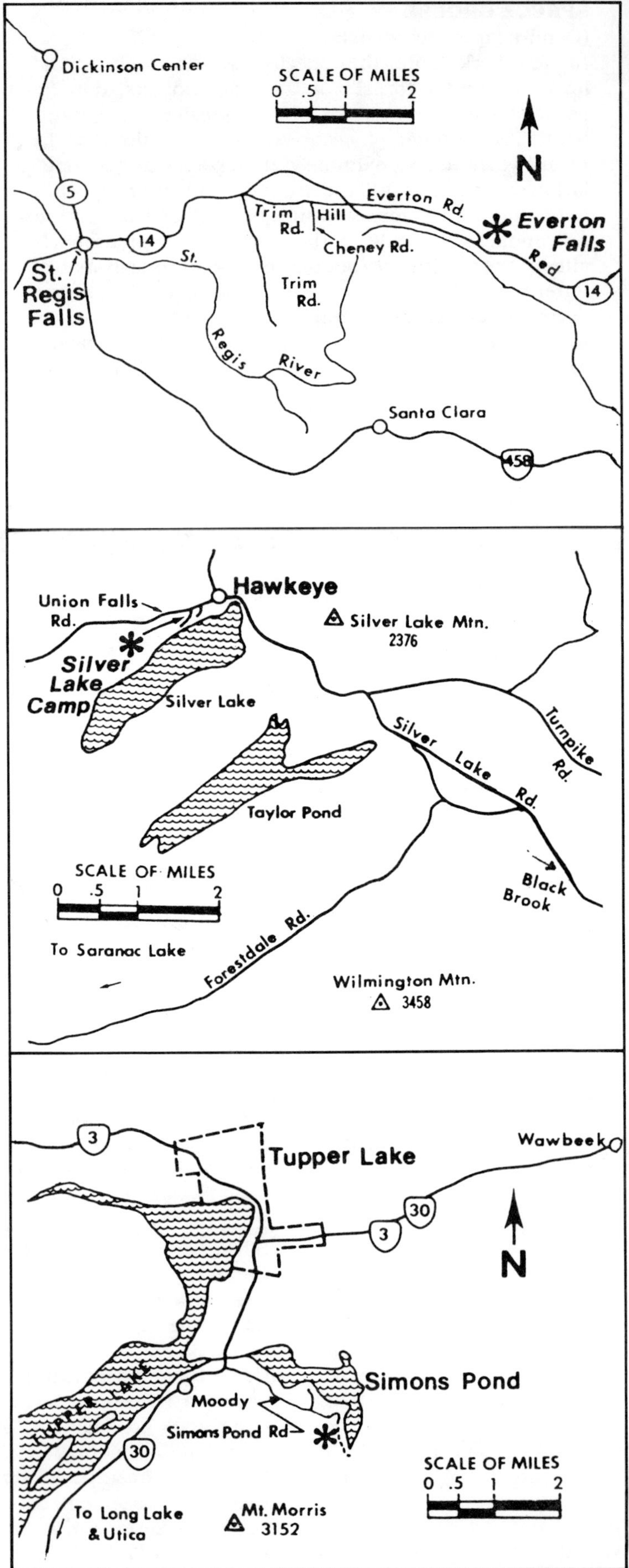

ARTS & CRAFTS

(68)
ARTS CENTERS AND COUNCILS

ADIRONDACK LAKES CENTER FOR THE ARTS, Blue Mountain Lake, NY 12812. Classes, demonstrations, films, performances and workshops throughout the year. Courses and workshops in photography, jewelry, pottery, weaving, batik, print making, wood working, dance, creative writing. Also sells crafts and art supplies. Elizabeth Folwell, Director. Information: (518)352-7715.

CENTER FOR MUSIC, DRAMA AND ART, Saranac Ave., Lake Placid, NY 12946. A vast number of programs and services available at the Center: professional theatre, art and dance classes, library, Lake Placid Sinfonietta, concerts, crafts, films, lectures, Fine Arts Gallery, Parson's School of Design's summer workshops, Performing and Visual Arts fellowship program. Offering workshops in watercolor, modern dance, woodcarving, calligraphy, etc. Joan Harvey, Director. Information: (518)523-2512.

COMMUNITY ARTS CENTER, Rt. 28, Old Forge, NY 13420. Monthly art exhibits, summer dance, drama and musical performances, classes in folk and fine arts, photography, films. Two-week national watercolor seminar, residency program in photography. Craft gift shop. Lorraine Stripp, Director. Information: (315)369-6411.

LAKE GEORGE ARTS PROJECT, INC., Canada St., Lake George, NY 12845. Art exhibits, poetry series, lecture series and summer concert series throughout Warren County. John Strong, Director. Information: (518) 668-2616.

LOWER ADIRONDACK REGIONAL ARTS COUNCIL, INC., (LARAC) PO Box 659, 10 Ridge St., Glens Falls, NY 12801. Information: (518)798-1144.

THE STUDIO: A CREATIVE ARTS CENTER FOR CHILDREN, 13 Church St., Saranac Lake, NY 12983. Year round classes for adults and children in music, arts and crafts, drama, aerobics, dance. Barbara Damp, Director. Information: (518)891-1011.

(69)
GALLERIES

ADIRONDACK ART ASSOCIATION SCHOOLHOUSE GALLERY, Rt. 22, Essex, NY 12936. Three shows of Essex county artists; each show lasting 3 weeks during the summer months. Paintings, sculptures, prints and crafts for sale. Information: (518)963-7270.

ADIRONDACK MUSEUM, Blue Mountain Lake, NY 12812. Two galleries have changing exhibits of paintings and photographs from the museum's collections; also special exhibitions every one-two years. Information: (518)352-7311 or 7312.

ADIRONDACK CENTER MUSEUM, Court St., Elizabethtown, NY 12932. Contemporary art exhibits by regional artists. Open May 15-October 15. Information: (518) 873-6466.

ADIRONDACK STORE AND GALLERY, Saranac-Lake Placid Road, (Rt. 86), Ray Brook, NY 12977. Largest commercial gallery in the Adirondacks featuring exhibits by local artists. Open June-September. Additional exhibit at Lake Placid Hilton open daily. Information: (518) 891-2880.

ADIRONDACK YESTERYEARS, INC., Lower Saranac Lake, NY 12983. Representative collection of vintage oil and watercolor paintings. Appointment preferred. Information: (518)891-3206.

ART COMPANY, THE, 6 Dorsey St., Saranac Lake, NY 12983. Contemporary and traditional Adirondack art. Information: (518)891-2270.

ARTISAN SHOP, Rt. 73, Keene Valley, NY 12943. Wood sculpture, Adirondack paintings and photographs. Information: (518)576-4510.

CARPENTER AND PAINTER GALLERY, 2 1/2 miles north off Rt. 9, Elizabethtown, NY 12932. Open year round, Monday-Saturday 10-5, Sunday 1-5 or by appointment. Information: (518)873-9830.

COMMUNITY ART CENTER, Rt. 28, Old Forge, NY 13420. Monthly exhibits of regional artists, photographers, crafts persons, painters. Seasonal hours, June-October, call for details. Information: (315)369-6411.

DEPOT THEATRE, Westport, NY 12993. Lobby art shows. May-September. Information: (518)962-4449.

FINE ARTS GALLERY, Center for Music, Drama and Art, Saranac Ave., Lake Placid, NY 12946. Gallery art shows, juried shows. Information: (518)523-2512.

JEANNE HASTINGS GALLERY AND WORKSHOP, Old Stone Schoolhouse, Middle Rd., Lake George, NY 12845. Painting, oil and water color classes. Information: (518) 668-5195.

LAKE PLACID GALLERY, 5 Main St., Lake Placid, NY 12946. Information: (518)523-2330.

THE STUDIO, 15 Main St., Lake Placid, NY 12946. Oil and water colors, unique crafts, woodcarvings, dolls, etc. Information: (518)523-3589.

SIGNIFICANT GALLERIES OUTSIDE THE ADIRONDACK PARK.

HYDE COLLECTION, 161 Warren St., Glens Falls, NY 12801. Paintings and sculptures from 5thC BC-20thC AD informally displayed among a large collection of European furniture and decorative arts. Closed January and major holidays. Admission fee. Information: (518) 792-1761. Fredrick Fisher, Director.

KENT GALLERY, S.U.N.Y. Plattsburgh, Plattsburgh, NY 12901. Permanent exhibit of paintings and drawings of Rockwell Kent. Ed Brohel, Director. Information: (518) 564-2288.

MUNSON-WILLIAMS-PROCTOR INSTITUTE, 310 Genesee St., Utica, NY 13502. The Institute is comprised of three major divisions: the Museum of Art, Performing Arts, and the School of Art. The Museum of Art's collection contains 19th and 20th century American and European paintings, drawings, prints, sculpture and decorative arts. The decorative arts collection is housed in Fountain Elms, a restored 1850 Victorian house-museum adjacent to the museum. The Performing Arts Division offers events ranging from major concerts to intimate dramatic readings. Approximately 40 events dealing with music, literature, drama and film were sponsored last year by the Performing Arts Division. The School of Arts enrolls nearly 2,000 students during the summer, fall and spring semesters. Classes are offered in painting, drawing, sculpture, pottery, ceramics, printmaking, photography, silkscreen, quilting and dancing. Museum of Art Director: Paul D. Schweizer. Performing Arts Coordinator: Douglas D. Himes. School of Art Director: Clyde McCulley. Information: (315)797-0000.

FREDERIC REMINGTON MUSEUM, 303 Washington St., Ogdensburg, NY 13669. Collection includes Remington's paintings and sculptures, library, personal memorabilia and a re-creation of his studio. The Remington Collection contains 14 bronzes, 7 oils, 140 original water-colors and several hundred pen and ink sketches by Fredric Remington. Hours: Monday through Saturday (open all year) 10:00 am-5:00 pm. Closed most major holidays. Donation $2.00 for Adults, $1.00 for students and Senior Citizens, Children 12 and under free of charge. Special rates for bus tours and groups. Executive Director, Mr. Bruce Eldredge. Director, Mildred Dillenbeck. Information: (315)369-2425.

(70)
OUTDOOR SCULPTURE AND ART

This listing includes those examples of larger outdoor sculpture and art which may be viewed from the roadside while driving through the Adirondacks.

WARRENSBURG BICENTENNIAL MURAL, Rt. 9N, Warrensburg, Warren County. Huge mural on the side wall of the Museum of Local History, approximately 70 feet long and 25 feet high, depicting 163 years (1813-1976) of progress in town of Warrensburg.

BEAR'S DEN RESTAURANT, Rt. 28, Inlet, Hamilton County. Forest mural over restaurant sign.

WOODEN PLATFORM SCULPTURE, Rt. 73, South of Lake Placid village, opposite Intervales Ski Jump, Essex County. 80 foot-long wooden sculpture, built for the 1980 Olympics.

FRONT FACADE, Blue Mt. Designs, Rt. 30, Blue Mt. Lake, Hamilton County. An architecturally interesting building facade, with cut-out entrance and painted design on front.

STAGE COACH ROCK, Rt. 73, at pull off on north side of road, just above Upper Cascade Lake, Essex County. Remarkably detailed image of team of horses and stage-coach chiseled into rock, commemorating early days of stage travel on this road.

SILO SCULPTURE, Old Military Rd., (Keene Rd.) Lake Placid, Essex County. Artist: Nancy Lyons. Commissioned for 1980 Olympics.

(71)
ADIRONDACKANA

The four stores below contain outstanding collections of books, antiques, art, crafts and other items pertinent to the Adirondacks. In all cases, the quality is high and the inventory is varied. For gifts, research or browsing they are all recommended. Collectively they have done much to add to our appreciation of the Adirondack region. (Stores that sell primarily Adirondack art and crafts are included in Section 74.)

ADIRONDACK MUSEUM BOOK SHOP, Adirondack Museum, Rt. 30, Blue Mt. Lake, NY 12812. Open to all museum visitors, June 15-October 15, 10am-5pm, daily. Books, slides, prints, maps, and souvenirs. Craig Gilborn, Director. (518)352-7311 or 7312.

ADIRONDACK STORE AND GALLERY, Saranac-Lake Placid Rd., Ray Brook, NY 12983. Art gallery, books, crafts, gifts, furniture. Open June-September. Sally Packard, proprietor. Also located at Hilton Hotel, Lake Placid.

WILDWOOD, Rt. 28, Old Forge, NY 13420. Adirondack specialists. Old and new books, paintings, prints, maps, pack baskets, antiques and old boats. Appraisals. Ted and Sara Comstock, proprietors. (315)369-3397.

WITH PIPE AND BOOK, 117 Main St., Lake Placid, NY 12946. Old and rare books, maps, paintings, prints and ephemera. Breck and Julie Turner, proprietors. (518) 523-9096.

(72)
ADIRONDACK ARTISTS

Listed below are the most famous and most important Adirondack artists, that is, acclaimed artists who painted a significant number of Adirondack subjects in their careers. Criteria for inclusion are: citation in historical texts, acclaim in art publications and current periodicals, frequency of display in Adirondack galleries, and editors' choice. To be included, they need not to have resided in the Adirondacks, nor made the Adirondacks the major subject of their work.

Artists in the first grouping are deceased. The second group are living and working today, which makes the selection much more difficult, more subjective, and without the benefit of historical perspective.

John W. Casilear (1811-1893)
Samuel Coleman (1832-1920)
Jasper Cropsey (1823-1900)
A.B. (Asher Brown) Durand (1796-1886)
Sanford R. Gifford (1823-1880)
James Hart (1821-1901)
William Hart (1823-1894)
Winslow Homer (1836-1910)
John F. Kensett (1816-1872)
Rockwell Kent (1882-1971)
Jonas Lie (1880-1940)
H.D. (Homer Dodge) Martin (1833-1909)
A. (Nelson Augustus) Moore (1824-1902)
L.W. (Levi Wells) Prentice (1851-1935)
Fredric Remington (1861-1909)
Sanford Robinson (1823-1880)
James N. Rosenberg (1874-1970)
J.D. (James David) Smillie (1883- 1909)
Roswell M. Shurtleff (1838-1915)
Gustav Stewart, dates unknown
Seneca Ray Stoddard (1844-1917)
A.F. (Arthur Fitzwilliam) Tait (1819-1905)
Alexander Wyant (1836-1892)

LIVING ARTISTS

Peter Jennerjohn, Jay
Ryland Loos, Albany
Bruce Mitchell, Keene Valley
Robert Plumb, Hannawa Falls
Jean Reynolds, Cranberry Falls
Mimi Rockerfeller, Ampersand Lake
Ruth Rumney, Mineville
Slayton Underhill, Wilmington
Don Wynn, formerly Blue Mt. Lake, now Potsdam

Seneca Ray Stoddard, artist and photographer.

(73)
ADIRONDACK PHOTOGRAPHERS

This listing includes photographers of Adirondack subjects whose work has been prominently featured in historical contexts (first grouping) or contemporary works (second grouping). Selection criteria: prominence in history; frequency of publication in contemporary magazines especially *Adirondack Life;* Adirondack stores and galleries; editors' choice.

Seneca Ray Stoddard	(1844-1917)
Edward Bierstadt,	dates unknown
Edward Gockeler	(1898-1972)
Fredrick A. ("Adirondack") Hodges	(1888-1959)
William Kollecker	(1879-1962)
George Baldwin,	dates unknown
Irving Stedman	(1875-1957)

Tony Atwill, Dorset, Vermont
Francis Bayle, Glens Falls, NY
Robin Brown, Plattsburgh, NY
George and Barrie Rolleston Cannon, Ithaca, NY
Albert Gates, Port Henry, NY
Anne LaBastille, Big Moose, NY
Richard Linke, Saratoga Springs, NY
Robert A. Lubeck, Rome, NY
Jean Marsh, Blue Mt. Lake, NY
Gary Randorf, Elizabethtown, NY
Clyde Smith, Wadhams, NY
Kenneth Wilson, Panama, NY

See also Eliot Porter, *Forever Wild: the Adirondacks* (Blue Mt. Lake/New York City: Adirondack Museum and Harper and Row, 1966).

(74)
ADIRONDACK CRAFT STORES AND STUDIOS

Many of the stores and studios listed below specialize in particular types of crafts, while others carry a more general selection of products. When the handcrafts featured are too numerous to list individually, these are usually described as "various crafts", and only specialties are identified. The establishments are open year-round unless otherwise noted. Demonstrations, tours and classes, if offered, often are not on a fixed schedule, and it is wise to call before visiting. Admission is free unless noted.

CLINTON

AUSABLE CHASM RECREATION CENTER, INC. Glassblowing. May 14-October 16, daily 10-5. Demonstrations. US Rt. 9, Ausable Chasm, NY 12911. (On grounds of Ausable Chasm on US 9 1.5 miles north of Keeseville) (518)834-7454.

ESSEX

ADIRONDACK STORE AND GALLERY. Various arts and crafts. Two locations: Rt. 86, Raybrook, NY 12977. Open June-September. Lake Placid Hilton, Lake Placid, NY 12946. Daily, year round. Write for free catalog. Drawer 991, Lake Placid, NY 12946. (518)891-2880.

BAILEY'S BOATS. Builder of wood-strip guide-boats. Keene, NY 12942. (518)576-9709.

CARRIAGE HOUSE MUSEUM AND MORIAH CRAFTS. Various crafts. June 20-October 12 daily 10:30-4. Moriah Center, NY 12961. (On NY 9N/NY 22 south of Port Henry)

ESSEX INDUSTRIES. Workshop for the mentally handicapped, making canoe seats, canoe chairs, carrying yokes, various other products. Mineville, NY 12956. (518) 942-6671.

JAY CRAFT CENTER AND SILVER LAKE POTTERY. Pottery studio and gift shop. Monday-Saturday 10-5. Quality handcrafts.Route 9N, Jay, NY 12941. (On NY 9N .1 mile south of junction with NY 86) (518)946-7824.

JIM ZYNSKY. Makes guide-boat oars, canoe seats, etc. Keene, NY 12942.

LA DUE'S ARTS AND CRAFTS SHOP. Various crafts. Daily 10-10. 334 Montcalm St., Ticonderoga, NY 12883. (From NY 9N, east on Montcalm St. .3 miles) (518) 585-7715.

NORTH COUNTRY CRAFT CO-OP. Various crafts. Year round, Monday-Saturday 10-5. Westport, NY 12993. (On Main St., i.e., NY 9N/NY 22, next to bank) (518)962-8905.

HORNBECK BOATS. Ultra-light pack canoes, fiberglass guide-boats. Daily 9-5. Demonstrations. Trout Brook Rd., Olmstedville, NY 12857. (From NY 28N to Olmstedville, east on Trout Brook Rd. .6 mi) (518)251-2764.

PENFIELD HOMESTEAD MUSEUM. Various crafts. May 15-October 15. Tuesday-Sunday 10-5; October 16-May 14 by appointment. Donation. Ironville National Historic District, Crown Point, NY 12928. (From NY 74, north on Corduroy Rd. to Ironville) (518)597-3804.

THE STUDIO. Various crafts. Open year-round. 15 Main St., Lake Placid, NY 12946. (On Main St. at Saranac Ave.) (518)523-3589.

WESTPORT TRADING COMPANY. Custom stained-glass windows, antiques. Tues-Sun 9-5 or by appointment. Westport, NY 12993. (518)962-4801.

FRANKLIN

ART COMPANY, THE. Works by local artists, art supplies and custom framing. 6 Dorsey St., Saranac Lake, NY 12983. (518)891-2270.

AVIS BROWN. Wildlife wood carving. Call ahead. Red Tavern Rd., Star Route, Malone, NY 12953. (From junction of NY 30 and NY 99, west on Red Tavern Rd. .2 miles) (518)483-4599.

CARL HATHAWAY. Traditional guide-boat builder. Saranac Lake, NY 12983. (518)891-3961.

LONG POND FORGE. Silver jewelry. Monday-Friday 11-5, call ahead. RD 1, St. Regis Falls, NY 12980. (From NY 72 in St. Regis Falls, north on Main St. 2 blocks, east on Duane St. or Red Tavern Rd. 3 miles, right on Trim Rd. .5 miles) (518)856-9926.

NORTH WOODS CRAFT CO-OP. Hand made clothing, toys, quilts, pillows and other crafts. Monday-Saturday 10-5. 33 Main St., Saranac Lake, NY 12983. (Across from town hall.) (518)891-5849.

FULTON

THE DEPOT. Antiques, handcrafts, doll house miniatures. June-December, Saturday 10-5, Sunday 12-5; July-August Monday-Friday 12-5. PO Box 217, Broadalbin, NY 12025. (From NY 29, north on S. Second Ave. .4 miles, east on W. Main St. .4 miles to Railroad St., in old railroad depot) (518)883-3928.

GREEN'S CUSTOM SNOW SHOES. Snow shoes. Monday-Friday 9-5pm; Saturday-Sunday 7am-9pm; call ahead. Demonstrations. RD 1, Broadalbin, NY 12025. (From Broadalbin, east on NY 29, 4 miles, north on CR 14 3.6 miles through Hagedorns Mills, left on Ryden Rd. .1 mile, right on Lampman Rd. 1.6 miles, left on CR 136 .2 miles) (518)883-3703.

HAMILTON

ADIRONDACK LAKES CENTER FOR THE ARTS. Crafts shop with various crafts. July-August Monday-Saturday 10-4; September-June Monday-Saturday 10-4; call ahead. Demonstrations and classes and workshops. Blue Mountain Lake, NY 12812. (On NY 28 .3 miles west of junction of NY 28 and NY 30) (518)352-7715.

BLUE MT. DESIGNS. Crafts in all media, watercolors, photography. May-October daily 10-5. Blue Mountain Lake, NY 12812. (On NY 28N/NY 30 .1 miles north of junction of NY 28 and NY 30) (518)352-7361.

CHIMNEY MOUNTAIN CRAFTSMEN. Pine furniture and decorative accessories. Indian Lake, NY 12842. (On Rt. 28, on western edge of town) (518)648-5255.

ED'S POT SHOP. Stoneware pottery. May-December, daily, 9-9pm. Demonstrations. PO Box 343, Long Lake, NY 12847. (.5 miles north of Long Lake on NY 30, northeast on Walker Rd. .1 mile) (518)624-4505.

MOUNTAIN TOY MAKERS. Wooden toys. Monday-Saturday 10-4, call ahead. Demonstrations. Box 51, Long Lake, NY 12847. (On Walker Rd., 4 houses past junction, Rice Rd. on left, gray house) (518)624-6175.

"OVER THE BRIDGE" CRAFTS. Various crafts. September 17-October 30 Saturday 10-5, Sunday 1-7; July-August Friday 10-6, Saturday 10-5, Sunday 1-7. PO Box 54, North River, NY 12956. (Off NY 28 3.3 miles north of North River). (518)251-3160.

JAMIE SUTLIFF. Rustic furniture. Long Lake, NY 12847. (518)624-3581.

WOODCARVINGS BY RICK AND ELLEN BUTZ. Regional wildlife and folk carvings of the Adirondacks. Please call in advance if possible, (518)352-7737. Blue Mountain Lake, NY 12812. (1/4 mile north of the Adirondack Museum).

HERKIMER

BANJO SHOP, THE. Banjos, dulcimers; repair and construction. July-August daily 9-9; September-June Saturday-Sunday 9-9. Box 44, Old Forge, NY 13420. (On NY 28 .5 miles north of railroad trestle in Thendara) (315)369-6872.

COMMUNITY ARTS CENTER. Pottery, silversmithing, weaving, macrame, jewelry and fine arts shop. Seasonal hours, call for details. Classes, preformances, demonstrations, exhibits and films. Old Forge, NY 13420. (On NY 28 .1 mile west of Hollister Rd. 1/4 mile north of the village.) (315)369-6411.

HAND OF MAN, THE. Main St., Old Forge, NY 13420. Pottery, wood carvings, St. Lukes glass, art & craft supplies. Open daily, July-August; Saturdays 9-5, year round except April. (315)369-3381.

HOLLY WOODWORKING. Wooden gift ware, decorative accessories, carvings. June-August 9-9; September-May 10-5. Old Forge, NY 13420. (On NY 28 at junction of Hollister Rd.) (315)369-3757.

MORNING SUN, THE. Goods from the woods, Native American and other crafts. June-September open 6 1/2 days. Off season-limited hours. Crosby Blvd., Old Forge, NY 13420. (315)369-3181.

OLD FORGE HARDWARE, INC. Various crafts. June 25-September 5 Monday-Saturday 8-9, Sunday 10-3; September 6-June 24 Monday-Saturday 8-5. Old Forge, NY 13420. (On NY 28 near junction with Crosby Blvd.) (315)369-6100.

OLD FORGE WOODMAKER. Wooden furniture and other crafts. Open year-round, 9am-4:30pm. Box 468, Old Forge, NY 13420. (One block west of Main intersection in center of town) (315)369-3535.

ST. LAWRENCE

LEATHER ARTISAN SHOP. Leather and silversmithing. Open year round: daily 10-6, June-August; closed Tuesdays September-December; closed Tuesday and Wednesday January-May. Childwold, NY 12922. (On NY 3 .2 miles west of Tupper Lake) (518)359-3102.

SARATOGA

BRUNO LA VERDIERE. Sculpture and drawing. By appointment only. Rt. 1, Box 268, Hadley, NY 12835. (From Hadley, north on Stony Creek Rd. 2.4 miles, left on dirt road, left fork to end) (518)696-3569.

WARREN

FIFE AND DRUM GIFT SHOPPE. Wooden furniture and other crafts. June-August daily 10-9; September-May Thursday-Tuesday 10-6. Demonstrations. Box 315, Chestertown, NY 12817. (On Main St. or US 9 .5 miles south of NY 8 junction).

HEITZ'S RUSTIC FURNITURE. Quality Adirondack rustic furniture. Look for rustic chair or bed sitting on north side of Rt. 28, half-way between Indian Lake and North Creek. Box 161, Indian Lake, New York, 12842. (518) 251-3327

MUSEUM OF LOCAL HISTORY. Various crafts. July-September Tuesday-Saturday 1-5, also Thursday-Friday 10-12; October-June by appointment. Demonstrations. Donations. 8 Orton Dr., Warrensburg, NY 12885. (I-87 Exit 23, east to US 9, north .6 miles to corner of Main St. and Horicon Ave.) (518)623-2928.

NATURAL STONE BRIDGE AND CAVES ROCK AND MINERAL SHOP. Jewelry, rocks, minerals, and gemstones; cutting and polishing. Memorial Day-Columbus Day. Demonstrations. Stonebridge Rd., Pottersville, NY 12860. (From US 9, west on Natural Stone Bridge Rd. 2 miles) (518)494-2283.

RED TRUCK CLAY WORKS. Pottery. March-December: Daily 9-5. January-February by appointment. Dennehy Rd., Chestertown, NY 12817. (From Rt. 9, east on Dennehy Rd.)

STONY CREEK YARN SHOPPE AND PETITE BOUTIQUE. Various crafts. July 1 to Labor Day. Monday-Saturday 10-5, Sunday 1-4. Winter Hours: closed Tuesdays. Wednesday-Saturday, 10-5. Demonstrations. 4565 Warrensburg Rd., Stony Creek, NY 12878. (On Warrensburg Rd. or CR 3 .5 miles southeast of Stony Creek).

Lewis, Oneida and Washington Counties have none in the Adirondack Park.

Original source: New York State, Office of Lt. Governor Mary Anne Krupsak, North Country Craft Trail Map, 1977. Many deletions and additional material added.

ENTERTAINMENT

(75)
CONCERTS AND THEATRES

ADIRONDACK FESTIVAL OF AMERICAN MUSIC, Adirondack Festival of Music, Box 562, Saranac Lake, NY 12983. A series of 25 concerts featuring American music, classical and contemporary, offered in different locations throughout the Lake Placid-Saranac Lake area. Information: (518)523-2512 or (518)891-1990.

ADIRONDACK LAKES CENTER FOR THE ARTS, Blue Mountain Lake, NY 12812. Series of traditional, classical and jazz concerts and professional theatre throughout the summer. Concerts at 8:30 pm Thursdays and theatre 8:30pm on Sundays. Coffee houses and square dancing year round. Information: (518)352-7715.

ADIRONDACK LAKES SUNSET CONCERTS, Chestertown, NY 12817. On Dynamite Hill. Early July through early August. Information: Sunset Concerts, Chamber of Commerce, Chestertown, NY 12817.

ADIRONDACK SUMMER MUSIC FESTIVAL, North Country Community College, Saranac Lake, NY 12983. Sponsored by Adirondack Studies Program, North Country Community College. Information: (518)891-2915.

BAND CONCERTS, Old Forge, NY 13420. Sunday nights, at lakefront. Summer months. Information: (315) 369-6983.

CENTER FOR MUSIC, DRAMA AND ART (CMDA), Saranac Ave., Lake Placid, NY 12946. Year-round theatre and concerts; nightly during the summer. Information: (518) 523-2512.

CONCERT SERIES, Saranac Lake, NY 12983. Riverside Park Bandshell. Every Friday evening, July and early August. Free. Information: Chamber of Commerce, (518) 891-1990.

DEPOT THEATRE, Westport, NY 12993. Dance recitals, concerts, cabarets, plays. Memorial Day weekend through Labor Day weekend. Information: (518)962-4449.

ELM TREE CONCERTS, Box 79, Westport, NY 12993. Chamber music concerts in an old fashioned farmhouse. Reservations suggested. Information: (518)546-8256.

JAVA JIVE COFFEEHOUSE, 68 Main St., Saranac Lake, NY 12983. Folk, jazz, blues, poetry and comedy programs. Food and drink. Open to all ages. No cover charge. Seasonal calendar available. Information: (518)891-4647.

JOHN VINTON, spellbinding storyteller featuring the all-time greats of Adirondack literature. Performs at many educational and entertainment events. Information: 167 Hicks St., Brooklyn, NY 11201. (212) 522-5588.

LAKE GEORGE DINNER THEATRE, Holiday Inn, Lake George, NY 12845. Smorgasbord dinner and professional Broadway theatre. Season begins the end of June through mid-October. Information: (518)668-5781 or 668-9258.

LAKE GEORGE OPERA SUMMER FESTIVAL, Box 425, Glens Falls, NY 12801. Performances during July and August at Queensbury Festival Auditorium, Glens Falls; Performing Arts Center, Saratoga Springs; Blenheim Mansion, Lake George and Opera-on-the-Lake Cruises, Lake George. Information: before July 1st: (518)793-3858, after July 1st: (518) 793-6642.

LAKE PLACID SINFONIETTA, Box 1242, Lake Placid, NY 12983. An ensemble of master musicians playing throughout the Lake Placid area for six weeks, special events, guest artists. Information: Center for Music, Drama and Art, (518)523-2512.

LUZERNE CHAMBER MUSIC FESTIVAL, Lake Tour Rd., Lake Luzerne, NY 12846. A series of weekly Tuesday evening concerts featuring members of the Philadelphia Orchestra in small ensembles. Early July-late August. Concerts held at The Grand Lodge at the Luzerne Music Center. Information: PO Box 35, Lake Luzerne, NY 12846. (518)696-2771.

MAPLEWOOD MUSIC FESTIVAL, Wadhams Rd., Elizabethtown, NY 12932. Year round concerts of classical music. Summer Festival of Baroque Music on original instruments at the Essex County Courthouse and other sites in Essex and Clinton Counties. Information: (518) 873-2169.

MEADOWMOUNT SCHOOL OF MUSIC, Wadhams-Lewis Rd., Westport, NY 12993. String concerts are held for the public on Wednesday and Sunday evenings during the summer, 7:30 pm at the Edward Lee and Jean Campe Memorial Music Hall. Information: (518)873-2063.

NORTH COUNTRY COMMUNITY COLLEGE CHORALE and COMMUNITY BAND, 20 Winona Ave., Saranac Lake, NY 12983. Two major annual concerts and numerous concerts throughout the region. Information: George Reynolds, (518)891-2915.

SENNET, 68 Main St., Saranac Lake, NY 12983. Theatrical productions by a coalition of professional and community artists. Full summer schedule; periodic winter productions. Available for bookings; flexible in terms of adaptation to available space and fee structure. Information: (518)891-1854.

TICONDEROGA FESTIVAL GUILD INC., Montcalm St., Ticonderoga, NY 12883. Concerts on the Green at the Community Building during July and August. Information: (518)585-6716.

WADHAMS PLAYERS, Wadhams United Church of Christ, Parish Hall, Wadhams, NY 12990. Productions at announced times. Information: (518)962-4826.

(76)
MOVIE THEATRES

Some of the theatres below are seasonal, with the length of the season sometimes varying, depending on the weather and level of tourism. Other than July and August, when all are open, it is advisable to call the theatre to check its schedule.

GAIETY THEATRE, Rt. 28, Inlet, NY 13360. (315) 357-4552.

HARBOR THEATRE, Mirror Lake Drive, Lake Placid, NY 12946. (518)523-8165.

PALACE THEATRE, 26 Main St., Lake Placid, NY 12946. (518)523-9271.

SKY-LINE DRIVE-IN, Crown Point, NY 12928.

STATE THEATRE, 181 Montcalm St., Ticonderoga, NY 12883. (518)585-6636.

STRAND THEATRE, Main St., Old Forge, NY 13420. (315)369-6703.

STRAND THEATRE, Main St., Schroon Lake, NY 12870. (518)532-9300.

In addition to these commercial theatres, a number of art centers and community centers offer various film series, at different times of the year.

ADIRONDACK LAKES CENTER FOR THE ARTS, Blue Mountain Lake, NY 12812. Movies shown year-round at the center and Blue Mt. Lake area. Information: (518) 352-7715.

CENTER FOR MUSIC, DRAMA AND ART, Saranac Ave, Lake Placid, NY 12946. Several six-week film series for adults and children. Spring, summer, fall. Information: (518)523-2515.

COMMUNITY ARTS CENTER, Rt. 28, Old Forge, NY 13420. Old-time classics movie series, Tuesday nights, summer months, 8pm. Information: (315)369-6411.

ELIZABETHTOWN SOCIAL CENTER, Rt. 9, Box 250, Elizabethtown, NY 12932. Silent film classics, Thursday evenings, summer months. Information: (518)873-6408.

LAKE GEORGE HISTORICAL ASSOCIATION, PO Box 472, Lake George, NY 12845. Wednesday Night Movie Festivals, 8pm, summer months. Information: (518) 668-5044.

RADIO AND TELEVISION STATIONS

Listed first are those radio stations with transmission headquarters inside the Adirondack Park. Following are those radio and television stations transmitting on the perimeter of the Park and received within the Blue Line. There are no television stations located within the Adirondacks.

TRANSMITTING FROM WITHIN THE ADIRONDACKS

WIPS-RADIO. AM 1250. 1kw. Adult contemporary, more than thirty hours of news weekly. Information: Lake George Ave., Ticonderoga, NY 12883. (518)585-2868.

WIRD-RADIO. AM 920 and FM 105.5 (WLPW). 5kw, daytime only. Located in Holiday Inn. Information: 1 Olympic Dr., Lake Placid, NY 12946. (518)523-3341.

WNBZ-RADIO. AM 1240. 1240kw, 6am-10:15pm. Located at Radio Park. Serving the northern Adirondacks. Information: Box 211, Saranac Lake, NY 12983. (518)891-1544.

WTPL-RADIO. FM 102.3. 75kw. News, weather, information and entertainment. Information: Moody Rd., Tupper Lake, NY 12986. (518)359-2900.

WXTY-RADIO. FM 103.9. 3kw, live 24 hours daily. Adult contemporary, advertising and broadcasting from all major events in the area. Information: Lake George Ave., Ticonderoga, NY 12883. (518)585-2868.

TRANSMITTING FROM OUTSIDE THE ADIRONDACKS

WADR-RADIO. AM 1480. 5kw. Country music, daytime only. Information: Box 1480, Remsen, NY 13438. (315) 831-3941.

WAES-RADIO. FM 93.5- Adult contemporary music, 24 hours daily. Serving all of Central New York from the Adirondack foothills. Hourly snowmobile and ski reports. Campsite reports during summer. Information: Box 1480, Remsen, NY 13438. (315)831-3941.

WASM-RADIO. FM 102.9. 3000w, beautiful stereo music. Information: 71 West Ave., Saratoga Springs, NY 12866. (518)584-1610.

WBZA-RADIO. AM 1230 and FM 107.1 (WNIQ). AM-1000w (day), 250w (night), FM-3000w. Information: PO Box 982, Everts Ave., Glens Falls, NY 12801. (518) 792-2151.

WEAV-RADIO. AM 960. 5kw., country-western music. Information: Rt. 9 South., Plattsburgh, NY 12901. (518)561-0960.

WEZF-RADIO. FM 92.7. 3600w, easy listening, 24 hours daily. Information: PO Box C-1093, Burlington, VT 05402. (802)655-3663.

WGFB RADIO. FM 100. 10kw, rock and roll music. Information: Rt. 9 South, Plattsburgh, NY 12901. (518) 561-0960.

WIBQ-RADIO. FM 98.7. 25 kw, 24 hours a day. Adult contemporary, relaxing music. Serving Central Adirondacks. Information: PO Box 950, Utica, NY 13503. (315) 736-9313.

WIBX-RADIO. AM 950. 5kw, 24 hours a day. News 6-9am, noon-1pm, 4-7pm, plus on the hour; sports in season; vacation travelers weather and road reports daily. To report news call Hotline (315)736-0780. Telephone talk 1-4pm, Monday-Friday, Big Bands 11pm-5am. Information: PO Box 950, Utica, NY 13503.

WIRY-RADIO. AM 1340. 24 hours. Contemporary music. Information: 301 Cornelia St., Plattsburgh, NY 12901. (518)563-1340.

WKAJ-RADIO. AM 900. 250w, contemporary rock. Information: 71 West Ave., Saratoga Springs, NY 12886. (518)584-1610.

WKDR-RADIO. AM 1070. 5 kw, sunrise to sunset. Country music. Information: PO Box 518, North Country Shopping Center, Plattsburgh, NY 12901. (518)561-7600.

WKTV-TELEVISION. Channel 2 (NBC), in the Utica area. Information: Smith Hill Rd., Utica NY 13503. (315) 733-0404.

WPTZ-TELEVISION. Channel 5 (NBC), in the eastern Adirondack region. Information: Old Moffitt Rd., Plattsburgh, NY 12901. (518)561-5555.

WRCK-RADIO. FM 107.3. 50kw, 24 hours daily. Rock music, American top 40 every Sunday evening. Information: Box 781, Utica, NY 13503. (315)797-1330.

WSCG-RADIO. FM 93.5. 3 kw, 24 hours. WSCG-Country 93. Modern-country format. Serving Saratoga, Warren, and Washington Counties. Information: 609A Palmer Ave., Corinth, NY 12801. (518)793-5421.

WSLU-RADIO. FM 96.7. 2.6kw, 6am-1am weekdays, 7am-1am weekends. North Country public radio station. Classical, jazz, folk, bluegrass, news and public affairs programs. Listener-supported. Program guide available. Information: WSLU-FM, Payson Hall, St. Lawrence University, Canton, NY 13617. (315)379-5356.

WSPN-RADIO. FM 91. 250 kw, 24 hours daily. Progressive rock and roll and jazz. Information: North Broadway, Saratoga Springs, NY 12866. (518)584-5770.

WTLB. AM 1310. 5 kw, 24 hours. Adult contemporary music.. Hourly local and national (ABC) news. Recreational, snowmobile and ski reports throughout the day. Telephone/talk program, "WTLB LIVE" ,weekdays 3-6pm. Information: Box 781, Utica, NY 13503. (315)797-1330.

WUTR-TELEVISION. Channel 20 (ABC), in Utica area. Eyewitness news. Information: PO Box 20, Smith Hill Rd., Deerfield, NY 13503. (315)797-5220 or 797-5332.

WWSC-RADIO. AM 1450. 1 kw, 24 hours daily. Adult contemporary. "The Station of Tri-Counties." Information: 217 Dix Ave., Glens Falls, NY 12801. (518)793-4444.

WYLR-RADIO. FM 96 (Y-96). 3kw, 24 hours daily. Full service rock radio. Information: 217 Dix Ave., Glens Falls, NY 12801. (518)793-4444.

(78)
THEME PARKS AND AMUSEMENT PARKS

ENCHANTED FOREST, Old Forge, NY 13420. Twenty-one rides including storybook favorites, train, balloon and skyrides. May 24-September 1. July-August daily 9:30am-5:30pm. May-June, Monday-Friday 10am-4pm, Saturday-Sunday 9:30am-5:30pm. Information: (315) 369-6145.

FRONTIER TOWN, North Hudson, NY 12855. Recreation of the American Frontier with two rodeos daily, largest operating stageline in the U.S., pony express and cavalry fort. Reconstructed Iroquois Village, water-powered grist mills, steam-powered saw mills and catalan forge. July-Labor Day, 9:30am-6pm. Spring and fall 10:30am-4pm. Exit 29 off I-87. Information: (518)532-7181.

GASLIGHT VILLAGE, Lake George, NY 12845. 40 rides and shows of the "Gay 90's". Cavalcade of cars, old time movies, ice show. Season: Mid-June- Labor Day. Hours 2pm-10pm. Exit 21 off I-87, take Rt. 9N. Information: (518)668-5459.

HOUSE OF FRANKENSTEIN, 213 Canada St., Lake George, NY 12845. Horror house. May, Saturday-Sunday 10am-10pm. June-October, daily 10am-10pm. Exit 21 off I-87, onto Rt. 9 North. Information: (518)668-3377.

MAGIC FOREST, Lake George, NY 12845. Home of Rex the high diving horse, Santa and his famous reindeer, bird show, and magic show. Late June-Labor Day, daily. One mile south of Lake George on Rt. 9. Information: (518)668-2448.

PAINTED PONY RODEO, Lake Luzerne, NY 12846. Oldest continuous weekly rodeo in U.S. Western bar and country dancing in the Saloon. Rodeo every Friday: July 1-September 2 at 8pm. Exit 21 off I-87, Rt. 9N. Information: (518)696-2421.

PINE LAKE AMUSEMENT PARK, Pine Lake, NY. Information: (518)835-4382.

SANTA'S WORKSHOP, Wilmington, NY 12997. Children's rides, puppet theatre and magic shows at the village home of Santa Claus and his helpers. Late June-Mid-October, daily. Located on Whiteface Mt. Highway. North Pole, NY. 12946. Information: (518)946-2211.

SHERMAN'S AMUSEMENT PARK, Caroga Lake, NY 12032. Arcade, beach, entertainment, rides, picnic area and restaurant. Information: (518)835-6171.

WATER SLIDE WORLD, Lake George, NY 12845. Three slides with over 1100 ft. of sliding, whirlpool, spas, snackbar, arcade, bicycle rentals, bumperboats and game room. Daily 10am-10pm weather permitting. Intersection of Rts. 9 and 9L. Information: (518)668-4407.

WAXLIFE, USA, Lake George, NY 12845. New York's largest wax museum featuring entertainment and historical figures. Westbrook Rd. For rates, operating hours and information: (518)668-2717. Group rates (518) 668-5459.

(79)
ANNUAL ENTERTAINMENT EVENTS CALENDAR

Note: See also Annual Educational Events Calendar (Section 43) and Annual Recreational Events Calendar (Section 101).

JANUARY

LAKE GEORGE WINTER CARNIVAL. Every weekend from mid-January to end of February. For exact times and locations of events: Greater Lake George Winter Carnival, Inc., PO Box 329, Lake George, NY 12845. (518)668-5755.

TUPPER LAKE WINTER CARNIVAL, Tupper Lake. Late January. Information: Chamber of Commerce, Tupper Lake, NY 12986. (518)359-3328.

FEBRUARY

WINTER CARNIVAL, Speculator, Lake Pleasant, Piseco. 1st weekend in February. Information: Office of Tourism, Speculator, NY 12165. (518)548-4521.

WINTER CARNIVAL, Saranac Lake. 2nd weekend in February. The oldest winter carnival in the USA. Information: Chamber of Commerce, Saranac Lake, NY 12983. (518)891-1990.

WINTER CARNIVAL, Raquette Lake. President's weekend in February. Competitions, snowsports, food. Information: P.T.F., Raquette Lake, NY 13436.

W.O.W.- WINTER OUTDOOR WEEKEND, Essex County. Weekend closest to Washington's Birthday. Information: Essex County Dept. of Tourism, Elizabethtown, NY 12932. (518)873-6301.

WINTER CARNIVAL, Hague. Last weekend in February. Snowmobile, cross country ski races, National Ice Auger Championships. Information: (518)543-6353.

MAY

RETURN OF CHIMNEY SWIFTS, Lake Luzerne. May 7th. At site of tannery chimney, Main St. Information: Chamber of Commerce, PO Box 222, Lake Luzerne, NY 12846. (518)696-3500.

MAPLE SUGAR FESTIVAL, Elizabethtown. Early May. Maple sugar making, demonstrations, games, lectures, exhibits, films, food. Information: Essex County Historical Society, Adirondack Center Museum, Elizabethtown, NY 12932. (518)873-6466.

ADIRONDACK FOLK SINGING AND STORYTELLING FESTIVAL, Sagamore Lodge and Conference Center, Raquette Lake, NY 13436. Fourth annual festival in 1984. Variety of performances, workshops, swap sessions and informal happenings. Information: (315)354-5311.

OPEN HOUSE, Blue Mt. Lake. 3rd Saturday in May, 1-4 pm. Held at Adirondack Lakes Center for the Arts. Free craft demonstrations, exhibitions, music, films, refreshments. Information: (518)352-7751.

HISTORICAL BOAT TOUR, Lake George. 3rd weekend in May. Annual tour on the "Ticonderoga". Speak-easy night on the lake with Dixieland band, food and drink, games. Benefit for Lake George Historical Society. Information: (518)668-5044.

JUNE

CORVETTE CLUB RALLY, Lake Luzerne. 1st weekend in June. Sponsored by Foothills Council Corvette Club, c/o Chamber of Commerce, Lake Luzerne, NY 12846. Information: (518)696-2431.

BLACK FLY FESTIVAL, Inlet. 1st weekend in June. Includes Black Fly Walk and Bite Contest. Specials offered by merchants. Cake decorating contest. Information: Chamber of Commerce, Inlet, NY 13360. (315) 357-5501.

SUN ARTS, CRAFTS AND MUSIC FAIR, Stony Creek. Information: Chamber of Commerce, Stony Creek, NY 12878. (518)623-2161.

NEW YORK STATE FIDDLERS CONTEST, Old Forge. 3rd weekend in June. At Enchanted Forest, Rt. 28, Old Forge, NY 13420. Information: (315)369-6145.

STRAWBERRY FESTIVAL, Hague. Last weekend in June. Shortcake, ice cream, various soda fountain delights and more. Information: Chamber of Commerce, Hague, NY 12836. (518)543-6353.

JULY

KIDDIE PARADE, Saranac Lake. July 4th. Information: Chamber of Commerce, Saranac Lake, NY 12983.

ANTIQUES, ARTS AND CRAFTS AUCTION, Blue Mt. Lake. Every July 4th weekend. Held at the Adirondack Lakes Center for the Arts. Information: Adirondack Lakes Center for the Arts, Blue Mt. Lake, NY 12812.

JULY 4TH CELEBRATION, Jay. Parade from Upper Jay to village square in Jay, morning. Events and booths, afternoon and evening. Fireworks display. Information: Chamber of Commerce, Jay, NY 12941.

CONCERT AND FIREWORKS, Old Forge. July 4th evening. Held at the lakefront. Information: Chamber of Commerce, Old Forge, NY 13420. (315)369-6983.

PING-PONG BALL DROP, Inlet. 1st weekend in July. Childrens' event, held at Loomis Field. Balls contain free gifts and services from local merchants. Information: Chamber of Commerce, Inlet, NY 13360. (315)357-5501.

CRAFT FAIR, Old Forge. 1st weekend in July. Held at the Community Arts Center. Juried craft fair. Information: (315)369-6411.

CRAFT FESTIVAL, Pottersville. 2nd weekend in July. Information: Chamber of Commerce, Chestertown, NY 12817.

WOODSMEN'S DAYS. Tupper Lake. 2nd weekend in July. Parades, competitions. Information: Chamber of Commerce, Tupper Lake, NY 12986. (518)359-2507 or 359-3328.

HIGHLAND/SCOTTISH GAMES, Ticonderoga. 2nd weekend in July. Highland dancing, music, competitions, crafts, food. Information: Chamber of Commerce, Ticonderoga, NY 12883. (518)585-6619.

ART SHOW, Speculator. 2nd Saturday in July. Information: Office of Tourism and Community Development, Speculator, NY 12164.

FLEA MARKET, Saranac Lake. Sponsored by Masons. Mid-July. Held at the Civic Center. Information: Chamber of Commerce, Saranac Lake, NY 12983. (518)891-1990.

STRAWBERRY FESTIVAL, Chestertown. 2nd weekend in July. Also a bazaar. Information: Chamber of Commerce. Chestertown, NY 12817.

ARTS AND CRAFTS SHOW, Bolton Landing. 2nd weekend in July. Held at Roger's Memorial Park. 150 artisans and craftspeople. Information: Chamber of Commerce, Bolton Landing, NY 12814.

ART SHOW AND EXHIBIT, Tupper Lake. Mid-July. Held at Goff-Nelson Library. Information: Chamber of Commerce, Tupper Lake, NY 12986.

STRAWBERRY FESTIVAL, Brant Lake. Mid-July. Held at Barrie House. Information: Adirondack Lakes Chamber of Commerce, Chestertown, NY 12817. (518)494-2722.

PAGEANT, Lake Luzerne. 2nd weekend in July. Miss Rodeo New York Pageant. Held at Painted Rodeo Ranch. Information: RD Box 283, Lake Luzerne, NY 12846. (518)696-2421 or 2422.

FLEA MARKET, Speculator. 3rd weekend in July. Information: Office of Tourism and Community Development, Speculator, NY 12164.

ARTS AND CRAFT FESTIVAL, Lake Luzerne. 3rd weekend in July. Held at Fairley Dickinson Farm. Benefit for public library. No charge. Information: PO Box 222, Lake Luzerne, NY 12846.

ANTIQUE SHOW AND SALE, Saranac Lake. Last Tuesday, Wednesday and Thursday in July. Held at Town Hall. Information: Chamber of Commerce, Saranac Lake, NY 12983.

SIDEWALK SALE, Saranac Lake. Last Thursday, Friday and Saturday in July. Sponsored by the Business Association. Information: Chamber of Commerce, Saranac Lake, NY 12983.

BAZAAR AND FOOD SALE, Tupper Lake. Late July. Sponsored by Senior Citizen Association. Information: Chamber of Commerce, Tupper Lake, NY 12983. (518)359-3328.

CIRCUS, Tupper Lake. Last week in July. Information: Chamber of Commerce, Tupper Lake, NY 12983.

CRAFT FAIR, Piseco. 4th Saturday in July. Information: Office of Tourism and Community Development, Speculator, NY 12164.

ARTS IN THE PARK, Inlet. At Arrowhead Park. Last weekend in July. Displays or purchases of homemade crafts. Information: (315)357-5501.

ANTIQUE SHOW, Bolton Landing. Last weekend in July. Under the Big Top Tent, 45 dealers. Information: Chamber of Commerce, Bolton Landing, NY 12814. (518)644-3831.

ARTS AND CRAFTS SHOW, Hague. Information: Chamber of Commerce, Hague, NY 12836. (518)543-6353.

BLUE GRASS FESTIVAL, Jay. Three day festival, in July. Information: Chamber of Commerce, Jay NY 12941.

PARADE/FLEA MARKET, Westport. Information: Chamber of Commerce, Westport, NY 12993.

FLOWER SHOW, Schroon Lake. Sponsored by Adirondack Mountain Garden Club. Information: Joyce Mangine, Olmstedville, NY 12857.

AUGUST

BRIDGE TOURNAMENT, Saranac Lake. 1st weekend in August. Held at The Saranac. Information: Chamber of Commerce, Saranac Lake, NY 12983.

QUILT AND COVERLET SHOW, Lake Luzerne. 1st Saturday in August. Held at Kinneau Museum, Main St. Sponsored by Historical Society. Information: (518)696-2732 or 696-3561.

MOUNTAIN DAYS AND LUMBERJACK COMPETITION, Stony Creek. 1st weekend in August. Rt. 418, west of Warrensburg. Information: (518)696-2394.

FIDDLERS ROUNDUP, Athol/Thurman. 1st weekend in August. Held at Toad Hall, Stud Farm. Information: Volunteer Fire Co., Athol, NY 12810. (518)623-9649.

ARTS AND CRAFTS SHOW, Hague. First weekend in August. Held at public beach and park area. Information: Chamber of Commerce, Hague, NY 12936. (518)543-6353.

ARTS AND CRAFTS SHOW, Lake Pleasant. 1st or 2nd Thursday in August. Held at Pine Cone Bowl. Information: Tourist Office, Speculator, NY 12164.

PAINT AND PALETTE FESTIVAL, Saranac Lake. 1st week in August. Held at Harrietstown Hall. Information: Chamber of Commerce, Saranac Lake, NY 12986.

OLD HOME DAYS, Wells. 1st weekend in August. Fair atmosphere with booths, rides, games, dances. Information: Wells Civic Improvement Group, Ms. Janet Scheider, Wells, NY 12190.

ANTIQUES MARKET, Warrensburg. 1st weekend in August. Held at the Recreation Field. Information: Chamber of Commerce, Warrensburg, NY 12885. (518) 623-2161.

ART SHOW, Old Forge. 1st week-3rd week in August. Held at Community Arts Center. Adirondack Regional Art Exhibit. Information: (315)369-6411.

ARTS AND CRAFTS SHOW, Bolton Landing. 2nd weekend in August. Held at Roger's Memorial Park. Information: Chamber of Commerce, Bolton Landing, NY 12814.

FLEA MARKET, Hadley-Luzerne. 2nd Saturday in August. Sponsored by Historical Society. Held on Rt. 9N. Information (518)696-3202.

HERITAGE DAYS, Crown Point. 3rd weekend in August. Held at the Penfield Homestead Museum. Barbecue and crafts. Information: (518)597-3084.

FAMILY FESTIVAL, Lake George. 3rd week in August. Sponsored by Lake George Volunteer Fireman's Company. Information: Chamber of Commerce, Lake George, NY 12845. (518)668-5755.

MONSTER RALLY, Lake George. Last weekend in August. Celebrate the birthday of the Lake George Seamonster. Costumes, parade, festivities. Information: Lake George Historical Society. (518)668-5044.

BLUE GRASS FESTIVAL, Tupper Lake. End of August. Information: Chamber of Commerce, Tupper Lake, NY 12986.

BLUE GRASS FESTIVAL, Long Lake. Held at Long Lake Ski Slope. Information: Alice Scivally, Long Lake Publicity Director, Long Lake, NY 12847.

ANTIQUE AND COLLECTIBLES AUCTION, Elizabethtown. Held at Adirondack Center Museum. Information: Adirondack Center Museum, Elizabethtown, NY 12932.

DESSERT PARLOR, Indian Lake. Information: Chamber of Commerce, Indian Lake, NY 12842. (518)648-5112.

PENNY AUCTION, Piseco. Held at Piseco Community Hall. Information: Tourism Office, Speculator, NY 12164.

FLEA MARKET, Bolton Landing. Under the Big Top Tent. Information: Chamber of Commerce, Bolton Landing, NY 12814.

COUNTY FAIRS- SUMMER

CLINTON COUNTY. Plattsburgh, NY. Early August. Information: Robert W. Rabideau, PO Box 62, Maple St., Morrisonville, NY 12962. (518)563-3039.

ESSEX COUNTY. Westport, NY. Mid-August. Information: Mr. Lyn Lobdell, Westport, NY 12993. (518)873-6494.

FRANKLIN COUNTY. Malone, NY. Mid-August. Information: William McCabe, 12 Jones St., Malone, NY 12953.

HERKIMER COUNTY. Frankfort, NY. Mid-August. Information: Eleanor S. Crouch, 76 W. Main St., Mohawk, NY 13407. (315)866-2361.

LEWIS COUNTY. Lowville, NY. Mid-July. Information: Jesse Shantz, RD 1, Box 158, Lowville, NY 13367. (315)376-3976.

ONEIDA COUNTY. Booneville, NY. Early August. Information: Mrs. Marion Sattler, Gorge Rd., Booneville, NY 13309. Or Newell Wagoner, (315)942-2251.

ST. LAWRENCE COUNTY. Gouverneur, NY. First full week in August. Information: Beulah C. Appleby, 85 E. Barney St., Gouverneur, NY 13642. (315)287-3010.

SARATOGA COUNTY. Ballston Spa, NY. Late July. Information: Marie Willard, RD 4, Geyser Rd., Ballston Spa, NY 12020. (518)885-9701.

WARREN COUNTY YOUTH FAIR, Warrensburg, NY. Early August. Sponsored by the Warren County Cooperative Extension Service Association. Information: Andrew Sprague, 17 Hudson St., Warrensburg, NY 12885. (518) 623-3291.

WASHINGTON COUNTY, Greenwich, NY. Late August. Information: Mrs. Gayle Smith, RFD 1, Box 340, Fort Edward, NY 12828. (518)747-3073.

SEPTEMBER

ART SHOW, OLD FORGE. Labor-Day weekend-4th Sunday in September. Held at Community Arts Center, Main Gallery. Adirondack National Exhibition of American Watercolors (ANEW). Information: (315)369-6411.

PIG ROAST, Indian Lake. September 4th. Held at the Firehall. Information: Chamber of Commerce, Indian Lake, NY 12842.

FIREMAN'S ANNUAL DANCE, Bolton Landing. 1st weekend in September. Information: Chamber of Commerce, Bolton Landing, NY 12814. (518)644-3831.

CLAM BAKE. Inlet. 2nd weekend in September. Tickets sold in advance. Sponsored by the Raquette Lake Fire Dept. Information: Raquette Lake Fire Dept., Raquette Lake NY 13436.

BALLOON FESTIVAL, Glens Falls. 3rd weekend in September. Held at Warren County Airport. Information: Chamber of Commerce, Glens Falls, NY 12801.

OKTUPPER FEST, Tupper Lake. 2nd or 3rd weekend in September. Big Tupper Ski Area, Tupper Lake. Food, music, dancing, crafts, chairlift rides. Sponsored by the Chamber of Commerce. Information: (518)359-3328.

SQUARE DANCE FESTIVAL, Lake Placid. Last weekend in September. Held at Olympic Center. Sponsored by the Hi Peak Squares. 500-600 couples. Information: Lake Placid Chamber of Commerce, Lake Placid, NY 12946.

ANTIQUE AUTO RALLY, Wilmington. Last weekend in September. Held at Whiteface Mountain Ski Center. Information: Chamber of Commerce, Box 277, Wilmington, NY 12997.

OCTOBER

FIDDLERS JAMBOREE, Lake George. 1st weekend in October. Held at the Top O' The World. Donation. Information: Top O' The World, Box 252, Lake George, NY 12845. (518)668-5415.

HISTORIC HOUSE TOUR, Lake George. 1st weekend in October. Begins at the Court House Museum. Information: (518)668-5044.

ANTIQUE SHOW AND SALE, Old Forge. 1st weekend in October. Held at Community Arts Center. Information: Community Arts Center, Old Forge, NY 13420. (315) 369-6411.

STREET SALE AND AUCTION, Warrensburg. "World's Largest Garage Sale". Columbus Day weekend in October. Town-wide Sale. Information: Chamber of Commerce, Warrensburg, NY 12885. (518)623-2161.

ANCESTOR DAY, Lake George. 3rd weekend in September. Re-enactment of the Battle of Lake George and Black Powder Day Parade. Held at the Top O' The World, Lake George. Information: Top O'The World, PO Box 252, Lake George, NY 12845. (518)668-5415.

HALLOWEEN PARTY, Blue Mt. Lake, Halloween Weekend, 7:30 pm. Held at the Adirondack Center for the Arts. Haunted house, games, costumes, films, refreshments. Information: (518)352-7715.

SKATE AMERICA, Lake Placid. Figure skaters from 15 countries compete in preparation for world competition. Information: Chamber of Commerce, Lake Placid, NY 12946.

FOLIAGE AND FUN WEEKEND, Speculator/Lake Pleasant/Piseco. Information: Tourism Office, Speculator, NY 12164.

NOVEMBER

BAZAAR, Old Forge. 1st weekend in November. Held at Community Arts Center. First weekend in November. Information: Community Arts Center, Old Forge, NY 13420. (315)369-6411.

DECEMBER

BAZAAR, Saranac Lake. 1st Saturday in December. Held at St. Lukes Parish House. Information: St. Lukes Church, Saranac Lake, NY 12983.

RECREATION

(80)
TRAIL GUIDES

ADIRONDACK MOUNTAIN CLUB, *Guide to Adirondack Trails: High Peak Region:* 10th edition (Glens Falls, NY: Adk. Mountain Club, 1980).

ADIRONDACK MOUNTAIN CLUB, *Guide to the Northville-Lake Placid Trail* (Glens Falls, NY: Adk Mt. Club, 1980).

BURMEISTER, Walter F. *Appalachian Waters 2: The Hudson River and Its Tributaries* (Oakton, VA: Appalachian Books, 1974).

COGGESHALL, Almy and Anne, *25 Ski Tours in the Adirondacks* (Woodstock, VT: Back Country Publications, 1979).

GOODWIN, Tony, *Northern Adirondack Ski Tours* (Glens Falls, NY: Adk. Mountain Club, 1982).

JAMIESON, Paul, *Adirondack Canoe Waters: North Flow:* Second Edition (Glens Falls, NY: Adk. Mountain Club, 1981).

MCMARTIN, Barbara, *Discover the Adirondacks, 1: From Indian Lake to the Hudson River* (Woodstock, VT: Back Country Publications, 1979).

MCMARTIN, Barbara, *Discover the Adirondacks, 2: Walks, Waterways and Winter Treks in the Southern Adirondacks* (Woodstock, VT: Back Country Publications, 1980).

MCMARTIN, Barbara, *Fifty Hikes in the Adirondacks: Short Walks, Day Trips and Backpacks Throughout the Park* (Woodstock, VT: Back Country Publications, 1980).

MCMARTIN, Barbara, *Guide to the Eastern Adirondacks: Lake George, Pharoah Lake and Beyond* (Glens Falls, NY: Adk. Mountain Club, 1981).

MCMARTIN, Barbara, *Old Roads and Open Peaks: Walks, Climbs, Canoe Routes, and Bushwacks in the Southeastern Adirondack Park* (Glens Falls, NY: Adk. Mountain Club, 1977).

REDINGTON, Robert J., *Guide to Trails of the West Central Adirondacks* (Glens Falls, NY: Adk. Mountain Club, 1980).

ROSECRANS, Thomas R., *Adirondack Rock and Ice Climbs* (Lake George, NY: Rosecrans Outing and Climbing Klub, 1976).

WADSWORTH, Bruce, *An Adirondack Sampler: Day Hikes for all Seasons* (Glens Falls, NY: Adk. Mountain Club, 1979).

WADSWORTH, Bruce, *An Adirondack Sampler II: Backpacking Trips* (Glens Falls, NY: Adk. Mountain Club, 1981).

(81)
20 OUTSTANDING DAY HIKES

The editors invited noted trail guide author Barbara McMartin to contribute a section on 20 excellent and varied hikes from around the Adirondacks. Ms. McMartin notes that many of her favorite trails would not lend themselves to short descriptions. She ruled out some High Peaks trails because of the danger of going there unprepared and a couple of others because of over-use. This listing, then, should not be read as the author's nominees for the 20 very best hikes in the Adirondacks, but as 20 outstanding hikes, many of which are Ms. McMartin's favorites. We thank her for this fine contribution.

All round trip distances are for out-and-back trails, except when described as a "loop". Times are stated for round trip distances.

ALGONQUIN. Essex County. 8 miles round trip; vertical rise, 2936 ft. to 5114 ft. summit; time, 6 hours; map, USGS 15' Mount Marcy; start, take Heart Lake Road south of NY 73 to parking area at end of road (nominal parking fee).
Strenuous walk to noblest summit deep in the High Peaks Wilderness. Special clothes and equipment may be needed, depending on the season. Be prepared for temperature extremes and check with ranger or caretaker at parking area to be certain you are properly equipped and prepared.

AMPERSAND. Franklin County. 6.2 miles round trip; vertical rise, 1790 ft. to 3352 ft. summit; time, 4 hours; maps, USGS 15' Santanoni and Saranac Lake; start, drive 7 miles east of the intersection of NY 3 and 30 on NY 3 to parking turnout on north, opposite trailhead.
Moderately strenuous climb, that is sometimes very steep, leads to open rock summit overlooking the Saranac Lakes and the western High Peaks.

AUGER FALLS. Hamilton County. Loop just over 1/2 mile; verical rise, minimal; time, 1 hour; maps, USGS 15' Lake Pleasant and Harrisburg; start, drive north of intersection of NY 8 and 30 along those joined routes for 1.5 miles to marked International Paper Company picnic site and trailhead.
Short, marked path begins from south end of dirt road that parallels the highway. Path leads to beautiful waterfalls on Main Branch Sacandaga River. Continuing unmarked footpath loops north along the falls and back beside calm stretch to start. Be careful near the falls; moss covered rocks and spray from the falls make slippery footing.

BALD/RONDAXE MOUNTAIN. Herkimer County. Less than two mile round trip; vertical rise, 400 ft. to 2350 ft. summit; time, 1 1/2 hours; map, USGS 15' Old Forge; start, take NY 28 east 4.6 miles from Old Forge to Rondaxe Road, then north .25 mile to trailhead.
The shortest, easiest climb in the Adirondacks with one of the greatest views. Exposed ledge seems to overhang the Fulton Chain. Views to the east to Blue Mountain and just north of east all the way to Mount Marcy and MacIntyre.

BLUE LEDGE. Essex County. 5 mile round trip; vertical rise, 230 ft.; time, 3 hours; map, USGS 15' Newcomb; start, drive 9.4 miles north from North Creek along NY 28N to North Woods Club Road and follow it 6.8 miles on a narrow, sometimes very bumpy dirt road to the trailhead.
Easy trail heads west then south to descend into the Hudson River Gorge at its deepest, opposite Blue Ledge. Handsome trail, wildflowers. Furious white water in spring; gentle, sometimes swimmable pools in the summer.

BLUE MOUNTAIN. Hamilton County. 4 miles round trip; vertical rise, 1750 ft. to 3759 ft. summit; time, 3 1/2 hours; map, USGS 15' Blue Mountain; start, from private trailhead just south of Adirondack Museum on NY 30 (minimal parking fee).
Fire tower mountain with superb views to west of the gentle Adirondack Lake district and to east and north toward the High Peaks. Moderate climb on a well-defined trail.

CRANE MOUNTAIN. Warren County. 4.8 mile loop; vertical rise, 1300 ft. to 3240 ft. summit; time 4 to 5 hours; map, USGS 15' North Creek; start, South Johnsburg Road to Thurman, west 1.2 miles to right fork, continue 1.5 miles bearing right on narrow woods road that leads to trailhead. Take trail to left to begin.
Spectacular walk; clockwise loop along Woods Road, up rock faces, past Crane Mountain Pond to abandoned fire tower summit. Panoramic views, ladies' slippers in spring, lots to see on and off trail.

DEBAR MOUNTAIN. Franklin County. 7 miles round trip; vertical rise, 1600 ft. to 3300 ft. summit; time, 6 hours; map USGS 7.5' Meacham Lake and Debar Mountain; start Meacham Lake Campsite off NY 30.
Moderately strenuous day-hike begins with a gentle uphill walk that culminates in a 1/2 mile, 800 ft. scramble. Abandoned fire tower summit with great views. One of the more exciting places in the far northern Adirondacks.

DEER LEAP. Warren County. 3.2 miles round trip; vertical rise, minimal; time, 2 1/2 hours; map, USGS 15' Bolton Landing; start, Northway exit 24 east to NY 9N, then 9 miles north to trailhead.
Views of Lake George from this promontory on the Tongue Mountain Range; wildflowers. Trail forks after .55 mile, Deer Leap to left. Best views are off the trail to right not far from intersection. Watch for paths leading to view spots all along the trail.

ECHO CLIFFS. Hamilton County. 1.4 miles round trip; vertical rise 600 ft.; time 1 1/3 hours; map, USGS 15' Piseco; start, opposite Little Sand Point State Campsite on NW shore of Piseco Lake.
Easy trail to perch on cliff top on Panther Mountain overlooking Piseco Lake and Silver Lake Wilderness.

HADLEY MOUNTAIN. Saratoga County. 4 miles round trip; vertical rise, 1550 ft. to 2700 ft. summit; time, 3 hours; map, USGS 15' Lake Luzerne; start, from County Rt. 4 along north shore of Sacandaga Reservoir, turn north on Hadley Hill Road, 5.2 miles, left to Tower Road 1.4 miles to trailhead.
Easy to follow fire tower trail. Summit and tower give views of both Catskill and Adirondack High Peaks and the mountains of Vermont. Lovely, partially open summit ridge to wander along for extended trip.

PEAKED HILL. Essex County. 4.4 miles round trip, plus short canoe trip across Paradox Lake; vertical rise, 780 ft. to 1880 ft. summit; time, 4 1/2 hours; map, USGS 7.5' Paradox Lake; start, boat ramp at Paradox Lake Campsite on NY 74.
The beginnings of many trails in the Adirondacks are reached only by boat; this one from a very short trip across the Paradox Lake narrows to the trailhead. Steep climb at first, then gentle walk past Peaked Pond. Final steep climb leads to promontory looking south over Schroon Lake.

PEAKED MOUNTAIN. Warren County. 7 miles round trip; vertical rise, 1245 ft. to 2919 ft. summit; time, 5 hours; map, USGS 15' Thirteenth Lake; start, boat launching site at the north end of Thirteenth Lake.
The trail follows the west shore of Thirteenth Lake for less than 3/4 mile, then turns northwest along Peaked Mountain Brook to beautiful Peaked Mountain Pond, 1 1/2 miles farther. Unmarked paths continue around the north shore of the pond where soon a marked trail will lead to the summit. (If trail markings are not yet up, use map, compass and guidebook for the mountain climb.)

PHAROAH LAKE. Essex County. 5 miles round trip, with option of much more hiking to explore lake as you wish; vertical rise, minimal; time, 2 hours; map USGS 15' Paradox Lake; start, NY 8 east to Palisade Road at head of Brant Lake, then north 1.6 miles to Beaver Pond Road, right at 1.5 miles onto Pharoah Road, then 1.4 miles to trailhead.
This trail from the south is an easy woods road walk to an outstandingly beautiful lake, overshadowed by Pharoah Mountain. Trails lead along both shores to rock ledges, pine covered knolls, camping and picnic sites.

PINE ORCHARD. Hamilton County. 4.8 miles round trip; vertical rise, minimal; time, 2 1/2 hours; map, USGS 15' Harrisburg; start, from NY 30 at Wells, turn onto Griffin Road .8 mile to Windfall Road, then 1 mile to unmarked right fork, follow it 1.9 miles to small parking turnouts on side of road bordered by State land.
Old logging road, now a snowmobile trail, crosses private land, then enters the Forest Preserve. Relatively level walk beside marshes and through deep woods culminates in a knoll covered with virgin pine stand. Trees to 6 ft. in diameter date possibly to hurricane circa 1815. Most accessible virgin stand in the Adirondacks.

POKAMOONSHINE. Essex County. 2 miles round trip; vertical rise, 1260 ft. to 2140 ft. summit; map, USGS 15' AuSable Forks; start, Pok-o-moonshine State Park, 3 miles south of Northway exit 33 on NY 9.
Short but steep walk to fire tower summit with superb views east over Lake Champlain to Vermont. Mountain is famous for its rock-climbing cliffs, visible from highway. Well marked trail.

ST. REGIS MOUNTAIN. Franklin County. 6 miles round trip; vertical rise, 1235 ft. to 2873 ft. summit; time, 4 hours; map, USGS 15' St. Regis; start, turn west off NY 30 past Paul Smith's College for 2.5 miles to turn south on narrow road that is marked for tower.
Moderate walk on well marked and well cared-for trail to bare summit with fire tower. Views all around, with High Peaks and a multitude of lakes dominating the landscape.

SNOWY MOUNTAIN. Hamilton County. 7.5 miles round trip; vertical rise, 2100 ft. to 3899 ft. summit; time, 6 hours; map, USGS 15' Indian Lake; start, opposite parking turnout on NY 30, 17 miles north of Speculator or 7 miles south of Indian Lake Village.
Moderate climb at first, then trail becomes very steep. Strenuous day trip to abandonded fire tower summit on highest peak in the southern Adirondacks. Dramatic cliffs give Snowy its famous profile.

STEWART AND INDIAN LAKES. Hamilton County. 4 miles round trip; vertical rise, 440 ft.; time, 2 hours; map, USGS 7.5' Canada Lake; start near NY 10 bridge over channel between Canada and Green Lakes, turn north along shore of Green Lake, stay left on narrow dirt road 100 yards to parking area.
These small lakes are typical of the hundreds of uninhabited and secluded lakes that dot the southern Adirondacks. Most are reached by unmarked or poorly marked trails and paths. An old logging road to this pair is currently marked as a ski touring route. It starts 200 yards along the dirt road from the parking area and winds uphill circling Stewart Lake at a distance. Leave the trail to explore both lakes.

TREADWAY MOUNTAIN. Essex County. 8 miles round trip; vertical rise, 930 ft. to 2240 ft. summit; time, 6 hours; map, USGS 7.5' Graphite; start, Putnam Pond Campsite south of NY 74.
Long, but not too strenuous hike to a windswept mountain offers one of the best views, with surprisingly lovely distant panorama of the High Peaks across the lakes and forests of the Pharoah Lake Wilderness. Trip can be shortened by nearly 3 miles if boat access to trailhead is used, because the first 1 1/2 miles of trip is circuit of southern shores of Putnam Pond.

Note: All the descriptions in this section are abridged by Ms. McMartin from her outstanding series of trail guides, described in Section 80. For a more complete description of any of these trails and scores of others, consult the appropriate trail guide.

ADIRONDACK 46'ERS: FACTS AND RECORDS

WHAT ARE THE 46'ERS?

The Adirondack 46'ers are climbers who have ascended the high peaks of the Adirondacks. The first persons to climb all of them (in 1925) chose those mountains with an elevation of 4000 feet or more. There were 46. From this came the name of the present group. While later surveys have indicated that a few of these are under 4000 feet, the Adirondack 46'ers retain the original listing.

HOW TO BECOME A 46'ER

To become a 46'er you must climb all 46 mountains of the original list (these peaks and their elevations can be found in Section 54 of The Adirondack Guide). 26 have marked trails. 20 are trailless. Before attempting to climb them you should become familiar with the mountain terrain by studying guidebooks, trail maps and USGS maps. USGS maps and a compass are essential for trailless climbs. Keep track of each mountain you climb. List the date and the persons with you. When you have completed the 46, attach your record to the "Questionnaire" the 46'ers will send you. This will be your formal application.

BECOMING AN ASPIRING 46'ER

An "Aspiring 46'er" is a climber who has ascended 30 of the 46. When you have accomplished this, notify the Adirondack 46'ers, Adirondack, NY 12808, and they will send you the questionnaire/application referred to above.

REGISTERING YOUR CLIMBS

On each of the trailless summits there is a register. Sign your name and address in the log book for these summits, as well as any other log books you pass on the trails, in campsites, etc. You are invited to write to the Adirondack 46'ers of your progress up the 46. If you do this, they appreciate it if you would include dates, names of others in your party, and also names of the previous party who signed any of the log books just before you.

FACTS AND RECORDS

The 46 peaks were first climbed by three men: Herbert K. Clark, George Marshall and Robert Marshall (namesake of the Bob Marshall Wilderness), on June 10, 1925. Since the Adirondack 46'ers list climbers alphabetically who finish at the same time, they are listed in the official roster as 46'ers #'s 1,2 and 3.

The name "46'ers" was not coined at the time. That came later when a group from Troy called themselves "The Forty-Sixers of Troy," organizing in 1936. That was when Grace Leach Hudowalski, 46'er Historian, began keeping the records and she's been doing it ever since!

Tommy (Thomas V.) Lamb of Lake Placid was the youngest 46'er. He started climbing in 1966 and finished about 15 months later. He was six when he became 46'er #451. He climbed with his family who all became 46'ers the year before Tommy.

As of February 1983, there were 1,830 Adirondack 46'ers.

The first woman to climb all 46 peaks was Grace Leach Hudowalski, who became 46'er #9 in 1937.

There were no records of how many times a person climbs 46 peaks. However, the record may be held by James A. Goodwin of West Hartford and Keene Valley (46'er #24), who has climbed them all 15 times.

The shortest time record for climbing all 46 peaks was set by a group of climbers from Camp Pok-O-Moonshine under the leadership of John Sharp Swan, Jr., 46'er #556. Swan had climbed the mountains several times and the entire expedition was carefully planned. Their time was 4 days, 18 hours, 18 minutes. The group were all experienced climbers who knew all the 46 peaks in advance. (CAUTION: Climbing for speed is extremely dangerous. The first attempt to climb the peaks in less than five days ended in death—a climber who was not a 46'er and did not correspond with the 46'ers. The 46'ers do not keep records of time because they feel this perverts the meaning of the climbing experience. "We feel climbers should enjoy the mountains and take their time. Too much is lost in rushing over them.")

The oldest person to finish climbing the 46 peaks was Harry Gamble of Pottersville who climbed his 46th peak, Mt. Cliff (3960 feet and trailless) on July 23, 1969 at the age of 70.

While climbing numbers were formerly assigned to dogs—and two canines achieved the distinction of becoming 46'ers—this practice no longer continues. The reason is that St. Huberts restricts dogs on their land, so climbing the mountain in this area necessitated taking different approaches that were difficult and trailless.

Thanks to Adirondack 46'er Historian Grace Leach Hudowalski for her assistance in compiling the information for this section.

(83)
HUNTING

REGULATIONS

The following information is excerpted from the *New York State Fishing, Small Game Hunting and Trapping Regulations Guide* and from the pamphlet "Big Game Hunting," both available from NYS Department of Environmental Conservation, 50 Wolf Rd., Albany, NY 12233 or any Regional D.E.C. office. These publications provide more details than does this summary of major regulations and seasons, and there are some changes in regulations each year. Therefore, it would be wise to consult the most recent publications available before hunting in the Adirondacks.

For big game hunting, the minimum age to obtain a license is 16. To obtain a license a 16 or 17 year old must show a hunter training certificate issued in his state of residence, or show proof of having been issued a license in a previous year. He may hunt only when accompanied by a licensed big game hunter at least 18 years old. Persons 18 years and over are subject to the same proof of qualification, but may hunt alone.

For small game hunting, minors under the age of 14 may not obtain a hunting license or hunt wild birds or animals. Minors 14 or 15 years of age may obtain a hunting license under certain conditions and must, when hunting, be accompanied by a parent, guardian or designated person over 18 who also possesses a current NYS hunting license.

Free hunting licenses are available to NYS residents 70 and over; members of the Six Nations, Shinnecock and Poospatuck tribes living on reservations in NYS; and honorably discharged disabled veterans.

All persons 16 years of age and over hunting migratory waterfowl must have a Federal Migratory Bird Hunting Stamp in addition to their NYS hunting license. Minors 14 or 15 years of age may hunt migratory waterfowl with a NYS license only.

Generally hunting hours for small and big game are from sunrise to sunset. Ducks and geese may be taken from one-half hour before sunrise to sunset. After opening day, furbearers may be taken at any time of the day.

It is unlawful to hunt or take any threatened or endangered species. Hawks, owls, song-birds and all other protected non-game birds may not be hunted or taken.

If you take an animal or bird carrying a Department of Environmental Conservation band or tag, please report it. If possible return the band or tag; but in any case, give the number stamped on it, the species of wildlife, and the place and date taken. Reports should be made to DEC, Division of Fish and Wildlife, 50 Wolf Rd., Albany, NY 12233.

SEASONS

The following chart gives general season time frames for the various big and small game species that are hunted in the Adirondacks. As stated earlier, exact opening and closing dates may change from year to year, and the Department of Environmental Conservation should be consulted for the most recent rules and regulations. The chart below, however, gives a good idea of the types and lengths of hunting seasons in the Adirondacks. With respect to big game hunting, sportspersons can calculate exact season dates by using the following formula.

Big Game: Deer and Bear

Early Bear Season:	Third Saturday in September through the day immediately preceding the opening of the muzzleloading season.
#Archery Season:	September 26 through the Thursday immediately preceding the next-to-last Saturday in October.
#Muzzleloading Season:	A seven day season ending at sunset on the Thursday immediately preceding the next-to-last Saturday in October.
Regular Firearm Season:	Next-to-last Saturday in October through the first Sunday in December.

= requires either an archery or muzzleloading stamp in addition to a big game license.

Small Game

Grouse:	mid-September -February 28
Pheasant:	October 1 - November 30
Cottontail rabbit:	October 1 - February 28
Squirrel:	October 1 - February 28
#Turkey	
Fall Season:	Washington County only. Mid-October to mid-November
Spring Season:	Washington County and eastern Essex County only. Early May - May 31

#Migratory Game Birds

##Ducks:	early October - early December
##Geese:	early October - early January
Woodcock:	mid-September - late November
Crows:	early September - mid-April (Hunting permitted only on Friday, Saturday, Sunday and Monday)
Snipe:	early September - late November
Virginia & Sora Rails:	early September - early November
Gallinules:	early September - early November

#Furbearers

Raccoon, Red and Gray fox, opossum, weasels, coyote, bobcat:	late October to either late February, mid-March or late March depending on location

= contact the N.Y.S. Department of Environmental Conservation for specific rules and regulations.

= Federal Migratory Bird Hunting Stamp required in addition to a small game license.

LICENSES

The license year runs from October 1 through September 30. License applications (shown below) and licenses are available from the Regional Offices of the Department of Environmental Conservation, town and county clerks, and many sporting goods stores. Licenses may also be purchased by mail by sending a completed application to a D.E.C. Regional Office (see Section 116).

Licenses for the new license year go on sale in late August. Individuals also receive a complete set of new rules and regulations when they purchase a license.

STANDARD LICENSE APPLICATION AND FEE SCHEDULE

PRINT CLEARLY ● USE BALL POINT PEN ● BEAR DOWN

NEW YORK STATE DEPARTMENT OF ENVIRONMENTAL CONSERVATION

SPORTING LICENSE APPLICATION

OFFICIAL USE ONLY

LICENSE YEAR October 1, 19______ to September 30, 19______

DATE Mo/Day/Yr | TIME ☐am ☐pm | CITY/TOWN/VILLAGE | ● TAG NUMBER

PROOF OF ELIGIBILITY FOR HUNTING/TRAPPING LICENSE(S) ☐ Hunting ☐ Big Game ☐ Bowhunting ☐ Trapping

AGENT SIGNATURE | ● AGENT NUMBER | ● CONTROL NO. 000000 1

INSTRUCTIONS

1. Complete all sections of the application except parts labeled **"For Official Use"**
2. If renewing by mail, include a **stamped, self-addressed envelope.**
3. Present completed application to license agent for license validation.
4. Previously issued humting/trapping license, stamp or training certificate must be submitted with application.

● LAST NAME

● FIRST NAME | ● MI

● STREET ADDRESS

● CITY | ● STATE

● ZIP CODE | ● AREA CODE | ● TELEPHONE NUMBER

● DATE OF BIRTH Mo / Day / Yr | ● SEX ☐ M ☐ F | EYE COLOR | HEIGHT ft. in.

STATUS OF LEGAL RESIDENCE

☐ Resident of New York State for more than 3 months.

☐ Non-Resident or Resident of New York State for less than 3 months.

CERTIFICATION

I hereby affirm under penalty of perjury that information provided on this form is true to the best of my knowledge and belief. False statements are punishable as a Class A misdemeanor pursuant to Section 7, 0921 (8) of the Environmental Conservation Law.

X________________

82-19-26 (4/83) SIGNATURE OF LICENSEE

Circle license type(s) you are applying for and fee:

● LICENSE TYPE		CODE	FEE
RESIDENT			
FISHING—SEASON		06	$ 9.50
*FISHING—3 DAY		26	$ 3.50
HUNTING		18	$ 8.50
HUNTING AND FISHING		35	$16.50
BIG GAME		11	$ 8.50
SPORTSMAN		31	$23.50
TRAPPING		07	$ 8.50
HUNTING AND BIG GAME		21	$16.50
JUNIOR ARCHERY		01	$ 7.50
JUNIOR TRAPPING		27	$ 3.50
NON-RESIDENT			
FISHING—SEASON		66	$20.50
*FISHING—3 DAY		76	$ 6.50
*FISHING—7 DAY		86	$12.50
HUNTING—SEASON		52	35.50
*HUNTING—3 DAY		54	$12.50
BIG GAME		71	$55.50
*List Consecutive Dates License To Be Validated: Beginning ______ Ending ______			
PRIMITIVE			
BOWHUNTING		23	$ 5.25
MUZZLELOADING		33	$ 5.25
FREE			
FISHING		36	—
SPORTSMAN		41	—
BOWHUNTING		43	—
TRAPPING		37	—
MUZZLELOADING		13	—
Residents must submit proof of eligibility for free licenses		**TOTAL FEE**	**$**

SAMPLE ONLY DO NOT USE

(84)

SPORT FISHING

REGULATIONS

The following information is excerpted from the *New York State Fishing, Small Game Hunting and Trapping Regulations Guide* published by and available from the New York State Department of Environmental Conservation, 50 Wolf Rd., Albany, NY 12233. The *Guide* has more details than does this summary of major regulations, and there are some changes in regulations each year. Therefore, it would be wise to consult the most recent edition of the *Guide* before fishing in the Adirondacks.

Fishing licenses are typically required for persons 16 years and older, with a few exceptions.

Free licenses are available to NY State citizen-residents 70 and older; members of Six Nations, Shinnecock and Poospatuck tribes living on reservations in NYS; honorably discharged veterans; and citizen-residents who are blind.

Licenses are required just about everywhere in the Adirondacks, including privately owned lakes. Exceptions are licensed fishing preserves and when owners of cultivated farms fish their own ponds.

Seasons, minimum lengths and limits may vary from year to year, but the general pattern has been consistent with the 1982-83 regulations which follow:

Species	Season	Minimum Length	Daily Limit
Brook Trout Brown Trout Rainbow Trout Splake	April 1-Sept. 30 (3rd. Sat. in April in Clinton, Essex and Franklin Counties)	Any Size	10
Lake Trout	Apr. 1-Sept. 30	21"	3
Kokanee—(Red Salmon)	April 1-Sept. 30	Any Size	10
Landlocked Salmon	Apr. 1-Sept. 30	15"	3
Largemouth Bass Smallmouth Bass	3rd Sat. in June- November 30	12"	5
Muskellunge	"	30"	1
Northern Pike	1st Sat. May- March 15	18"	5
Pickerel	"	15"	5
Tiger Muskellunge	"	30"	1
Walleye	"	15"	5

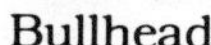

Bullhead

Brook Trout

Largemouth Bass

SPECIAL REGULATIONS BY COUNTY

There are different regulations for Lake Champlain and for the different Adirondack counties. The following ones are taken directly from the *Guide*.

COUNTY		Species	Open Season	Minimum Length	Daily Limit	Method
CLINTON	All waters except those covered by Lake Champlain regulations and others as listed below	Trout	3rd Sat. in April-Oct. 15	Any size	10	
	Lake Champlain and tributaries to first barrier	All species	SEE Lake Champlain Regulations pages 24-25			
	Upper Chateaugay Lake, Chazy Lake	Lake trout	All year	21"	3	Ice fishing permitted
		Trout	All year	Any size	10	
	Great Chazy River from Rt. 11 at Champlain upstream to Perrys Mills Dam		Fishing prohibited March 16 through 1st Friday in May to protect spawning walleye			
	Saranac River from Rt. 22B in Morrisonville upstream to Union Falls Dam	Largemouth and Smallmouth bass Northern pike	3rd Sat. in April-Oct. 15	Any size	Any number	
	North Branch Saranac River from mouth of Cold Brook upstream to Alder Brook	Trout	3rd Sat. in April-Oct. 15	12"	3	Artificial lures only
ESSEX	All waters except those covered by Lake Champlain regulations and others as listed below	Trout	3rd Sat. in April-Oct. 15	Any size	10	
	Lake Champlain and tributaries to first barrier and Bouquet River	All species	SEE Lake Champlain Regulations pages 24-25			
	East Branch Ausable River, West Branch Ausable River, Bouquet River from Willsboro Dam upstream	Largemouth and Smallmouth bass	3rd Sat. in April-Oct. 15	Any size	Any number	
	West Branch Ausable River except section below	Trout	3rd Sat. in April-Oct. 15	9"	10	
	West Branch Ausable River from Monument Falls downstream 2.2 miles	Trout	All year	12"	3	Artificial lures only
	Bigsby Pond, Copperas Pond, Crane Pond	Lake trout	April 1-Sept. 30	15"	3	Tip-ups prohibited
	Eagle Lake	Trout	All year	Any size	10	Ice fishing permitted
	First Lake of Essex Chain	Lake trout	April 1-Sept. 30	15"	3	
		Trout	April 1-Sept. 30	Any size	10	
	Lake George and tributaries to first barrier	Lake trout, Landlocked salmon, Trout	SEE Lake George under Warren County page 52			
	Ticonderoga Creek from Lower Falls upstream to Lake George	Lake trout, Landlocked salmon, Trout	Regulations in effect for Lake Champlain apply; SEE page 24			
	Hudson River	Largemouth and Smallmouth bass, Northern pike	All year	Any size	Any number	Ice fishing permitted
	Mirror Lake, Lake Placid	Lake trout	April 1-Oct. 15	15"	3	
	Moose Pond in town of St. Armand	Largemouth and Smallmouth bass	April 1-Nov. 30	Any size	Any number	
		Lake trout	April 1-Sept. 30	15"	3	
	Paradox Lake, Schroon Lake, Schroon River from Schroon Lake upstream to Alder Meadow Road	Lake trout	All year	21"	3	Ice fishing permitted
		Landlocked salmon	All year	15"	3	Ice fishing permitted
		Pickerel	All year	Any size	Any number	Ice fishing permitted
		Trout	All year	Any size	10	Ice fishing permitted
	Schroon River from Alder Meadow Road upstream to County Road 2B in North Hudson, The Branch from mouth upstream to Palmer Dam	Landlocked salmon	April 1-Oct. 15	15"	3	

COUNTY		Species	Open Season	Minimum Length	Daily Limit	Method
FRANKLIN	All waters except as listed below	Trout	3rd Sat. in April-Oct. 15	Any size	10	
	Big Fish Pond, Big Pine Pond, St. Regis Pond	Lake trout	April 1-Sept. 30	15"	3	
	Black Pond, Long Pond	Trout	3rd Sat. in April-Oct. 15	Any size	5	Artificial lures only
	Lower Chateaugay Lake, Lake Clear	Lake trout	All year	21"	3	Ice fishing permitted
		Trout	All year	Any size	10	
	Chateaugay River from The Forge downstream, East Branch St. Regis River	Largemouth and Smallmouth bass Northern pike	3rd Sat. in April-Oct. 15	Any size	Any number	
	Lake Colby	Kokanee	All year	Any size	10	Ice fishing permitted; use or possession of fish for bait prohibited
		Trout	All year	Any size	10	
	Deer Pond, Ledge Pond	Lake trout	April 1-Sept. 30	15"	3	Tip-ups prohibited
	Indian Lake, Mountain View Lake	Trout	All year	Any size	10	Ice fishing permitted
	Little Clear Pond and tributaries	Fishing prohibited to protect landlocked salmon brood stock				
	Little Green Pond	Kokanee	3rd Sat. in April-Oct. 15	Any size	Any number	
	Mountain Pond	Trout	All year		No kill	Artificial lures only
	Saranac River from Hough Brook at Union Falls Flow upstream to Franklin Falls Flow Dam	Fishing prohibited March 1 through May 15 to protect spawning walleye				
	Upper Saranac Lake	Lake trout	April 1-Sept. 30	23"	3	Tip-ups prohibited
	West Pine Pond	Fishing permitted 1) 3rd Sat. in April through June 15 and 2) Sept. 1 through Sept. 30				
	Whey Pond	Trout	3rd Sat. in April-Oct. 15	12"	3	Artificial lures only
FULTON	All waters	Pickerel	All year	Any size	Any number	
	Canada Lake	Lake trout	All year	21"	3	Ice fishing permitted
		Trout	All year	Any size	10	
	East Caroga Lake, West Caroga Lake, Green Lake, Lily Lake, West Lake	Trout	All year	Any size	10	Ice fishing permitted
HAMILTON	All waters	Pickerel	All year	Any size	Any number	
	Abanakee Lake, Indian River	Lake trout	All year	Any size	3	Ice fishing permitted
		Landlocked salmon	All year	Any size	3	
		Trout	All year	Any size	10	
	Adirondack Lake	Northern pike	1st Sat. in May-March 15	Any size	5	Ice fishing permitted
	Lake Algonquin, Hudson River from mouth of Boreas River downstream, Limekiln Lake, Sacandaga Lake, Sixth Lake	Trout	All year	Any size	10	Ice fishing permitted
	Blue Mountain Lake, Forked Lake, Gilman Lake, Long Lake, Lake Pleasant, Lewey Lake, Piseco Lake, Raquette Lake, Seventh Lake, South Pond	Lake trout	All year	21"	3	Ice fishing permitted
		Trout	All year	Any size	10	
	Fawn Lake	Lake trout	April 1-Sept. 30	18"	3	Tip-ups prohibited
	First Lake of Essex Chain, West Canada Lake	Lake trout	April 1-Sept. 30	15"	3	
	Fourth Lake of Fulton Chain	Lake trout	All year	21"	3	Ice fishing permitted
		Trout	All year	9"	10	

COUNTY		Species	Open Season	Minimum Length	Daily Limit	Method
	Hudson River, Indian River from Abanakee Lake Dam downstream, Kunjamuk River, East Stony Creek from Middle Lake outlet upstream	Largemouth and Smallmouth bass	All year	Any size	Any number	Ice fishing permitted
		Northern pike	All year	Any size	Any number	
	Indian Lake, Lake Eaton	Lake trout	All year	21"	3	Ice fishing permitted
		Landlocked salmon	All year	15"	3	
		Trout	All year	Any size	10	
	Sagamore Lake	Lake trout	April 1-Sept. 30	18"	3	
HERKIMER	Beardsley Lake, Kyser Lake, Mohawk River (Barge Canal)					Ice fishing permitted
	First Bisby Lake, Little Moose Lake	Lake trout	All year	15"	3	Ice fishing permitted
		Trout	All year	9"	10	
	First, Second, Third and Fourth Lakes of Fulton Chain	Lake trout	All year	21"	3	Ice fishing permitted
		Trout	All year	9"	10	
	Unadilla River	Trout	April 1-Sept. 30	9"	10	
	Horn Lake	Fishing prohibited to protect brook trout brood stock				
	Limekiln Lake	Trout	All year	Any size	10	Ice fishing permitted
	Moose River, Middle Branch Moose River, South Branch Moose River, West Canada Creek from mouth upstream to Cincinnati Creek	Trout	April 1-Nov. 30	Any size	10	
	West Canada Creek from bridge at Trenton Falls downstream 2.5 miles to Cincinnati Creek	Trout	April 1-Nov. 30	12"	3	Artificial lures only
	Stillwater Reservoir	Trout	All year	9"	10	Ice fishing permitted
	Woodhull Lake	Lake trout	April 1-Sept. 30	15"	3	
LEWIS	Black River, Crystal Creek, Otter Creek	Trout	April 1-Sept. 30	9"	10	
	Black River	Walleye	1st Sat. in May-March 15	18"	3	Ice fishing permitted
	Black River, Deer River, West Branch Deer River	Largemouth and Smallmouth bass	3rd Sat. in June-Nov. 30	10"	5	
	East Branch Fish Creek from Rome Reservoir Dam downstream, Moose River	Trout	April 1-Nov. 30	Any size	10	
	Lake Bonaparte	Trout	All year	9"	10	Ice fishing permitted
ONEIDA	Big Creek, Black River, Cincinnati Creek from Remsen downstream, Lansing Kill, Mad River, Mohawk River from Delta Dam downstream to Barge Canal, Oriskany Creek from College Street bridge in Clinton upstream, Sauquoit Creek from Pinnacle Road upstream, Sconondoa Creek	Trout	April 1-Sept. 30	9"	10	
	East Branch Fish Creek from Rome Reservoir Dam downstream, West Branch Fish Creek, Mohawk River from Delta Lake upstream to Lansing Kill, Moose River, Nine Mile Creek, Oneida Creek, Oriskany Creek from College Street bridge in Clinton downstream, Sauquoit Creek from Pinnacle Road in Sauquoit downstream, West Canada Creek except section below	Trout	April 1-Nov. 30	Any size	10	
	West Canada Creek from bridge at Trenton Falls downstream 2.5 miles to mouth of Cincinnati Creek	Trout	April 1-Nov. 30	12"	3	Artificial lures only
	Fish Creek from Barge Canal upstream to junction of East and West Branches of Fish Creek	Fishing prohibited March 16 through 1st Friday in May to protect spawning walleye				
ST. LAWRENCE	All rivers and streams except those covered by Great Lakes Regulations	Largemouth and Smallmouth bass	3rd Sat. in June-Nov. 30	10"	5	
	St. Lawrence River and tributaries to first barrier	All species	SEE Great Lakes Regulations pages 18-21			
	Plumb Brook, Van Rensselaer Creek	Trout	April 1-Sept. 30	9"	10	
	Little River, Oswegatchie River from Cranberry Lake Dam downstream	Trout	April 1-Nov. 30	Any size	10	

COUNTY		Species	Open Season	Minimum Length	Daily Limit	Method
	Pleasant Lake	Walleye	1st Sat. in May-March 15	18"	3	Ice fishing permitted
	Portaferry Lake and tributaries	Smelt fishing prohibited				
	Trout Lake	Lake trout	All year	21"	3	Ice fishing permitted
		Trout	All year	9"	10	
SARATOGA	All waters except Mohawk River	Pickerel	All year	Any size	Any number	
	Mohawk River	General Angling Regulations apply; SEE page 17				
	Hudson River from Glens Falls Bridge upstream, Sacandaga River from Stewarts Bridge Reservoir downstream	Largemouth and Smallmouth bass	3rd Sat. in June-Nov. 30	10"	5	
	Hudson River from Troy Dam upstream to Fort Edward and tributaries in this section to first barrier impassable by fish	Fishing prohibited				
	Kayaderosseras Creek from Saratoga Lake upstream to first R.R. bridge	Fishing prohibited March 16 through 1st Friday in May to protect spawning walleye				
WARREN	All waters	Pickerel	All year	Any size	Any number	
	Brant Lake, Hudson River, Lake Luzerne, Round Pond in Town of Thurman	Trout	All year	Any size	10	Ice fishing permitted
	Lake George	Lake trout	All year	23"	3	Ice fishing permitted except as noted
		Landlocked salmon	All year	15"	3	
		Trout	All year	Any size	10	
		Note: Ice fishing prohibited in zone near Dome Island. Contact DEC Region 5 Office at Warrensburg for boundary; see page 86. Use of smelt for bait prohibited. Possession of smelt prohibited except April 1 through May 15; see dip netting, page 14-15.				
	Lake George tributaries upstream to first barrier impassable by fish	Fishing prohibited October 1 through March 31; in addition, from April 1 thorugh May 15 no fishing between 10:00 P.M. and 5:00 A.M. Foul-hooked trout, lake trout and landlocked salmon must be released without unnecessary injury.				
	Glen Lake	Walleye	1st Sat. in May-March 15	18"	3	
	Hour Pond, Jabe Pond, Little Jabe Pond, Peaked Mountain Pond and their tributaries	Trout	April 1-Sept. 30	12"	3	Artificial lures only
	Hudson River from Glens Falls bridge upstream to Thurman bridge, Lily Pond, Pack Forest Lake	Largemouth and Smallmouth bass	3rd Sat. in June-Nov. 30	10"	5	
	Hudson River from Thurman bridge upstream	Largemouth and Smallmouth bass	All year	Any size	Any number	Ice fishing permitted
	Schroon Lake, Schroon River from Schroon Lake downstream to Starbuckville Dam	Lake trout	All year	21"	3	Ice fishing permitted
		Landlocked salmon	All year	15"	3	
		Trout	All year	Any size	10	
	Schroon River from Starbuckville Dam downstream	Largemouth and Smallmouth bass	3rd Sat. in June-Nov. 30	10"	5	Ice fishing permitted
		Lake trout	All year	Any size	3	
		Landlocked salmon	All year	Any size	3	
		Trout	All year	Any size	10	
	Thirteenth Lake and tributaries and outlet downstream to first road crossing	Trout	April 1-Sept. 30	12"	3	Artificial lures only
		Landlocked salmon	April 1-Sept. 30	18"	1	
	Trout Lake	Lake trout	All year	21"	3	Ice fishing permitted
		Trout	All year	Any size	10	
WASHINGTON	Batten Kill from Vermont state line downstream to covered bridge at Eagleville	Trout	All year	10"	3	Artificial lures only
	Lake Champlain and tributaries to first barrier	All species	SEE Lake Champlain Regulations pages 24-25			
	Lake George and tributaries to first barrier	Lake trout, Landlocked salmon, Trout	SEE Lake George under Warren County page 52			
	Hudson River from Troy Dam upstream to Fort Edward and tributaries in this section to first barrier impassable by fish	Fishing prohibited				

TAGGED FISH

DEC fishery biologists sometimes tag fish to gain information about fish populations in selected study waters. If you catch a tagged fish, write down the tag number, length of the fish, date and location of capture; send this information to the address on the tag. You will receive note by return mail that describes the tagging program and gives an account of the individual fish reported. Also don't remove tags from fish you release.

MAJOR FISHING STREAMS

This listing, published by the Department of Environmental Conservation, cites major warmwater sections of streams and rivers open to public fishing. The * indicates rivers with sections of major cold water significance, as well as warmwater significance—especially in headwaters. The mileage figures reflect only those miles open to public fishing. Total mileage is not available.

County	Mileage
CLINTON	
*Ausable River (also in Essex Co.)	6 mi.
*Great Chazy River	7 mi.
*Saranac River	6 mi.
ESSEX	
*Ausable River (also in Clinton Co.)	6 mi.
*Cold River	2 mi.
*Hudson River	8 mi.
Saranac River	8 mi.
*Schroon River	6 mi.
FRANKLIN	
*Fish Creek	2 mi.
*Osgood River	5 mi.
*Raquette River	16 mi.
Saranac River	4 mi.
FULTON	None in the Adirondacks.
HAMILTON	
*Cedar River	2 mi.
*Indian River	1 mi.
*Kunjamuk River	10 mi.
Raquette River	5 mi.
*Sacandaga River	6 mi.
HERKIMER	
*Beaver River	8 mi.
*Moose River, Middle Br.	12 mi.
*Moose River, North Br.	12 mi.
LEWIS	
Beaver River	18 mi.
Moose River	14 mi.
ONEIDA	
*Black River	8 mi.
ST. LAWRENCE	
*Grass River	12 mi.
*Oswegatchie River	12 mi.
*Raquette River	35 mi.
SARATOGA	
Hudson River (also in Warren Co.)	8 mi.
WARREN	
Hudson River (also in Saratoga Co.)	37 mi.
Schroon River	12 mi.
WASHINGTON	None in the Adirondacks.

REGION 5 TOP FISHING WATERS

The listing below is published by the Department of Environmental Conservation (undated). For a more recent and more comprehensive listing of Adirondack fishing waters, see Francis Betters, *Fishing The Adirondacks* (Adirondacks Sports Publication, 1982), available from Adirondack Sporting Goods, Rt. 86, Wilmington, NY 12997. (518)946-2605. A few changes to the D.E.C. list have been made in light of Betters' and other information.

BROOK TROUT

Essex County
Bailey Pond
Barnes Pond
Center Pond
Crab Pond
Grizzle Ocean
Livingston Pond
Marion Pond
Oxshoe Pond
Spectacle Ponds

Franklin County
Bessie Pond
Black Pond
Grass Pond
Kit Fox Pond
Little Trout River
Whey Pond

Hamilton County
N Lake
Lost Ponds
Spruce Pond

Warren County
Big Jabe Pond
Hour Pond
Thirteenth Lake
Sacandaga River (E. Branch)

BROWN TROUT

Clinton County
Little Ausable River
North Branch Great Chazy River
North Branch Saranac River
Saranac River (main stem)

Essex County
Bouquet River
West Branch Ausable River

Franklin County
Chateaugay River
Little Salmon River
Salmon River

Warren County
Mill Creek
Glenn Creek

Washington County
Battenkill River

RAINBOW TROUT

Clinton County
Chazy Lake
Taylor Pond
Upper Chateaugay Lake

Essex County
Hudson River
Lake Placid
Mirror Lake
Paradox Lake
West Branch Ausable River

Franklin County
Lake Kushaqua
Lower Chateaugay
Saint Regis River

Hamilton County
Eighth Lake
Seventh Lake

Warren County
Lake George

LAKE TROUT

Clinton County
Chazy Lake
Lake Champlain
Taylor Pond
Upper Chateaugay

Essex County
Lake Champlain
Lake Placid
Paradox Lake
Schroon Lake

Hamilton County
Blue Mountain Lake
Indian Lake
Piseco Lake
Raquette Lake

Warren County
Lake George

KOKANEE SALMON

Franklin County
Lake Colby
Little Green Pond

Hamilton County
Bug Lake
Mitchell Ponds

SPLAKE

Essex County
Goose Pond

Franklin County
Lake Colby
Little Long Pond
Upper Saint Regis Lake

Hamilton County
Seventh Lake

LANDLOCKED SALMON

Clinton County
Lake Champlain

Essex County
Bouquet River
Lake Champlain
Schroon Lake
McKensie Pond

Franklin County
Little Green Pond

Hamilton County
Lake Eaton

Warren County
Lake George
Thirteenth Lake

NORTHERN PIKE

Clinton County
Chazy Lake
Lake Champlain
Union Falls

Essex County
Franklin Falls Pond
Lake Champlain
Lake Flower

Franklin County
Franklin Falls Pond
Raquette River
Raquette Pond
Saranac Lake Chain
Tupper Lake
Union Falls Pond
Upper Saint Regis Lake

Fulton County
Great Sacandaga Res.
Peck Lake

Hamilton County
Long Lake

Saratoga County
Great Sacandaga Res

Warren County
Lake George
Loon Lake
Schroon River

WALLEYE

Clinton County
Lake Champlain
Union Falls Pond

Essex County
Lake Champlain

Franklin County
Raquette River
Tupper Lake
Union Falls

Fulton County
Great Sacandaga Res.

Saratoga County
Great Sacandaga Res.

SMALLMOUTH BASS

Clinton County
Chazy Lake
Upper Chateaugay Lake

Essex County
Eagle Lake
Lake Placid
Paradox Lake
Schroon Lake

Franklin County
Long Pond
Lower Chateaugay Lake
Raquette Pond
Raquette River Saranac Lake Chain
Tupper Lake

Fulton County
Great Sacandaga Reservoir
Peck Lake

Hamilton County
Eighth Lake
Forked Lake
Indian Lake
Lake Eaton
Lake Pleasant
Long Lake
Piseco Lake
Raquette Lake
Sacandaga Lake
Seventh Lake

Saratoga County
Great Sacandaga Reservoir

St. Lawrence County
Cranberry Lake

Warren County
Brant Lake
Lake George
Schroon River

LARGEMOUTH BASS

Essex County
Eagle Lake
Paradox Lake

Franklin County
Osgood Lake
Upper Saint Regis Lake

Fulton County
Peck Lake

Warren County
Brant Lake
Lake George
Loon Lake

Washington County
Cossayuna Lake

TIGER MUSKELLUNGE

Hamilton County
Lake Durant

Warren County
Brant Lake
Loon Lake

(85)

ICE FISHING

Any person holding a fishing license or entitled to fish without a license may fish through the ice in waters not inhabited by trout and in certain trout waters designated by the Department of Environmental Conservation. See Section 116 for regional offices of D.E.C.

Check with the *New York State Fishing, Small Game Hunting and Trapping Regulations Guide* pertaining to the water you intend to fish. Unless noted otherwise, fish may be taken where ice fishing is permitted as follows:

November 15-April 30: Those species in the General Angling Regulations table, for which there is no closed season and no minimum length.

November 15-March 15: Northern pike, pickerel, tiger muskellunge, walleye.

During Open Season: Other species.

Information: Fisheries Division of the Department of Environmental Conservation at Warrensburg. (518)623-3671.

Source: *NY State Fishing, Small Game Hunting and Trapping Regulations Guide*, 1982-83.

(86)

LICENSED ADIRONDACK GUIDES

The following is the most recent (1979) listing of Adirondack guides. Complete listings, consisting of guide's name, address and territory for which licensed, are periodically published by the Department of Environmental Conservation. Information is also available from the New York State Outdoor Guides Association, PO Box 4337, Albany, NY 12204.

Aiello, Joseph Sr.
Aird, Arvin C.
Alden, Cecil R.
Angerosa, Richard V.
Andrews, John Wm.
Andros, Charles H.
Archard, Malcolm W.
Arndt, Bernard
Atwill, Lionel
Azzue, Anthony

Balogh, William A.
Barlow, Edward A.
Barth, Francis F.
Batchelder, Warren E.
Beckley, Kenneth
Bell, Stanton
Berry, James L.
Betters, Edward J.
Blatter, Roger
Bold, Glen

Bortle, Frank S. Jr.
Boyer, Robert
Brannen, Richard
Brockney, Lloyd J.
Brockway, Larry E.
Brown, Robert E.
Brust, Russell Jr.
Burtch, Lewis P.
Butler, George T.
Byczek, Joseph A.

Cadieux, Ronald E.
Campbell, Karlton F.
Campbell Harold J. Jr.
Canaday, Douglas B.
Carman, William E.
Carter, Gary W.
Chase, S. Tice Jr.
Cheney, Loren
Chesebro, William F.
Chrysler, Ray W.

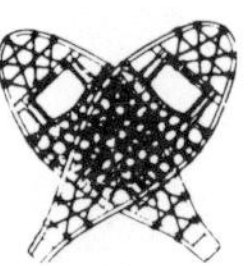

Cinquina, Marlo L.
Cipriano, Angelo J.
Cobane, P. Stanley
Cole, Edward D.
Collins, Harry T.
Comeau, Jules J.
Conklin, Carl K.
Conklin, Daniel L.
Connolly, William R.
Connor, David R.

Cookinham, Edward S.
Coon, Sidney
Cooper, Wayne W.
Corell, Philip B.
Corrigan, William J.
Corse, David G.
Cox, Donald H.
Crandall, Richard A.
Cranker, James S.
Cranker, William G.

Cromie, William J.
Cure, Clinton F.
Czwakiel, Frank A.
Danchak, Jack
Dassa, Morris,
Davis, Ralph J.
Davis, Richard O.
Davis, William J.
Day, Major Jr.
Deming, John A.

Dewyen, John C. Sr.
Dhumm, Donald J.
Dice, Robert
Dixon, William M. Jr.
D'Onofrio, Salvadore
Drake, Roger T. Sr.
Drury, John K.
Duffy, Gerald W.
Duprey, Dennis B.
Eberley, Robert G.

Ellsworth, James L.
Evans, Donald J.
Exford, Myron K.
Faelten, William
Fehsal, Raymond
Farmer, Steven L.
Faulkner, Albert
Ferrusi, Ralph J.
Finch, Donald F.
Fish, Terrance J.

Fisher, Edward C.
Fleury, Roy P.
Foote, DeWitt Wm.
Ford, Wayne K.N.
Fowler, Richard C.
Fox, Ronald Basil
Fraser, Roderick
Frasier, Eugene O.
Frantanton, Anthony
Friedow, Ernest C.

Frisbie, Daniel J.
Frishmuth, Ronald E.
Games, Roy Victor III
Garhartt, Raymond
Garwig, William E. Jr.
Gasiorowski, John S. Jr.
Geandreau, Robert A.
Gethehead, John J.
Giddings, Jay D.
Gleasman, Harley

Goodemote, Russell
Goodrow, John F. Sr.
Goodwin, James A.
Goodwin, James A. Jr.
Gould, Nelson A.
Graff, Edward S. Jr.
Graves, Rollin A.
Green, John T. Sr.
Griffen, Clark D.
Grund, William C.

Grzyb, Richard
Hackett, Joseph
Haines, Howard
Hall, Larry F.
Hamilton, Douglas W. Jr.
Hance, Peter G.
Hance, Richard Lee
Havas, Daniel
Harvey, Gary
Hastings, John T.

Hayes, Harold R.
Hendrecks, Timothy
Herman, Frances
Hickey, Howard
Hickson, Alfred J.
Hill, Charles B.
Hinman, Jack K.
Hogancamp, Paul Jr.
Holt, Melvin E.
Houmiel, Hubert

Howard, David A.
Howard, Joel M.
Hughes, Robert C.
Hundley, Albert T.
Hunt, James O.
Hutton, Jerry
Irish, Arthur
Ives, Willard G. Jr.
Jacobsen, Jacques Noel Jr.
Jandreau, Bernard L.

Jarvis, Francis L.
Jacques, Lynworth E. Sr.
Jerry, Harold A. Jr.
Johnson, Edgar L.
Hones, Russell W.
Kanaby, Andrew W.
Kearney, David L.
Kelly, Larry
Kerr, Randolph E.
Ketchum, Vern

Keyser, Edwin
Kiniry, Owen E.
Klein, Herbert Jr.
Klein, Jerry
Knight, John C.
Kolocotronis, James
Kromko, Steve
LaBastille, Anne
Lacombe, Ignatius
Lambrigger, Robert
Langton, Dudley D.

Larison, Robert
Larow, Fred
Lathrop, Douglas G.
Lawrence, Russell B. III
Leach, John J. III
LeBlanc, Bernard J.
LeClair, Ernest J.
LeClair, Penny J.
Lee, Arthur C. Jr.
Leege, William W.

Lehr, Daniel
Loffler, Harold J.
Loucks, Raymond A.
Lucci, Robert J.
McAvoy, Howard
McCarthy, Joseph A.
McCulley, Frederick
McCutcheon, Charles A.
McFaul, Lloyd
McGrath, W.J. James

McInerney, Joseph J.
McIntosh, Charles F.
McIntyre, Donald R.
McLymond, Clayton
McPhilmy, John L.
Majo, Lynn A.
Maly, Lance F.
Mance, Ernest J. Jr.
Manfred, Thomas W.
Manning, John J. Jr.

Manning, Wesley
Marchese, James J.
Marrone, Robert M.
Maslyn, Paul
Maxfield, Jerald J.
Maya, Waldemar D.
Mayes, Dean
Mensink, Robert A.
Mesmer F. Dan
Miller, Jack C.

Miller, James A.
Miller, Lawrence
Minchin, Thomas M.
Ming, John S.
Mitchell, Donald C.
Monteleone, Stephen A.
Montroy, Lawrence F.
Moody, Robert W.
Morgan, Alexander L.
Morris, Brian Lee

Morse, Robert F.
Murat, Donald S.
Murat, William P.
Newell, Nora J.
Newman, Jack K.
Nichols, David Ross
Norton, Charles R.
Norton, David R.
O'Brien, Howard
O'Connor, William

Oliver, Everett F.
Olkowski, Melvin D.
Olton, Marc B.
O'Neill, Karen
Orr, Charles Andrew
Ostrander, Richard
Oudekerk, John N. Jr.
Paluck, David Martin
Panchyshyn, George J.
Panchyshyn, Henry T.

Parent, Richard L.
Parrott, Gary G.
Pasco, Merwyn
Passer, Jerry E.
Pearsall, Robert E.
Perkins, Robert D.
Peroni, George P.
Petit, Richard B.
Pfeiffer, Jack
Phillips, Thomas R.

Pisaneschi, Roger
Plete, Philip W.
Porter, Hugh M.
Pratt, Neil F.
Prestopnik, Richard
Provoncha, Thomas N.
Puglia, Frank
Quick, Russell W.
Quinones, David L.
Rapant, Robert
Raub, Lawrence

Record, Timothy
Reed, Willard Leland
Reynolds, David
Richer, William A.
Rinaldi, Paul G.
Ritzmann, Edward A.
Robertson, Lewis
Robinson, James L.
Robinson, Stephen M.
Rock, Raymond F.

Rockwell, Landon G.
Rodd, Robert Adelore
Roller, Albert
Romeo, Thomas A.
Rommel, Richard
Ross, Harold E.
Rowe, Dennis
Rumrill, Burton D.
Russell, Albert E.
Sadler, Edward

St. John, Charles A.
Salton, Stanley W.
Sandberg, Hector R.
Schrader, Andrew Jr.
Schrader, Raymond
Schunk, Friedel
Seaman, Clark J.
Sears, Dexter C.
Schring, George T.
Seymour, William L.

Shaw, Robert G.
Shayne, Robert F.
Shea, Michael E.
Sherwood, Kenneth W.
Short, Leroy W.
Simmons, James E. Sr.
Simpson, Kenyon Ray
Sipe, Robert M.
Slingerland, Russell G.
Smith, Charles Allen

Smith, DeForrest
Smith, Donald E.
Smith, Edwin Thomas
Smith, Gregory Nye
Smith, James A.
Smith, John J.
Smith, Ray H.
Smith, Timothy V.G.
Smith, William B.
Snyder, Robert R.
Sobolewski, Thomas E.

Sorensen, Ralph
Sprague, Andrew C.
Stanton, Welford E.
Stark, Raymond P. Jr.
Stiles, Bruce E.
Stout, James P.
Strack, Thomas H.
Stuart, David F. Sr.
Suddaby, Gary
Sweeter, John F.

Tefft, Tim
Thaotte, Richard L.
Tompkins, George F.
Tormey, Hayden C.
Tornetta, Paul
Trumpbour, William H. Jr.
Tucker, Sherwin R.
Turner, Alfred H.
Turner, Brian B.
Tybush, Frank L.

Ulinski, William S.
Van Zandt, Jeffrey G.
Vienna, David J.
Virkler, M.C.
Visscher, W.
Vodron, John
Wallace, Donald S.
Wands, H.A.
Ward, Peter J.
Warne, Steven P.

Warren, John N.
Wells, Howard E.
Wells, Llewellyn
Wemple, Dick
West, Alan G.
Wharton, William Jr.
Wheeler, Gregg R.
White, Bruce D.
Wilkes, William G.
Wilkins, Dillman F.

Williams, Donald R.
Woodard, Clarence Ben
Wolfe, Ralph E.
Woodruff, Alan R.
Wriston, George W. Jr.
Yonke, J. John
Yost, A.J.
Young, Jonona S.
Yurgartis, Stanley
Zampella, Ralph
Zukovsky, Alexander

(87)
FLYING SERVICES

These services generally specialize in scenic flying tours and in taking hunters and fishing people to remote Adirondack lakes. However, they also provide air transportation—in all seasons—both on land and water,between the Adirondacks and other areas and states.

ADIRONDACK FLYING SERVICE, Cascade Rd. (Rt. 73), Lake Placid Airport, Lake Placid, NY 12946. (518)523-2473.

BIRD'S SEAPLANE SERVICE, Inc., off Rt. 28, Inlet, NY 13360. (315)357-3631.

HELM'S AERO SERVICE, Rt. 30, Long Lake, NY 12847. (518)624-3931 or 624-3561.

PAYNE'S AIR SERVICE, off Rt. 28, Seventh Lake, NY 13360. (315)357-3971.

TRI LAKES FLYING SERVICE, INC., Lake Clear Rd., Adirondack Airport, Saranac Lake, NY 12983. (518)891-3114.

STATE CAMPGROUNDS

The following is a list of New York State public campgrounds in the Adirondack Park. Most operate Memorial Day to Labor Day; one should call in advance for spring and fall camping. For further information call the campground or the regional Department of Environmental Conservation headquarters, listed in Section 116. An asterick (*) indicates boat access only.

CLINTON COUNTY

AUSABLE POINT CAMPGROUND, Rt. 9, 12 miles south of Plattsburgh. 121 sites, swimming. (518)561-7080.

ESSEX COUNTY

CROWN POINT RESERVATION CAMPGROUND, off Rt. 9N, 8 miles north of Crown Point. 64 sites, swimming, boat launching. (518)597-3264.

LAKE HARRIS CAMPGROUND, off Rt. 28N, 3 miles north of Newcomb. 90 sites, swimming, boat launching. (518) 582-2503.

LINCOLN POND CAMPGROUND, 6 miles south of Elizabethtown on county Rt. 7. 15 sites, swimming. (518)942-5292.

MEADOWBROOK CAMPGROUND, Rt. 86, 4 miles east of Saranac Lake. 62 sites. (518)891-4351.

PARADOX LAKE CAMPGROUND, Rt. 74, 2 miles east of Severance. 58 sites, swimming, boat launching. (518) 532-7451.

POKE-O-MOONSHINE CAMPGROUND, US Rt. 9, 6 miles south of Keeseville. 25 sites. (518)834-9045.

PUTNAM POND CAMPGROUND, off Rt. 74, 6 miles west of Ticonderoga. 56 sites, swimming, boat launching. (518) 585-7280.

SHARP BRIDGE CAMPGROUND, US Rt. 9, 15 miles north of Schroon Lake. 37 sites. (518)532-7538.

WILMINGTON NOTCH CAMPGROUND, Rt. 86, 3.5 miles west of Wilmington. 50 sites. (518)946-7172.

FRANKLIN COUNTY

BUCK POND CAMPGROUND, off Rt. 30, 12 miles east of Paul Smiths. 114 sites, swimming, boat launching. (518) 891-3449.

FISH CREEK CAMPGROUND, Rt. 30, 12 miles east of Tupper Lake. 351 sites, swimming, boat launching. (518)891-4560.

MEACHAM LAKE CAMPGROUND, Rt. 30, 19 miles north of Clear Lake Junction. 222 sites, swimming, boat launching. (518)483-5116.

ROLLIN'S POND CAMPGROUND*, same as FISH CREEK. 288 sites. (518)891-3239.

SARANAC LAKE ISLANDS*, off Rt. 3, near Village of Saranac Lake. 62 sites. (518)891-4590.

FULTON COUNTY

CAROGA LAKE CAMPGROUND, Rt. 29A, 9 miles north of Gloversville. 164 sites, swimming, boat launching. (518) 835-9451.

NORTHHAMPTON BEACH CAMPGROUND, Rt. 30, 1.5 miles south of Northville. 224 sites, swimming, boat launching. (518)863-6000.

HAMILTON COUNTY

BROWN TRACT POND CAMPGROUND, Rt. 28, 7 miles east of Eagle Bay. 90 sites, swimming, boat launching. (315)354-4412.

EIGHTH LAKE CAMPGROUND, Rt. 28, 5 miles west of Raquette Lake. 118 sites, swimming, boat launching. (315)357-3132.

FORKED LAKE CAMPGROUND, off Rt. 30, 3 miles west of Deerland Village. 78 sites, boat launching. (518)624-3346.

GOLDEN BEACH CAMPGROUND, Rt. 28, 3 miles east of Raquette Lake. 206 sites, swimming, boat launching. (315)354-4230.

INDIAN LAKE ISLANDS CAMPGROUND*, Rt. 30, 14 miles north of Speculator. 50 sites, boat launching. (518) 648-5300.

LAKE DURANT CAMPGROUND, Rt. 28, 3 miles east of Blue Mt. Lake. 60 sites, swimming, boat launching. (518)352-7797.

LAKE EATON CAMPGROUND, Rt. 30, 2 miles west of Long Lake. 139 sites, swimming, boat launching. (518) 624-2641.

LEWEY LAKE CAMPGROUND, Rt. 30, 14 miles north of Speculator. 206 sites, swimming, boat launching. (518) 648-5266.

LIMEKILN LAKE CAMPGROUND, off Rt. 28, 3 miles southeast of Inlet. 272 sites, swimming, boat launching. (315)357-4401.

LITTLE SAND POINT CAMPGROUND, off Rt. 8, 3 miles west of Piseco. 78 sites, swimming, boat launching. (518)548-7585.

MOFFIT BEACH CAMPGROUND, Rt. 8, 4 miles west of Speculator. 258 sites, swimming, boat launching. (518) 548-7102.

POINT COMFORT CAMPGROUND, off Rt. 8, 4 miles west of Piseco. 77 sites, swimming, boat launching. (518) 548-7586.

POPLAR POINT CAMPGROUND, off Rt. 8, 2 miles west of Piseco. 34 sites, swimming, boat launching. (518) 548-8031.

SACANDAGA CAMPGROUND, Rt. 30, 4 miles south of Wells. 143 sites, swimming. (518)924-4121.

TIOGA POINT CAMPGROUND*, Raquette Lake. 15 sites. (518)354-4101.

HERKIMER COUNTY

ALGER ISLAND CAMPGROUND*, off Rt. 28, 8 miles east of Old Forge. 15 sites. (315)369-3415.

FOURTH LAKE PICNIC AREA, off Rt. 28, 8 miles east of Old Forge. (315)369-3224.

HINCKLEY RESERVOIR PICNIC AREA, off Rt. 365, 5 miles east of Hinckley. Swimming. (315)826-3800.

NICKS LAKE CAMPGROUND, off Rt. 28, 1.5 miles southwest of Old Forge. 112 sites, swimming, boat launching. (315)369-3314.

ST. LAWRENCE COUNTY

CRANBERRY LAKE CAMPGROUND, off Rt. 3, 1.5 miles south of Cranberry Lake Village. 173 sites, swimming. (315)848-3614.

WARREN COUNTY

EAGLE POINT CAMPGROUND, US Rt. 9, 2 miles north of Pottersville. 71 sites, swimming, boat launching. (518) 494-2220.

HEARTHSTONE POINT CAMPGROUND, Rt. 9N, 2 miles north of Lake George Village. 254 sites, swimming. (518)668-5193.

LAKE GEORGE BATTLEFIELD PICNIC AREA, off US Rt. 9, 1/4 mile east of Lake George Village.

LAKE GEORGE BATTLEGROUND CAMPGROUND, US Rt. 9, 1/4 mile south of Lake George Village. 68 sites. (518)668-3348.

LAKE GEORGE BEACH, US Rt. 9, 1/4 east of Lake George Village. (518)668-3352.

LAKE GEORGE ISLANDS*, Bolton Landing. 212 sites, swimming. (518)644-9696.

LUZERNE CAMPGROUND, Rt. 9N, 8 miles southwest of Lake George Village. 165 sites, swimming, boat launching. (518)696-2031.

ROGERS ROCK CAMPGROUND, Rt. 9N, 3 miles north of Hague. 304 sites, swimming, boat launching. (518) 585-6746.

LEWIS, ONEIDA, SARATOGA AND WASHINGTON COUNTIES have no state campgrounds in the Adirondack Park.

CHILDREN'S SUMMER CAMPS

CAMP ASSOCIATIONS

AASC - Association of Adirondack Scout Camps, PO Box 350, Dayton, NJ 08810.

ACA - American Camping Association, Bradford Woods, Martinsville, IN 46151.

AIC - Association of Independent Camps, 157 W. 57th St., New York, NY 10019. (212)582-3540.

CCI - Christian Camping International, PO Box 646, Wheaton, IL 60189.

NYSCDA - New York State Camp Directors Association, c/o Ruth Wortman, President, 80 Neptune Ave., Woodmere, NY 11598.

NYSOEA - New York State Outdoor Education Association, 196 Morton Ave., Albany, NY 12202.

ADIRONDACK CAMPS

ADIRONDACK SWIM & TRIP, Rainbow Lake, Franklin County, ACA, 80 boys, 8-14. Specialties: outdoor living skills, sailing, canoeing, swimming, canoe and mountain trips. Joseph Reiners, Jr., 39 Mill Valley Rd., Pittsford, NY 14534. (716)248-5331.

ADIRONDACK WOODCRAFT, Old Forge, Herkimer County, ACA, AIC, 150 boys, 6-16, 8 weeks. Specialties: rock climbing and canoe and mountain trips, campcrafts, environment, sports, watersports. John or David Leach, Box 219, Old Forge, NY 13420. (315)369-6031/3816.

BACO, Minerva, Essex County, ACA, AIC, NYSCDA, NYSOEA, 200 boys, 6-16, 8 weeks. Specialties: academic, arts & crafts, tennis, music, campcrafts, backpacking, dramatics, horseback riding, sailing, gymnastics, pioneering, sports, watersports. Ruth & Melvin Wortman, 80 Neptune Ave., Woodmere, NY 11598. (516)374-7757.

BRANT LAKE, Brant Lake, Warren County, ACA, AIC, NYSCDA, 320 boys, 7-16, 8 weeks. Specialties: arts, tennis, land sports, watersports. Karen Meltzer/Robert Gersten, 19 E. 80th St., New York, NY 10021. (212) 734-6216.

BRANT LAKE DANCE CENTER FOR GIRLS, Brant Lake, Warren County. Two 3-week sessions. Specialties: Ballet, modern, jazz, tap, tennis and watersports. Karen Meltzer/Robert Gersten, Directors, 19 East 80th St., New York, NY 10021. (212)734-6216.

BULLOCK FARM, Ticonderoga, Essex County, NYSCDA, 40 girls, 8-18, 2, 4, 6, and 8 weeks. Specialty: horseback riding. Susan McIntyre, Bullock Farm, Ticonderoga, NY 12883. (518)585-9808.

CEDARLANDS, Long Lake, Hamilton County, AASC, 200 boys, 11-18, 2 weeks. Specialties: outpost camping, aquatics, logging, wilderness survival, sailboarding, waterskiing. AASC Voyageur Trek Program, wilderness, high adventure, Scout camp. Land of the Oneida Council, 1401 Genesee St., Utica, NY 13501. (315)735-4437.

CHATEAUGAY, Merrill, Clinton County, AIC, 125 boys & girls, 7-16, 7 weeks. Specialties: water skiing, sailing, water and land sports, horseback riding, hiking, arts & crafts.John & Judy Golden, 1833 Kenyon Rd., Ontario, NY 14519. (315)524-5654.

CHE-NA-WAH, Minerva, Essex County, ACA, AIC, NYSCDA, 160 girls, 6-16, 8 weeks. Specialties: academic, arts & crafts, campcrafts, health, horseback riding, performing arts, sports, watersports. Alice & Les Sternin, 51 Planting Field Rd., Roslyn Heights, NY 11577. (516)621-5333.

CHEROKEE, Saranac Inn, Franklin County, 70 boys & girls, 9-19, 4-6 weeks. Specialties: Bible study, arts & crafts, horseback riding, sports, watersports. New York Conference of Seventh Day Adventists, Box 67, Syracuse, NY 13215. (315)469-6921.

CURTIS S. READ, Brant Lake, Warren County, AASC, 250 boys, 11-15, 7 weeks. Specialties: arts & crafts, campcrafts, environment, sports, watersports. Westchester-Putnam Council BSA, 1111 Westchester Ave., White Plains, NY 10604. (914)949-6180.

DEERFOOT LODGE, Speculator, Hamilton County, ACA, CCI, 100 boys, 8-16, 9 weeks. Specialties: wilderness skills, academic, campcrafts, environment, sports, watersports, arts & crafts. Deerfoot Lodge, RD 2, PO Box 159 B, Greenville, NY 12083.

DUDLEY YMCA, Westport, Essex County, ACA, NYSCDA, 465 boys, 10-15, 8 weeks. Specialties: arts & crafts, drama, music, hiking, canoeing, sports. William J. Schmidt, Camp Dudley, Westport, NY 12933. (518) 962-4720.

EAGLE ISLAND CAMP, Upper Saranac Lake, Franklin County, ACA, 135 girls, 10-18, 7 weeks of 1 and 2 week sessions. Specialties: sailing, aquatics, canoe tripping, backpacking and camping. Girl Scout Council of Greater Essex County, 120 Valley Rd., Montclair, NJ 07042. (201)746-8200.

ECHO, Raquette Lake, Hamilton County, ACA, NYSCDA, 95 girls, 5-16. Specialties: academic, arts & crafts, environment, health, horseback riding, performing arts, sports, watersports. Virginia Pope, Echo Camp for Girls, PO Box 606, Saratoga Springs, NY 12866. (518)587-8363.

ECHO LAKE, Warrensburg, Warren County, ACA, NYSCDA, 375 campers, 7-17, 8 weeks. Specialties: arts & crafts, campcrafts, environment, performing arts, sports, watersports. Amy & Morry Stein, 49 Clubway, Hartsdale, NY 10530. (914)472-5858.

FLOODWOOD MOUNTAIN SCOUT RESERVATION, Saranac Inn, Franklin County, 250 boys, 11-17, 6 weeks. Specialties: canoeing,rock climbing, rappelling, waterskiing, backpacking, environmental science, Scouting outdoor advancement program, watersports. Bergen Council-BSA, 1060 Main St., River Edge, NJ 07661. (201)342-8600.

FOREST LAKE, Warrensburg, Warren County, 150 boys, 7-16, 8 weeks. Specialties: hobbies, horseback riding, land sports, watersports. Philip H. Confer, 27 Baltimore Ave., Massapequa, NY 11758. (516)798-4156.

4-H SACANDAGA, Speculator, Hamilton County, 100 boys & girls, 8-19, 7 weeks, one week sessions. Specialties: academic, creative arts, campcrafts, environment, sports, watersports, counselor training. Cooperative Extension Association 4-H, 17 Hudson St., Warrensburg, NY 12885. (518)623-3291.

FOWLER, Speculator, Hamilton County, 104 children & adults, 9 weeks. Specialties: academic, arts & crafts, campcrafts, health, performing arts, religious study, sports, watersports. Particular Synod of Albany, 1790 Grand Blvd., Schenectady, NY 12309. (518)374-4573.

GUGGENHEIM, Saranac Lake, Franklin County, ACA, 76 boys & girls, 12-15, 4 weeks. 16-18, 2 weeks. Specialties: academic, arts & crafts, campcrafts, environment, religious study, sports, watersports. Mrs. Carol Patton, 604 Washington St., PO Box 369, Ogdensburg, NY 13669. (315)393-0368.

HIDDEN LAKE, Lake Luzerne, Warren County, 230 girls, 8-14. Specialties: arts & crafts, campcrafts, environment, horseback riding, team and individual sports, watersports, backpacking, cycling, canoeing. Mohawk Pathways Girl Scout Council, 945 Palmer Ave., Schenectady, NY 12309. (518)374-3345.

HUMAN RELATIONS YOUTH ADVENTURE CAMP, Raquette Lake, Hamilton County, NYSCDA, NYSOEA, 33 boys & girls, 11-14, two 16-day sessions. Specialties: arts & crafts, campcrafts, environment, human relations, watersports. Sagamore Lodge and Conference Center, Sagamore Rd., Raquette Lake, NY 13436. (315)354-5311.

IDYLWOLD, South Schroon, Essex County, AIC, NYSCDA, 150 boys 6-16, 8 weeks. Specialties: academic, arts & crafts, campcrafts, environment, performing arts, sports, tennis, soccer, watersports. George Edelman, 64 Polo Rd., Great Neck, NY 11023. (516)487-5824.

JEANNE d'ARC, Merrill, Clinton County, NYSCDA, 130 girls, 6-17, 6 weeks. Specialties: arts & crafts, academic, sailing, water skiing, horseback riding, camping, land sports, performing arts, Catholic Chapel. Mr. & Mrs. C.C. McIntyre, Box 83-H, Scarsdale, NY 10583. (914)472-4041.

LAKE CLEAR GIRL SCOUT, Lake Clear, Franklin County, 100 girls, 6-17, 1-4 weeks. Specialties: outdoor awareness, arts & crafts, campcrafts, horseback riding,sailing, watersports. North Country Girl Scout Council, Inc., Box 882, Plattsburgh, NY 12901. (518)563-1560.

LAKE COLBY ENVIRONMENTAL EDUCATION, Saranac Lake, Franklin County, 50 boys & girls, 12-14, 8 one-week sessions. Specialties: environmental education. NYS Dept. of Environmental Conservation, 50 Wolf Rd., Room 509, Albany, NY 12233. (518)457-3720.

LITTLE NOTCH, West Fort Ann, Washington County, ACA, 188 girls, 6-17, 5 one-week sessions. Specialties: rock climbing, backpacking, canoeing, sailing, biking, horseback riding, outdoor living skills. Frances Plummer, Hudson Valley Girl Scout Council, 750 Delaware Ave., Delmar, NY 12054. (518)439-4936.

LONG LAKE CREATIVE ARTS, Long Lake, Hamilton County, ACA, AIC, 130 boys & girls, 9-17, 7 weeks. Specialties: arts & crafts, horseback riding, performing arts, sports, watersports. David Katz, 67-42 Ingram St., Forest Hills, NY 11375. (212)520-8433. Summer: Walker Rd, Long Lake, NY 12847. (518)624-4831.

LUZERNE MUSIC CENTER, Lake Luzerne, Warren County, girls and boys, 10-18. Specialties: music-learning experience combined with recreation program. Staffed by members of the Philadelphia Orchestra. Bert Phillips and Toby Blumenthal, Directors. 5 East Brookhaven Road, Wallingford, PA 19086.

MASSAWEPIE SCOUT, Piercefield, St. Lawrence County, 600 boys, 11-18, 7 weeks. Specialties: arts & crafts, campcrafts, environment, health, sports, watersports. Otetiana Council- BSA, 474 East Ave., Rochester, NY 14607. (716)244-4210.

NORTH COUNTRY CAMPS (Lincoln for boys, Whippoorwill for girls), Keeseville, Essex County, ACA, 80 boys 9-15, 70 girls 9-15, 7 1/2 weeks. Specialties: mountain climbing, canoe, backpack, and bicycle trips, sailing, horseback riding, swimming, field sports, woodworking and crafts, tennis and archery. Peter L. Gucker, 36 Wellwood Road, Demarest, NJ 07627. (201)768-6198.

NORTHERN FRONTIER, Indian Lake, Hamilton County, ACA, CCI, 130 boys, 8-18, 8 weeks. Specialties: arts & crafts, campcrafts, horseback riding, religious study, sports, watersports. Brigade Camp Association, 83 Coach Lane, Newburgh, NY 12550. (914)564-2567.

PENIEL BIBLE CONFERENCE, Lake Luzerne, Warren County, CCI, 125 children & adults, 8 weeks. Specialties: arts & crafts, religious studies, sports, watersports. Ronald Stimers, Box 177, Schenectady, NY 12301. (518) 374-0811.

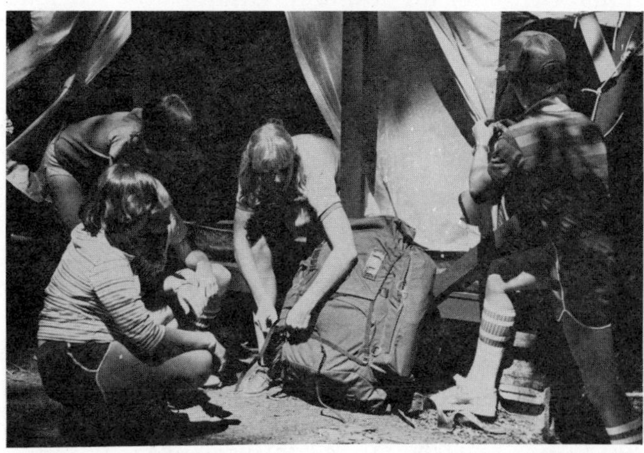

PILGRIM CAMP, Brant Lake, Warren County, boys & girls, 6-15 and adults 16 and over. Specialties: watersports, sports. Gordon P. Gardiner, Rt. 1, Box 134, Brant Lake, NY 12815. (518)494-2547.

POINT O'PINES, Brant Lake, Warren County, ACA, AIC, NYSCDA, 240 girls, 7-15, 8 weeks. Specialties: arts & crafts,athletics, tennis, watersports, outdoor camping. Hobart E. Rosen, 86 Spruce Lane, Greenwich, CT 06830. (203)322-1414.

POK-O-MAC CREADY CAMPS, Willsboro, Essex County, ACA, 200 boys & girls, 7-16, 6 weeks. Specialties: arts & crafts, rock climbing, backpacking, campcrafts, horseback riding, sailing, pottery, sports, watersports. Jack Swan, Box 16C, Brookfield Center, CT 06805. (203)775-9865.

RAQUETTE LAKE BOYS, Raquette Lake, Hamilton County, ACA, 180 boys, 6-15, 8 weeks. Specialties: Team sports, tennis, aquatic sports. Tripping and mountaineering options available. Rennie and Jerry Halsband, 140 Larchmont Ave., Larchmont, NY 10538. (914)833-0171.

RAQUETTE LAKE GIRLS, Raquette Lake, Hamilton County, ACA, 200 girls, 6-15, 8 weeks. Specialties: all aquatic sports, tennis, gymnastics, dance, theatre, arts and crafts. English riding available. Rennie and Jerry Halsband, 180 Larchmont Ave., Larchmont, NY 10538. (914)833-0171.

REGIS APPLE JACK, Paul Smiths, Franklin County, ACA, 160 girls & boys, 6-16, 8 weeks. Specialties: drama, arts & crafts, campcrafts, environment, health, horseback riding, tennis, computers, performing arts, sports, watersports. Humes Family, 107 Robinhood Rd., White Plains, NY 10605. (914)997-7039.

SABATTIS ADVENTURE SCOUT CAMP, Long Lake, Hamilton County, 300 boys, 11-17, 4 weeks. Specialties: archery, rifle, campcrafts, environment, hiking, swimming, canoeing, sailing. Watchung Area Council- BSA, 905 Watchung Ave., Plainfield, NJ 07060. (201)753-1976.

SABATTIS SCOUT, Long Lake, St. Lawrence County, 300 boys per week, 11-18, 6 weeks. Specialties: wilderness trips, campcraft, environment, watersports. Hiawatha Council- BSA, 600 W. Genesee St., Syracuse, NY 13204. (315)474-8574.

SKYE FARM, Bolton, Warren County, 160 girls & boys, 8-18, 8 weeks. Specialties: academic, arts & crafts, campcrafts, environment, health, performing arts, religious study, watersports. Rev. Harold Shippey, Sherman Lake Rd., Warrensburg, NY 12885. (518)494-2137.

SOMMERHILL, Athol, Warren County, ACA, NYSCDA, 150 girls & boys, 8-17, 4-8 weeks. Specialties: arts & crafts, campcrafts, horseback riding, performing arts, sports, watersports. Lawrence Singer, 20 Huntley Rd., Eastchester, NY 10709. (914)793-1302.

SON RISE/RETREAT CENTER, Pottersville, Warren County, children & adults. Peter Strom, Director, Box 51, Pottersville, NY 12860. (518)494-2620.

TAPAWINGO, Speculator, Hamilton County, CCI, 64 girls, 8-16, 8 weeks. Specialties: arts & crafts, campcrafts, health, religious study, sports, watersports. Camp-of-the-Woods, Speculator, NY 12164. (518)548-4311.

TREETOPS, Lake Placid, Essex County, ACA, NYSCDA, 165 boys & girls, 8-13, 7 weeks. Specialties: nature, campcrafts, farming, horseback riding, creative arts, canoeing, waterskills, sailing. Non-competitive. Mrs. Gail Schumacher, 53 University Ave., Hamilton, NY 13346. (315)824-1408.

WALDEN, Diamond Point, Warren County, AIC, NYSCDA, 190 girls & boys, 7-16, 8 weeks. Specialties: arts & crafts, performing arts, sports, watersports. Martin Muster, 478 Whitewood Rd., Union, NJ 07083. (201)687-8321.

WOODSMOKE, Lake Placid, Essex County, ACA, NYSOEA, Adirondack Mountain Club-46'ers, 45 girls & boys, 7-15, 7 weeks. Specialties: outdoor living skills, water sports, hiking and climbing, land sports, leadership program. Kris Hansen, Box 628, Lake Placid, NY 12946. (518)523-9344 and 523-3868.

WORD OF LIFE ISLAND, Schroon Lake, Essex County, 340 girls & boys, 13-25, 10 weeks. WORD OF LIFE Ranch, Pottersville, Warren County, 770 girls & boys, 6-13, 10 weeks. Specialties: academics, campcrafts, horseback riding and horsemanship, religious study, sports, watersports. Kenneth Dobbel, Administrator, Fellowship, Inc., Schroon Lake, NY 12870. (518)532-7111.

YMCA CAMP, Gorham, Eagle Bay, Herkimer County, ACA, 165 girls & boys, 8-15, 8 weeks. Specialties: arts & crafts, campcrafts, backpacking, horseback riding, sports, water skiing. YMCA Resident Camps, 444 East Main St., Rochester, NY 14605. (716)325-2889.

Source: New York State Department of Commerce; additional material added.

(90)

TEN POPULAR CANOE ROUTES

OLD FORGE TO TUPPER LAKE, Herkimer, Hamilton and Franklin Counties. 84 miles, with 6.8 miles of carry. For canoeists of average ability. A canoe-camping trip of six days on the Moose River's Fulton Chain of Lakes and on the Raquette River and the lakes it connects. Provisions can be purchased at Raquette Lake and Long Lake villages. Put-in, near the Information Center in Old Forge; take-out, the public dock at Moody on Tupper Lake.

OLD FORGE TO SARANAC LAKE VILLAGE, Herkimer, Hamilton and Franklin Counties. 90 miles, with 8.4 miles of carry. Canoeists of average ability. This follows the route of the above trip to the mouth of Stony Creek on the Raquette; there it swings north and east through Stony Creek and the Stony Creek Ponds, then via Indian Carry to the Saranac Lakes and the Saranac River. Take-out, the public beach on Lake Flower in Saranac Lake Village.

WEST BRANCH OF THE SACANDAGA RIVER, Hamilton County. A quiet downstream float of 10 miles in smooth water through meadows and woods. Put-in, the Rt. 10 bridge; take-out, Shaker Place.

KUNJAMUK RIVER, Hamilton County. 23 miles round trip, upstream and return, in stillwater and moderate flow with no carries except perhaps for fallen trees. Overnight camping on state land at the upstream end. Suitable for novices. Put-in and take-out, just off Rt. 8, 2 miles east of Speculator at the confluence with the Sacandaga. (We have received reports that recent blow-downs and dams have detracted from the pleasantness of this trip. Eds.)

HUDSON RIVER, Warren and Saratoga Counties. 14 miles of placid flow and riffles, with no carries. A beautiful section suitable for practiced beginners, unlike the upper river, which calls for whitewater skills. The only danger point is the approach to the falls above Lake Luzerne village. Put-in, below the Rt. 418 bridge at Thurman Station; take-out, above Luzerne Falls on the left shore at the Warren County canoe access site on the River Rd.

BLUE MOUNTAIN LAKE TO RAQUETTE LAKE, Hamilton County. 14 miles through the Eckford Chain of Lakes, the Marion River, and Raquette Lake to the hamlet on the southwest shore. One carry of 1/2 mile between Utowana Lake and the Marion River landing. Suitable for novices. Put-in, the public bathing beach in hamlet of Blue Mountain Lake; take-out, the hamlet of Raquette Lake.

UPPER OSWEGATCHIE RIVER (EAST BRANCH), St. Lawrence and Herkimer Counties. 36-mile round trip upstream from Inlet in the Five Ponds Wilderness Area. A short carry at High Falls and possibly some lining at one or two mild rapids during low water levels. Suitable for a canoe-camping trip of several days, mixed with hiking to numerous trout ponds on branching trails. Put-in and take-out, Inlet, a state canoe access site at the end of a 3.5-mile dirt road off Rt. 3, about 3.2 miles east of Star Lake village.

FISH CREEK PONDS, Franklin County. A circular tour of 10.5 miles through the Fish Creek Ponds, Fish Creek, Little Square Pond, Fish Creek again, Floodwood, Rollins, Whey and Copperas ponds back to the start. Three short carries totaling 0.6 miles. Put-in and take-out, the public parking lot at the south end of Follensby Clear Pond (the latter is connected with the Fish Creek Ponds by Spider Brook). Many other pond-hopping trips are possible in this area at the headwaters of the Saranac River and also the numerous ponds of the St. Regis Canoe Area to the north. Power boats are prohibited in the latter.

SARANAC RIVER, FROM SARANAC LAKE VILLAGE TO UNION FALLS, Essex and Franklin Counties. 21 miles. One carry of 0.4 miles between Franklin Falls Pond and Union Falls Pond. Impressive mountain views from the two backwater ponds. For inexperienced canoeists a second carry of 1.3 miles may be necessary at Class I-II-III rapids 10 miles below the start. Put-in, below the Lake Flower dam in Saranac Lake village or at the north-eastern end of the village; take-out, state land at the right of Union Falls Dam.

WEST BRANCH OF THE AUSABLE RIVER, RIVERSIDE DRIVE TO THE CONSERVATION MONUMENT, Essex County. 7 miles. Notable for mountain views, especially of Whiteface. One carry of 0.2 miles near the end of the run. Put-in, an iron bridge off Riverside Dr. 1 mile north of the Olympic Ski Jump; take-out, the Conservation Monument on Rt. 86 (1.1 miles east of the Rt. 86 bridge). Memorial Day races are held on this segment of the river each year.

This section is contributed by Paul Jamieson, author of *Adirondack Canoe Waters: North Flow*, published by the Adirondack Mountain Club, Inc., 172 Ridge Street, Glens Falls, NY 12801.

(91)

WHITE WATER RAFTING

Four Adirondack rivers provide rafting adventures.

In spring, THE HUDSON RIVER at North Creek and North River is one of the great white water rivers in the eastern United States. Spring freshets pour off the mountains and the Hudson becomes a raging torrent of haystacks, chutes and rock gardens. In fall the river often rises to near spring time levels.

THE SACANDAGA RIVER in Lake Luzerne is primarily a family fun watercourse that is a training ground for more adventuresome rivers.

THE SCHROON RIVER provides seasonal rafting trips for all ages. Families particularly will find this waterway exciting fun.

THE MOOSE RIVER provides significant white water in spring and sometimes in fall.

The following outfitters provide guided trips:

ADIRONDACK RIVER OUTFITTERS, Inc., PO Box 649, Old Forge, NY 13420. (315)369-3525, 369-6099.

ADIRONDACK WHITEWATERS, Inc., PO Box 801, Corinth, NY 12822. (518)654-2640 (winter), (518)696-2953 (summer).

HUDSON RIVER RAFTING CO. CUNNINGHAM'S SKI BARN, North Creek, NY 12853. (518)696-2964 (summer), (518)251-3215 (winter).

HUDSON WHITE WATER WORLD, Route 903, Jim Thorpe, PA 18229. (717)325-3657.

MAINE WHITEWATER, Inc., Gadabout Gaddis Airport, Bingham, Maine 04920. (207)672-4814 (summer), (207) 622-2260 (winter).

NORTHERN WHITEWATER EXPEDITIONS, Inc., PO Box 100, The Forks, Maine 04985. (207)663-2271 (summer), (518)648-5881 (spring).

UNICORN RAFTING EXPEDITIONS, Inc., PO Box 50, The Forks, Maine 04985. (207)663-2258.

WILDERNESS TOURS, Inc., PO Box 89, Beachburg, Ontario, Canada KOJ 1CO. (613)582-3351, or (613) 582-3805.

PUBLIC BEACHES

Some of the beaches listed below have dressing rooms and rest rooms; others do not. Call or write for further information.

ESSEX COUNTY

BULWAGGA BAY BEACH AND CAMPSITE, Moriah, NY 12960. May 15 through week after Labor Day. Lifeguard 10-6pm.

ESSEX TOWN BEACH, Essex, NY 12936. Open July 1st through the week after Labor Day. Lifeguard noon-5pm.

MIRROR LAKE BEACH, Lake Placid, NY 12946. July 1 through Labor Day. Life guard on duty.

PORT DOUGLAS BEACH, Chesterfield, NY 12944. Open July 4th weekend through Labor Day weekend, noon-8pm, weekends 9am-8pm. Lifeguards on duty.

PORT HENRY MUNICIPAL BEACH AND CAMPSITE, Port Henry, NY 12974. Open Memorial Day through Labor Day weekend. Lifeguards 10-6pm. Beach closes 10pm.

SCHROON LAKE PUBLIC BEACH, Schroon Lake, NY 12870. Open June 15 through September 7, 10am-6pm. 5 lifeguards on duty. (518)532-9079 or 7737, town office; (518)532-7338, beach.

WESTPORT BEACH AND PARK, Westport, NY 12993. Open Memorial Day through Labor Day, sunrise to sunset. Lifeguards on duty. (518)962-4419.

WILMINGTON RECREATION AREA, Wilmington, NY 12997. Open July 1 through August 31. Lifeguard 1pm-6pm. Picnic area available. (518)946-2255.

FRANKLIN COUNTY

LAKE COLBY, Harrietstown, NY 12983. Open June 25 through Labor Day, 9-5 daily. (518)891-9819.

LITTLE WOLF BEACH, Tupper Lake, NY 12986. Open June 20 through Labor Day; beach closes 8 pm. Lifeguards on duty. (518)359-3000.

HAMILTON COUNTY

BLUE MOUNTAIN LAKE BEACH, Blue Mountain Lake, NY 12812.

EIGHTH LAKE BEACH AND CAMPSITE, Rt. 28, Inlet, NY 13360. NYS Public Campsite. Lifeguards. Information: (315)357-3132.

GOLDEN BEACH CAMPSITE, Raquette Lake, NY 13436. NYS Public Campsite. Lifeguards. Information: (315) 354-4230.

INLET PUBLIC BEACH, Arrowhead Park, Inlet, NY 13360. Lifeguards on duty. Information:(315)357-5501.

LONG LAKE BEACH, Long Lake, NY 12847.

RAQUETTE LAKE BEACH, Raquette Lake, NY 13436.

SPECULATOR PUBLIC BEACH, Speculator, NY 12164. Open mid-June through Labor Day, daily 10-5.

HERKIMER COUNTY

FIRST LAKE, Old Forge, NY 13420. Open 9am-6pm. (315)369-6983.

WARREN COUNTY

BIXBY BEACH, Lake Shore Dr., Bolton Landing, NY 12814.

BRANT LAKE TOWN BEACH, Brant Lake, NY 12815.

ECHO LAKE BEACH, Warrensburg, NY 12885.

FARLEIGH DICKINSON BEACH, Lake Ave., Lake Luzerne, NY 12846.

FAXON'S BEACH, off Rts. 8 and 9, Chestertown, NY 12817.

GARNET LAKE NATURAL BEACH, Rt. 8, North Creek, NY 12853.

HADLEY BEACH, Old Corinth Rd., Lake Luzerne, NY 12846.

HAGUE PUBLIC BEACH, Rt. 9N, Hague, NY 12836.

HUDDLE BEACH, Lake Shore Dr., Bolton Landing, NY 12814.

HUDSON GROVE BEACH, Terrace Ave., Lake Luzerne, NY 12846.

LAKE AVE. BEACH, Lake Ave., Lake George, NY 12845.

LUZERNE HEIGHTS PUBLIC BEACH, Pierpont Rd., Lake Luzerne, NY 12846.

MILLION DOLLAR BEACH, Beach Rd., Lake George, NY 12845.

NORTH CREEK BEACH AND PICNIC AREA, North Creek, NY 12853.

SHEPARD PARK, Canada St., Lake George, NY 12845.

THIRTEENTH LAKE BEACH, Thirteenth Lake Rd., North River, NY 12856.

VETERANS MEMORIAL PARK AND BEACH, Lake Shore Dr., Bolton Landing, NY 12814.

WASHINGTON COUNTY

WASHINGTON COUNTY BEACH, Huletts Landing, NY 12841. Information: (518)499-2788, summer only. 747-0477, year round.

HADLOCK INN BEACH, Hadlock Pond, Fort Ann, NY 12872. Lifeguard on weekends.

(93)
SKI CENTERS AND INFORMATION

Up-to-date information on ski conditions, weather, etc. may be obtained from the following sources:

BIG TUPPER SKI AREA. 24 hours. (518)359-3651.
GORE MOUNTAIN. (518)251-2523.
LAKE PLACID. Monday-Friday, after 9:30 am. (518)523-2445.
OLD FORGE AREA. Daily snow report. (315)369-6983.
WARREN COUNTY. Weather, events, gas. (518)793-1300.
WHITEFACE MOUNTAIN. (518)946-7171.

WGY— 810 AM. Broadcasts ski reports in Capital District.
WIRD— 920 AM. Broadcasts ski reports 4 times daily in Lake Placid.
WNBZ— 1240 AM. Broadcasts ski reports 4 times daily in Saranac Lake.

The following ski centers are located in the Adirondack Park. XC = Cross Country, D = Downhill.

ESSEX

XC ADIRONDAK LOJ, Box 867, Lake Placid, NY 12946. 12 km marked groomed trails, connecting to hundreds of miles of wilderness, marked trails in High Peak area. Ski instruction, hotel, lean-tos, lodge, campsites, cabins, restaurant. Operated by Adirondack Mt. Club. Reservations suggested. Information: (518)523-3441, 8am-8pm.

XC AUSABLE CHASM SKI TOURING CENTER, Ausable Chasm, NY 12911. 20 kilometers of trails. Trails marked according to difficulty, instruction available, shops, rentals. Connects to unlimited wilderness trails. Member of National Ski Touring Operators' Association. Open daily 9am; nights, Wednesday-Sunday. Information: (518)834-9990 or 834-7454.

XC BARKEATER LODGE AND SKI TOURING CENTER, Alstead Mill Rd., Keene, NY 12942. 25 miles of trails (15 groomed). Ski instruction, lodging, restaurant, rentals, shop, guided tours. Nominal fee. Open daily. Information: (518)576-2221.

XC CASCADE CENTER FOR TOURING, Rt. 73, Lake Placid, NY 12946. 30 miles of trails. Instruction available, restaurant, shop, rentals, tours, lodge. Nominal fee. Open daily; nights Friday and Saturday. Information: (518)523-9605.

XC CRAIG FARM CROSS COUNTRY SKI CENTER, Craig Rd., east off Rt. 22, Putnam Station, NY 12861. (6 miles south of Ticonderoga). 10-12 mile groomed trails. Instruction available, rentals, lodge. Information: (518)547-8336.

XC K.O.A. (AT WHITEFACE MOUNTAIN), Wilmington, NY 12997. Log cabins, ski dorm for groups, kitchen meal plan.25 miles of trails. Information: (518) 946-7878.

XC LAKE PLACID CLUB RESORT, Mirror Lake Dr., Lake Placid, NY 12946. 12 miles of trails. Basic and Telemark instruction available, rentals, lodging. Nominal fee. Information: (518)523-3361 or 800 (518)342-9501, toll free.

XC MARCY SKI TOURING SCHOOL, Marcy Hotel, 122 Main St., Lake Placid, NY 12946. Certified instruction, rentals, repair. Information: (518)523-2569.

XC MT. VAN HOEVENBERG, Rt. 73, Lake Placid, NY 12946. 33 miles of trails (29 groomed). Warming hut, waxing room, marked trails, guided tours, rentals, sales, meals, snacks. Nominal fee. Open daily. Information: Olympic Center (ORDA), Lake Placid, NY 12946. (518)523-1655.

D MT. WHITNEY, Mt. Whitney, Lake Placid, NY 12946. 5 trails; 2 T-bars, base 1700 ft., vertical drop 408 ft. Ski school (American method), Telemark instruction, cafeteria, lounge, rentals, repairs, lodge. Information: (518)523-3361 or 523-2031. Open daily; Wednesday, Friday and Saturday nights.

D XC OTIS MOUNTAIN, Rt. 9S, South Elizabethtown, NY 12932. 3 trails, T-bar, rope tow, and some XC trails. 375 ft. vertical drop. Ski school, rentals and snacks. Open weekends, holidays and Wednesday nights. Information: (518)873-6448.

XC WESTPORT SKI TOURING CENTER, Liberty St., Westport, NY 12993. 21.1 miles of trails (15 groomed). Rentals, sales, meals, lodging. Nominal fee. Open daily. Information: (518)962-8313 or 962-8666.

D WHITEFACE MOUNTAIN SKI CENTER, Rt. 86, Wilmington, NY 12997. 28 trails; 3225 ft. vertical drop. Snowmaking, ski school (American method), 3 cafeterias, lounge, nursery, rentals, repairs, ski shop and 2 lodges. Open daily. Information: (518) 946-2223.

XC WHITEFACE RESORT, Box 231, Whiteface Inn Rd., Lake Placid, NY 12946. 8.5 miles of trails. Instruction available, rentals, guided tours, sales. Nominal fee. Open daily. Information: (518)523-2551.

FRANKLIN

XC ADIRONDACK SKI TOURS, Saranac Lake, NY 12983. Week-long back country ski tours, all inclusive program with guides, instructions, rentals, lodging, meals. Information: (518)891-1080.

D XC BIG TUPPER SKI AREA, P.O. Box 820, Tupper Lake, NY 12986. 23 downhill trails; 1,152 ft. vertical drop. 14 miles cross country trails. Snowmaking, group rates, ski school, rentals, cafeteria, ski patrol, lodge, ski shop. No charge for cross country. Open daily; nights Wednesday, Friday and Saturday. Information: (518)359-3651.

XC COLD RIVER RANCH, Coreys, Tupper Lake, NY 12986. 230 kilometers of trails adjoining property. Guided outings, snowshoeing, ice fishing. Lodging for up to 9 people. Information: (518)359-7559. Open daily.

XC HARRIETSTOWN CROSS COUNTRY SKI CENTER, 30 Main St., Saranac Lake, NY 12983. Located 1 mile east of Saranac Lake on Rt. 30. 7 miles of trails. No charge, lodge. Open 9am-10pm during winter months. Information: (518)891-1990.

D XC MT. PISGAH (also called VETERANS MEMORIAL SKI CENTER), Trudeau Rd., Saranac Lake Village, NY 12983. 6 miles of trails; 300 ft. vertical drop. Lodge, night skiing, snack bar. Open Tuesday-Friday, 2pm-9pm (closed Monday except on holidays), Saturday and Sunday 10am-6pm. Information: (518)891-0970 or 891-9942.

FULTON

D ROYAL MOUNTAIN, Rt. 10, Johnstown, NY 12095. 7 trails; 550 ft. vertical drop. Instruction available, rentals. Open Saturday, Sunday and holidays. Information: (518)835-6445.

HAMILTON

XC ADIRONDACK HUT TO HUT, Box 7008, Albany, NY 12225. 160 kilometers of trails. Guided wilderness ski tours, instructions, lodging, rentals, sales, snacks and meals. Basic trail fee. Open at varying times. Information: (518)449-5098 or 828-7007.

D XC INDIAN LAKE, Rt. 30, Indian Lake, NY 12842. 3 downhill trails; 215 ft. vertical drop. 88 kilometers of cross country trails. Free. Open daily for cross country; Saturday, Sunday and holidays for downhill. Information: (518)648-5112.

XC INLET SKI TOURING CENTER, South Shore Rd., Inlet, NY 13360. 75 kilometers of trails; no trail fee. Rentals, sales, guides, instruction available, lodging nearby. Open daily 9am-6pm. Information: (315) 357-6961.

XC IRONDEQUOIT CLUB, Piseco Lake, NY 12139. Over 6 miles of trails, other trails nearby. Meals and lodging. Open daily. Information: (518)548-5500. Closed spring and late fall.

XC LAPLAND LAKE NORDIC SKI AND VACATION CENTER, c/o Olavie Hirvonen, Benson, NY or RD 2, Northville, NY 12134. 40 kilometers of trails. Trails connect to other trails on state land. Lodging, instruction available, guided tours, rentals, sales, night skiing, snowshoeing, ice skating. Nominal fee. Open daily, nights at varying times. Information: (518)863-4974.

D XC OAK MOUNTAIN, Oak Mountain Ski Center, Inc., Dept. A, Speculator, NY 12164. 12 trails; 650 ft. vertical drop. Sport shop, cafeteria, rentals, PSIA member ski school, "family center". Open daily when conditions permit, December-March 15, 9am-4pm. Information: (518)548-7311.

XC SAGAMORE LODGE, Sagamore Rd., Raquette Lake, NY 13436. 18 miles of trails. Former Vanderbilt estate. Weekend and week-long packages and programs. Instruction, guided tours, lodging, rentals. Information: (315)354-5311.

XC SPECULATOR CROSS COUNTRY SKIING/KUNJAMUK LOOP, Office of Tourism, Speculator, NY 12164. Over 10 kilometers of trails. Instruction available, guided tours, meals, snacks lodging. Free. Open when conditions permit, daylight hours, December-March 15. Information: (518)548-4521.

HERKIMER

XC ADIRONDACK WOODCRAFT, Box 219, Old Forge, NY 13420. 10 kilometers of groomed and set trails. Instruction available, guided tours, rentals, sales, snacks and lodging. Nominal fee. Open daily, Friday and Saturday nights. Night skiing on lighted 2 kilometer loop. Information: (315)369-3816.

XC COVEWOOD LODGE, Big Moose Lake, Eagle Bay, NY 13331. Lodging, 50 kilometers of trails. Open daily. Information: (518)357-3041.

D XC McCAULEY MOUNTAIN SKI CENTER, Ski Information Center, Old Forge, NY 13420. 9 downhill trails; 633 ft. vertical drop. 24 kilometers of cross country trails. Chalet with cafeteria, ski school, rentals, repairs. Open daily. Information: (315) 369-3225 (downhill); (315)369-6983 (cross country).

WARREN

XC CUNNINGHAM SKI BARN/GORE MT. SKI TOURING CENTER, North Creek, NY 12853. Features Hudson River trail system - 50 kilometers of trails that parallel Upper Hudson River. Ski school, guide service and trips into Siamese Ponds Wilderness Region, sales, rentals, warm-up lounge. Open daily, Friday and Saturday nights, and full moon weeks. Information: (518)251-3215.

XC GARNET HILL SKI TOURING CENTER, North River, NY 12856. 100 kilometers of trails (30 groomed) adjoining state wilderness trails. Groomed trails are graded and marked according to NSTOA standards. Garnet Hill Lodge, food, rentals including snowshoes, instruction available, guided tours. Nominal fee. Open daily Thanksgiving to mid-April. Information: (518)251-2821.

D XC GORE MOUNTAIN SKI CENTER, Rt. 28, North Creek, NY 12853. 41 downhill slopes and trails, 2,100 ft. vertical drop. 20 miles of cross-country trails. Ski school, ski patrol, beginners to experts, rentals, nursery, skating rink, 2 lodges, snowshoe trails, snowmaking. Open daily 9am-4:30pm. Information: (518)251-2411 or 251-2523.

D HICKORY SKI CENTER, Hickory Hill Rd., Rt. 418, Warrensburg, NY 12885. 15 trails; 1200 ft. vertical drop. Ski school, ski patrol, lodge, cafeteria, beginners to experts. Open Saturday, Sunday and holidays, 9pm-4pm. Information: (518)623-9866.

D XC HIDDEN VALLEY SKI CENTER, Hidden Valley Ranch Resort, Lake Luzerne, NY 12846. 110 ft. vertical fall; 4 miles groomed cross country trails with connecting trails. Snowmaking, rentals, lodging facilities, horseback riding, ice skating, restaurant, horse-drawn sleigh rides, instruction available. No charge for cross country. Open everyday. (518)696-2431 or (212)757-4711.

XC QUEENSBURY COUNTRY CLUB, Rt. 149, Lake George, NY 12845. 10 kilometers of trails. Trails for novice to expert skiers, rentals, clubhouse with food and drinks, some ski instruction. Nominal fee. Open daily. Information: (518)793-3711.

CLINTON, LEWIS, ONEIDA, ST. LAWRENCE, SARATOGA and WASHINGTON COUNTIES have no ski centers in the Adirondack Park.

(94)
SNOWMOBILING

The Adirondack Park is one of the major snowmobiling centers in the Northeast. The Old Forge area alone, for example, boasts of 500 miles of groomed trails. As specific snowmobile trails and locations would be too numerous to mention, we have provided below the major maps, guides and sources for snowmobile information in the Adirondacks. Other chambers of commerce throughout the Adirondacks may have additional information.

COUNTIES

TRAILS IN CLINTON COUNTY. Plattsburgh and Clinton County Chamber of Commerce, 135 Margaret St., PO Box 310, Plattsburgh, NY 12901. (518)563-1000.

SNOWMOBILE TRAILS IN ESSEX COUNTY. Essex County Department of Tourism, Elizabethtown, NY 12932. (518) 873-6301.

TRAILS IN FRANKLIN COUNTY. Franklin County Tourism, 63 West Main St., Malone, NY 12953. (518)483-6767. ext. 230.

WARREN COUNTY SNOWMOBILE TRAIL MAP. Warren County Department of Tourism, Department 567, Municipal Center, Lake George, NY 12845. (518)761-6366.

SNOWMOBILE TRAILS IN WASHINGTON COUNTY. Washington County Planning Board, Washington County Bldg., Ft. Edward, NY 12828.

TOWNS

INLET SNOWMOBILE TRAILS. Inlet Chamber of Commerce, Inlet, NY 13360. (315)357-5501.

SNO-MOBILE MAP OF OLD FORGE AND CENTRAL ADIRONDACKS. Northwoods Sno-Travelers Club, Inc., PO Box 150, Old Forge, NY 13420.

TRAILS IN PISECO, LAKE PLEASANT, SPECULATOR AREA. Office of Tourism and Community Development, Speculator, NY 12164. (518)548-4521.

RAQUETTE LAKE AREA TRAIL MAP. Raquetteers, Raquette Lake, NY 13436. Available in local stores and restaurants.

MAP OF SARANAC LAKE'S SNOWMOBILE TRAILS. Chamber of Commerce, 30 Main St., Saranac Lake, NY 12983. (518)891-1990.

SNOMOBILER'S MAP AND GUIDE. Bolton Chamber of Commerce, Bolton Landing, NY 12814. (518)644-3831 (3311).

SCHROON LAKE SNOWMOBILE TRAILS. Chamber of Commerce, Schroon Lake, NY 12870. (518)532-7675.

NEW YORK SNOWMOBILE COORDINATING GROUP, PO Box 490A, RD. 2, Norwich, NY 13815. Membership organizations and magazine, *NYSCG Snowmobile News*.

SNOWMOBILING IN NEW YORK STATE. Informative booklet with snowmobile regulations and maps. Available from local chambers of commerce and Department of Environmental Conservation offices (see Sections 36 and 116).

(95)
ICE-SKATING

The following ice-skating rinks are open to the public usually, but not always, at no cost. Of course there are many more ice-skating rinks in the Adirondacks connected with private lodges and resorts.

Arrowhead Park, Inlet, Hamilton County. Outdoor. (315) 357-5501.

Big Moose Lake, Big Moose, Herkimer County. Outdoor.

Civic Center, Harrietstown, Franklin County. Indoor, daily noon-9pm. Saturday 9am-1pm, no charge. (518) 891-9836.

Fourth Lake, Inlet, Herkimer County. Outdoor.

Gore Mt. Ice Skating Rink, North Creek, Warren County. Outdoor, daily 9am-4:30pm. (518)251-2411.

Municipal Ice Rink, Tupper Lake, Franklin County. Outdoor, Tuesday-Friday 2-5 and 7-9, Saturday and Sunday 1-5, 7-9.

Olympic Arena, Lake Placid, Essex County. Call for hours and rental information. Indoor. (518)523-3325.

Olympic Speed Skating Oval, Lake Placid Village, Essex County. Outdoor. 7-9pm, weather permitting. (518) 523-3325.

Raquette Lake Village Skating Rink, Hamilton County. Outdoor.

Saranac Lake Civic Center, Saranac Lake, Franklin County. For daily schedule: (518)891-1990.

Schroon Lake Town Skating Rink, Schroon Lake, Essex County. Outdoor, lighted, closes 10pm. (518)532-7737.

Speculator Ballfield, Speculator, Hamilton County. Outdoor, closes 10pm. (518)548-4521.

Westport Beach and Campsite, Westport, Essex County. Outdoor.

Wilmington Recreation Area, Wilmington, Essex County. Outdoor, daily. Maintained 4-9pm weekdays, 1-9pm weekends.

GOLF COURSES

Adirondack golf courses are typically open from mid-May to mid-October. To be safe, one should call or write to verify seasons, days or hours for a particular course.

CLINTON COUNTY

INDOLE GOLF COURSE, AuSable Forks, NY 12921. 9 holes.

ESSEX COUNTY

COBBLE HILL GOLF COURSE, Elizabethtown, NY 12932. 9 holes. (518)873-9974.

CRAIG WOOD GOLF AND COUNTRY CLUB, Cascade Rd., Lake Placid, NY 12946. 18 holes. (518)523-9904.

LAKE PLACID CLUB RESORT, Mirror Lake Dr., Lake Placid, NY 12946. 3 golf courses, two 18-hole, one 9-hole executive course. (518)523-3361. Numerous tournaments held May-September.

PORT HENRY TOWN GOLF COURSE, Port Henry, NY 12974. 9 holes. (518)546-9979.

SARANAC LAKE GOLF COURSE, Rt. 86, Ray Brook, NY 12977. 9 holes. (518)891-2675.

SCHROON LAKE GOLF CLUB, Schroon Lake, NY 12870. 9 holes. (518)532-9062.

TICONDEROGA GOLF COURSE, Ticonderoga, NY 12883. 18 holes. (518)585-7435.

TOWN OF MORIAH COUNTRY CLUB, Moriah, NY 12960. 9 holes. Information: (518)546-7472; clubhouse (518) 546-9979.

WESTPORT COUNTRY CLUB, Westport, NY 12993. 18 holes. (518)962-4470.

WHITEFACE RESORT, Whiteface Inn Rd., PO Box 231, Lake Placid, NY 12946. 18 holes. (518)523-2551.

WILLSBORO GOLF CLUB, Willsboro Point Rd., Willsboro, NY 12996. 9 holes.

FRANKLIN COUNTY

LOON LAKE GOLF CLUB, Loon Lake Inn, Rt. 99, Loon Lake, NY 12951. 18 holes. (518)891-3249.

SARANAC INN GOLF AND COUNTRY CLUB, Saranac Inn, NY 12982. 18 holes. (518)891-1402.

TUPPER LAKE COUNTRY CLUB, Rt. 30, Tupper Lake, NY 12986. 18 holes. (518)359-3701.

FULTON COUNTY

NICK STONER MUNICIPAL GOLF COURSE, Caroga Lake, NY 12032. 18 holes. (518)835-4211.

SACANDAGA GOLF CLUB, Rt. 30, Sacandaga Park, NY 12134. 9 holes. Coin telephone: (518)863-8994.

HAMILTON COUNTY

CEDAR RIVER CLUB, Indian Lake, NY 12842. 9 holes.

DEER RUN GOLF COURSE, Rt. 28, Inlet, NY 13360. 9 holes. Formerly the Inlet Golf Course. (315)357-5596.

LAKE PLEASANT GOLF CLUB, Rt. 8, Lake Pleasant, NY 12108. 9 holes. (518)548-7071.

WAKELY LODGE GOLF COURSE, Cedar River Rd., Indian Lake, NY 12842. 9 holes. (518)648-5011.

HERKIMER COUNTY

THENDARA GOLF CLUB, Rt. 28, Thendara, NY 13472. 18 holes. (315)369-3136.

LEWIS COUNTY

BRANTINGHAM GOLF COURSE, Brantingham, NY 13312. 9 holes.

ST. LAWRENCE COUNTY

CLIFTON FINE MUNICIPAL GOLF COURSE, Rt. 3, Star Lake, NY 13690. 9 holes.

SAYLES MEMORIAL GOLF COURSE, Star Lake, NY 13690.

WARREN COUNTY

CRONIN'S GOLF COURSE, Hudson Ave., Warrensburg, NY 12885. 18 holes. (518)623-9336.

GREEN MANSIONS GOLF AND TENNIS FACILITIES, Rt. 9, Chestertown, NY 12817. 9 holes. (518)494-3721.

1000 ACRES, Rt. 418, Stony Creek, NY 12878. 9 holes. (518)696-2444.

QUEENSBURY COUNTRY CLUB, Rt. 149, Lake George, NY 12845. 18 holes. (518)793-3711.

SAGAMORE GOLF COURSE, Bolton Landing, NY 12814. 18 holes.

TOP O' THE WORLD RESORT, INC., Rt. 9, Lake George, NY 12845. 9 holes. (518)668-5415.

WASHINGTON COUNTY

HULETT'S ON LAKE GEORGE, Hulett's Landing, NY 12841. 9 holes. (518)499-1234 and (518)499-1819.

(97)
TENNIS COURTS

This listing include mostly tennis courts open to the public at no charge. Tennis courts which the public may use for a fee are so designated.

ESSEX COUNTY

HOLIDAY INN, Olympic Dr., Lake PLacid, NY 12946. 6 outdoor courts. (518)523-2556.

ELIZABETHTOWN SOCIAL CENTER, Elizabethtown, NY 12932. 2 outdoor courts. (518)873-6408.

INN ON THE LIBRARY LAWN, Westport, NY 12993. 2 outdoor all weather courts. Fee. (518)962-8666.

LAKE PLACID CLUB RESORT, Mirror Lake Dr., Lake Placid, NY 12946. 4 Har Tru and 2 all-weather courts. Fee. (518)523-3361.

LAKE PLACID PUBLIC TENNIS COURTS, Parkside and Shore Dr. intersection, Lake Placid, NY 12946. Fee. 4 outdoor courts.

SCHROON LAKE TOWN PARK, Schroon Lake, NY 12870. 7 outdoor courts. (518)532-7737.

WESTPORT CENTRAL SCHOOL, Westport, NY 12993.

WHITEFACE CHALET, Wilmington, NY 12997. One outdoor court. Fee. (518)946-2207.

WHITEFACE RESORT, Whiteface Inn Rd., Lake PLacid, NY 12946. 4 outdoor courts. Fee. (518)523-2551.

FRANKLIN COUNTY

MUNICIPAL TENNIS COURTS, Saranac Ave., Saranac Lake, NY 12983. 5 outdoor courts. (518)891-1990.

MUNICIPAL TENNIS COURTS, Tupper Lake, NY 12986. 2 lighted outdoor courts, blacktop. (518)359-3328.

PINE TERRACE MOTEL, Tupper Lake, NY 12986. 3 clay Har Tru courts, 2 lighted courts. Fee. (518)359-9258.

SARANAC LAKE TENNIS CLUB, Trudeau Rd., Saranac Lake, NY 12983. 3 outdoor courts. Fee. (518)891-5200.

HAMILTON COUNTY

ARROWHEAD PARK PUBLIC TENNIS COURTS, Inlet, NY 13360. Fee. (315)357-5771 or 5501.

MUNICIPAL TENNIS COURTS, Lake Pleasant, NY 12108. 2 courts. Information: (518)548-4521.

MUNICIPAL TENNIS COURTS, Speculator, NY 12164. 2 courts. (518)548-4521.

HERKIMER COUNTY

MUNICIPAL TENNIS COURTS, Old Forge, NY 13420. 2 courts. (315)369-6983.

WARREN COUNTY

BOLTON BALL FIELD, Bolton Landing, NY 12814.

GREEN MANSIONS GOLF AND TENNIS FACILITIES, Rt. 9, Chestertown, NY 12817. 5 clay courts. Fee. (518) 494-3721.

HIGH SCHOOL, Lake George, NY 12845.

LIBRARY AVENUE COURTS, Warrensburg, NY 12885.

MAIN STREET PARK, Lake Luzerne, NY 12846.

MIDDLE SCHOOL, Lake Luzerne, NY 12846.

NORTH CREEK TOWN BEACH, North Creek, NY 12853.

NORTH WARREN SCHOOL, Chestertown, NY 12817.

ROGERS MEMORIAL PARK, Bolton Landing, NY 12814.

TOP O' THE WORLD, Rt. 9L East, Lake George, NY 12845. One court fee. (518)668-5415.

USHER PARK, Rt. 9L, Lake George, NY 12845.

(98)

HORSE TRAILS

This section, first, describes the major horse trail systems in the Adirondacks and, second, lists various additional trails on public land throughout the Park.

LAKE GEORGE HORSE TRAIL SYSTEM, Washington County, Towns of Ft. Ann and Dresden. 3 parking areas readily accessible from either I-87 Exit 20, or Rt. 4 and Rt. 149 in the Village of Ft. Ann. From Ft. Ann travel west on Rt. 149 5.1 miles to Buttermilk Falls Rd., then north 5.7 miles to lower Hogtown parking lot. By continuing west on Rt. 149 to Rt. 9L, then north to Pilot Knob Road a total of 7.1 miles, you will approach the Pilot Knob parking area. From Exit 20 east on Rt. 149 it is 3.9 miles to Rt. 9L and 1.3 more miles to Buttermilk Falls Rd. This system has trails for single lane and side by side riding on a variety of loops. The trails follow streams with waterfalls, past vistas overlooking Lake George and large forested areas, and have appropriately located leantos on small ponds for the rider who would like to camp overnight.

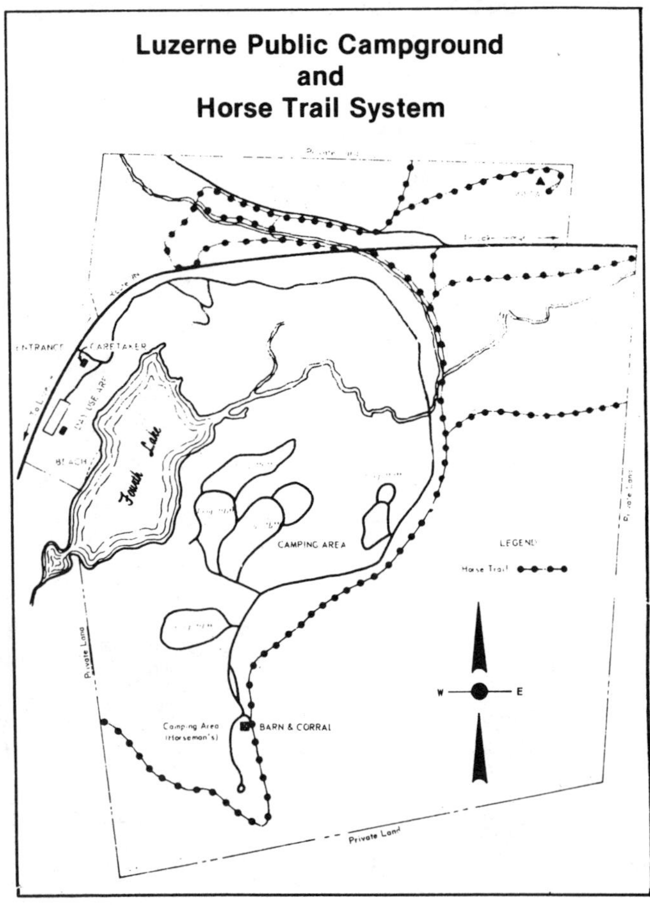

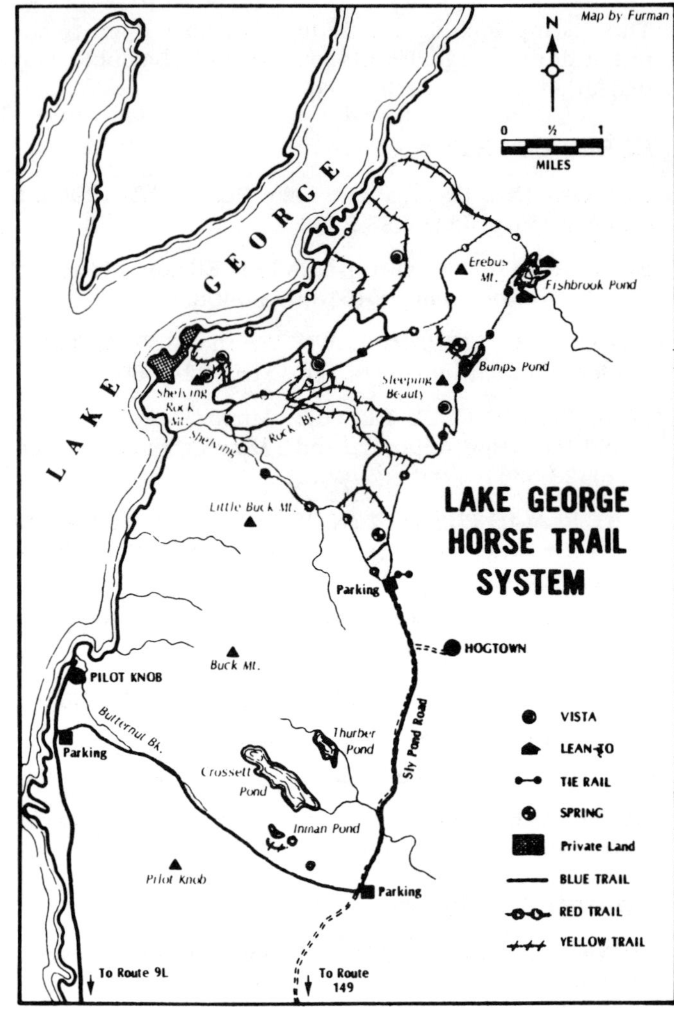

LUZERNE CAMPGROUND AND HORSE TRAIL SYSTEM, Warren County. Access point: 8 miles southwest of Lake George Village on Rt. 9N. Special camping area on site for horsepersons, including barn, corral, tent and trailer sites. 5 miles of trails on state land continuing on to private lands used by nearby dude ranches. From open hardwoods to groves of white pine, the trails traverse a variety of terrain, such as the flat easy going along the Stewart Creek or a rather stiff climb which leads to a vista where one may look back over the campground and Fourth Lake. Note: Horses are not allowed on campground road or through camping area; there is a camping service charge at Luzerne.

MEACHAM LAKE HORSE TRAIL SYSTEM, Franklin County. Access point: off Rt. 30, 3.5 miles north of Paul Smith's College, turn right onto gravel road at intersection of Rt. 30 and Slush Pond Road; proceed .1 mile to unloading area. There are two dead-end trips in this system.

(1) From the unloading area, travel southwesterly, across Route 30 and on to Slush Pond Road about 1.3 miles. Turn right. The trail continues northwesterly through the forest a distance of 1.5 miles where it intersects with a town road. Turn right onto town road. The trail continues on the town road a distance of 1.9 miles to Rt. 30 where it terminates. Total distance is 4.7 miles.

(2) From the unloading area, travel southeast on the gravel road a short distance. Here the trail leaves the road and turns left onto a gated truck trail. The route continues along the truck trail a distance of 1.5 miles to its terminus at Hays Brook. Turning left off the truck trail, the trail heads easterly crossing Hays Brook on a plank bridge and continues northerly a distance of 2.4 miles to an old sheep meadow where 2 leantos and a horsebarn are located.

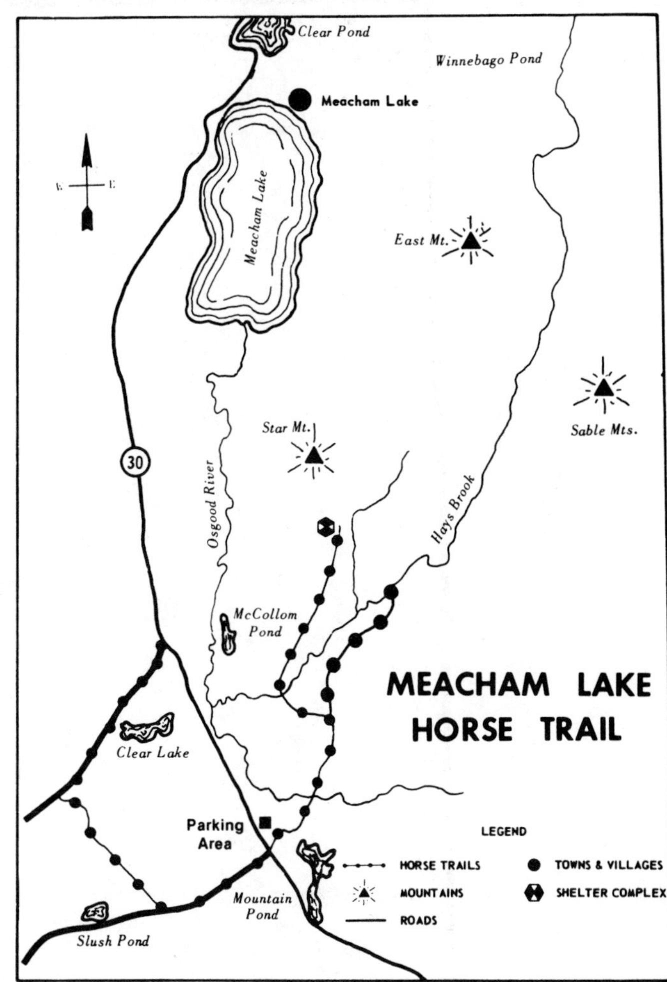

PHARAOH LAKE HORSE TRAIL SYSTEM, northern Warren County and southern Essex County. SUCKER BROOK HORSE TRAIL. Access site: At the general store in Adirondack (which is on the east shore of Schroon Lake), proceed due east for 0.2 miles to a Y fork; turn left and continue to a T intersection. Take the left fork again. The road shortly dead-ends in a parking lot at the start of the Sucker Brook horse trail. From the unloading area the trail leads north past Pine Hill and on to Sucker Brook. Here the trail turns easterly, continues along the south side of Sucker Brook, past Number 8 Hill, crosses Desolate Brook, continuing in an easterly direction crossing Pharaoh Lake Outlet where it intersects with the Pharaoh Lake Horse Trail. Total distance 5.8 miles.

PHARAOH LAKE ROAD HORSE TRAIL. Access point: From Northway Exit 25, take Rt. 8 toward Brant Lake. Follow around the shore of Brant Lake to its further end. Turn left on Palisades Road which will continue around the end of the lake. The road will veer to the left again. Two-tenths of a mile beyond this turn, or 1.2 miles from Route NY 8, turn right onto the Beaver Pond Road and proceed northerly a distance of one mile to an intersection with the Pharaoh Lake Road. Turn right and travel 1.1 miles to the unloading area. From the unloading area, the trail leads northerly to the crossing of Mill Brook and follows the south side of Pharaoh Lake and the intersection with the Sucker Brook horse trail to the left. The trail continues up the southern side of Pharaoh Lake for about a mile to 2 leantos and a horse shelter. From here the trail turns easterly and then southerly terminating at the Springhill Ponds. Total distance is 6.5 miles.

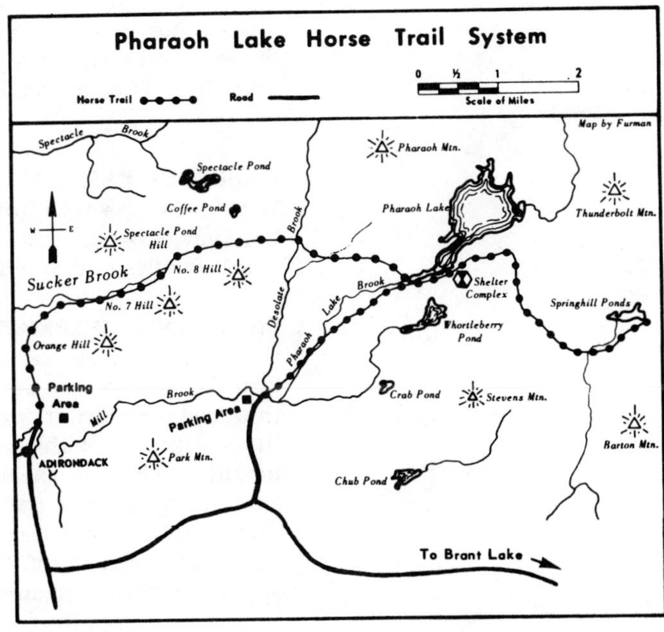

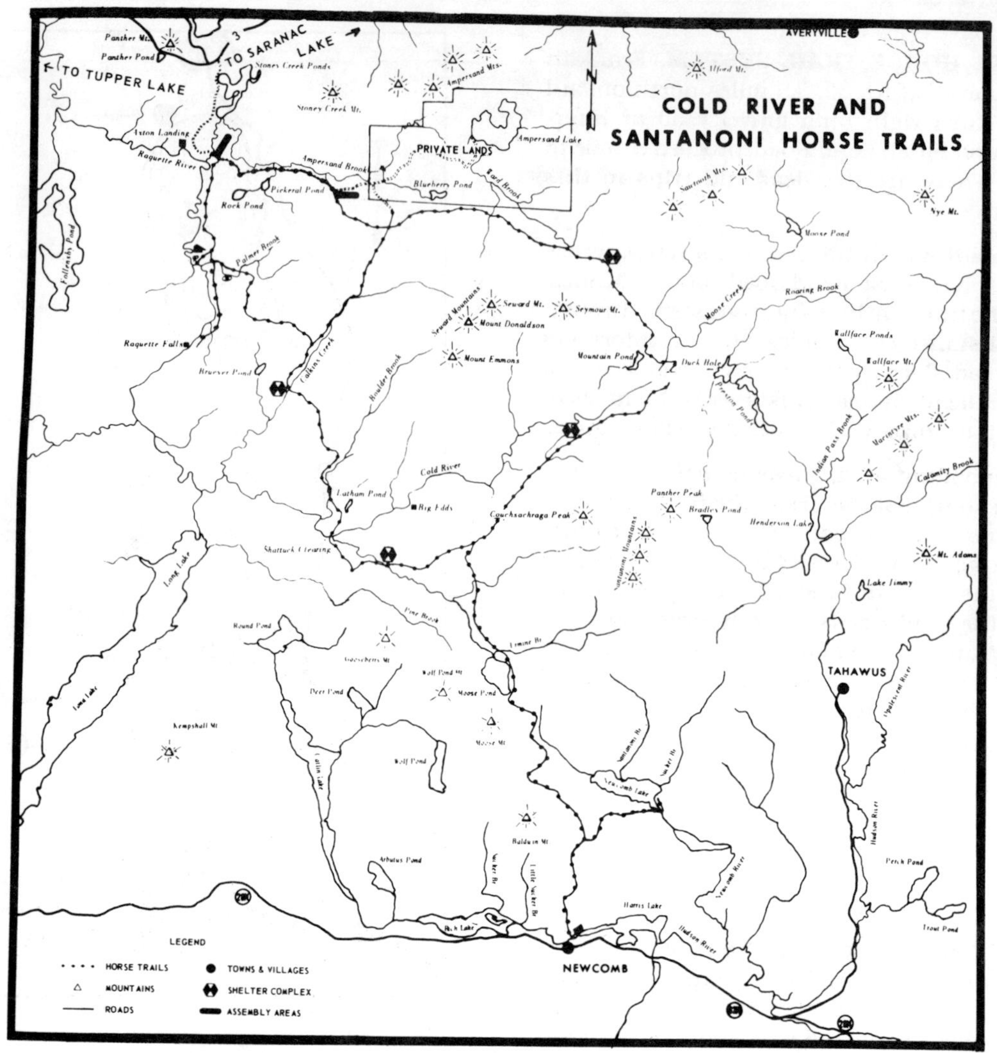

SANTONONI HORSE TRAIL, Franklin County. Access point: Take Rt. 28N to Newcomb. Turn onto dirt road and proceed to parking lot just north of the gate house. Description: Follow gravel road 2.3 miles to junction of Moose Pond Rd. Follow east fork to Newcomb Lake 2.7 miles or north fork 4.7 miles to Moose Pond. Trail beyond Moose Pond continues 5.1 miles to the junction of the Cold River Trail. Newcomb Lake Trail is 10 miles round trip.

RAQUETTE FALLS HORSE TRAIL, Franklin County. Trail branches south from Cold River Trail, 3 miles from the Ampersand Assembly Area and follows an old wagon road 1.6 miles to Raquette Falls Outpost.

COLD RIVER HORSE TRAIL SYSTEM, Franklin and Essex Counties. Access point: 2.6 miles from Hamlet of Corey's, off Rt. 3. At a distance of 3.1 miles further along this road an alternate parking lot has been provided on the south side of the road. Description: trail complex includes two loops, the shorter loop being 12.7 miles in length, about a one-day ride, and the longer one 32.1 miles long, a two or three-day ride. Shelters for riders and horses provided along the route. Numerous vistas with superb views of surrounding mountains along the trail.

SARANAC INN HORSE TRAIL SYSTEM, Franklin County. Access point: Just west of the Saranac Inn D.E.C. Field Operations Headquarters on Rt. 30. Several trails extend from one another varying in length from one mile to 11 miles round trip.

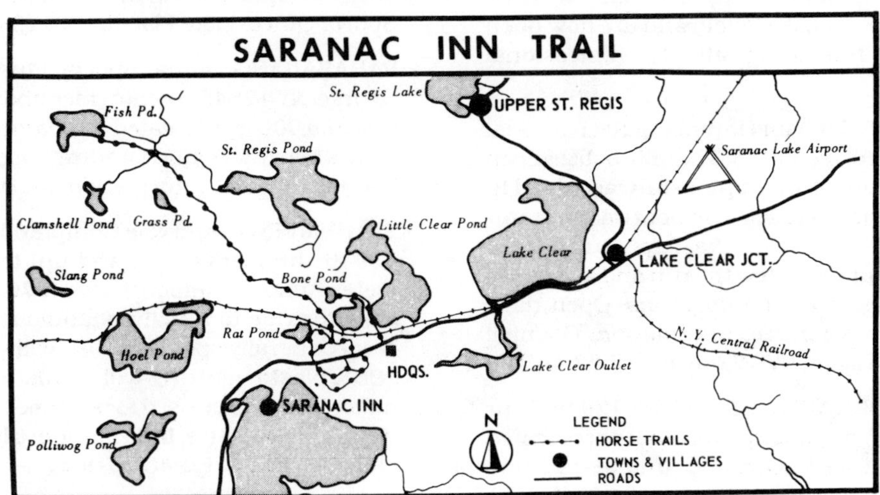

The following routes and mileages are available for the equestrian on public lands within the region. More precise information may be obtained from the Department of Environmental Conservation Regional Forester's Office (see Section 116 for D.E.C. listings).

CLINTON COUNTY

Terry Mountain State Forest Areas. Two areas, 6 miles.

ESSEX COUNTY

South Meadows-Marcy Dam Forest Preserve Lands. 3 miles.
Connery Pond Forest Preserve Lands. 5 miles.

FRANKLIN COUNTY

Deer Run State Forest Area. 18 miles.
Bombay State Forest Area. 6 miles.
Titusville Mountain State Forest Area. 2 miles.
DeBar Mountain Game Management Area. 10 miles.

FULTON COUNTY

Rockwood State Forest Area. 2 miles.

HERKIMER COUNTY

Thendara-Big Otter Lake Forest Preserve Lands. Ha-De-Ron-Dah Wilderness. 8 miles.
McKeever-Woodhull Lake Forest Preserve Lands. Black River Wild Forest Area. 6 miles.
Big Moose Road-Cascade Lake Forest Preserve Lands. Pigeon Lake Wilderness. 1.5 miles.
Moss Lake Forest Preserve Lands. Fulton Chain Wild Forest Area. 2.5 miles.

LEWIS COUNTY

Brantingham-Chases Lake Forest Preserve Lands. 25 miles.

ST. LAWRENCE COUNTY

Aldrich-Streeters Lake Forest Preserve Lands. 6 miles.

WARREN COUNTY

Siamese Ponds, 11th Mountain, John's Pond, Baldwin, Spring Fullers Forest Preserve Lands. 24 miles.

This section was excerpted from *Horse Trails in New York State*, published by the Department of Environmental Conservation, 50 Wolf Rd., Albany, NY 12233.

(99)
OTHER SPORTS ACTIVITIES

Additional sporting activities in the Adirondacks, not listed in any other section, are listed here. The first three listings are of facilities built or improved for the 1980 Winter Olympic Games in Lake Placid and are now open for public use as well as being sites for professional training.

BOBSLEDDING/LUGE, Mt. Van Hovenberg Recreational Area, Rt. 73, Lake Placid, NY 12946. The only bobsled run in the Western Hemisphere. Championship races held in the winter; passenger rides available on Bobrun; spectator walk-way follows the length of the run. During the summer open to the public to view the run and aspects of construction. Displays, films, photographs. Open daily except Mondays. Admission fee. Information: Olympic Center (ORDA), Lake Placid, NY 12946. (518)523-1655.

OLYMPIC CENTER (ORDA), Lake Placid, NY 12946. Four ice surfaces and ORDA administrative offices are located within the center. The 1980 Olympic Rink seats 5,000 with accommodation for an additional 3,000 in the bleachers. The rink is utilized for many international events and was the site of the 1980 Winter Olympic figure skating and hockey events. The U.S. Rink is primarily used for hockey, figure skating and curling. The 1932 Olympic Arena, used during the 1932 Winter Olympics, has a seating capacity of 1,200. Local high schools and youth progams use this surface on a regular basis (for public skating see Section 95). The Lussi Rink is used for convention meetings and is also used occasionally for public skating. Information: (518)523-1655.

ADIRONDACK LAKERS COMPETITIVE SWIM CLUB. U.S. certified swim club for ages 6-25. Competitions in divisions. Year- round and summer programs. Held at North Country Community College. Information: Janine Du Mond, (518)891-4286.

LAKE PLACID ROWING CLUB. Formed in 1980, open to all ages. Sponsors the annual Lake Placid Regatta and other events. Information: North Elba Park District, Sports Office, Lake Placid, NY 12946. (518)523-2591.

PARASAILING, Aqua Sports Plus, PO Box 743, Lake George, NY 12845. Scenic rides above Lake George at 300, 600 and 900 feet. Located at 1 James St., Lake George and Chic's Marina, Bolton Landing. Open May 15-October 12, 9 am until dark. Information: (518)668-3280.

SKI JUMPING, Intervale Complex, Rt. 73, Lake Placid, NY 12946. Jumpers (age 5 and up) train on 15, 25 and 40 meter jumps. Competitions on 70 and 90 meter jumps. Elevator ride to top gives fabulous view of surrounding area. Generally open daily 9-5, call to verify. As of summer 1983, plastic matting will be installed on the 40 and 70 meter jumps to be used for summer training and competition. Admission fee. Information: Olympic Center (ORDA), Lake Placid, NY 12946. (518)523-1655.

SLEIGH RIDES/DOG SLED RIDES, Mirror Lake, Lake Placid. Sled rides across Mirror Lake pulled by a team of dogs. Open: weather and conditions permitting. Rates on request. Information: Chamber of Commerce, Lake Placid, NY 12946. (518)523-2445.

TOBOGGANNING, Parkside Dr., Lake Placid, NY 12946. A four- lane chute on to frozen Mirror Lake; rentals available, nominal fee. Information: North Elba Park District, Sports Office, Lake Placid, NY 12946. (518)523-2591.

UNITED STATES LUGE ASSOCIATION. Formed in the summer of 1976 in anticipation of the 1980 Olympics in Lake Placid it continues today with over 210 members, promoting interest in the sport. Information: U.S.L.A., 1 Wilmington Rd., Lake Placid, NY 12946. (518)523-2071.

(100)
RECREATIONAL COURSES AND SCHOOLS

ALPINE SKI RACING

NEW YORK ALPINE TRAINING CENTER AT WHITEFACE, Wilmington, NY 12997. "Recognized as a major development program by the U.S. Ski team." Rigorous admission standards. Training sessions Dec. 1- April 1.

CANOEING

ADIRONDACK BOUND, Sagamore Lodge & Conference Center, Raquette Lake, NY 13436. Canoeing expeditions for adults, women and teenagers. Canoeing programs offered spring, summer and fall. Information: (315) 354-5303.

ADIRONDACK MOUNTAIN CLUB, 172 Ridge St., Glens Falls, NY 12801. Canoe camping and water safety course. Held at the end of July. Information: (518)793-7737.

CLIMBING

ADIRONDACK BOUND, Sagamore Lodge & Conference Center, Raquette Lake, NY 13436. Workshops for beginners focus on basic techniques and skills of rock climbing and rappelling. Information: (315)354-5303.

LAKE PLACID CLIMBING SCHOOL, INC., Sundog Ski and Sport, 90 Main St., Lake Placid, NY 12946. Full-day lessons, small group and individual instruction, group rates available. Information: (518)523-2752 or (518) 523-3984.

DIVING

UNDERWATER WORLD, RD #1, Box 63A, Lake George, NY 12845. Half day, one day, and 5-day courses on scuba diving skills, basic and advanced. Information: (518) 668-5882.

ORIENTEERING

THE AMERICAN LAND NAVIGATION INSTITUTE, Friends Lake Rd., Chestertown, NY 12817. Courses of various lengths in the use of Map and Compass, classroom instruction, day and night field training exercises. Courses may be custom tailored to suit any need or previous level of experience. All classes taught by a New York State Forest Ranger and former military instructor. No prerequisites. Michael B. Hagadorn, Director. Information: (518)494-2023.

OUTDOOR LEADERSHIP TRAINING

INTERNSHIP PROGRAM, Adirondack Bound, Sagamore Lodge & Conference Center, Raquette Lake, NY 13436. Fall, winter, and spring internships offer outdoor leadership skills and training, experience in leading groups as well as in administrative and logistical aspects of program. Information: (315)354-5303.

THE SAFETY NETWORK, Adirondack Bound, Sagamore Lodge & Conference Center, Raquette Lake, NY 13436. Workshops in Safety Management Systems for Outdoor Education Programs. Also offers on-site inspections. Information: (315)354-5303.

WILD/WATERS (Wilderness Institute for Leadership Development/Wilderness Adventures Training, Education and River School). Outdoor program near North Creek. Doug Azert, Director. Information: South Johnsburg and Glen Creek Rds., Warrensburg, NY 12885. (518)623-3278.

FISHING

FLYCASTING COURSE. Adirondack Sporting Goods, Rt. 86, Wilmington, NY 12997. Weekend course with Francis Betters, Adirondack fishing expert. Information: (518) 946-2605.

GRAND SLAM FISHING SCHOOL, c/o Warren County Tourism Dept., Lake George, NY 12845. Three-hour mini-course taught by local fishing experts on how and where to fish. Several sessions held during the summer. Information: (518)761-6366.

ADIRONDACK BOUND, Sagamore Lodge & Conference Center, Raquette Lake, NY 13436. Annual fishing weekend with instruction. Especially for beginners. Information: (315)354-5311.

FLYING

ADIRONDACK FLYING SERVICE, Lake Placid Airport, Cascade Rd. (Rt. 73), Lake Placid, NY 12946. Information: (518)523-2473.

TRI-LAKES FLYING SERVICE, INC., Lake Clear Rd., Adirondack Airport, Saranac Lake, NY 12983. Information: (518)891-3114.

PAYNE'S AIR SERVICE, off Rt. 28, Seventh Lake, NY 13360. Information: (315) 357-3971.

SAILING

LAKE GEORGE SAILING SCHOOL, RD 1, Box 99, Lake George, NY 12845. Intensive 2-day and 3-day course covering knowledge and skills to handle own sailboat. Information: (518)668-2805.

WATERSKIING

TOM'S WATER SKI SCHOOL, Rt. 9N, Lake Shore Dr., Lake George, NY 12845. Water ski lessons with professional instructors. Information: (518)668-3950.

WINTER MOUNTAINEERING

BEGINNERS WINTER MOUNTAINEERING SCHOOL, Adirondack Mountain Club, 172 Ridge St., Glens Falls, NY 12801. Two sessions, each lasting one week, mid-January and mid-March. Information: (518)793-7737.

WINTER SCHOOL, Adirondack Mountain Club. Week-long winter camping for beginners and experienced hikers. Held last week of December. First aid, winter ecology, ice axe use and other topics covered. Courses held in Adirondack Mountains. For information and application send a self-addressed stamped envelope (2 1st class stamps) to Winter School, Adirondack Mountain Club, 172 Ridge St., Glens Falls, NY 12801.

ANNUAL CALENDAR OF RECREATIONAL EVENTS

As distinguished from the Calendar of Entertainment Events (Section 79), this section includes events most commonly associated with "sports"—both for participants and spectators. Sometimes there was a very fine line between classifying an event as recreational or entertainment, and an arbitrary choice was made. If in doubt, check both sections.

When recreational events are contingent upon weather conditions (e.g., amount of snow for ski events; spring run-off for canoe races, etc.), it is advisable to check with the sponsor before planning to attend an event.

For further information on snow conditions, two other sections of *The Adirondack Guide* have telephone numbers one might call: Ski Centers (Section 93) and For More Information (Section 116).

JANUARY

SKI JUMP COMPETITION, Lake Placid. New Year's Day. Olympic Ski Jump Complex. 70 Meter ski jump competition. Information: Lake Placid, NY 12946. (518)523-2445.

SKI JUMP CHAMPIONSHIPS, Lake Placid. New Years weekend in January. National 70 Meter Ski Jump Championships, Intervale Complex. Information: Chamber of Commerce, Lake Placid, NY 12946.

FROSTBITE RUN, Lake Placid. 1st Saturday in January, unless it falls on January 1st. Around Mirror Lake, 2.5 and 5 miles. Information: Dr. Robert Lopez, Westport, NY 12993. (518)962-8228.

EQUITABLE FAMILY RACING CHALLENGE, Gore Mountain. Every Sunday from end of December to mid-February. Information: Gore Mt. Ski Center, Rt. 28, North Creek, NY 12853. (518)251-2411.

CROSS COUNTRY RELAY RACES, North Creek. Every weekend through March. Teams of Four. Information: Cunningham's Ski Barn, North Creek, NY 12853. (518) 251-3215.

SNOWSHOE RACE, Tupper Lake. 2nd weekend in January. Big Tupper Ski Area. Information: Tupper Lake, NY 12986. (518)359-3651.

LUMBERJACK SCRAMBLE, Tupper Lake. Mid-January. 10K citizen's race. Entrance fee. Information: Jim Frenette (518)359-3261.

HANDICAP RACE, Gore Mountain. Mid-week of the second week or 3rd weekend in January. Race for amputees. Information: Gore Mt. Ski Center, Rt. 28, North Creek, NY 12853. (518)251-2411.

RACE, Speculator. Second Saturday in January. Pleasant Riders, Poker Run—snowmobile event. Information: Office of Tourism and Community Development and Tourism, Speculator, NY 12164. (518)584-4521.

CHILDREN'S DAY, North Creek. Co-sponsored by the Warren County 4-H and Cunningham's Ski Barn. No charge. Information: (518)251-3215.

CITIZENS RACES AND EVENTS, Gore Mountain. 3rd weekend in January. Sponsored by Newport Cigarettes. Information: Gore Mountian Ski Center, Rt. 28, North Creek, NY 12853. (518)251-2411.

INTERNATIONAL DOG SLED CHAMPIONSHIPS, Saranac Lake. Last weekend in January. Includes races, parties and awards ceremony. Information: Saranac Lake Chamber of Commerce, Saranac Lake, NY 12983. (518) 891-1990.

GORE MOUNTAIN SKI CLUB RACE. 4th weekend in January. An official South Adirondack Council race for Junior III and II racers. Information: Gore Mt. Ski Center, Route 28, North Creek, NY 12853. (518)251-2411.

FEBRUARY

DOWNHILL RACE, Gore Mountain. 1st weekend in February. New York State Junior I and II class. Information: Gore Mt. Ski Center, North Creek, NY 12853. (518)251-2411.

POKER RUN, Piseco. 2nd Saturday in February. Snowmobile event. Information: Office of Tourism and Community Development, Speculator, NY 12164.

CROSS COUNTRY RELAY RACES, North Creek. Every weekend through March. Teams of four. Information: Cunningham's Ski Barn, Rt. 28, North Creek, NY 12853. (518)251-3215.

TOBOGGAN CHAMPIONSHIPS, Lake Placid. 3rd or 4th weekend in February. Held at Lake Placid Toboggan Chute. Information: Chamber of Commerce, Lake Placid, NY 12946. (518)523-2445.

CROSS COUNTRY SKI RACE, Inlet. Last Saturday in February. 10, 20 and 30 km races. Information: Chamber of Commerce, Inlet, NY 13360.

CROSS COUNTRY SKI RACE, Speculator. Last Saturday in Febraury. 10km race. Held at Speculator Ballfield. Information: Office of Tourism and Community Development, Speculator, NY 12164.

SWEETHEART SKI RACE, Tupper Lake. Last Saturday in February. Fun downhill ski race. Information: Big Tupper Ski Area, Tupper Lake, NY 12986. (518)359-3651.

SNOWMOBILE RACES, Hague. Sponsored by Hague Sno-Goers Club. All Classes. Information: Box 271, Hollow Rd., Hague, NY 12836.

CROSS COUNTRY RACE/MARATHON, Tupper Lake. 35km/40km races. Held at Big Tupper Ski Area. Information: Jim Frenette. (518)359-3261.

MARCH

RUN FOR YOUR LIFE, Keene. 1st Saturday in March. 50, 20, and 10 km races. Lake Placid Road Runners and American Cancer Society. Information: Dr. Robert Lopez, Westport, NY 12993. (518)962-8228.

EMPIRE STATE WINTER GAMES, Lake Placid. 1st and 2nd weeks in March. Information: Chamber of Commerce, Lake Placid, NY 12946. (518)523-2445.

GELANDESPRUNG JUMPING CONTEST, Tupper Lake. 1st Sunday in March. Free style jumping contest. Information: Tupper Lake Ski Area, Tupper Lake, NY 12986. (518)359-3651.

ST. PATRICKS CELEBRATION, Gore Mountain. St. Patrick's Day Weekend. Tournaments, parties, races. Information: Gore Mt. Ski Center, Rt. 28, North Creek, NY 12853. (518)251-2411.

POLE-PEDAL-PADDLE RACE, Gore Mt. Last weekend in March. Sponsored by Gore Mt. Ski Club. 4-way challenge race. Relay race includes cross country, downhill skiing, bicycling and whitewater canoeing. Information: Barron Clancy, (518)668-5819.

SKI RACE, North Creek. 15km, cross country citizen ski race, open and classified skiers can receive FIS points. Information: Cunningham's Ski Barn, North Creek, NY 12853. (518)251-3215.

APRIL

TROUT CONTEST, Ausable River. April 15-September 15. Either branch of the AuSable River in Essex County. Information: Chamber of Commerce, Box 277, Wilmington, NY 12997.

WHITEWATER RACE, Keene/Upper Jay. Last Sunday in April. 6-mile course on East Branch of the Ausable River. Information: Chamber of Commerce, PO Box 300, Ausable Forks, NY 12912.

MAY

SARA - PLACID RUN, Saranac Lake - Lake Placid. 1st Saturday in May. 5 and 10 mile runs. Information: Dr. R. Lopez, Westport, NY 12993.

WHITEWATER DERBY, North Creek. 1st full weekend in May. Held on Hudson River. Both slalom races and downhill river events in canoeing and kayaking. Subdivided into classes with sometimes as many as 11 different categories from novice through experienced paddlers. Information: Thomas Pierson, North Creek, NY 12853.

BED RACE, Bolton Landing. Last Sunday in May. Bed race down Main St. 4 pushers, one passenger, audience of 5,000. Information: Chamber of Commerce, Bolton Landing, NY 12814.

CHILDREN'S FISHING TOURNAMENT, Inlet. May 27th-noon May 31st. Ages 15 and under. No entrance fee, prizes, fishing tackle. Entry blanks at any local business.

TROUT CONTEST, Ausable River. April 15-September 15. Either branch of the Ausable River in Essex County. Information: Chamber of Commerce, Wilmington, NY 12997.

JUNE

GOLF TOURNAMENT, Thendara. 1st weekend in June. Sponsored by the NYS American Legion. Information: Thendara Golf Course, Thendara, NY 13472. (315) 369-3136.

CANOE RACE, Lake Placid. Early June. 7.5 mile races on West Branch of the Ausable River. Nominal entry fee. Information: North Elba Parks District, Sports Office. (518)523-3325.

CROSS COUNTRY RUN, Lake Placid. 1st Saturday in June, also in early October. Held at Mt. Van Hoevenberg Recreation Center. Information: North Elba Park District, Sports Office, Lake Placid, NY 12946. (518)523-1710.

CROSS COUNTRY RACE, Old Forge. 2nd Sunday in June. "Adirondack Deer Run." 10 km race. Information: Chamber of Commerce, Old Forge, NY 13420.

OPEN GOLF TOURNAMENT, Westport. 2nd weekend in June. Tom Tanneberger Memorial Tournament. Information: Country Club, Westport, NY 12993.

UPHILL FOOTRACE, Wilmington. 2nd Sunday in June. 8 miles up Whiteface Mt. Memorial Highway. Information: Whiteface Mt. Chamber of Commerce, Box 277, Wilmington, NY 12997.

BASS TOURNAMENT, Hague. 3rd weekend in June. Sponorsed by NYS Bass Federation. Spectators invited to official weigh-in and ceremonies. Information: (518) 543-6353.

FROG JUMPING CONTEST, Old Forge. 3rd weekend in June. Held at lakefront. Information: Office of Tourist Information, Old Forge, NY 13420.

TROUT CONTEST, Ausable River. April 15-September 15. Either branch of the Ausable River in Essex County. Information: Chamber of Commerce, Wilmington, NY 12997.

HORSE SHOW, Lake Placid. Last weekend in June. Information: North Elba Park District, Sports Office, Lake Placid, NY 12946. (518)523-1710.

GUIDEBOAT/CANOE RACE & MARATHON, Tupper Lake. Last weekend in June. Entry fee. Information: Chamber of Commerce, Tupper Lake, NY 12986. (518)359-2507 or 359-3328.

BASS TOURNAMENT, Ticonderoga. Meet at Boat Launching Site. Information: Chamber of Commerce, Ticonderoga, NY 12883. (518)585-6619.

FIREMAN'S FIELD DAY, Nicholville. Information: Nicholville Fire Department, Nicholville, NY 12965.

JULY

SOFTBALL TOURNAMENT, Tupper Lake. July 4th weekend. "Old Home Week." Information: Chamber of Commerce, Tupper Lake, NY 12986. (518)359-2507 or 3328.

GUIDEBOAT AND CANOE RACES, Saranac Lake. Sunday closest to July 4th. Willard Hanner Memorial Race. Eight classes. Entry fee. Information: Chamber of Commerce, Saranac Lake, NY 12983. (518)891-1990.

INTERVALE SKI JUMP, Lake Placid. July 4th summer jump at 40 meter ski jump. Information: Chamber of Commerce, Lake Placid, NY 12946. (518)523-2445.

OPEN GOLF TOURNAMENT, Inlet. Early in July. Sponsored by Utica Sporting Goods. Contact Pro, Deer Run Golf Course, Inlet, NY 13360.

BATHTUB RACES, Pine Lake. 1st week in July. Information: (315)866-1500.

MONTY ARTO 3 AND 6 MILE RACES, Upper Jay and Keene. 1st Saturday in July, unless it falls on 4th, then Sunday. Information: Lake Placid Road Runners, Dr. Robert Lopez, Westport, NY 12993.

MAYOR'S CUP SAILING RACES, Lake Champlain. 2nd weekend in July. Information: Clinton County Chamber of Commerce, 135 Margaret St., Plattsburgh, NY 12901.

LAKE GEORGE-BOLTON RUN, Lake George. Mid-July. 10 mile run. Information: Chamber of Commerce, Lake George, NY 12925. (518)668-5755.

FREE SKATING COMPETITION, Lake Placid. Mid-July. Olympic Arena. Information: Chamber of Commerce, Lake Placid, NY 12946.

SAILING REGATTA, Lake Placid. Every other Sunday during July and August. Sailboats and windsurfers. Information: Whiteface Country Club, Lake Placid, NY 12946. (518)523-4424.

MIXED DOUBLES TENNIS SERIES, Lake Placid. Every other Sunday in July and August. Information: Whiteface Inn Country Club, Lake Placid, NY 12946. (518)523-4424.

WHITEFACE OPEN GOLF TOURNAMENT, Lake Placid. Late July/early August. Information: Chamber of Commerce, Lake Placid, NY 12946.

WET AND WILD WEEKEND/ GREAT SACANDAGA OPEN REGATTA. Late July. Sponsored by Fulton County Chamber of Commerce. Held at Great Sacandaga Lake, Mayfield. Information: Fulton County Chamber of Commerce, 40 N. Main, Gloversville, NY 12078. (518)762-4128 or 725-0641.

CANOE RACE, Blue Mt. Lake. 3rd week of July. Blue Mt. Marathon, 34 miles from Old Forge to Blue Mt. Lake, including 4 carries. Many classes, trophies, and a finish-line chicken barbecue. Information: Tom Warrington, PO Box 112, Blue Mt. Lake, NY 12812. (315)352-7732.

AAU SWIM MEET, Lake Placid. 3rd weekend in July. Held at Mirror Lake. Information: North Elba Park District, Sports Office, Lake Placid, NY 12946. (518)523-1710.

24 HOUR MARATHON RELAY, Westport. 3rd weekend in July. Held at the Fairgrounds, Westport. County-wide event. Information: Dr. Robert Lopez, Westport, NY 12993. (518)962-8228.

TRIATHLON EVENTS, Corinth. Last weekend in July. Canoe related competitions. Information: Jeff Towers, c/o Corinth Aquarium, West Maple St., Corinth, NY 12822. (518)654-9871.

I LOVE NY HORSESHOW, Lake Placid. Information: Chamber of Commerce, Lake Placid, NY 12946.

AUGUST

CAN-AM RUGBY TOURNAMENT, Saranac Lake. 1st weekend in August. Information: Chamber of Commerce, Saranac Lake, NY 12983.

FIRE DEPARTMENT FIELD DAYS, Star Lake. 1st weekend in August. AAU/TAC Sanctioned 26.2 mile Marathon. Information: Chamber of Commerce, Star Lake, NY 13690.

TENNIS CLASSIC, Old Forge. 1st weekend in August. Information: Tourist Information Center, Old Forge, NY 13420.

WATERSKI MEET, Lake Placid. 1st weekend in August. Information: North Elba Parks District, Sports Office, Lake Placid, NY 12946. (518)523-1710.

GENESEE LIGHT LAKE RUN, Lake Pleasant. 1st or 2nd Sunday in August. 10km run. Information: Chamber of Commerce, Speculator, NY 12164.

RUNNING RACE, Lake Placid. 2nd Saturday in August. "Over Hill and Dale". Also run-swim race. Information: Whiteface Inn Country Club, Whiteface, NY 12946. (518) 523-4424.

REGATTA DAY, Long Lake. 2nd weekend in August. Held at Long Lake Town Beach. Sailboat, guideboat, rowboat, canoe and war canoe races. Information: Hamilton County Publicity Bureau, Long Lake, NY 12847. (518)624-4151.

MINI-MARATHON, Westport. 2nd Sunday in August. 15 km run. Information: Dr. Robert Lopez, Westport, NY 12993. (518)962-8228.

FLAT WATER RACES, Brant Lake. Early-August. Amateurs. Sponsored by Brant Lake Trailers Snowmobile Club. Information: Robert Newton, Brant Lake, NY 12815. (518)494-2246.

OPEN GOLF TOURNAMENT, Tupper Lake. 2nd weekend in August. Information: Chamber of Commerce, Tupper Lake, NY 12986.

OPEN TENNIS TOURNAMENT, Inlet. 2nd-3rd weekend in August. Must pre-register by noon, August 13th. Information: Chamber of Commerce, Inlet, NY 13360.

GOLF TOURNAMENT, Lake Pleasant. 2nd Friday in August. Sponsored by Chamber of Commerce. Information: Chamber of Commerce, Speculator, NY 12164.

TENNIS TOURNAMENT, Lake Pleasant. 2nd Friday in August. Information: Chamber of Commerce, Speculator, NY 12164.

OPEN GOLF TOURNAMENT, Lake Placid. 3rd weekend in August. Sponsored by Michelob and Yamaha. Held at Lake Placid Club Resort. Information: Lake Placid Club Resort, Lake Placid, NY 12946.

BASS FISHING CONTEST, Lake Champlain. Information: Clinton County Chamber of Commerce, 135 Margaret St., Plattsburgh, NY 12901. (518)563-1000.

SUMMER-RUN, Schroon Lake. Run through town. Information: Chamber of Commerce, Schroon Lake, NY 12870. (518)532-7675 or 7379.

SEPTEMBER

TRIATHALON, Lake Placid, Keene, Wilmington. Labor Day weekend in September. Information: Sundog Ski and Sports, Main St., Lake Placid, NY 12946. (518) 523-2752.

MARATHON, Lake Placid. 2nd Saturday in September. Information: Dr. Robert Lopez, Westport, NY 12993. (518)962-8228.

MARATHON AND HALF-MARATHON, Lake Placid. 2nd week in September. Run from Paul Smiths to Lake Placid. Information: Chamber of Commerce, Lake Placid, NY 12946. (518)523-2445.

OPEN GOLF TOURNAMENT, Lake Placid. 2nd weekend in September. Held at Craig Wood Golf Course. Information: Craig Wood Golf Course, Lake Placid, NY 12946. (518)523-2591 or 523-9811.

LARRY MCNEIL GOLF TOURNAMENT, Inlet. 17th and 18th of September. Information: Inlet Golf Course (Deer Run), Inlet, NY 13360.

MUZZLE LOADING SHOOTS, Fort Ticonderoga. 3rd weekend in September. Sponsored by Fort Ticonderoga Muzzle Loading Association. A gathering of over 250 muzzle loading enthusiasts. Divided ranges, medals and trophies awarded. Information: Chamber of Commerce, Ticonderoga, NY 12883. (518)585-6619.

BARFLY OPEN GOLF TOURNAMENT, Lake Placid. Last weekend in September. Held on a rotating basis at Craig Wood, Whiteface Inn and Lake Placid Club Resort. Information: Lake Placid Club Resort, Lake Placid, NY 12946.

TURKEY SHOOT, Inlet. Held at Loomis Field. Information: Chamber of Commerce, Inlet, NY 13360.

OCTOBER

OPEN GOLF TOURNAMENT, Inlet. 1st weekend in October. Information: Inlet Golf Course (Deer Run), Inlet, NY 13360.

FALL FESTIVAL, Lake Luzerne. Early October. Held at the Sacandaga River. White water races. Information: George Conable, Lake Luzerne, NY 12846. (518)696-3197.

FALL FOLIAGE CLASSIC, North Creek. Columbus Day weekend in October. 10 km, "The Colors Run." Sponsored by North Creek Athletic League. Pre-race clinic. Information: Chamber of Commerce, North Creek, NY 12853.

WHITEWATER CANOE RACE, Old Forge. Mid-October. Held on the Moose River. Slalom and down river races, various classes. Singing Waters to Moose River. Information: Central Adirondack Association, Old Forge, NY 13420.

AMATEUR OPEN GOLF TOURNAMENT, Lake George. 4th weekend in October. Held at the Top O' the World. Calloway Handicap System. Registration. Information: Top O'The World, Box 252, Lake George, NY 12845. (518)668-5415.

MUZZLE LOADING BLACK POWDER SHOOT, Inlet. Held at Big Moose Fish and Game Range on Big Moose Road. Information: Chamber of Commerce, Inlet, NY 13360.

DECEMBER

X-COUNTRY RELAY RACES, North Creek. Every weekend through March. Teams of four. Sponsored by Cunningham's Ski Barn. Information: North Creek, NY 12853. (518)251-3215.

EQUITABLE FAMILY SKI CHALLENGE, North Creek. Every Sunday from December to mid-February. Information: Gore Mt. Ski Center, Rt. 28, North Creek, NY 12853. (518)251-2411.

CROSS-COUNTRY CITIZEN'S RACE, Lake Placid. 2nd weekend in December. Information: Cascade Ski Touring Center, Lake Placid, NY 12946.

SNODEO, Old Forge. 2nd weekend in December. Snowmobile contests and events. Information: Tourist Information Center, Old Forge, NY 13420.

FORT TO FORT, Crown Point. Early December. Crown Pt. to Ft. Ticonderoga. 30 km (18.5 miles). Information: Box 390, Westport, NY 12993.

TRANSPORTATION

(102)
RAILROADS

AMTRAK. "The Adirondack" runs daily between New York City and Montreal along the west side of Lake Champlain. It is a passenger service line, and the route is approximately 70 miles (112km) in length through the Adirondack Park. Information: (800)523-5700.

The schedule is subject to change. However AMTRAK informed us that the schedule has changed very little in the past six years, with only minor variations in what time the train leaves New York or Montreal. Please note that Port Kent, Willsboro, Westport, Port Henry, and Ticonderoga stops are "flag stops". Use toll-free number for reservations and schedule times.

READ DOWN/DE HAUT EN BAS — READ UP/DE BAS EN HAUT

68				Train Number/Numero Du Train		69
Daily				Frequency of Operation Frequence De Circulation		Daily
⊠				Type of Service/Service		⊠
10 15A	km 0	Mi 0	Dp	*(Delaware & Hudson)* **Montreal, QUE.** *(ET)* *-Windsor Sta./Gare Windsor*	Ar	7 13P
R 10 21A	3	2		Westmount, QUE. •		**D** 7 01P
R 10 27A	8	5		Montreal West, QUE. •		**D** 6 56P
	56 56	35 35		Lacolle, QUE. 🛃	Dp Ar	(42) 5 59P (43) 5 50P
11 15A 11 30A	65 65	41 41	Ar Dp	Rouses Point, NY • 🛃	Dp Ar	5 41P 5 39P
12 00N	102	64		**Plattsburgh, NY**		5 11P
⚑ 12 15P	123	77	Ar	Port Kent, NY •	Dp	⚑ 4 53P
⚑ 12 37P	144	90		Willsboro, NY •		⚑ 4 31P
⚑ 12 57P	167	104		Westport, NY • *(Elizabethtown)* *(Lake Placid And Saranac Lake)* (71)		⚑ 4 11P
⚑ 1 15P	185	115		Port Henry, NY •		⚑ 3 54P
⚑ 1 38P	212	132		Fort Ticonderoga, NY •		⚑ 3 31P
2 08P	247	154		Whitehall, NY • *(Rutland)*		3 01P
2 34P	283	176		Fort Edward, NY *(Glens Falls And Lake George)*		2 36P
3 05P	313	195		Saratoga Springs, NY		2 13P
3 46P	345	215		*(Conrail)* Schenectady, NY		1 42P
4 08P 4 25P	374	233	Ar Dp	**Albany-Rensselaer, NY**	Dp Ar	1 15P 1 02P
4 48P	418	260		Hudson, NY		12 37P
5 08P	460	286		Rhinecliff, NY *(Kingston)*		12 13P
D 5 25P	484	301		Poughkeepsie, NY *(Highland)*		**R** 11 59A
D 6 05P	548	341		Croton-Harmon, NY		**R** 11 18A
6 57P	603	375	Ar	**New York, NY** *(ET)* *-Grand Cent. Tml./Gare Grand Cent.*	Dp	10 35A

(103)
BUS LINES

GREYHOUND BUS LINES

Although there has been some discussion about eliminating parts of their route, Greyhound Bus Lines continues to serve the eastern Adirondacks and the Lake Placid-Saranac Lake region. There are several runs a day between Albany and Montreal, including stops at Glens Falls, Lake George, Warrensburg, Chestertown, Loon Lake, Pottersville, Schroon Lake, Elizabethtown, Saranac Lake, Lake Placid, Wilmington, Keeseville, Peru, Ausable Chasm and Plattsburgh. For exact schedules and routes call Albany: (518)434-0121 or Glens Falls: (518)793-5052, as there is no toll free listing, and most individual stops do not have a phone number.

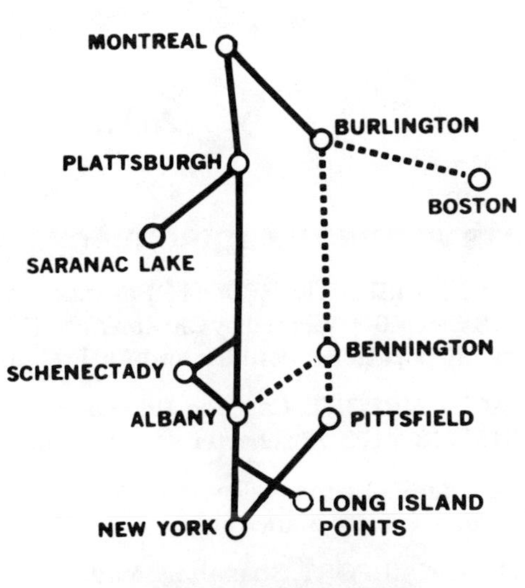

ADIRONDACK TRAILWAYS

During the off-season, Adirondack Trailways generally has three daily buses serving the Adirondacks: one between Massena and Albany, via Malone, Tupper Lake, Saranac Lake, Lake Placid and the Northway; one between Tupper Lake and Albany, via the same route as above; and one between Warrensburg and Albany. In the summer, additional service is added through the Central Adirondacks, via Albany, Warrensburg, Indian Lake, Blue Mountain Lake, Long Lake, Tupper Lake and other points. Albany connects to all other major cities. For exact schedules and routes, call (800)-342-4101 or the various passenger service centers listed below located in the Adirondack Park.

#Blue Mountain Lake, Steamboat Landing, (518)352-7323.
#Bolton Landing, Chamber of Commerce, (518)644-3831.
Chestertown, The Corner Store, (518)494-2091.
#Hague, Village Center, (518)543-2181.
#Indian Lake, Adirondack Trail Motel, (518)648-5044.
Keene, Monty's Elm Tree Inn, (518)576-9998.
Keene Valley, Gregory's Service Center, (518)576-2222.
Lake George, Fife and Drum Shop.
Lake Placid, Main St. Deli, (518)523-4309.
#North Creek, Smith Restaurant, (518)251-9965.
Pottersville, Wells House, (518)494-9937.
Saranac Lake, Oxford Market, 69 Broadway, (518)891-3300.
Schroon Lake, Sugar Bowl Restaurant, (518)532-9083.
#Ticonderoga, Bevilaqua's Grocery, 112 Champion Ave., (518)585-6680.
Tupper Lake, Miss Tupper Diner, (518)359-9621.
Warrensburg, Marco Polo, 161 Main St., (518)623-2786.

— seasonal summer agents.

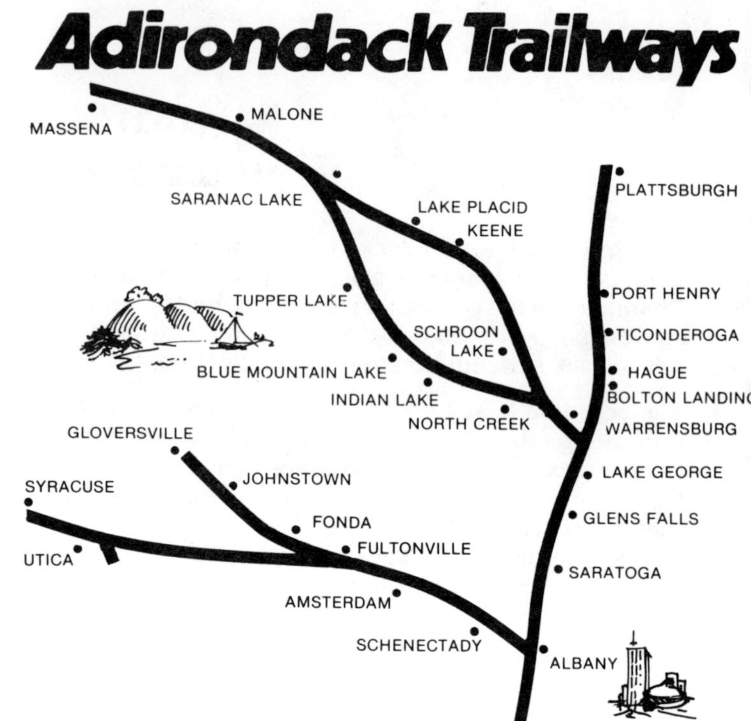

(104)
AIRPORTS AND AIR SERVICES

AIRPORTS WITHIN THE ADIRONDACKS

ADIRONDACK AIRPORT, RFD #1, Saranac Lake, NY 12983. (518)891-4600. Served by Clinton Aero, (518)891-5551. Local airport ticket counter and Air Freight.

LAKE PLACID AIRPORT, Cascade Rd., Lake Placid, NY 12946. (518)523-2473. Air charter service available.

MARCY AIRPORT, Keene Valley, NY 12943. (518)576-2214, evenings. Private planes only.

TICONDEROGA AIRPORT, Shanahan Road, Ticonderoga, NY 12883. (518)585-3375.

AIRPORTS BORDERING THE ADIRONDACKS

BURLINGTON AIRPORT, PO Box 2302, South Burlington, VT 05401. Served by Clinton Aero, Delta, Air North, Air Florida, Air Vermont, United, USAir, Precision, and People Express airlines.

CLINTON COUNTY AIRPORT, 198 Airport Road, Plattsburgh, NY 12901. (518)561-4350. Served by Clinton Aero Airlines.

MALONE DUFORGE AIRPORT, North Bangor Rd., Malone, NY 12953. (518)483-9892.

MASSENA TOWN AIRPORT, Hanger Rd., Massena, NY 13662. (315)769-9719. Served by Clinton Aero.

ONEIDA COUNTY AIRPORT (Utica/Rome), NY 13424. Served by Empire Airlines.

WARREN COUNTY AIRPORT, RD 1, Glens Falls, NY 12801. (518)792-5995. Housing Glens Falls Flight Center. (518)793-5605.

WATERTOWN AIRPORT, Watertown, NY 13601. Served by Clinton Aero.

AIRLINES SERVING THE ADIRONDACKS AREA

AIR FLORIDA. (800)327-6519.

AIR NORTH. (800)451-3432.

AIR VERMONT. (800)343-8828.

CLINTON AERO. (800)342-9100.

EMPIRE. (800)962-5665

PEOPLE EXPRESS. (800)526-9235.

PRECISION. (800)451-4221.

UNITED. (800)336-0123

USAIR. (800)428-4253.

FLYING SERVICES

In addition to the air services and airlines described above, there are the flying services located within the Blue Line. These services generally specialize in scenic flying tours and taking hunters and fishing people to remote Adirondack lakes. However, they also provide air transportation—in all seasons, both on land and water, between the Adirondacks and other areas and states. For complete listing of these independent flying services, see section 87.

(105)

LAKE CHAMPLAIN FERRIES

The first three ferries listed are operated by the Lake Champlain Transportation Company, c/o King Street Dock, Burlington, VT 05401, (802)864-9804. The Fort Ticoderoga Ferry is operated by Shorewell Ferry Co., Larrabee's Point, Shoreham, VT 05770, (802)897-7999.

PLATTSBURGH FERRY. Operates year round between Grand Isle, VT and Cumberland Head (Plattsburgh) NY. From Vermont Interstate 89 use Exit 17, 12 miles from the ferry. From New York Interstate 87 use Exit 39, five miles from the ferry. Crossing time is 12 minutes.

BURLINGTON FERRY. Mid-May through mid-October between Burlington, VT and Port Kent, NY. From Vermont Interstate 89 use Exit 14W, two miles from the ferry. From New York Interstate 87 use Exit 34 or 35, six miles from the ferry. Crossing time is one hour.

ESSEX FERRY. Operates early April through late November between Charlotte, VT and Essex, NY. From Vermont U.S. 7 take Route F-5 at Charlotte, three miles from the ferry. From New York Interstate 87 take Exit 32, 10 miles from the ferry. Crossing time is 20 minutes.

FORT TICONDEROGA FERRY. Operates mid-April through late October between Shoreham, VT and Ticonderoga, NY. In Vermont, take Route 74 from the north or Route 73 from the south. In New York, take Route 74 east from Ticonderoga to the lake. Crossing time is 6 minutes.

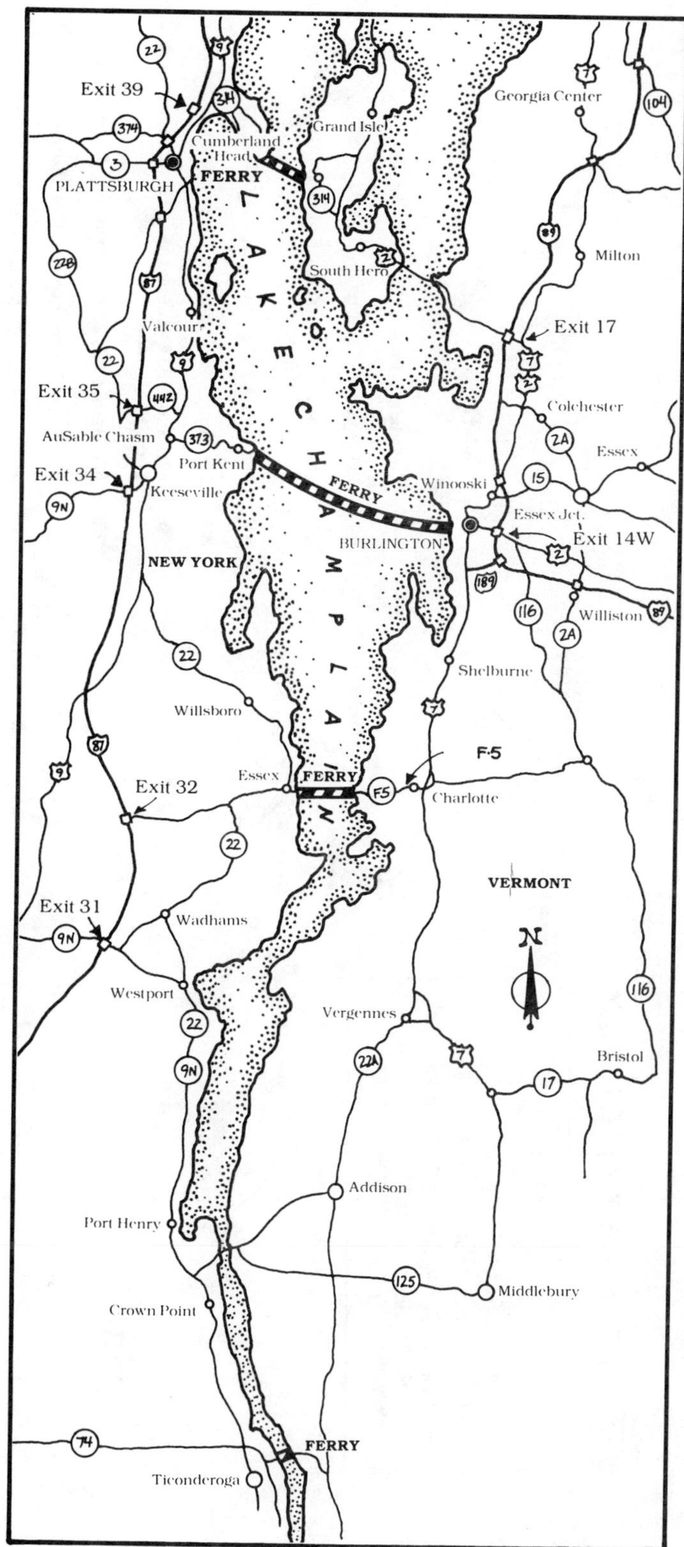

(106) ADIRONDACK NORTHWAY MAP AND INFORMATION

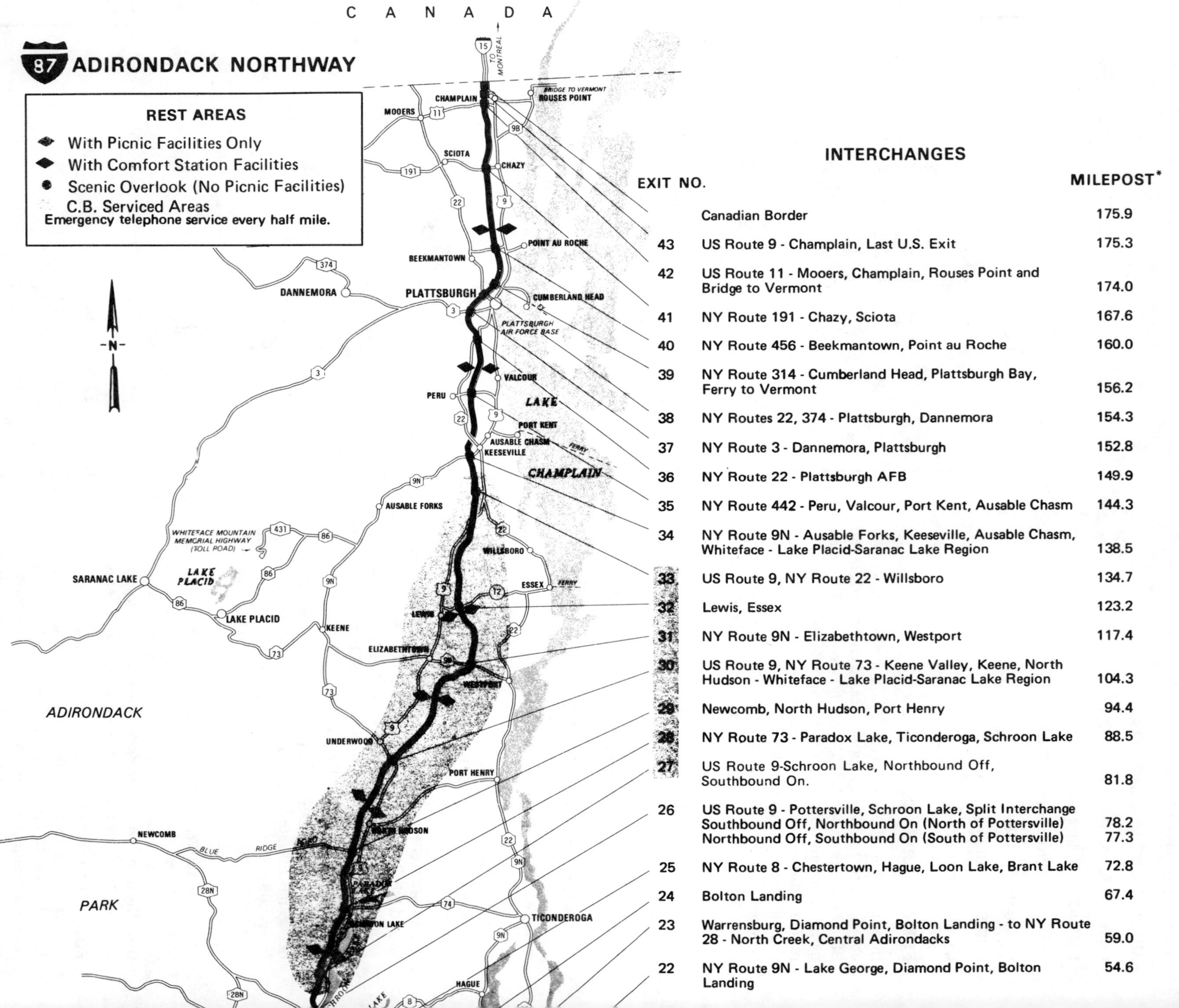

INTERCHANGES

EXIT NO.		MILEPOST*
	Canadian Border	175.9
43	US Route 9 - Champlain, Last U.S. Exit	175.3
42	US Route 11 - Mooers, Champlain, Rouses Point and Bridge to Vermont	174.0
41	NY Route 191 - Chazy, Sciota	167.6
40	NY Route 456 - Beekmantown, Point au Roche	160.0
39	NY Route 314 - Cumberland Head, Plattsburgh Bay, Ferry to Vermont	156.2
38	NY Routes 22, 374 - Plattsburgh, Dannemora	154.3
37	NY Route 3 - Dannemora, Plattsburgh	152.8
36	NY Route 22 - Plattsburgh AFB	149.9
35	NY Route 442 - Peru, Valcour, Port Kent, Ausable Chasm	144.3
34	NY Route 9N - Ausable Forks, Keeseville, Ausable Chasm, Whiteface - Lake Placid-Saranac Lake Region	138.5
33	US Route 9, NY Route 22 - Willsboro	134.7
32	Lewis, Essex	123.2
31	NY Route 9N - Elizabethtown, Westport	117.4
30	US Route 9, NY Route 73 - Keene Valley, Keene, North Hudson - Whiteface - Lake Placid-Saranac Lake Region	104.3
29	Newcomb, North Hudson, Port Henry	94.4
28	NY Route 73 - Paradox Lake, Ticonderoga, Schroon Lake	88.5
27	US Route 9-Schroon Lake, Northbound Off, Southbound On.	81.8
26	US Route 9 - Pottersville, Schroon Lake, Split Interchange Southbound Off, Northbound On (North of Pottersville) Northbound Off, Southbound On (South of Pottersville)	78.2 77.3
25	NY Route 8 - Chestertown, Hague, Loon Lake, Brant Lake	72.8
24	Bolton Landing	67.4
23	Warrensburg, Diamond Point, Bolton Landing - to NY Route 28 - North Creek, Central Adirondacks	59.0
22	NY Route 9N - Lake George, Diamond Point, Bolton Landing	54.6

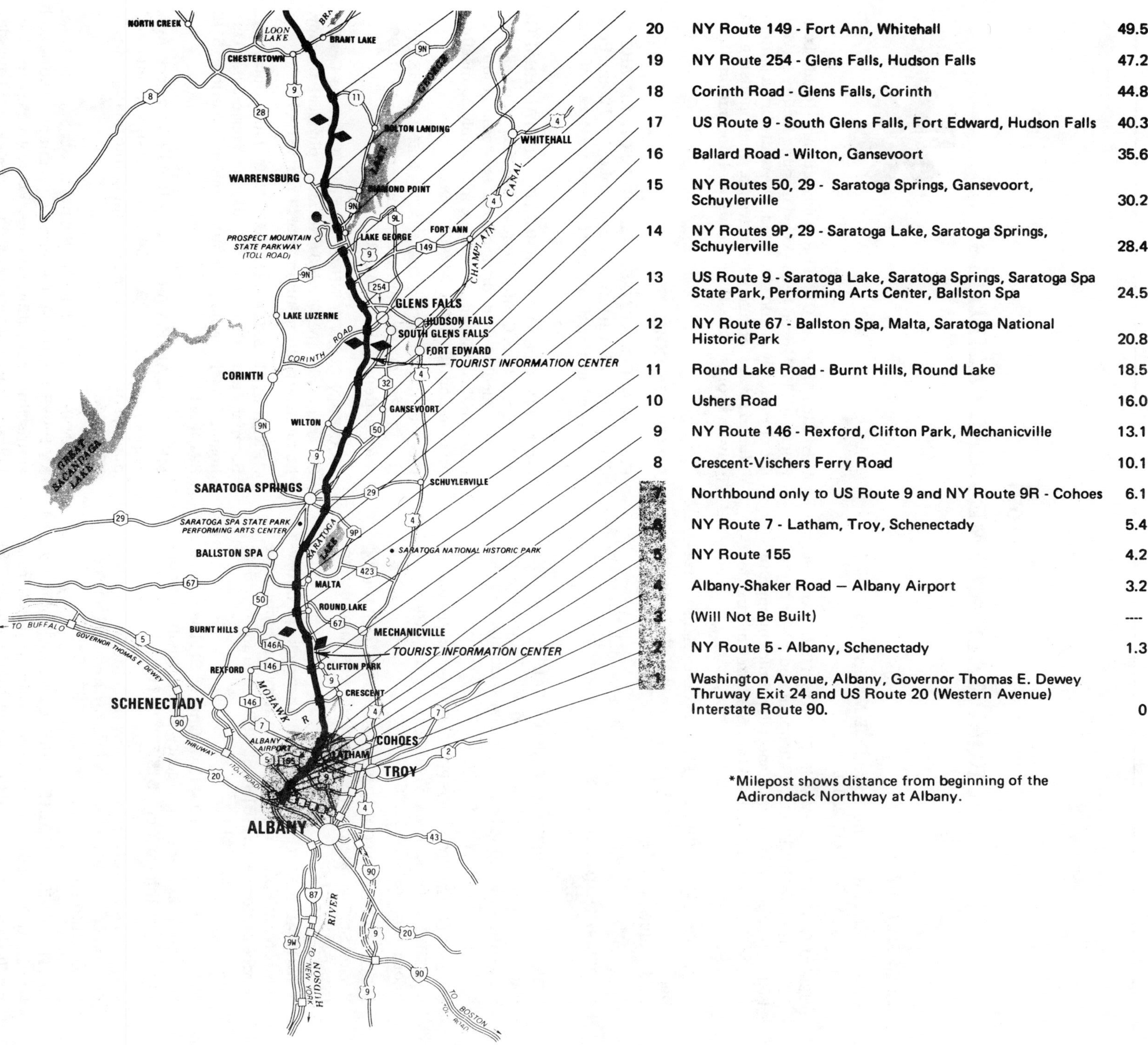

Exit		Milepost*
20	NY Route 149 - Fort Ann, Whitehall	49.5
19	NY Route 254 - Glens Falls, Hudson Falls	47.2
18	Corinth Road - Glens Falls, Corinth	44.8
17	US Route 9 - South Glens Falls, Fort Edward, Hudson Falls	40.3
16	Ballard Road - Wilton, Gansevoort	35.6
15	NY Routes 50, 29 - Saratoga Springs, Gansevoort, Schuylerville	30.2
14	NY Routes 9P, 29 - Saratoga Lake, Saratoga Springs, Schuylerville	28.4
13	US Route 9 - Saratoga Lake, Saratoga Springs, Saratoga Spa State Park, Performing Arts Center, Ballston Spa	24.5
12	NY Route 67 - Ballston Spa, Malta, Saratoga National Historic Park	20.8
11	Round Lake Road - Burnt Hills, Round Lake	18.5
10	Ushers Road	16.0
9	NY Route 146 - Rexford, Clifton Park, Mechanicville	13.1
8	Crescent-Vischers Ferry Road	10.1
7	Northbound only to US Route 9 and NY Route 9R - Cohoes	6.1
6	NY Route 7 - Latham, Troy, Schenectady	5.4
5	NY Route 155	4.2
4	Albany-Shaker Road — Albany Airport	3.2
3	(Will Not Be Built)	----
2	NY Route 5 - Albany, Schenectady	1.3
1	Washington Avenue, Albany, Governor Thomas E. Dewey Thruway Exit 24 and US Route 20 (Western Avenue) Interstate Route 90.	0

*Milepost shows distance from beginning of the Adirondack Northway at Albany.

ASSISTANCE

(107)
HOSPITALS AND MEDICAL FACILITIES

ESSEX COUNTY

CARE CENTER, at the Town Hall. Minerva, NY 12851. Information: (518)251-2510.

ELIZABETHTOWN COMMUNITY HOSPITAL, Park St., Elizabethtown, NY 12932. 29 hospital and 15 long term beds, 18 physicians on staff, specialty clinics by appointment only. Visiting hours 11am-8:30pm. Information: (518)873-6377.

ESSEX COUNTY NURSING SERVICE, Court House, Elizabethtown, NY 12932. Nursing, physical therapy, home-health aides. Information: (518)873-6301.

HEALTH CARE CENTER, Mineville Hospital, Mineville, NY 12956. Outpatient family medical care. Information: (518)942-6661.

HORACE NYE INFIRMARY AND HEALTH RELATED FACILITY, Park St., Elizabethtown, NY 12932. 60 bed skilled nursing and 40 bed health related facility. Operated by Essex County. Information: (518)873-6301.

MOSES-LUDINGTON HOSPITAL, Wicker St., Ticonderoga, NY 12883. 45 beds. Visiting hours 12 noon-8 pm. Information: (518)585-2831.

MOSES-LUDINGTON NURSING HOME COMPLEX, Wicker St., Ticonderoga, NY 12883. 40 beds. Information: (518)585-6771.

NEWCOMB MEDICAL CENTER, Winebrook Hills, Newcomb, NY 12852. X-ray, EKG, laboratory and ambulance services. Information: (518)582-2991. If no answer: (518) 582-2321 or 582-2414.

PLACID MEMORIAL HOSPITAL, Church St., Lake Placid, NY 12946. 29 beds, Emergency Room. Visiting hours 11am-8pm. Information: (518)523-3311.

PLANNED PARENTHOOD, Crown Point, NY 12928. Pregnancy testing and counseling, birth control services, by appointment. Information: (518)597-3033.

SMITH HOUSE HEALTH CARE CENTER, Point Rd., Willsboro, NY 12996. Rural health care center offering medical care on an outpatient basis. Information: (518) 963-4275.

UIHLEIN MERCY CENTER, Old Military Road, Lake Placid, NY 12946. 96 beds skilled nursing facility serving the chronically ill and sick aged. The white brick patient "clusters" are octagonal in design, each housing 14 private rooms. Rate is all inclusive. Information: (518) 523-2464.

FRANKLIN COUNTY

FRANKLIN COUNTY ASSOCIATION FOR RETARDED CHILDREN, 85 Park St., Tupper Lake, NY 12986. Residential, educational and recreational services. Information: (518)359-2840.

FRANKLIN COUNTY COMMUNITY MENTAL HEALTH SERVICES, Pius Center, Petrova Ave., Saranac Lake, NY 12983. Alcohol and drug abuse services, group and individual counseling, marriage and family counseling. Information: (518)891-2470.

FRANKLIN COUNTY COMMUNITY MENTAL HEALTH SERVICES, 60 Pleasant Ave., Tupper Lake, NY 12986. Information: (518)359-3282.

FRANKLIN COUNTY NURSING SERVICE, Pius Center, Saranac Lake, NY 12983. Nursing, physical therapy, home-health aides. Information: (518)891-4471.

GENERAL HOSPITAL OF SARANAC, Lake Colby Dr., Saranac Lake, NY 12983. 91 beds, short term-acute care hospital. Visiting hours 11am-8 pm. Information: (518) 891-4141.

MERCY HEALTH CARE CENTER, 114 Wawbeek Ave., Tupper Lake, NY 12986. 54 beds, nursing facility and diagnostic and treatment center. Information: (518) 359-3355.

PLANNED PARENTHOOD, 8 Church St., Saranac Lake, NY 12983. Contraceptive services, pregnancy testing and counseling, education services, VD testings, Pap tests. Fully confidential. Open Monday, Tuesday, and Thursday from 10-3. Information: (518)891-0046.

SUNMOUNT DEVELOPMENT CENTER, Sunmount Developmental Center, Tupper Lake Highway, Tupper Lake, NY 12986. State operated facility for the developmentally disabled. It serves up to 257 children and adults. Services are provided for Franklin, St. Lawrence, Clinton, Jefferson, Essex and Hamilton counties. Information: (518)359-3311.

TRI-LAKES SHELTER FOR WOMEN, Box 102, Saranac Lake, NY 12983. Offers alternatives to women who have been abused or battered, including private shelter or medical, legal or social referral. 24 hour hotline. Information: (518)891-3173.

HAMILTON COUNTY

INDIAN LAKE HEALTH CENTER, Main St., Indian Lake, NY 12842. Monday and Wednesday 9am-5pm, Tuesday and Friday 1-5pm, Thursday 2-5pm, Every other Saturday 9am-1pm. Information: (518)648-5707.

LONG LAKE MEDICAL CENTER, Newcomb Rd., Long Lake, NY 12847. Monday-Friday, 9am-3pm. Information: (518)624-2301.

PISECO HEALTH CENTER, at Community Hall. Old Piseco Rd., Piseco, NY 12139. Information: (518)548-8155.

PLANNED PARENTHOOD OF HAMILTON COUNTY, Indian Lake Health Center, Main St., Indian Lake, NY 12842. Contraceptive counseling, pregnancy testing and counseling and adolescentcounseling. Tuesday and Friday, 9am-4pm. Information: (518)648-5415.

HERKIMER COUNTY

OLD FORGE HEALTH CENTER, South Shore Rd., Old Forge, NY 13420. Physician services available 24 hrs/ daily by appointment. Dental services available 5 days/ week by appointment. Information: (315)369-6619.

ST. LAWRENCE COUNTY

CLIFTON-FINE HOSPITAL, Star Lake, NY 13690. Acute care municipal hospital, 22 beds. Visiting hours, 11:30am-8pm. Information: (315)848-3351.

SARATOGA COUNTY

ADIRONDACK REGIONAL HOSPITAL, 200 Smith Dr., Corinth, NY 12822. Acute inpatient care and outpatient services, 38 beds. Information: (518)654-9041.

WARREN COUNTY

ADIRONDACK TRI-COUNTY NURSING HOME, PO Box 500, North Creek, NY 12853. 60 beds, nursing service to inpatients, physical therapy to outpatients. Information: (518)251-2447.

CHESTERTOWN HEALTH CENTER, Main St., Chestertown, NY 12817. Monday-Saturday, 9am-5pm; Thursday, 9am-8pm. Information: (518)494-2761.

NORTH CREEK HEALTH CENTER, Rt. 28, North Creek, NY 12853. Monday-Wednesday, 9am-5pm; Thursday and Friday, 9am-8pm; Saturday, 9am-12noon. Information: (518)251-2541.

WARRENSBURG HEALTH CENTER, Health Center Plaza, Main St., Warrensburg, 12885. Monday-Saturday, 8am-10pm; Sunday, 10am-8pm by appointment. Information: (518)623-2844.

(108)
STATE POLICE

Following are the headquarters for troops covering portions of the Adirondacks.

Troop B
Ray Brook, NY 12977
(518)897-2000

Troop D
Rt. 5, Genesee St.,
Oneida, NY 13421
(315)363-4400

Troop G
Box 67
504 Loudon Rd.
Loudonville, NY 12211
(518)783-3211.

Other State Police phone numbers, which are not always staffed 24 hours a day, are listed below.

Bolton Landing	(518)644-2555
Chestertown	(518)494-3201
Crown Point	(518)597-3421
Dannemora	(518)492-7195
Ellenburg	(518)594-3848
Indian Lake	(518)648-5757
Keeseville	(518)834-9049
Lowville	(315)376-6513
Old Forge	(315)369-3322
Westport	(518)962-8235
Wilmington	(518)946-7181
Tupper Lake	(518)359-3221

FIRE DEPARTMENTS

CLINTON COUNTY

Dannemora. Walter N. Thayer Hose Co. No. 1, Box 123, 12929.
Ellenburg Center. Ellenburg Center Volunteer Fire Department, 12934.
Lyon Mountain. Lyon Mountain Volunteer Fire Department, Inc., 12952.
Saranac. Saranac Volunteer Fire Department, 12981.

ESSEX COUNTY

AuSable Forks. AuSable Forks Fire Department, Box 566, 12912.
Bloomingdale. Bloomingdale Volunteer Fire Co., 12913.
Crown Point. A.E. Phelps Engine Co., No. 1, 12928.
Crown Point. A.E. Phelps Engine Co., No. 2, 12928.
Elizabethtown. Elizabethtown Fire Co., 12932.
Keene. Keene Fire Department, 12944.
Keene Valley. Keene Valley Hose Co., 12943.
Lake Placid. Lake Placid Volunteer Fire Department, Box 569, 12946.
Mineville. Mineville and Witherbee Volunteer Firepartment, 12987.
Willsboro. Willsboro Fire District, 12996.
Wilmington. Wilmington Volunteer Fire Department, 12997.

FRANKLIN COUNTY

Gabriels. Paul Smith's-Gabriels Volunteer Fire Department, Inc., Box 145, 12936.
Owls Head. Owls Head-Mountain View Volunteer Fire Department, Inc., 12969.
St. Regis Falls. St. Regis Falls Volunteer Fire Department, 12980.
Saranac Lake. Saranac Lake Fire Department, Box 509, 12983.
Saranac Lake. Woodruff-Miller Hose Co., 99 Broadway, 12983.
Tupper Lake. Tupper Lake Volunteer Fire Department, 64 McLaughlin Ave., 12986.

FULTON COUNTY

Caroga Lake. Caroga Lake Volunteer Fire Department, Box 87, 12032.
Mayfield. Mayfield Fire Department, No. 1, 12117.
Stratford. Stratford Volunteer Fire Company, Box 217, 13470.

HAMILTON COUNTY

Blue Mountain Lake. Blue Mountain Lake Fire Department, 12812.
Cold Brook. Morehouse Fire Co., Inc., Star Route, 13224.
Indian Lake. Indain Lake Fire Department, 12842.
Inlet. Inlet Volunteer Fire Department, 13360.
Long Lake. Long Lake Fire Department, 12847.
Lake Pleasant. Lake Pleasant Fire Company, 12108.
Piseco. Piseco Volunteer Fire Department, 12139.
Raquette Lake. Raquette Lake Volunteer Fire Department, 13436.
Speculator. Speculator Volunteer Fire Department, Engine Co. No. 1, 12164.
Wells. Wells Volunteer Fire Company, 12190.

HERKIMER COUNTY

Eagle Bay. Eagle Bay Volunteer Fire Department, 13331.
Old Forge. Old Forge Volunteer Fire Department, Inc., 13420.

ST. LAWRENCE COUNTY

Hopkinton. Hopkinton-Fort Jackson Volunter Fire Department, Inc., 12940.
Star Lake. Star Lake Volunteer Fire Department, Box 96, 13890.

SARATOGA COUNTY

Corinth. Corinth Fire Department, Inc., Box 613, 12822.

WARREN COUNTY

Bolton Landing. Bolton Fire Department, 12814
Brant Lake. Horicon Volunteer Fire Co., Inc., 12815.
Chestertown. Chestertown Volunteer Fire Company, 12817.
Garnet Lake. Garnet Lake Fire Department, Inc., Johnsburg, 12843.
Hague. Hague Volunteer Fire Department, Inc., 12836.
Lake George. Lake George Fire Department, Box 828, 12845.
Lake Luzerne. Van R. Rhodes Volunteer Fire Company, Inc., Box 215, 12846.
North Creek. North Creek Volunteer Fire Co., Inc., 12853.
Pottersville. Pottersville Volunteer Fire Dept., Inc., 12860.
Riparius. Riverside Volunteer Fire Department, Inc., 12862.
Stony Creek. Stony Creek Volunteer Fire Company, 12878.
Warrensburg. Warrensburg Fire Company, 12885.

LEWIS, ONEIDA and WASHINGTON COUNTIES have none in the Adirondack Park.

Most of the information in this section is excerpted from the section on County Organization Members—1981, in the *Book of Proceedings of the Fireman's Association of the State of New York.* Our thanks to the Fireman's Association for their assistance.

(110)
24-HOUR GAS STATIONS

ESSEX COUNTY

Central Mobile Garage, 249 Main St., Lake Placid, NY 12946. AAA wrecker service. (518)523-3378; if no answer, 523-2050.

Lake Shore Garage, Hague, NY 12836. 24-hour towing service only. 8-5pm, Monday-Saturday. (518)543-6556.

Schroon Lake Service Center, Rt. 9, Schroon Lake, NY 12870. (518)532-7344. 24-hour towing service only. Summer: Monday-Saturday 7am-11pm, Sunday 9am-6pm; Winter: 8am-7pm, Monday-Saturday.

FRANKLIN COUNTY

Double "N" Service Station, Box 859, Saranac Lake, NY 12983. 24-hour AAA road service. Hours are 8-6 Monday-Saturday. Telephone answer machine on after closing with two numbers for road service. (518)891-0677.

HAMILTON COUNTY

Chamber's Inlet Garage, Rt. 28, Inlet, NY 13360. 24-hour towing, open 8am-6pm. (315)357-2501.

Day's Garage, Long Lake, NY 12847. AAA wrecker service. (518)624-3111.

HERKIMER COUNTY

Brussell's Thendara Garage, Thendara, NY 13472. AAA service station. (315)369-3755.

C & H Mobil, Old Forge, NY 13420. (315)369-3678.

WARREN COUNTY

Thomson's Garage, Lake George Rd. (Rt. 9 South), Lake George, NY 12845. 24-hour towing only. (518)668-5337.

Warrensburg Mobile Service, South Main St. (Rt. 9N), Warrensburg, NY 12885. Exit 23 off Northway. (518) 623-9492.

The following branch offices of the American Automobile Association cover areas within the Adirondack Park:

Fulton County Branch, Box 685, 338 North Comrie Ave., Johnstown, NY, 12095. (518)762-4619.

Glens Falls Branch, 30 South St., Glens Falls, NY 12801. (518)792-0088.

Plattsburgh Branch, 48A Oak St., Plattsburgh, NY 12901. 24- hour towing service. (518)563-3830.

Saratoga Branch, 376 Broadway, Arcade Building, Saratoga Springs, NY 12866. 24-hour towing service. (518)587-8449.

Utica Branch, 409 Court St., Utica, NY 13502. 24-hour towing service. (315)797-5000.

MISCELLANEOUS

(111)
MISCELLANEOUS AND LITTLE KNOWN FACTS

Of the 6 million acres making up the Adirondack Park, 3.7 million (62%) are privately owned, and the remaining 2.3 million (38%) are state owned.

In 1875, in Lewis County there were 6,979 horses and 26 blacksmiths.

In 1900, approximately 30,000 vacationers visited the Adirondack Mountains. By 1935, State campsites alone registered almost 400,000 visitors.

The Adirondack Park has 2,800 lakes and ponds. 1,200 miles of rivers and over 30,000 miles of brooks, streams and rivers.

In both the villages of Saranac Lake and Lake Placid, you do not see the body of water from which the village took its name. In Saranac, you see Lake Flower; in Placid you see Mirror Lake. In the village of Tupper Lake you are nearer to Raquette Pond than you are to the actual lake named Tupper Lake, which is 2 miles away.

During the 1920's and 30's Speculator, in Hamilton County, was the training camp for famous heavyweight boxing champions, such as Gene Tunney, Max Baer, Max Schmeling, Jim Slattery, Maxie Rosenbloom and Knute Hanson.

There are 42 mountains over 4,000 feet high in the Adirondacks. Mt. Marcy is the highest peak at 5,344 feet.

Whiteface Memorial Highway was constructed in 1936 as a memorial to the servicemen of WWI.

An informal poll by the editors found that the five most annoying Adirondack bugs are the Black fly, mosquito, deer fly, "no see-um" or punkie, and the house fly, in that order.

"GORP", the name of the omnipresent hiker's snack, is derived from " Good Old Raisins and Peanuts." (Granted not exclusively an Adirondack term, but no doubt of interest to many Adirondack hikers.)

In the town of Gabriels, Franklin County, guides at one time made enough money to work only three months of the year. As they all resided on the same street, it became known as Easy Street.

It cost a million dollars to build a man-made beach along the southern shoreline of Lake George.

During the summer of 1904, Lake George was the scene of a minor hoax when someone created an artificial sea monster, had it rise to the surface of the lake on selected occasions, and drew many tourists and visitors to the area as a result.

The Raquette River travels some two hundred miles before it empties into the St. Lawrence River.

Rev. Cyrus Comstock, an Adirondack resident, revolutionized 19th century passenger travel with his adaptation of the Buckboard Wagon; the idea spread throughout the country.

Ice cutting at Raquette Lake

At Old Forge and Raquette Lake, one of the oldest icing operations in the State existed between 1906-1922. It supplied the New York Central Railroad with 50-100,000 tons of ice for its icehouses. Icing for local use continues at Raquette Lake today.

Fort William Henry, used during the French and Indian War, was the fort in James Fenimore Cooper's novel *The Last of The Mohicans.*

In 1910, Warren County had 1,865 farms consisting of 250,349 acres, which was 44.5% of the area of the county. By 1969 the figure was down to 0.6%.

The first automobile came into the Adirondacks in July, 1902, as Mr. and Mrs. Herbert J. Sackett drove through on their honeymoon. They spent time at Lower Saranac Lake and at Paul Smiths. It is said that as the car rambled and puffed along, both terror and a sense of awe were left in its path.

On October 13, 1912, the first aeroplane flew into the area over Whiteface Mountain. It landed in a wheat field northeast of Bloomingdale Village. After staying overnight, and attracting much attention, George A. Gray of Boston flew his biplane on to Saranac Lake. There he stayed for several days giving rides, exhibitions, and delivering packages.

On February 12, 1927, in the village of Willsboro, Winifred "Waiter" Hathaway, saved the lives of four men and two young boys. Ice fishing on Lake Champlain, their lives were in danger when the ice began to break up. For canoeing out amidst pieces of ice, Waiter received the Carnegie Medal for life-saving heroism.

While being driven from Tahawus Club to North Creek — in the early morning hours of September 14, 1901, Theodore Roosevelt learned that President William McKinley had died. At North Creek station he was sworn in as the 26th President of the United States.

There are no poisonous snakes in the Adirondacks except in the Tongue Mountain area on Lake George, and on a narrow strip along Lake Champlain.

In the early days of the movie industry, the Saranac Lake area was a major location for filming motion pictures, and a major studio was located there.

The first winter ascent of Mt. Marcy was in March of 1893, made on snowshoes.

Honorable Amelia M. Murray, Maid of Honor to Queen Victoria, became the first woman to cross the Adirondacks by stagecoach, foot and boat, in the summer of 1855. Her guide was New York State Governor Horatio Seymour.

In 1912, Fridtjof Nansen, the famous Norwegian scientist, explorer and author, conquered Whiteface. It was the first known winter ascent of an Adirondack Peak on skis.

The lowest point in the Adirondack Park is the surface of Lake Champlain, 95 feet above sea level.

Lake George is 32 miles in length, making it the longest lake entirely in the Adirondacks. It has 225 islands, of which 154 are owned by the state. The lake goes to depths of 190 feet.

Dr. C. Hart Merriam, naturalist, reported in 1884 that the last moose killed in New York was an 800 pound female (7 feet tall at the hump) shot near Raquette Lake in 1861. In recent years, as moose have begun to occasionally wander into the Adirondacks from Vermont and Canada, there have been a few more shootings.

16% of the Adirondack Park—or over 40% of the state owned lands—is designated as official "wilderness".

The Adirondack Park is larger than any of the seven smallest states in the United States. It would take these five national parks added together to equal the size of the Adirondack Park: Yellowstone, Grand Canyon, Yosemite, Everglades and Great Smoky National Parks.

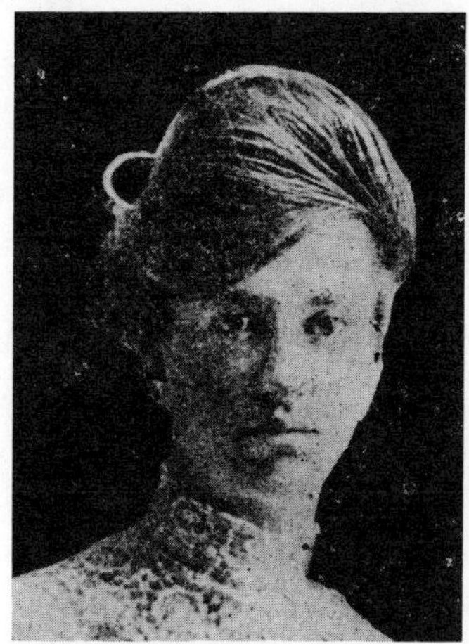

Grace Brown

Chester Gillette

On July 12, 1906 Chester Gillette killed Grace Brown at Big Moose. The fictionalized story of this event was popularized worldwide in Theodore Dreiser's novel *An American Tragedy.*

There are no traffic lights in Hamilton County (only one yellow blinking light in Long Lake).

President Cleveland often stayed at the Saranac Inn. President Harrison had a summer camp on Second Lake near Old Forge. President McKinley's favorite summer vacation spot was the Hotel Champlain, 2 miles south of Plattsburgh. Theodore Roosevelt frequented the Tahawus Club.

In 1908, President William Howard Taft visited the Adirondacks to attend ceremonies at the opening of the restored Fort Ticonderoga. President Coolidge once summered in the Adirondacks. President Franklin D. Roosevelt dedicated the Whiteface Mountain Memorial Highway in 1935.

From 1895 to 1903, a 7392 foot cable railroad ran from Lake George Village to the summit of Prospect Mountain. Cars operated every half-hour, at a cost of $.50 per passenger. Wages averaged $3.00/week then, and the railroad was unable to make it financially.

At one time, Prospect Mountain House stood at the top of Prospect Mountain. Built in the 1870's by Dr. James Ferguson, a retired physician from Glens Falls, the original building was destroyed by a forest fire in 1880. It was rebuilt, but burned again. People would hike, ride in horse-drawn carriages or ride the cable railroad cars up and back.

Benjamin Pond and J.W. Otis made the first winter ascent of Mt. Marcy on March 18, 1893, on snowshoes.

The first North Creek White Water Derby was held on May 3, 1958.

The first 4000 foot ascent in the Adirondacks was made on Giant Mountain by Charles Broadhead on June 2, 1797.

Dr. Alphonzo Goff flew the first airmail from the Adirondacks on May 19, 1938.

On June 29, 1916, C.M. Daniels played 228 holes of golf on his Sabattis course.

The Adirondack 46ers held their charter meeting on May 30, 1948.

On July 1, 1912 Richard Collier flew a Curtiss Biplane off Raquette Lake.

In 1783 General George Washington made a victory inspection of Crown Point and Fort Ticonderoga.

The War of 1812 reached the Adirondacks. The British sailed on Lake Champlain, up the Boquet River, seized flour and destroyed property near Willsboro. They were driven back by the militia.

Abolitionist Gerrit Smith, who had inherited nearly a million acres of the Adirondacks, gave land to any Negro who would clear and farm it. The all-black settlement of Timbucto was established in North Elba. Abolitionist John Brown moved there to teach the new black residents northern farming techniques. The experiment failed and, later, after he was hanged for attempting to organize a slave's rebellion at Harper's Ferry, John Brown's body was returned to the Adirondacks, lay in state at the County Court House in Elizabethtown, and is buried at his farm in North Elba.

Gifford Pinchot, later first chief of the U.S. Forest Service, developed the first large-scale scientific forestry management plan for George Vanderbilt's Biltmore in North Carolina. In 1896 Pinchot developed a similar plan for Vanderbilt's brother-in-law William Seward Webb's enormous Adirondack estate, Nehasane Park.

The map prepared in 1775 for Gen. John Burgoyne by Claude Joseph Southies was the first to depict features of the interior Adirondack region.

Lewis and Clark charted the Northwest Territory three decades before the first ascent of Mt. Marcy.

The Adirondacks are within a day's drive of some 60 million people.

In 1916, the National Park Service adopted the Adirondack rustic architectural style and modeled some of its grand lodges in the national parks of the West after this design.

In less than 40 miles, the Adirondacks rise one full mile, from the 95 foot elevation of Lake Champlain to 5344 foot Mt. Marcy.

The Adirondacks cover an area of 9,375 square miles.

The Village of Saranac Lake lies within three towns (Harrietstown, St. Armand, North Elba) and two counties (Essex and Franklin).

(112)
FIRE TOWERS

Observation stations on the tops of 15 Adirondack mountains were officially established in 1909. They were crude platforms of wood and concrete and connected by phone with the neareast settlement. Later the Department of Environmental Conservation changed to substantial steel towers with enclosed shelters at the top. Most tower facilities were placed at locations arrived at by verbal agreements, with the lands on which they were located often changing ownership many times over the years. In some instances, the present owners of lands under or adjoining the non-staffed tower sites cite public liability problems and are opposed to continued public access.

Today the fire tower detection program is under evaluation, as a more reliable combination of fire tower and aircraft detection is sought. Towers now listed as active may or may not be staffed in the near future.

The public is provided trail access to those towers listed as active and to those non-active towers located on state-owned lands. Some non-active towers and the trails leading to them have deteriorated, creating a potential public safety hazard.

In the following listing, the fire tower name and the name of the mountain are always the same. Elevation figures are published by D.E.C. and do not necessarily match the more precise figures in Section 54, the 100 Highest Peaks.

RAY BROOK JURISDICTION (REGION 5)

Active:	
Belfry Mountain	1,892 ft.
Lyon Mountain	3,830 ft.
Palmer Hill	1,146 ft.
Pharaoh Mountain	2,557 ft.
Pok-O-Moonshine	2,162 ft.
St. Regis Mountain	2,882 ft.
Vanderwhacker	3,385 ft.
Non-Active:	
Azure Mountain (On State Land)	2,518 ft.
Boreas Mountain (Public Access Denied)	3,815 ft.
Hurricane Mountain (On State Land)	3,687 ft.
Loon Lake Mountain (Public Access Denied)	3,355 ft.

NORTHVILLE JURISDICTION (REGIONS 5)

Active:	
Blue Mountain	3,759 ft.
Cathead Mountain	2,700 ft.
Kane Mountain	2,200 ft.
Pillsbury Mountain	3,626 ft.
Wakely Mountain	3,700 ft.

Non-Active:

Owls Head Mountain (On State Land)	2,740 ft.
Snowy Mountain (On State Land)	4,000 ft.
Tomany Mountain (On State Land)	2,600 ft.

WARRENSBURG JURISDICTION (REGION 5)

Active:

Black Mountain	2,646 ft.
Gore Mountain	3,583 ft.
Hadley Mountain	2,700 ft.
Spruce Mountain	2,003 ft.

Non-Active:

Crane Mountain (On State Land)	3,250 ft.
Swede Mountain (On State Land)	1,904 ft.

CANTON JURISDICTION (REGION 6)

Active:

Arab Mountain	2,539 ft.
Number Four	1,630 ft.

HERKIMER JURISDICTION (REGION 6)

Active:

Rondaxe	2,350 ft.
Stillwater	2,264 ft.
Dairy Hill	1,812 ft.

Non-Active·

Ft. Noble	2,338 ft.
Woodhull	2,362 ft.

Source: Department of Environmental Conservation listing.

(113)
LOST HIKERS AND CANOEISTS

This section is a grim reminder that the Adirondack Park contains the largest wilderness area in the eastern United States. The geodesic quadrangle in which the present writer resides, West Canada Lakes, contains 220 square miles of forests and lakes and less than two miles of paved road. From Rt. 30 between Long Lake and Tupper Lake, one can travel east for over 37 miles crossing only a few woods roads. Throughout the Adirondacks, a broken ski, a forgotten map and compass, a sudden change in temperature can mean the difference between life and death.

Thanks to excellent efforts of local citizens, Department of Environmental Conservation officers, State Police and various search and rescue squads, most lost hikers are found before it is too late. But not always. Sometimes help arrives too late. Sometimes the wilderness swallows up a victim, never to be seen again.

The following listing includes both lost hikers and those who perished on the trail before help could arrive. It is both a memorium to those who died and a caution to those of us who venture, especially alone, into the Adirondack wilderness.

As no state agency or organization we contacted keeps records on lost hikers, the listing below, gathered from random sources, is unfortunately far from complete. The editors invite correspondence containing additional information on this subject.

1956
Norman Nissen, about 20; died of hypothermia climbing in the High Peaks on Thanksgiving weekend.

1971
Douglas Legg, 8; wandered away from his grandparent's Camp Santanoni on July 10 and was never seen again. Over 650 people joined the largest search ever in Adirondack history, to no avail.

1972
Pat Griffin; died from effects of over-exertion, in June, attempting to set a speed record for climbing the 46 Adirondack High Peaks.

1973
George Atkinson; died in Panther Gorge on Mt. Marcy, March 14. His body was found three years later by searchers looking for Steven Thomas.

1976
Steven Thomas, 19; disappeared climbing Mt. Marcy on April 11. Exhaustive search, continuing still, failed to uncover a trace.

1976
Michael Aurilio, 25; died of hypothermia, October 26, after he and a companion wrecked their open canoe in the Hudson Gorge about one-half mile below Blue Ledge.

1977
Christopher Coyle, 17; drowned May 8 after falling from a raft in Harris Rift in the Hudson Gorge.

1982
Robert Gilpin; died on Algonquin, in February:

(114)

ADIRONDACK RECORDS & ADIRONDACK FIRSTS

Hamilton County has the smallest population, 5,034, of any county in New York State. It also has the lowest population density with 2.9 people per square mile.

Mt. Van Hoevenberg Recreational Area,in Essex County, is the site of the only luge and bobsled run in the Western Hemisphere.

The regulations governing land use within the Adirondacks—for both public and private lands—have often been called the most stringent and geographically expansive zoning regulations in the United States.

North Creek is the site of the first calico mill in New York State.

The first public campsite in New York State was established in 1923 on the Sacandaga River, near Wells.

In 1880, at Lake George, 23 men met to organize and hold canoe races. This became the founding of the ACA, the American Canoe Association.

St. Lawrence is the largest county in New York State with 2,768 square miles.

The theme park, "Frontier Town", in Essex County operates the biggest stageline in the country.

The Adirondack Park is the largest park in the contiguous 48 states. It is larger even then Yellowstone, Glacier, Yosemite and Olympic National Parks combined.

The Marion River Carry Railway

The Marion River Carry Railway (1900 to 1929), running from the Marion River to Utowana Lake, Hamilton County, was the shortest standard gauge railway in the world, running a total distance of about 1300 yards. It also had the wealthiest board of directors, including William Seward Webb, J. Pierport Morgan, Harry Payne Whitney, Reginald C. Vanderbilt, Collis P. Huntington, and others.

Camp Dudley, in Westport, is the oldest boys camp in the United States. Founded in 1884, it continues today, in full operation during the summer.

There are no cities within the Blue Line—the largest area without a city in New York State.

Lake Placid, five miles long and two miles wide, is the largest lake at 1,800 feet above sea level east of the Rockies.

The Ausable River has been rated the number one trout stream in New York State by the Department of Environmental Conservation and *Field and Stream* Magazine.

The largest open pit titanium mine in the world is at Tahawus, Essex County.

The Forest Technician Program, Wanakena Campus, is the oldest forest technician school in the country. It is located in Wanakena, in St. Lawrence County, and was originally called the Ranger School.

The first of New York State's licensed female hunting guides was Julia Burton (1896-1969).

The Adirondack Mountains are the oldest mountain range in North America (see Section 50).

The 1932 Olympic Winter Games, in Lake Placid, were the first Winter Olympics on man-made snow.

In 1898, Ne-ha-sa-ne was the site for the first scientific forest management plan for private lands in U.S. history. Ne-ha-sa-ne was William Seward Webb's estate of over 100,000 acres in Hamilton County, near Sabattis.

The Painted Pony Rodeo in Lake Luzerne is the oldest continuous weekly rodeo in the United States (according to the Painted Pony Rodeo).

The Adirondack Forest Preserve is the only constitutionally protected forest land in the United States.

The village of Tupper Lake had a sawmill which boasted the highest daily production of lumber in the world.

In the Winter of 1904-05, ten men and women skied, tobaganned, and snowshoed during the first open season of the Lake Placid Club. Lake Placid is credited as a focal point for making winter sports popular in America.

In 1920, the Sno Birds of Lake Placid were formed. Harry Wade Hicks, their outstanding member, became a legend in the history of organized cross-country skiing. At least 80 competitions were held each winter in those early seasons, leading the U.S. in this sport.

The Enchanted Forest, at Old Forge, has the largest public collection of authentic totem poles in the East.

On September 15, 1940, Pete Dubuc caught the world record pike (46 lbs., 2 oz.) in Sacandaga Reservoir. (Subsequently his catch was down-graded to the North American record.)

The last cougar reported to have been killed in New York was shot in Hamilton County in 1894.

Prospect House in Blue Mt. Lake, was considered by some as the finest hotel in America (1882-1903). It was the first hotel in the world to have electric lights in every guest bedroom. Each of the 300 rooms also had running water, and there was a two-story outhouse on the back, so guests on the upper floor did not have to descend to ground level. Later it was torn down. The Prospect Point Cottages now stand where it was located.

The first known use of electricity in industry took place at the Irondale iron works in what is now the Town of Crown Point. Allen Penfield bought a large electromagnet from Professor Joseph Henry, who had been conducting experiments with it in the late 1820's in Albany. Penfield used the electromagnet in his local iron works.

When Crown Point was built after British General Amhearst's 1759 victory over Fort St. Frederic, during the French and Indian Wars, it cost 10 million dollars and was the most expensive fortification in North America at the time.

The first important naval battle of the American Revolution took place off Valcour Island, Lake Champlain in the fall of 1776.

The oldest wild bear ever caught in New York was 42 years old. It was taken near the town of Newcomb, in 1974. Black bears' age can be counted by sectioning a small premolar tooth and counting the rings.

The heaviest bear recorded in New York was shot in 1975, near the town of Altamont, in Franklin County. He topped 660 pounds dressed and was estimated to have weighed 750 pounds while living.

At the North Creek Ski Bowl, the nation's first "ride up-slide down" ski center was organized. Ski Patrol service also began there.

(115)
OPERATING MAILBOATS

LAKE	START	STOP	LENGTH	PASSENGERS
Upper Saranac	6/15	9/15	20 mi.	No
Raquette	7/1	Labor Day	26 mi.	Yes
Fulton Chain	6/15	9/15	20 mi.	No
Cranberry	6/15	9/15	20 mi.	Yes
Twitchell	7/1	9/30	4 1/2 mi.	No
Big Moose	5/15	10/1	10 mi.	No
6th & 7th	6/15	9/15	15 mi.	Yes
Placid	7/1	9/15	5 mi.	No
George	6/1	Labor Day	6 mi.	No

(116)
FOR MORE INFORMATION

Several organizations and agencies have proved to be invaluable sources of information about the Adirondacks. These organizations, listed below, can provide residents and visitors alike with major quanities of information, brochures, maps and pamphlets. In Section 36 of *The Guide,* county and local chambers of commerce are listed. These are good sources of information for particular areas in the Adirondacks.

ADIRONDACK MOUNTAIN CLUB. Major publisher of Adirondack trail and field guides. For a listing of their publications, contact: Adirondack Mountain Club, 172 Ridge St., Glens Falls, NY 12801. (518)793-7737.

ADIRONDACK MUSEUM. Major source for information on the history of the Adirondacks. Museum and bookstore (see Section 14). Information: Blue Mt. Lake, NY 12812. (518)352-7311 or 7312.

ADIRONDACK PARK AGENCY. Information on Adirondack region, zoning and use of state and private lands, nature, economy, etc. Information: Box 99, Ray Brook, NY 12977. (518)891-4050.

DEPARTMENT OF ENVIRONMENTAL CONSERVATION. Information on camping, boating, hunting, fishing, trapping, fish and wildlife, forestry, plants, etc. Numerous free pamphlets available. New York State Headquarters: 50 Wolf Road, Albany, NY 12233. Offices for Regions 5 and 6 (see attached map), which serve the various Adirondack counties, are listed below:

Region 5
Headquarters:
Ray Brook, NY 12977
(518)891-1370.

Sub-headquarters:
Hudson Street
Box 220
Warrensburg, NY 12885
(518)623-3671

Forestry Offices:
Clinton, Essex, Franklin Counties
Ray Brook, NY 12977
(518)891-1370

Saratoga, Warren, Washington Counties
Hudson Street
Box 220
Warrensburg, NY 12885
(518)623-3671

Fulton, Hamilton Counties
Northville, NY 12134
(518)863-4545

Region 6
Headquarters:
State Office Building
317 Washington St.,
Watertown, NY 13601
(315)782-0100, ext. 262

Sub-headquarters:
State Office Building
Utica, NY 13501
(315)797-6120

Forestry Offices:
Jefferson, Lewis Counties
Rt. 812
PO Box 31
Lowville, NY 13367
(315)376-3521

St. Lawrence County
30 Court St.
Canton, NY 13617
(315)386-4546

Herkimer, Oneida Counties
225 North Main St.
Herkimer, NY 13350
(315)866-6330

OLYMPIC REGIONAL DEVELOPMENT AUTHORITY (ORDA), Olympic Center, Lake Placid, NY 12946. The Authority is responsible for the promotion and management of all the Olympic venues. Information regarding all upcoming events at the Olympic facilities can be obtained by calling (518)523-1655.

TOURIST INFORMATION CENTERS

I LOVE NEW YORK TOURISM OFFICE, 90 Main St., Lake Placid, NY 12946. Operated by the New York State Department of Commerce. (518)523-2412.

TOURISM INFORMATION CENTER, I-87 (Adirondack Northway) between Exits 11 and 12 Northbound. Open 9am-5pm daily.

ADIRONDACK INFORMATION CENTER, I-87 (Adirondack Northway) between Exits 17 and 18, Northbound. Open daily, year-round except Thanksgiving, Christmas, and New Year's. 9am-5pm, winter and 9am-9pm summer. Operated by the Warren County Tourism Department. (518)792-1050.

These tourist information centers have a large collection of brochures, maps, guides and information available on where to stay and eat and what to do in the Adirondacks.

CREDITS

Grateful acknowledgement to the following individuals and institutions is made for use of photographs and illustrations:

Cover	Albert Gates, "Clear Pond from Sunrise"
17-20	National Survey, Chester, VT.
26	Virginia Conard
30	Adirondack Museum
33	Adirondack Museum
38	Susan Schafstall
41	Adirondack Museum
49	Susan Schafstall
54	Robert Venables
57	Adirondack Museum
58	Adirondack Museum
59	Adirondack Museum
60	Adirondack Museum
62	Adirondack Museum
63	Seneca Ray Stoddard
67	(top) Adirondack Museum (bottom) Nancie Battaglia
83	Howard Kirschenbaum
90	Al Stripp, *Central Adirondack Guide*
92	Adirondack Museum
94	Howard Kirschenbaum
95	NYS Geological Survey, Educational Leaflet #23, "New Mountains from Old Rocks: The Adirondacks"
99	Adirondack Museum
101	Loomis Room, Keene Valley Library and *Adirondac*, April 1983
105	*An Environmental Education Resource Manual for Adirondack Schools*, by D.E.C. and A.P.A., 1979
113	Scott Weaver, Courtesy of Dr. E.W. Cupp,Cornell University
124	Adirondack Museum
137	Howard Kirschenbaum
153-156	Kris Hansen, Camp Woodsmoke, Lake Placid
158	Adirondack River Outfitters, Thendara
171	Ann Beck
186	Linda Smith
187	Adirondack Museum
190	Adirondack Museum

INDEX

Included in this name index are primarily: historical figures; organizations, agencies, clubs and associations; historic sites, hotels and "Great Camps"; book authors and titles (the latter in italics); and major scenic attractions. Not included are the names within sections that are discrete and obvious, e.g., hospitals, golf courses, summer camps, etc. In other words, a person wondering, "Now what was the name of that hospital?" or "Where did I see that listing on the Whiteface Resort Golf Course?" would not need the Index, but could use the Table of Contents to go right to the Hospitals or Golf Courses section. Also not included are the names of towns, rivers, mountains, or chambers of commerce (which are given throughout as sources of more information), as these would have enlarged the index to unwieldy proportions and in most cases would not have proved very useful to the reader.

About the publisher . . .

SAGAMORE INSTITUTE is a non-profit educational organization with headquarters in Saratoga Springs and its Sagamore Lodge and Conference Center in Raquette Lake, New York. The Institute works locally, nationally and internationally in the fields of education, professional training and development, environmental education and social change. In the Adirondack Mountains, Sagamore operates a major conference center, museum tours of its historic Adirondack "Great Camp", the Adirondack Bound outdoor recreation and education program, and a children's summer camp.

About the editors . . .

HOWARD KIRSCHENBAUM is Director of Sagamore Institute in Saratoga Springs and Sagamore Lodge and Conference Center in Raquette Lake, where he resides. Dr. Kirschenbaum is author of eleven books in the fields of education and psychology and a nationally known educational consultant. He is also a board member of the Raquette Lake Free Library and an Adirondack guide, taking groups on hikes throughout the Adirondacks and on tours of "Great Camps" and historic sites.

SUSAN SCHAFSTALL is the Conference Coordinator at Sagamore Lodge and Conference Center. She is a former fifth grade teacher from Toledo, Ohio and has worked actively with the Girl Scouts, her church and Sagamore Institute's College Awareness Expedition leading cross-country trips for teenagers. She is also author of an article for teachers: "Photography: A Unit Worth a Thousand Words."

JANINE STUCHIN, a special project coordinator at Sagamore Lodge and Conference Center, is a recent graduate of the State University of New York at Albany, in the field of sociology. During her junior year of college, in Israel, she compiled a directory of women's health resources in Jerusalem. She recently returned from a 200 mile kayak trip in Utah and hopes to work in a field that combines her interests in human services and the outdoors.

NOTES

NOTES